OPERATIONS HANDBOOK FOR THE SMALL ACADEMIC LIBRARY

Recent Titles in
The Greenwood Library Management Collection

Strategic Marketing for Libraries: A Handbook
Elizabeth J. Wood, with assistance from Victoria L. Young

The Smaller Academic Library: A Management Handbook
Gerard B. McCabe, editor

Operations Handbook for the Small Academic Library

EDITED BY

Gerard B. McCabe

THE GREENWOOD LIBRARY MANAGEMENT COLLECTION

Greenwood Press
NEW YORK • WESTPORT, CONNECTICUT • LONDON

Library of Congress Cataloging-in-Publication Data

Operations handbook for the small academic library.

(The Greenwood library management collection,
ISSN: 0894–2986)
Bibliography: p.
Includes index.
1. Libraries, University and college—Administration.
2. Small libraries—Administration. I. McCabe, Gerard B.
II. Series.
Z675.U5066 1989 027.7 88–34811
ISBN 0–313–26474–0 (lib. bdg. : alk. paper)

British Library Cataloguing in Publication Data is available.

Library of Congress Catalog Card Number: 88–34811
ISBN: 0–313–26474–0
ISSN: 0894–2986

First published in 1989

Greenwood Press, Inc.
88 Post Road West, Westport, Connecticut 06881

Printed in the United States of America

The paper used in this book complies with the Permanent Paper Standard issued by the National Information Standards Organization (Z39.48–1984).

10 9 8 7 6 5 4 3 2 1

Contents

Abbreviations

AACR2	Anglo American Cataloging Rules. 2nd edition
ACRL	Association of College and Research Libraries
ALA	American Library Association
AMIGOS	Amigos Bibliographic Council
ANSI	American National Standards Institute
ARL	Association of Research Libraries
ASCII	American Standard Code for Information Interchange
AV	audiovisual
BI	bibliographic instruction
BPO	British Post Office
CAP	Collection Analysis Project
CD	compact disc
CD-ROM	Compact disc–read only memory
CIJE	*Current Index to Journals in Education*
CIP	cataloging in publication
CLIP	College Library Information Packet
COM	computer output microform
CONTU	Commission on New Technological Uses of Copyright Works
CPI	Consumer Price Index

CPM	Critical Path Method
DDC	Dewey Decimal Classification
DOS	Direct Operating System
ERIC	Educational Resources Information Center
F&E	furniture and equipment
FTE	full-time equivalent
FY	fiscal year
GHZ	gigahertz
GRC	General Research Corp.
HEA	Higher Education Act
HEGIS	Higher Education General Information Survey
HSG	High Sierra Group
HVAC	heating, ventilating, and air conditioning
ICAN	Iowa Computer Assisted Network
IFTS	Instructional Fixed Television Service
ILL	interlibrary loan
ILL ME	Interlibrary Loan Micro Enhancer
IMC	Instructional Materials Center
IPS	inches per second
ISBN	International Standard Book Number
ISI	Institute for Scientific Information
ISPN	International Standard Program Number
LAMA	Library Administration and Management Association
LAN	local area network
LC	Library of Congress
LCC	Library of Congress Classification
LCS	Library Circulation System
LIRN	Library and Information Resources of the Northwest
LISA	*Library and Information Science Abstracts*
LRC	Learning Resource Center
MARC	Machine Readable Cataloging (program)
MEDLINE	Medlars online (Medical literature analysis & retrieval service)
MINITEX	Minnesota interlibrary telecommunications exchange
MLC	minimal level cataloging
MUGLNC	Microcomputer Users Group for Libraries in North Carolina
NAAL	Network of Alabama Academic Libraries
NAD	OCLC Name-Address Directory

NEDCC	Northeast Document Conservation Center
NISO	National Information Standards Organization
NOTIS	Northwestern Online Total Integrated System
NTIS	National Technical Information Service
OATS	Original Article Text Service
OCLC	Online Computer Library Center
OJT	on-the-job training
OMS	Office of Management Studies
O.P.	out-of-print
OPAC	on-line public access catalog
PBS	Public Broadcasting System
PC	personal computer
PCRs	primary collection responsibilities
RAM	random access memory
RF	radio frequency
RH	relative humidity
RIE	*Resources in Education*
RLG	Research Library Group
RLIN	Research Libraries Information Network
RTSD	Resources and Technical Services Division of the American Library Association
SOLINET	Southeastern Library Network
TRLN	Triangle Research Libraries Network
TVRO	Television Receive Only
TWX	teletypewriter exchange service
UL	Union Listing
UMI	University Microfilms International
USBE	Universal Serials and Book Exchange, Inc.
USC-Coastal	University of South Carolina-Coastal Carolina College
WLN	Western Library Network

Preface

This new volume in the Greenwood Library Management Collection is intended for readers who work in small academic libraries or who have an interest in these libraries; it is not aimed at managers but at all library staff. The operations handbook is not a sequel to *The Smaller Academic Library: A Management Handbook*, which was also edited by this editor and published by Greenwood Press, but is intended to complement the earlier book by providing a series of chapters on practical day-to-day operations, with subjects that come up for consideration in such libraries and for which librarians and staff require some information.

In the past, librarians working in small academic libraries emulated the larger academic libraries, frequently because of library school influence. With the large academic library used as a laboratory, library science students who went on to work in smaller academic libraries could hardly help but emulate the role model for which they had received their training. The smaller academic library is not a microcosm of the larger institution; it is an entity in its own right. The smaller academic libraries are the majority, and when the small, subject-specialized libraries are added to the group, the numbers increase greatly. Small libraries have their own peculiar needs, and it is not wise to use the larger libraries as a role model today because they also have their own unique needs. Very often the larger libraries have superior financial support and they emphasize objectives not characteristic of the role that the smaller academic library fulfills on its campus.

The large academic library, with its assemblage of highly trained, very specialized professionals, can establish goals and objectives that are far beyond the means of the minimally staffed small academic library. In the latter, the broadly trained professional who moves without regard to prior academic training from the needs of one discipline to another, and who relates very quickly to the competing aspirations of the library's services and supporting units, cannot focus the skills of an expert on a service or a technical requirement, and will not have the time to do so, rather, such a person must react quickly, effectively, and with an economical resolution.

Small academic libraries exist to meet the fundamental needs of their clientele. Their system of financial support does not permit what would be a luxury for them: the employment of a staff of specially trained individuals with limited areas of responsibility, each giving their undivided attention to very specific concerns. The management of larger academic libraries, often consisting of several individuals each with a different area of expertise, has the responsibility to coordinate the diverse efforts of all of the units that comprise the library. In the small academic library, only one such individual may have that responsibility.

Chapters are arranged in subject sections for the reader's convenience. In the section on material selection, two related chapters by Hastreiter and Tomczyk discuss periodicals and serials. The cost of continuation items and their central importance to the collections of academic libraries requires depth, so two chapters were planned. As in the case of other chapters, each author was asked to discuss specifically certain aspects of the subject. This section also has chapters on microform periodicals and other formats.

The chapters on microcomputers, software, and CD-ROM (Compact Disc–Read Only Memory) in the technology section are intended to complement each other. By deliberate choice, the public services section lacks a chapter on reference service as I believe the subject is adequately covered elsewhere.

Small academic libraries deserve consideration in their own right and this book, like the earlier volume, is another effort to do so. In closing, I wish to acknowledge the assistance of Dr. Rashelle Karp, College of Library Science, with the organization of this book, and Peggy Postlewait, Carlson Library's administrative secretary, who provided much technical assistance.

PART I

Administration

1

Practical Presentation of Cost Data in the Smaller Academic Library

Edward D. Garten

As academic libraries have grown and diversified in the services they offer, they have required new management postures, strategies, and cost analysis approaches. Contemporary management notions regarding resource allocation compel library directors to have complete and accurate information regarding the financial and nonfinancial aspects of their library operations. On virtually every college or university campus today, library directors are required to offer more sharply focused background information in order to justify budgetary requests both to their superiors and to individuals who serve on campus budget hearing committees.

Within an increasingly more complex academic environment, with ever increasing competing interests, library directors need simple and politically expedient ways to enhance the efficiency and financial viability of the library and its services. Many books and articles are available that offer a range of scientific methodologies for data gathering and cost interpretation. Such resources may be of value within certain institutional frameworks and political climates; however, the basic contention behind this chapter on cost analysis in the small academic library is that in our experience most funding decisions in academe are given the nod based on simple and straightforward cost analysis presentations. The simple linkage of financial data to nonfinancial data—often ''people data''—is essential to making informed presentations to senior administration. Too often extensive studies are done to convince college administrators of a correct course of action with many of these presentations going unread, barely scanned, or read inaccurately. Both clarity and conciseness should be sought when tying cost studies to either oral presentations or accompanying memoranda.

Clearly, while it is vital to understand what particular library programs cost, this information is often less likely to be used in making decisions than in selling those decisions to the vice-president, budget review bodies, or the larger campus community. Decisions in libraries typically are not based on "rational" economic considerations. More often than not, policy in libraries and the institutions in which they reside is simply a reflection of a complex political process studded with the values and power relationships of various interest groups on campus, all operating within an environment where they are trying to distribute limited resources in an efficient, if not completely fair, fashion. It is unfortunate that individuals often determine the premises behind the gathering of cost information and then use the quantitative data that results from a study to justify positions that have in fact already been assumed.

Even within such working environments, which are often characterized as "organized anarchies," it is wise not to fall victim to the belief that cost data will be unattainable or unproductive to gaining resources for programmatic efforts. The lack of comprehensive data on long-term library benefits should not inhibit the effort to obtain at least recognizable and useful cost information. An inventory of benefits should be developed for all programs and activities even if this information is premised largely on anecdotal information from patrons and staff. In the end, the best assessment of the benefits of any library activity incorporates the judgments of library patrons. Costs associated with these benefits, however, can and should be monitored by all staff members associated with a particular programmatic effort. Monitoring should be done on a regular basis so as to establish trend lines and determine departmental or unit costs.

Most of all, you should remember: The ultimate standard for conducting a cost-finding effort is not the gathering of data; rather the standard is the usefulness of the information received, and that is often predicated on the manner in which it is presented.

WHAT IS MEANT BY COSTS?

Librarians make a range of purchasing decisions, financial investments in the future of their services, and, ultimately, decisions with respect to the use of personnel. Costs may be defined simply as the amount of capital exchanged in order to provide a service, program, activity, or function. The aggregate of all costs associated with a program or activity is known as total cost. To determine the total cost of an activity within the library, two important elements need to be understood: direct costs and indirect costs.

Costs are often distinguished as being either fixed or variable. This distinction is important not only in cost accounting but throughout managerial accounting as a whole. If costs in a library are to be properly estimated and controlled, it is necessary to know whether the cost can be expected to change under given conditions and, if so, by what dollar amount.

Fixed costs refer to costs that do not change in total amount with changes in volume of output or activity. Another way of viewing fixed costs is to describe them as those costs that remain constant regardless of changes in the activity level or method of providing the activity. For example, a small college library is part of a consortial van delivery system and must pay $8,000 per year as a share in the system. One year the library uses the shuttle extensively, while the next year the use of the system is down by 40%. Even with the downturn in use of the system, the library still must pay its share of the van cost. Fixed costs are sometimes classified as being either committed or programmed costs. A library manager may commit a library to a cost pattern that will extend several years into the future. For example, the consortium noted above may require that each participating library enter a binding contract for three years at a fixed rate per year. Other costs, referred to either as programmed or discretionary costs, are determined as part of a general college or university budget. For example, custodial or classified salaries may be set by the personnel office once a year, and the library manager may have little control over this cost. It is a fixed cost, but one determined at another level within the institution.

In the strict sense, variable costs are costs that vary in direct proportion to changes in productive output. For example, direct materials and on-line cataloging costs are usually variable costs with each additional book acquired. Thus, the materials, or overhead costs, will vary in direct proportion to the number of books processed. In other words, variable costs in a library are those that change directly with changes in the activity level of performing the activity.

Some costs, however, may be semivariable. The cost may change, but not in direct proportion to the changes in output or activity. Very often semivariable costs, which can have the attributes of both variable and fixed costs, are falsely called variable costs. Repairs by the university physical plant which are quite commonly charged to the library's budget often will not be fixed in amount but will increase as building operations and services expand.

Both direct and indirect costs are the primary elements in developing cost information. These costs relate to activities that the library performs. Each task becomes an element toward determining the total cost of a library activity.

For example, I will use the costs attached to purchasing and cataloging a book, as this is a cost question often asked by senior administrators or library directors. Within this technical service activity, a number of discrete tasks must be performed. A direct or indirect expenditure is made for the resources needed to perform each task, and the sum of these expenditures provides an approximate cost of purchasing a book. A matrix that may be helpful is given in table 1.

By using this matrix you can determine the approximate cost of acquiring and cataloging a book by task and by the total activity. Additionally, the direct and indirect cost elements can be identified and compared.

The selection of appropriate unit cost information should be guided by your

Table 1
Book Acquisitions and Cataloging Costs Grid

	Direct		Indirect		Total
	People +	Materials +	Facilities +	Services =	Total
	Salary Fringe	Supplies	Computer	Admin.	
ACTIVITY					
Select					
Purchase					
Acquire					
Receive					
Catalog					
Process					
TOTAL					

capacity to obtain information. As was suggested earlier, if complex accounting mechanisms must be put into place to obtain such information, it is best to use alternative units of measure. This is especially true for smaller academic libraries, which often lack the staff to secure detailed cost information. A number of books are available, however, both within and without the library field, that offer formulas and suggest elements that may be useful in gathering usable information.

THE IMPORTANCE OF COST FINDING

Senior university administrators generally are deliberative individuals, yet are pressed from all sides by competing claims on resources. While there are certainly times when library directors may find it advantageous to prepare elaborate cost analysis presentations for their superiors, experience would suggest that the simplest presentations are often the most attractive and persuasive in the long term. Thus, any system of costing library services must begin with a clear understanding of how the cost data are to be used. Is the material to be simply educational background forwarded to the vice-president as information, or is the material to be used for immediate persuasion?

Certainly it can be useful to have quantitative data to support decisions in that the notion of costs in general is a concept that has broad meaning to many within the academic community, well beyond specific cost considerations attached to the specific library program. However, the library director who believes that this kind of detailed information will determine the course of library funding is likely to become frustrated and disappointed.

Clearly, the linkage of financial to nonfinancial data is essential to making more informed management decisions. Such data puts into a necessary perspective the financial resources requested to support a new or continuing library initiative, and offers usable and typically persuasive data on productivity and performance.

APPROACHES TO THE EFFECTIVE PRESENTATION OF COST DATA

Given the ostensibly collaborative yet competitive environment in which most academic library managers find themselves working, I would suggest that there are, in reality, only a handful of useful approaches to cost benefit presentation. Here I suggest four approaches with illustrations.

The experience of many small academic library directors would suggest that they are often found in the "petitioner" mode of interaction with respect to senior university administrators. The first two examples and illustrations arise out of this posture. The third type of simple cost analysis presented here is one which might be called the "trade-off" presentation where cost comparisons are made between two alternative and equally viable choices. Finally, I offer a fourth type of cost analysis which I have termed the "narrative, iterative approach."

Costing an Additional Workload

College librarians are, if not frequently, at least periodically faced with the pleasant responsibility of accepting gifts from individuals for the acquisition of library materials. In most instances, donor monies are given directly to the university, placed in a restricted account, and drawn upon over time to pay invoices for books acquired. In some instances, however, the donor may open a line of credit with a preferred book vendor. In any case, however, it is rare that funds to offset the additional technical-service overhead costs accompany the gift. It is up to the library to assume the additional processing burden associated with the gift; if the library cannot assume the burden within existing staff lines and supply budgets, a "petition" must be made to senior administration. It is often useful to ground such petitions on cost-impact information. What is it costing to acquire this "free" gift in personnel terms, and in computer and cataloging costs? What is not being done because of the impact of this gift on technical services?

At the smaller college or university, the academic dean or vice-president is likely to know at least the general framework of every librarian's, and many support staff members', job descriptions and responsibilities. What is important in making the case for new funds to support the integration of a gift into the library is not so much a complex costing of effort, but rather a simple, straightforward, and honest presentation of the proportion of effort the new undertaking will demand from the individuals involved. Often you as the library director are asking for new, temporary staff, to augment effort being applied in the technical processing of a continuing or short-term gift. A simple, straightforward presentation such as noted in table 2 gives library managers an opportunity to have something concrete to use as they explain the new initiative and its impact on present staff. Who is working on this project? How much time is being expended? How does this project impact on overall acquisition and cataloging costs? What are the long-standing projects and activities of the library which are not being accomplished because of this gift?

Costing an Ongoing Activity

College librarians often enter standing agreements with their business or budget offices to receive what is often referred to as an "allocated expense credit" or, in simple terms, a reimbursement for labor expended on a permanent, ongoing library activity. Often, such services are of benefit to the entire university but occupy significant library staff time as well as consuming library-purchased supplies and materials. For example, the college may choose to compensate the library for a librarian on sabbatical leave by allowing the director a certain percent of the librarian's salary. Thus, the director may hire part-time or interim staff to assist with projects while the permanent staff member is on sabbatical. In a fashion, the "absent" librarian is costing the library, and the director is simply asking for or being granted compensatory funding. Another common example occurs when a library asks the college for an allocated expense credit to compensate for labor applied to a photocopy operation which, from both a service perspective and a fiscal perspective, benefits the larger college. Table 3 is an example of a cost analysis of this type.

Trade-Off Analyses

It is rare to encounter a smaller academic library where the director is not on occasion called on to compare costs associated with locating a project, equipment, or operation in one of two possible sites. In recent years a good example might be the cost trade-offs associated with locating library automation support hardware in the library or in the computer center on campus. Clearly, looking at the costs associated with each location is important in

Table 2
Overhead Costs to Acquire and Catalog Monographs Acquired through the Robert Smith Gift 1987–1988

Overhead Costs Projected Through June 30, 1988

Value of Purchases Made Through Smith Line-of-Credit with Johnson & Jones Vendors July 1, 1987 through June 30, 1988	$95,000
Overhead	
Personnel Applied in Technical Services	
1. Raymond Mason (50% effort)	20,832
2. Jackie Day (40% effort)	6,052
3. Bertie Louis (33 1/3% effort)	5,835
4. Fred Williams (10% effort)	2,300
Cataloging Costs	
5. OCLC On-Line Computer Costs	5,557
	40,576

1. Approximately half of Mason's workload is an ''intellectual cost'' attached to the acquisition of the Smith Gift, i.e., reading reviews, analyzing present holdings, making selections, and interacting with other librarians and various teaching faculty in the departments.

2. Mrs. Day has continued to devote approximately 40% of her effort to the Smith Gift work, i.e., pre-order searching, verification, correspondence and phone interaction with the vendor, and the sundry tasks associated with the receipt of orders.

3. Miss Louis, a technical support person in Bibliographic Control, has had her normal workload impacted by a gift which has increased overall volume of workflow by 33%. Without Smith's impact, she has borne a workflow of approximately $180,000 per year in books. With the Smith Gift, however, the volume passing Louis is close to $270,000. She has assumed a ⅓ greater workload above and beyond normal workload.

4. Dr. Williams interacts with a certain percentage of Smith Gift acquisition books depending on the complexity of cataloging problems involved.

5. Minimum costs to catalog the approximately 4,700 books to be acquired through Smith through the end of the fiscal year. This reflects ''first time use charges'' of OCLC of $1.17 per item cataloged, but does not include the incidental book preparation costs associated with making the book ready for the shelf.

reaching a final implementation decision. Other ''trade-off cost studies'' may compare costs associated with hiring professional staff against those of clerical staff to perform particular projects; clerical staff against costs of student workers; or costs associated with housing particular collections in one library

Table 3
Maintenance Hours for Photocopy Machines Fiscal Year 1988–89: 245 Working Days, Plus Weekends and Holidays = 351 Days for Eight Photocopy Machines

	Minutes
1. Service machines and collect money; 5 minutes x 6 machines x 351 days	10,530
2. Roll money, record amounts; 60 minutes x 245 days	14,700
3. Refill safe and prepare deposit; 60 minutes x 245 days	14,700
4. Order wrappers; 20 minutes x 12 months	240
5. Service calls, operator attention; 70 minutes x 200 days	14,000
6. Meter reads; 30 minutes x 12 days	360
7. Monthly billing for photocopy service; 120 minutes x 12 months	1,440
8. Monthiy statistical reports; 200 minutes x 12 months	2,400
9. Issue xerox key and charge card to patrons; 30 minutes x 351 days	10,530
10. Train new personnel; 110 minutes x 3 academic terms	330
11. Prepare record sheets for next month; 60 minutes x 12 days	720
12. Semi-annual inventory reports; 90 minutes x 2 days	180
13. Fill machines twice a day; 60 minutes x 351 days	21,060
14. Deliver paper to stations; 90 minutes x 52 weeks	4,680
Total Minutes	95,870

ALLOCATED EXPENSE CREDIT REQUESTED
95,870 Minutes or 1,598 hours x $4.20 per hour = $6,711.60

location over another. From both a good management perspective and a simple political standpoint it is just good judgment to show senior administrators and fellow staff members the costs associated with chosing among options. "Trade-off cost studies" lend themselves to spread-sheet display quite readily, and table 4 is of this type.

Narrative and Iterative Cost Studies

In implementing a major (and typically costly) program within the library, most library managers are asked to work and plan in conjunction with other constituencies on campus who may be affected by the program. This is true above all in the case of library automation. An automation project likely will bring into play key individuals from the library, the computer center, the academic affairs office, the physical plant office, and, typically, the vice-president for administration. The latter involvement may, in turn, trigger the involvement of the college chief fiscal officer.

Narrative cost studies typically arise out of a series of planning meetings where alternatives are examined, costs compared, and funds available to a project agreed on. Readers who have been involved in such planning processes know that while these kinds of meetings are often protracted, they are also generally iterative; that is, the achievement of the desired results or parameters of the project are better achieved after the sequential meetings. Typically, as new information and cost understandings are gained from meeting to meeting, planners arrive at a closer approximation of the final, real costs of the project. Commonly, one member of the planning group takes responsibility for recording the highlights of all movement in the discussions, concisely states areas where consensus has been gained, and updates cost projections from meeting to meeting as new data is brought in following investigations or conversations with vendors and suppliers. In this type of "rolling" costing approach, the person responsible for the tasks noted here will, following each meeting, forward an updated iteration of the process to each team member along with a spreadsheet of costs. The narrative or iterative type of cost analysis is especially valuable if one places much emphasis on consensus building within the development of a project. The appendix presents "pages" from a hypothetical narrative cost study illustrating this approach. In this example, it is likely that several versions of this document will have been prepared before mutual understanding and agreement are reached.

CONCLUSION

Any system of costing library services must start with a clear understanding of how the cost data are to be used. Are the data to be used as a weapon in the library's seemingly endless quest for funds? Are cost data primarily to help library management decide which services to back, or are such studies to be used to make staff members aware of the costs attached to a particular effort?

Table 4
Library Automation, Pro Forma Expenses, and Comparison of Sites

I. CAPITALIZATION	LIBRARY	COMPUTER CENTER
(A) Library Preparation		
(1) Site Preparation		
(a) AC/Electric	$ 4,000	$ 4,000
(b) Furnishings	6,000	6,000
(2) Tape Preparation		
(a) De-duping	1,000	1,000
(b) Flipping	33,000	33,000
(c) Cross Reference Creation	2,500	2,500
(d) Accession Number Extract	3,000	3,000
(e) Wanding/Linking of Books	20,000	20,000
(3) Wiring/TELECOM		
(a) Cabling	17,375	6,575
(b) Modems (4 ports)	5,000	5,000
(c) Aims Boxes (4 ports)	200	200
(B) Serials/Acquisitions (INNOVACQ)	73,000	73,000
(C) On-Line Catalog and Circulation		
(1) DYNIX	111,280	111,280
(2) PRIME/DATATEL	211,000	211,000
(3) Extra Printer		4,200
(4) Laser Readers	7,742	7,742
(5) FAST FILE Maintenance Utility	2,500	2,500
(D) Other Costs		
(1) Interfaces		
(a) INNOVACQ/DYNIX Interface	7,500	7,500
(b) Administrative Computing		
Patron File Generation	500	500
G.L. Accounting	1,500	1,500
Student Holds/Blocks	1,000	1,000
(2) Ms. Case's fees (Consultant)	4,200	4,200
SUBTOTAL	512,297	505,697
(E) CONTINGENCY (1.5% OF Subtotal)	7,684	7,585

Presentation of cost data, along with benefit analysis, must be kept simple and understandable. Management of any library, whether small or large, will always be an exercise in striking balances, recognizing opportunities for further service, and avoiding costly disasters. Information about costs can, itself, be expensive to create, and a director will always want to balance any effort to create cost information against its usefulness.

Appropriately used, cost information should reinforce a concern for the quality of service and help a library focus its energies on its fundamental purposes. Cost analysis, of course, has value beyond the simple identification of costs. The process requires staff to examine how they perform tasks. It is often this consultative process, accompanied by straightforward and often iterative cost data, that is of most value to the costing process.

APPENDIX: LIBRARY COMPUTERIZATION PROPOSAL—NARRATIVE COST ANALYSIS (REVISION DATE 10/26/88—THIRD ITERATION)

Team Members: Lewis, Donatelli, Walker, McAdams, Smith, and Ploeger

The purpose of this proposal is to suggest the strategy that we believe should be pursued in the automation of the various library systems. Since extensive documentation has been prepared by members of the Library staff about the most appropriate software, this proposal concentrates on the questions of hardware, operations, and the financing of the proposed acquisition. The proposal is divided as follows:

A. System Purchases
- 1. Serials/Acquisitions
- 2. On-line Catalogue and Circulation
  - a. Software
  - b. Hardware

B. System Placement and Networking (Pros/Cons)
- 1. Placement
  - a. Introduction
  - b. Pro Location in Library
  - c. Pro Location in Computer Center
- 2. Networking
  - a. Introduction
  - b. Pro Networking with Other Campus Computers
  - c. Cons to Networking with Other Campus Computers

C. Factors Which Are Independent of Computer Location and Networking

D. Five Year Financial *Pro Forma* for the Automation of the Library

E. Proposed Computer Center/Library Service Agreement

F. Summary Recommendations and Conclusions

G. Appendix—Work Plans and Assignments (Note—In final proposal this will not appear)

A. System Acquisition

1. Serials/Acquisitions

During the summer of 1988, a Contact System was purchased for this purpose. It was bought as a stand-alone software/hardware system and is housed on the first floor of the Library. The cost was $87,000 with a yearly maintenance cost of $8,000.

2. Online catalogue and circulation.
   a. Software
      i. All agreed that Smith Automated Systems is the best choice for us.
      ii. Ms. Jane Case (a nationally recognized software negotiator) was contacted and has negotiated the contract with Smith for us.
   b. Hardware
      i. The hardware Smith suggested in its original proposal was a PPC–100. While this is a good machine, our collection is sufficiently large at present that it would absorb all the capabilities of the system. We want room for expansion since there are a number of situations where adding to the basic catalogue would be advantageous (e.g., Law Library, Marian Library). The next larger size PPC Computer would cost approximately $100,000 more.
      ii. Roemer has been able to negotiate an agreement with Datatel whereby if we make a joint purchase of Library Administrative computing equipment, we will be able to acquire a much larger LIBROS computer for the Library at a price comparable to the PPC.
      iii. Though the Prime LIBROS configuration we recommend is far superior to the PPC in nearly all performance standards, there are ways in which the operating system of the Prime is not optimal for the running of the Smith software.
         —The PPC operating system compiles subroutine calls in an order which is the inverse of the way in which the Smith software is written.
         —The PPC operating system segments very large files into smaller files rather than allowing files of very large size.

B. System Placement and Networking (Pros and Cons)

1. Placement
   a. Introduction—We have investigated the placement of the LIBROS system either in the Library as a stand-alone facility or on the third floor of the Computer Center as a part of the University's computer center. To help understand the rationale of our final recommendation, the pros and cons we developed are summarized here. Note that placement is heavily influenced by the possibility of networking which, itself, poses greater costs.
   b. Pro Location in the Library
      i. At present, the Computer Center and the Library keep different hours. If located in the Computer Center, it would have to stay open at least the same length of time that the Library does. If located in the Library, no interdivisional scheduling would be required. To determine how serious a conflict this is, we would need to determine whether the hours of each center are determined by the same underlying student usage patterns and needs. We need cost figures here since the Computer Center would need longer hours.
      ii. Cabling from the Computer Center to the Library introduces a small possibility of transmission errors.

iii. Located at the Library, the Library is better able to control its own destiny vis-à-vis Computer Center charges.
iv. Located in the Computer Center, costs are likely to be increased in the following areas:
—Annual Computer Center operating charges.
—Purchase of a second console for the Library.
—Cabling charges from Computer Center to the Library.

c. Pro Location in Computer Center
i. In the event something out of the ordinary happens with the LIBROS, in the Computer Center there would be persons with more experience.
ii. While the Library facilities for the LIBROS are adequate, because of all the other computing equipment in the Computer Center, more money has been invested in environmental controls in the Computer Center.
iii. If all LIBROS were located in the Computer Center, certain costs would likely be lessened: (a) Networking; (b) initial setup for the phone ports (for "call-ins" to the catalog system); (c) tape drives (since they would be shared).
iv. If the Library LIBROS and the Administrative LIBROS or Academic and Research Vaxs are to be networked, it is much better to do this if all are in the same location. Costs will decrease.
v. In the past, the University has opted for the centralization of computer equipment.

2. Networking of Library LIBROS with Existing Computers
a. Introduction—With the addition of the Library computer, we will have three major systems on campus—the other two being the Administrative LIBROS and the Academic/Research Vax Cluster. There may be an advantage to networking the Library LIBROS to one or both of these systems. To help understand the rationale of our final recommendation, the pros and cons we developed are summarized here.
b. Factors Which Favor Networking of Library LIBROS with Other Campus Computer
i. If the Library LIBROS is networked to other existing campus computers, then those persons who are hardwired to an existing computer will have access to the Library LIBROS. This appears to be especially advantageous to Vax Cluster users who would be students, faculty, and members of the Research Institute. The above only applies to users who are hardwired to an existing computer. If the Library LIBROS is equipped with modern and aim ports, then users with modems or aim boxes, respectively, would be able to access it no matter where it is located. On the other hand, if the Library LIBROS is networked to a computer already having modem or aim ports, these would not have to be duplicated. Ploeger must get better cost data here.
ii. Data transfer between the two LIBROS systems would be greatly enhanced if they were networked. The major data transfer is the update of authorized patrons after each registration period.
c. Factors Which Discourage Networking
i. Since Networking almost certainly implies that the computers be in the same location, all reasons for not being in the same location apply.

ii. Networking will increase costs. Will the benefits derived from this justify these costs?

C. Five-Year Financial Forma

The attached pages show our best estimate of a five-year operating pro forma for two possible configurations of the Library computing system:

1. Stand-alone system in the Library. In this case, we assume the Library LIBROS is equipped with four modem ports and with four aim ports.
2. System networked to the Vax Cluster in the Computer Center. In this case, we assume that there are four hardwired ports from the Library LIBROS to the Vax Cluster. We also assume that four modem ports are installed in the Library LIBROS so that persons with a modem anywhere in the city can access our catalogue. (The projections are on the attached spread-sheets. The scenario titled ''Library'' refers to the first case and ''Computer Center'' to the second).

D. Proposed OCA/Library Service Agreement

To avoid misunderstandings and to clarify expectations if the Library Prime were located on the third floor of the Computer Center, we developed an agreement that outlines the conditions that would apply in this instance. The agreement is attached as a separate piece. Financial agreements are attached.

E. Summary Recommendations and Conclusions (To be completed by Walker)

F. Appendix—Working Plans and Assignments (To be mailed to you next week)

2

The Library Advisory Committee

Henry R. Stewart and
Ronald P. Haselhuhn

If one were to determine the importance of a topic by the number of citations in the literature, then the role of the "library advisory committee" in academic institutions would be considered unimportant. However, this topic should be one of interest to library directors and their staff because of the importance such a committee should play as a communication channel between the library and the faculty, students, and administration in an academic institution. We have served on such committees either as a librarian or as a faculty representative, and realize the importance of such a committee to both the library and to the faculty and students. We also realize that service on such a committee can at times be both rewarding and frustrating. It is our hope that through this chapter we can share their experience and research so that the library advisory committee can become an effective administrative tool for the academic library.

A library advisory committee is defined as a committee that is advisory to the library director and is primarily composed of persons external to the library. Although this is a generalized definition of the historic role of a library advisory committee, it does not define completely the importance such a committee can play as a legitimized means of communication between the library and its immediate environment composed of faculty, students, and administration.

This chapter will (1) begin with a brief review of the available literature, then (2) see how the standards for academic libraries treat this topic, and finally (3) use information from a previous study by the authors to recommend a useful structure and role for the library committee to make it an effective liaison device for communication between the faculty, students, and the library in the academic environment.

LITERATURE REVIEW

A review of the literature uncovered very few citations relating directly to the role of the library advisory committee in academic institutions. A study by Raymound Kilpela (1968: 141–43) of large universities' library committees in sixty-four Association of Research Libraries (ARL) institutions is somewhat relevant to this chapter. The findings indicate that the library director was usually an ex-officio committee member, the committee's duties were largely advisory, and the committee concerned itself with the establishment of policies and liaison activities among the faculty, administration, and the library. An unpublished survey of faculty library committees conducted for the College and University Section of the Virginia Library Association echoed many of the Kilpela findings (Stewart 1979). The most recent research on library advisory committees was performed by the authors of this chapter (Stewart and Haselhuhn 1986: 22–47). The findings from that study will form the basis for the section on committee structure in this chapter.

A review of the information in texts directed either to academic institutions or the subject of library management again found very little information directly related to the topic. Louis Round Wilson and Maurice F. Tauber (1956: 43) noted that a faculty committee on the library was common and that normally it is intended to serve in an advisory capacity. Rutherford D. Rogers and David C. Weber (1971: 12–13) state that the library committee can be an immensely useful group in an advisory capacity. They then list several functions of the committee, including establishment of major operational policies, support for the total library budget, advice on the allocation of the book budget (if departmental allocations exist), and counsel to the library and university administration on the general library program. Rogers and Weber also state that the library committee can be a major source of support for the total library budget to the university administration in the section on budgeting and fiscal management. Guy R. Lyle (1974: 28–29), in his now dated classic on academic library administration, agrees that the committee should be advisory in nature and can serve a useful liaison role, and states that size and term of service for members vary. He also says that the librarian usually is a member and most frequently serves as chair or secretary.

It is interesting to note that two of the more recent textbooks on library administration, one by Robert D. Stueart and John Taylor Eastlick (1987) and the other by John R. Rizzo (1980) make no mention of the library advisory committee. These two textbooks take a scientific management approach to the subject of library management and are not directed toward one specific type of library as were the preceding texts. While these are excellent books on management, they seem to miss a major topic: how a library director can interface with a major component of the immediate environment—the faculty and students.

STANDARDS FOR ACADEMIC LIBRARIES

We also reviewed the standards for academic libraries to determine their position on library committees and to what extent the standards could be used to make recommendations for such a committee.

Standard II.C. of the revised "Guidelines for Two-Year College Learning Resources Programs" (Association of College and Research Libraries, 1982: 8) states that the membership of the library committee should be composed of faculty and students, should be advisory in nature, and should not concern itself with details of administration. The commentary to this section of the standard states that the committee members should either be appointed by the appropriate administrative officer of the college, elected by the faculty, or selected by the procedure for the formation of a faculty committee at the particular institution. The members should represent the various academic divisions of the college and be composed of both senior and junior faculty. The committee acts as a connecting link between the faculty as a whole and the Learning Resources Program.

Standard 7.3, Administration, of the "Standards for College Libraries, 1986" (Morris 1986: 198) is similar in that it states that there shall be a standing advisory committee with members from the student body and the teaching faculty, and that it shall serve as a formal channel of communication between the library and its user community. It recommends that the librarian serve as an ex-officio member, and also asks that the duties of the committee be stated in writing.

The commentary to Standard E.1 of the "Standards for University Libraries" (Association of College and Research Libraries, 1979: 105) mentions that there has long been a recognized need to involve faculty in library matters because of the importance of the library to instruction and research. The existence of a library committee is valuable for close, continuing interaction between the faculty and the library. This standard also states the need for the duties of the committee to be defined clearly in writing and says that the committee's duties should be advisory.

The wording used in the three standards is interesting and seems to reflect the results of the study we conducted (Stewart and Haselhuhn 1986). The two-year college standards use terms such as "are essential" and "as a rule," and are not nearly as prescriptive as the wording in the college library standards, which state that "there shall be a committee." The university standards only mention the library committee in a commentary under administration and governance, but these institutions have the highest percentage of library committees of all institutions. The standards, taken together, do give some insight into the formation, composition, duties, and role of the committee.

STRUCTURE OF THE COMMITTEE

The following information was extracted from the Stewart and Haselhuhn study (1986) and is intended to give the librarian some practical help in the formation, structuring and assignment of duties to a library advisory committee.

Name of the Committee

The most popular name found by the study was ''library committee,'' with several institutions adding the name of the library to the committee's title. Several were named ''library advisory committee,'' while the two-year institutions used terms such as learning resource, Instructional Materials Center (IMC), Learning Resource Center (LRC), media, or instructional. Four- and five-year institutions often added terms such as faculty or faculty senate to the title of the committee. In keeping with the purpose of the committee, it is recommended that the word ''advisory'' be part of the title of the committee, and furthermore that the committee be entitled ''library advisory committee.'' The word library should be replaced with the term used on that campus for a library; that is, LRC, media, or instructional.

Size of the Committee

The size of the library advisory committee should be related to the intended purpose of the committee. If the purpose of the committee is problem solving, then according to Harold Koontz and Cyril O'Donnell (1972: 392), the committee should be no larger than five, as five is the ideal size for decision-making committees. However, if the purpose of the committee is to be advisory and liaison then, according to the standards and the literature, the size of the committee should be structured to ensure adequate representation of all academic areas and the student body. The study indicated that most of the committees exceeded six in number. It is recommended that the duties of the committees be advisory and liaison, and the size of the committee must ensure adequate representation of all areas of the academic community.

Composition of the Committee: Faculty

The number of faculty represented on the committee ranged from one to sixteen, with committees of five or six faculty members being the most common number. Larger institutions tended to have larger committees to insure adequate representation of different areas of the campus. Of 41% of the committees the faculty were at-large representatives, on 28% the faculty represented departments, and 31% of the committees had representation from a combination of divisions, divisions and schools, schools, and at-large. Faculty members were appointed to committee membership 87% of the time, with the appointing authority being mainly upper administration (meaning presidents, academic vice-presidents, or deans). The remainder were appointed by area administration or faculty governing body; three were appointed by the librarian. For the thirty committees where representatives were elected, nine were elected by all faculty, and ten by academic areas; the remainder were either elected by the senate or no indication was given. It is recommended that selection of faculty for membership on the committee follow the procedure for the formation of a faculty committee at that institution, and that the number of faculty representatives to the committee be maintained at a manageable number and be consistent with the size of similar campus committees.

Composition of the Committee: Student

Students were members of 73% of the committees. Five- and seven-year institutions have the highest ratio of student representatives, with four-year schools having students on the committee 61% of the time. The number of student representatives ranged from one to six, with the majority of the committees having one or two student members. Student members were generally appointed by the student governing body, and most were designated at-large members. It is recommended that the committee, as stated in the standards, have representation from the student body and that these student members be appointed or elected by the student governing association and be designated at-large members.

Composition of the Committee: Librarian and Library Staff Members

The survey indicated that the head librarian was a member of 91% of the committees with several including both the head librarian and other members of the library staff. In most of these instances, specific staff or staff positions were designated for membership. It is recommended that there should be a library faculty representative on the committee, and that for smaller institutions this representative should normally be the head librarian serving as an ex-officio member, as recommended in the standards.

Written Charge for Committee

Although the standards strongly recommend a written charge that delineates the committee's duties, only 56% of the committees have such a charge. Thirty-five percent of the two-year institutions have a written charge, as do 61% of the four-year institutions, 66% of the five-year institutions, and 77% of the seven-year institutions. It is recommended strongly that the committee's duties be specified in writing, although this statement need not be extremely detailed.

Chair of Committee

This is the area of greatest variance between types of institutions. Twenty-six library directors of two-year institutions were chair of the committee versus nineteen committee members. Four-year institutions had a ratio of twenty-two library directors to twelve committee members serving as chair. In five-year institutions, only five library directors served as chair versus twenty-one committee members. No library directors of the nineteen committees of seven-year institutions served as chair. Fifty-two of the chairs were elected by their committee, with forty chairs being appointed. In most cases these appointments were made by the same appointing authority that appointed members to the committee. It is recommended that the chair of the committee be elected by members of the committee, and that the chair should not be the head of the library. It is also recommended that the chair be responsible for the preparation of the agenda (usually in communication with the library director). The study revealed that the librarian assisted with the development of the agenda when not the chair, and that committee members were encouraged to add items of concern to the agenda.

Frequency of Meetings

The study indicated a range of meeting frequencies from weekly to infrequently, with one that indicated no meeting in four years. Respondents would indicate a frequency, and also note "at the direction of the chairperson." Thirty-four indicated monthly, and fifty reported a range of meeting times from weekly to four meetings per term or semester. It is recommended that the committee meet no less than two or three times a semester or term, with additional meetings at the direction of the chairperson.

Functions and Powers of the Committee

The study revealed that the primary function of the committee was overwhelmingly advisory and liaison. Few of the committees had the power to make decisions or determine policy, with the majority of the committees indicating that the powers of the committee were mainly advisory to either the librarian or upper administration. This would reinforce the statements in the various standards that the committees are to be advisory in nature. The study also indicated an advisory role of the committee in the establishment of the library's operational policies, and in book selection. The committee has mainly an advisory role in the establishment of the book budget allocation, if an allocation process is used at the institution, with only eight involved in establishing the final allocation. In like manner, only two committees were involved in the approval of the general library operating budget. It is recommended that the committee perform an advisory function in these matters. It is recommended further that the committee be aware of policy debates in the library and that their opinion on policy changes and review be solicited. The committee should be informed about the library budget so they can provide the necessary liaison to the areas they represent.

Liaison Role of the Committee

The standards indicate that liaison is to be a major role of the committee, and our study indicates a strong responsibility in liaison with only 6.6% of the respondents indicating no liaison role. The committee can and should be extremely helpful in communicating to its constituents the support that the library can provide. Additionally and importantly, the committee can help explain the financial, personnel, and other needs of the library. It is beneficial for the library to have the entire campus understand the role the library plays and therefore its needs. Also important is the responsibility of the committee members to express the needs of their constituents to the library. The committee members must understand that they have to fill a two-way communications role.

Committee Role in the Selection of Librarians

While the study showed that 55% of the committees had no role in the selection of key librarians (department heads or higher), 15% of the committees fulfilled an advisory role, and 19% were part of a selection committee. Eight percent were involved only in the selection of a new library director. It is recommended that at least one of the external members of the committee be involved in the search for key librarians.

SUMMARY

The library advisory committee should be an integral part of the operation of academic libraries. It is a device that can be of great benefit to the library and the academic community. An advisory committee is generally recommended by standards. Specific recommendations to follow are:

1. There must be a written charge for the committee.
2. The committee's size should ensure adequate representation from all areas of the academic community, elected or appointed according to the normal campus procedures.
3. The chair should be elected by the committee and should not be the director of the library.
4. The agenda should be set by the chair.
5. Meetings of the committee should be held at least two times per semester or term, with additional meetings at the direction of the chair.

6. The committee should have an advisory role in policy formulation and should be informed on budgetary matters.
7. At least one external member of the committee should be involved in the selection process for librarians of department-head level and higher.

If these recommendations are followed, the library advisory committee will be an effective administrative tool for the academic library.

REFERENCES

Association of College and Research Libraries. "Guidelines for Two-Year College Learning Resources Programs." (Rev.) 1982. *College and Research Libraries News* 43, no. 1 (January): 8.

Association of College and Research Libraries. "Standards for University Libraries." 1979. *College and Research Libraries News* 40, no. 4 (April): 105.

Kilpela, Raymond. 1968. "The University Library Committee." *College and Research Libraries* 29 (March): 141–44.

Koontz, Harold, and Cyril O'Donnell. 1972. *Principles of Management: An Analysis of Managerial Functions*, 5th ed. New York: McGraw-Hill.

Lyle, Guy R. 1974. *The Administration of the College Library*. 4th ed. New York: H. W. Wilson Company.

Morris, Jacquelyn M. 1986. "Standards for College Libraries, 1986." *College and Research Libraries News* 47, no. 3 (March): 198.

Rizzo, John R. 1980. *Management for Librarians: Fundamentals and Issues*. Westport, Conn: Greenwood Press.

Rogers, Rutherford D., and David C. Weber. 1971. *University Library Administration*. New York: H. W. Wilson Company.

Stewart, Henry R. 1979. "The Faculty Library Committee in Virginia." Paper presented to the College and University Section of the Virginia Library Association, Richmond, April 1979. The questionnaire used in that survey was revised for this study.

Stewart, Henry R., and Ronald P. Haselhuhn. 1986. "Status of the Library Committee in Academic Institutions of the Mountain Plains Library Association." In *Preparing for the 21st Century: Proceedings of the Mountain Plains Library Association Academic Library Section Research Forum*. Edited by V. Sue Hatfield, pp. 22–47. CLA/MPLA Joint Conference, October 11–15, 1986.

Stueart, Robert D., and John Taylor Eastlick. 1987. *Library Management*, 3d. ed. Littleton, Colo: Libraries Unlimited, Inc.

Wilson, Louis Round, and Maurice F. Tauber. 1956. *The University Library*, 2d ed. New York: Columbia University Press.

3

An Overview of the History of Bibliographic Networks Focused on the Impact of the National and Regional Networks

J. J. Hayden III

THE OLD PLAN—REGIONAL DATABASES LINKED TO A NATIONAL DATABASE

The history of the formation of the current national, regional, and state bibliographic networks can provide the observer with insights on how the current situation evolved. The original plan was that there would be several regional networks established, and that these networks would provide access to computer-based bibliographic databases. The libraries in a region would make use of the regional database for cataloging purposes. Bibliographic information for these regional databases would come from a few select cataloging centers, such as the Library of Congress. Conversely, titles that were not found in a regional database and that were added to it would be sent to the national center for inclusion in the next transmission of the national database. The basic reasons for the desirability of a national bibliographic database were the completeness, uniformity, and accuracy of the cataloging that could be obtained from such a database. This would enable any subsequent user of the bibliographic information to be able to build on the cataloging work already done, and hopefully would minimize the amount of work required to catalog an item.

OHIO COLLEGE LIBRARY CENTER—FROM PLANS TO ACTUALITY

Fred Kilgore decided to put the theory of an on-line cataloging database into practice. By establishing the Ohio College Library Center and connecting libraries from Ohio into the system, he provided real proof that such a system was feasible. Over the last twenty-five years, OCLC (now the Online Computer Library Center) has grown into a database of over eighteen million records, with terminals across the United States and in several other countries. The establishment of OCLC and the regional networks, as well as some of the state networks, went hand in glove; without the creation of the national database and the regional centers to provide access and support to the database, it is possible that today there would be no national database.

FOUNDING OF REGIONAL NETWORKS

The founders of the regional networks were the large academic and public libraries. These organizations were in the forefront of the move to automate the process of handling library materials. In addition to the desire to have a uniform description of bibliographic material in a database that could be used to build local databases, several technological events fostered the establishment of the national and regional networks. The development of computer systems that could support large numbers of terminals and allow users to share access to databases was one of the most important developments. The Machine Readable Cataloging program, MARC, formalized the format and identification of information in bibliographic records. The development of library automation systems in the academic and research environment was another important development. The convergence of these forces plus countless hours of work by catalogers has produced today's national bibliographic database. The networks provided the support for this movement toward library automation, and in so doing gained a wealth of experience both in working with a large bibliographic database and in assisting libraries with the creation of local library automation systems.

Reasons for the establishment of a national bibliographic database are much easier to define in retrospect. The vast majority of cataloging done via the OCLC database involves the addition of local information to the basic bibliographic record. This implies that the goals of uniform cataloging and increased productivity gained by using a pre-cataloged record have been realized. However, serendipity does strike, the ability to carry out interlibrary loans of materials, an activity that was not high on the list of requirements for a national database, is now one of its major uses.

EXPANSION OF THE ACTIVITIES OF OCLC

It is true that any system that is not growing is declining. The directors of OCLC have understood this principle and have attempted to keep expanding the organization. Because the networks have provided access to the OCLC system and support for its products, it is necessary to understand the direction OCLC is taking with respect to library automation products in order to see how this has affected the role of the networks, especially the regional networks.

In addition to the core on-line cataloging services described, OCLC is the vendor of several types of local library automation systems, from partial components such as acquisitions and serials control, to complete integrated systems such as the LS2000 product. In 1984, OCLC was granted a copyright to its database and began to use it to create by-products such as printed lists and optical disc–based reference systems. In addition, the IBM PC (personal computer) replaced the custom-built terminals that had been connected to the OCLC system. Together with a new set of software to access the OCLC database, this marked the beginning of the bibliographic workstation. As the development of the microcomputer has progressed, the PC has given way to more powerful micros, and OCLC has kept pace by introducing more capable workstations as terminals for the network. The IBM AT-class microcomputer that makes up the M310 series terminals is more powerful than many of the minicomputer-based library automation systems of the early 1980s. This computer capacity will serve as the foundation for one of the stated OCLC goals, the electronic delivery of documents to the end user. The technology is in place to facilitate the use of computers to access bibliographic databases, search for specific information, and download that information to be published on a local laser printer.

CHANGING POSITION OF REGIONAL NETWORKS

An examination of the membership of networks reveals that the vast majority are large academic and public libraries and have little need for the services of most networks, state or regional. This is due in large part to the fact that network membership and OCLC membership are synonymous, and the majority of members have completed the retrospective conversion of their primary bibliographic records and have established online library automation systems. When asked, "What can the regional network do for you?" the reply most often given is to continue to send a bill every month along with a tape containing the OCLC MARC cataloging records that have been changed (transaction archives). This response comes at a time when OCLC wants the networks to expand their role as dealers of OCLC services and add a sales staffperson specifically for the various OCLC products. This step takes the network significantly beyond the role of a broker and provider of support services.

THE PLIGHT OF THE NETWORK

The largest libraries need little from national and regional networks, while the smaller libraries cannot afford the recurring communications costs of being on-line. The smaller libraries are in need of the same type of resource sharing that the large libraries needed ten to fifteen years ago. The statistics show that a majority of the total library community, including academic, public, and special libraries, are not part of the OCLC/Regional/State networks. This is due to one basic factor: cost. Even when using the very best telecommunications access rates—dial-up, 2,400-baud, non–prime time—a library can spend thousands of dollars each year on this method of cataloging. This cost does not count the initial investment of an IBM XT-class computer, which is the minimum requirement for accessing the OCLC system. Given the cost of these initial requirements, and the fact that there are now several local cataloging products that provide access to the Library of Congress database, there seems to be little incentive for libraries to become part of this national database.

IMPACT OF NEW TECHNOLOGY ON THE LIBRARY COMMUNITY

The irony is that with the advent of the Micro-Mainframe, (such as the Compacq 386) and IBM upper-end PS/2 computers, the prospect for automating the smaller academic and public library has never been brighter. This puts these smaller libraries in the same position the large academics were in when OCLC was just starting. The needs are the same now as they were then: a large database for retrospective conversion, training on how to use the various MARC formats, support when loading these records into local systems, and answers to questions about the various library automation options available.

THE ROLE OF THE REGIONAL NETWORK

What then is the role of the regional network? It can be summed up in a few words: to provide services that cross local, area, or state boundaries. The extension of the existing services to libraries not using OCLC, and facilitating the participation of these libraries in the national database even though they may never be connected directly to OCLC, is a prime example of such activities. How do the regional, state, and area networks interact? The regional network should augment and coordinate services between the library organizations in the region in order to promote resource sharing. In this sense the term "resource" is not limited to library materials, but includes access to specialized programs and staff that the regional network can support and employ because the regional geographic coverage can encompass sufficient demand for the service to make support of such activities feasible. The most important area of development of services and focus of activities should be in defining and carrying out programs, projects, and services that can be used by the smaller library. This is not too difficult a task because, once updated to take into account changes in technology, the same processes that were developed and used to meet the needs of the large libraries are now needed by the smaller libraries. If the networks ignore the calls for assistance from this group, then the days of the network, be it national, regional, or state-based, appear to be numbered.

4

Library Cooperative Activity: Common Characteristics of Successful Efforts

Fred Heath

Library cooperation is a term that has entered into common parlance in recent years. It is a broad concept, and covers in one nuance or another almost all activities between and among libraries. Its origins lie in the efforts of similar types of libraries to overcome the limitations of local budgets and collections by pooling resources (DeGennaro 1980: 353–55; Holicky 1984: 146). In recent years, higher-minded sentiments have been used to justify the rush to cooperative activity. To some, networking efforts are the means by which we facilitate access of the individual to information resources (Segal 1987: 42–58). For others, cooperative activity is seen as a better way to accommodate the "human right" of universal access to information (Dowlin 1987: 64–67). These and other factors have fostered the rapid growth of formal cooperative ventures of all kinds. A 1986 study by Martin Cummings recalled that of the 125 academic library consortia in place in 1970, 75% of them had come into being since 1965. Even more impressive has been the growth of more than 500 structures of varying complexity in the past fifteen years (Cummings 1986: 47).

Applying organizational theory to this outbreak of cooperative activity, Ed Walters has categorized five types of networking activity. Of necessity, types he identified vary greatly in size and complexity, exhibit different governance structures, and undertake a broad range of programs. Nevertheless, they are all part of that complex mosaic that serves as a surrogate for a national library network. Almost all libraries are members of more than one type of library cooperative, and it is difficult to discuss one type of network without defining its relationships to the others (Walters 1987: 15–29). Embracing the notion that resource sharing is a general good, and straining under the twin pressures of declining purchasing power and a rapidly growing information universe, library directors have turned to cooperative activity for relief. At this time, it is important that close scrutiny be given to their motivations. Despite the flush of good feelings that normally accompanies the birth of cooperative activity, and given the difficulty of quantifying the actual costs of interinstitutional activity, there is a slowly emerging awareness that library cooperation is not without significant costs (Ballard 1985: 257; Kantor: 1985a,b). Recently, Charles Lowry called for librarians to give closer attention to the costs of cooperative undertakings, suggesting that failure to better access the cost benefit of such activities "is naive at best and irresponsible at worst" (Lowry 1988: 6).

The purpose of this chapter is not to access the costs of library cooperation. Such an assessment across the broad spectrum of activities cataloged by Walters would be difficult. Accurate studies are probably feasible only when specific activities are analyzed. Rather, the purpose of this chapter will be to use the example of some cooperative efforts that are generally recognized as successful. From those examples, the focus will be on motivations that led to their establishment, as well as those organizational characteristics that have distinguished them from other efforts. These examples may serve as an informal guide for those library administrators who are currently assessing their own participation in cooperative activity, or are seeking to ensure the success of organizations of which they are a part.

Because it is the type of networking activity that seems to enjoy the broadest support among academic librarians, this chapter will focus on cooperative collection development and similar resource-sharing ventures. Even a casual glance at abstracting and indexing sources will reveal to the inquirer a skyrocketing interest over the past decade in cooperative collection development and related activities. Whether cooperation takes place at the local or subregional levels, or at the broader state, regional, or national levels, the concept of sharing responsibilities for the development and management of collections is one of the most challenging issues confronting libraries at this time. It is a particularly complicated topic, as it moves collection development from the exclusive sphere of the specialist and introduces as players administrators and others for whom collection development is often not an area of expertise. This chapter, developed from the perspective of an administrator, undertakes to review cooperative resource sharing from three aspects. The first part will review some of the factors contributing to the growing interest in cooperative activity. The middle section will identify some significant efforts at shared collection development that have emerged. The examples are intended to serve as models for others considering cooperative activity. The chapter will conclude with a search for some commonalities, and will attempt to summarize the shared aspects of successful cooperative ventures. Perhaps these key considerations will serve as a useful checklist for emergent organizations.

THE ENVIRONMENT FOR COOPERATIVE ACTIVITY

Cooperative collection activity is not a new movement in libraries. Joseph Branin, formerly of the University of Georgia, tells an amusing story of how, when he was deeply immersed in the initial efforts to establish the Southeastern Association of Research Libraries' Union List of Serials, he paused from his feverish efforts long enough to accept a gift of dusty tomes from an emeritus professor. In that stack of books, he found a 1936 ALA publication entitled *Libraries of the South: A Report on Developments, 1930–1935* (Branin 1986: 2). As he thumbed through the book, a committee report on Southern library resources caught his eye. In that report, the compiler Robert Downs observed that better coordination of bibliographic and location information was badly needed, and that among the remedies for the bibliographic deficiencies plaguing the South would be the completion of a projected union list of serials even then under development. Branin recalled his surprise at seeing his own efforts at cooperative resource-sharing activity preceded by fifty years. Even today, Mr. Branin says he wonders if that 1936 document was historical evidence of a half-century of cooperation in the region, or whether it was merely a further demonstration of futility—that after all these years, librarians were still trying to solve the same problems.

Despite strong critics who cite the costs of cooperation (such as Paul B. Kantor and Charles B. Lowry), the call for renewed resource-sharing efforts among libraries has continued to be issued periodically throughout the years. The need for a national library and information network to serve the needs of the American people was recognized well in advance of the 1979 White House Conference on Library and Information Services, and was discussed in one of the earliest statements of the National Commission on Libraries and Information Science (Galvin 1978: 1). The White House Conference subsequently addressed, but never fully resolved, the need for a national network (White House Conference on Library and Information Services 1979: 64, 84). The unfolding of this decade, however, has revealed a steady evolution toward effective networks which are attempting to husband scarce resources by sharing collection responsibilities, and are putting larger numbers of people into contact with the information they seek.

Why is there so much interest in cooperative activity today? Why does it enjoy such a high priority in almost every library? By recognizing that the overall problem is the pressing information needs of library clients and understanding that cooperative activity is but one strategy employed to meet those information needs, it is possible to catalog the factors at work.

The Economic Environment

I recall my first paper on collection issues. It was delivered at a Collection Development Institute in Richmond, Virginia, about a decade ago. At that time,

I worked in the library of a regional university, where funds were extremely limited. I specifically remember the contrast between the thrust of my own paper and that of one of the presenters from a major research library. Coming as she did from the perspective of a large university, I thought that her concerns for a comprehensive collection-building program, utilizing far-reaching foreign acquisitions, out-of-print want lists and other techniques, were far removed from my own context, where inadequate collections, soaring prices, and exploding print universes were problems I shared in common with my increasingly sophisticated client group and with most of the other librarians in the room that day. However, in the past decade, large libraries have come to share these limitations. For the past several years, all academic libraries have been operating in an environment of scarcity. From 1979 through 1982, for example, the number of volumes added to Association of Research Libraries (ARL) libraries declined (Branin 1986: 9). Similarly, among small liberal arts colleges, the average acquisitions budget increased by about 50% between 1975 and 1981 yet the number of volumes added and periodicals received decreased (Farber 1982: 3).

Subsequently, regional economic dislocation caused by the decline in the price of oil visited hardship on many institutions. Nationwide, the past three years have recorded a sharp decline in the dollar against foreign currencies, driving up the price of foreign titles and subscriptions along with other imports. To cite but one example, the same dollar that would purchase 3.8 Dutch guilders at the beginning of 1985 was worth only 1.8 guilders in March of 1988 (Kels 1988: 3). Driven by devaluation and fueled by other factors, European scientific journals have increased as much as 30% per year during this period. Budget cuts have been felt from Kansas to Massachusetts and from Louisiana to California, and administrators of institutions of higher education in many states continue to guard against the fearful prospect of taxpayer-led initiatives which could cut operating funds still further (Jascik 1986: 11). It is precisely this kind of environment that has led Paul Gherman to observe that cooperative activity has become ‘‘more an economic decision than one of ‘apple pie and motherhood’ ’’ (Gherman 1987: 51–57).

Economic disequilibrium has rekindled academic interest in cooperative resource sharing. The Research Library Group (RLG) emerged in its current form in the late 1970s. It is a member-owned cooperative of twenty-five research universities and independent research libraries, attempting to achieve collectively ‘‘what they can no longer afford or hope to achieve individually using traditional technology—namely, the continued provision of adequate research collections and services to their users’’ (DeGennaro 1981: 1049). Organizations such as the Research Library Group evolved in part because those libraries realized that it would be impossible in the future to keep up with user demands or to acquire research materials at the local level as they had in the past (Branin 1986: 8). These same motivations were surely in the minds of the Triangle Research Libraries Network (TRLN) when that North Carolina consortium was founded, and they certainly were a driving factor in the creation of the Network of Alabama

Academic Libraries (Byrd, Davis, Gosling, and Herman 1985: 71; Hewitt 1986: 140–43; Medina 1986).

The Information Explosion

Librarians who write in this field are fond of citing Fremont Rider and his studies of the rate at which the availability of published information doubles (Shera 1967: 746). Suffice it to say that it is an astonishing phenomenon in general, and in some disciplines it is overwhelming. Scientific journals are a case in point. It is not unusual today to find major libraries without monograph budgets as they struggle to maintain serial subscriptions. At the same time heroic efforts are being made to hold on to these subscriptions, there is a radical shift away from monographs to journals as the medium of publication. Again, to cite a single example, in 1965 there were 28,000 serials listed in *Ulrich's Periodical Directory*, while by 1981 that publication carried 63,000 listings (Branin 1986: 13).

As if that were not enough, entire new formats are arising that tax budgets, extend staff, and overwhelm expertise. Recently a conference was held in Racine, Wisconsin, on the future of information resources in higher education. At the conference, nonlibrarians, including the president of Carnegie Mellon, warned of the dangers of libraries failing to capture and make available the leading edge of research: computerized information. Unless libraries prove themselves better able to supply such data, the critics warned, they will diminish in value to researchers. "Books are not critical for research in most fields;" one observer warned, "yet that is the primary concern and investment of most libraries" (Turner, 1986: 34).

The primary theme of the Racine conference was that there is a growing body of research information accessible only by computer and that it is essential that research libraries begin to grapple with the problems of acquiring such data and making it available through cataloging. Librarians and libraries seem to have difficulty responding to this responsibility, perhaps because they lack the time or expertise to judge what is worth saving. Consequently, there seems to have emerged an "electronic word of mouth" where researchers in fast-moving fields have developed their own networks to share data, thus circumventing the limitations of libraries (Turner 1986: 34).

The obvious needs to tap available expertise wherever it exists in library circles and to share the responsibilities for acquiring and making available such materials are the occasion for the consideration of a third environmental factor: the general shift in attitude toward support of cooperative activity.

The Shift in Attitude

Resource sharing is but one strategy employed by libraries to meet the pressing information needs of clients. The twin pressures of rising costs and the even more rapid increase in the volume and variety of information have given cooperative activity a credibility in recent years that it had not previously enjoyed. The idea of sharing resources as a way to improve the effective use of public funds has gained favor at the municipal, state, and even interstate levels. Technological advances—which have permitted the increasingly rapid transfer of data and the linkage of local systems—have contributed to the shift to a more favorable attitude toward resource sharing by library and campus administrators. Similarly, libraries are becoming more adept at handling the intricacies of the management agreements required to handle complicated resource sharing agreements that cut across many lines of authority. Finally, in the face of mounting complexities, there remains an entrepreneurial spirit determined to explore every possible library organizational arrangement in the effort to provide clients with the information they are seeking (Library and Information Resources of the Northwest 1985: 1).

Among the many factors that play a role, there is also a negative influence at work: a lingering crisis of confidence in the public mind regarding all government activity. Arthur Curley observed at a 1983 Collection Development and Management Institute that tensions were growing in the public mind as the idealism and activism of earlier times gave way to a deep skepticism about the value of government services. In a curious way, this skepticism fosters cooperation. Curley observed that cooperation offered government officials at every level the prospect of cutting costs. Librarians should always bear in mind that government authorities promote cooperation as a way to save money, and should advance their arguments regarding cooperation with great care (Fletcher 1983: 881).

In addition to disruptions caused by a poor economy that have forced budget cuts for higher education in many parts of the country, there have been taxpayer-led initiatives, usually defeated, which would have reduced allocations still further. That distressing aspect of public attitudes is mirrored by the press. Just as colleges and universities have fought on one front to preserve state funding for higher education, so too have they attempted to reverse the restrictive fiscal policies of Ronald Reagan's administration in Washington. There was a long period of time when the popular press was supportive of such activity on the part of higher education. That sentiment is no longer preponderantly in education's corner, however. Recently, for example, as colleges and universities lobbied to overcome what they felt were some of the most crippling aspects of the recent income tax reform initiative, they found their efforts opposed in the editorials of the *Wall Street Journal*, the *New York Times*, and the *Washington Post*. As one of the editorials concluded: "Institutions of higher learning should be asking themselves how it happened that what's good for society and what's good for them came to be so different" ("Opinion" 1986: 38–39). If American higher education had not yet come under siege, in this increasingly hostile atmosphere it was only natural that libraries would begin to draw closer to other libraries with whom they once practiced a certain rivalry.

COOPERATIVE COLLECTION DEVELOPMENT: NATIONAL, REGIONAL, AND STATE BACKGROUND

This section will briefly describe the activities of library cooperatives at the national, regional, and local (state) level. The Research Libraries Group (RLG), The Library and Information Resources for the Northwest Program (LIRN), and the Network of Alabama Academic Libraries (NAAL) will be reviewed, along with a cursory look at other ventures.

National Activities

In the aftermath of the White House Conference on Library and Information Services, there was optimism about national collection efforts. The final report of the conference gave a major emphasis to centralized national efforts, including a National Library and Information Service system, which would build national collections and establish national networks to share resources. Prominent among the recommendations was the call for a national periodicals system, with collections, services, and facilities designed to enhance access (White House Conference on Library and Information Services 1979: 19). In the current political environment, there is little sentiment for centralized educational activities and not much remains of the fond dream of nationwide resource-sharing efforts.

The national models we still have are essentially decentralized. RLG did emerge in part due to pressures on major research libraries to share some collection development responsibilities. As its charter observes:

> RLG is founded on the recognition that neither significant increases in library purchasing power nor reductions in demand for library services are likely in the foreseeable future, that the volume of information on which scholarship depends will continue to grow, and that in the decades ahead, individual collections, regardless of their size and history, will be forced to move increasingly away from the concept of comprehensive acquisitions practices. (Mosher 1986: 28)

RLG was founded in 1975 by several eastern research libraries which recognized that "the combination of economic and information inflation spelled trouble" (Martin 1982: 1). Although plagued throughout its history by financial problems, RLG is nonetheless an organization with an impressive budget. Membership fees are formidable and there are additional charges for database maintenance. Through its formative period, the stature of the participants was sufficient to entice large grants from such foundations as Sloan, Ford, and Carnegie, which permitted the maintenance of a pooled acquisitions budget. In the early 1980s, the annual RLG budget exceeded ten million dollars per annum (Beyers 1983: 576). By 1986, the organization had approximately thirty members around the nation (Cummings 1986: 50). The Research Libraries Information Network

(RLIN) is the automated information structure upon which RLG mounts its impressive array of services. Programs that have developed over time include collection development, interlibrary loan, shared cataloging of East Asian materials, public service programs, and preservation (Shurkin 1982: 454).

Certainly there remain other efforts near the national level. The Linked Systems Project, involving Western Library Network (WLN), Research Libraries Group (RLG), the Library of Congress, and OCLC (the Online Computer Library Center), promises to facilitate the online distribution of records among utilities (Avram 1986: 44; Buckland 1987: 83). OCLC remains intent on building an international bibliographic database, and the erstwhile Oxford Project (now renamed New Online System) and the European initiatives are symbolic of the role to be played by this national utility in cooperative collection development and resource-sharing activity (Melin 1986: 38; OCLC 1987). However, at the national level, it seems the future holds less of actual consortia—which are likely to be too large to ever work effectively—than the common language, data sets, and other components that cooperatives of varying size and complexity will need to work together.

One such example is the *RLG Conspectus*, a tool that is being used with some modifications all around the nation. As Joe Branin expertly explains, the conspectus is an attempt to provide a national standard to permit libraries to use a single language to describe their strengths and weaknesses to each other. It is a simple idea in concept. Based on the Library of Congress classification system, the world of knowledge is compartmentalized into roughly 5,000 subject categories. For each division, the conspectus provides the Library of Congress range of call numbers and the description of the subject. A library is asked to rate its collection two ways for each of these categories. First of all, existing collecting strength is rated on a scale of zero to five. The assigned rating becomes a statement of the relative strength of that part of the collection as it has evolved over time. Secondly, libraries are asked to evaluate current collecting intensity. For example, in a given year, collecting intensity can suddenly soar if the parent institution determines to add a doctoral program in a particular area. It can just as suddenly plummet when the price of oil drops to fifteen dollars a barrel or other external factors impact the library (Branin 1986: 27–28).

The rating scale allows comparisons among collections. With a zero assigned to a conspectus number, a library is saying that it collects nothing in that area. Surprisingly, zero is a number that pops up often in such exercises. In a current assessment being performed by AMIGOS for the state of Alabama, it was necessary to collapse the conspectus because of the large number of empty sets. The conspectus had to be similarly tailored for the Fred Meyer project in the Pacific Northwest for the same reasons (Førcier 1988: 43–45). With a rating of five, a library makes the statement that it collects everything published—this is a rare number at any university. At the fourth level, a library states that it is maintaining a research collection and probably buying 75 to 80% of the major publications in that area (Branin 1986: 28).

The conspectus was intended to provide a means by which research libraries could identify collection strengths nationally, to determine collecting levels at other libraries, and to establish a system for locating needed material in a more timely fashion. It was not produced for the exclusive use of RLG, but was designed to help all research libraries understand and map the interrelationships of their collections (Mosher 1986: 29, 31). Certainly the conspectus has been used by collection development librarians in most of the RLG libraries for purposes of collective acquisitions decisions. The RLG librarians assemble periodically after conspectus-based analysis to assign primary collection responsibilities (PCRs) among themselves. Where there are particularly strong collections, libraries may be asked to continue buying at that level, and the assigned PCRs are tested in RLG publications. The arrangement is not legally binding, and a library can elect not to exercise these PCR responsibilities (Branin 1986: 26–30). Similarly, libraries that belong to the Association of Research Libraries use the conspectus as part of the North American Collection Inventory Project. Already, in Phase II of that project, research libraries are beginning to develop approaches to coordinated collection management (Farrell 1986: 47). These projects are probably as close as we come to collection assessment activities at the near national level (Branin 1986: 27).

RLG participants in the ongoing use of the conspectus can contribute their assessments to an on-line database, which is accessible to others (Farrell 1986: 55). There have also been important enhancements. AMIGOS, the Southwestern regional component of OCLC, has adapted the conspectus for computer-based collection assessment. That conspectus has been used to complete a pilot project of Texas library materials, and other projects are underway for Alabama and Florida libraries.

The North American Collection Inventory Project was initiated in July 1983 as an undertaking involving both the Association of Research Libraries and RLG (Mosher 1986: 31–32). It is similar to the informal practices of the RLG libraries. Intended to involve research libraries throughout the United States and Canada, the long-term goal is to develop an on-line inventory of research collections, thus helping researchers locate needed materials. It is expected that the inventory will identify strengths and weaknesses, and thus will facilitate coordinated management of national research collections. The goal is the determination of shared responsibilities for maintaining these research collections (Farrell 1986: 47, 51).

Regional Activities

In 1984, the Fred Meyer Charitable Trust in Portland, Oregon, with assets exceeding $170,000,000 and annual grants in the neighborhood of $8,000,000, turned its attention to libraries as part of its commitment to strengthen educational and economic opportunities in the Pacific Northwest. The resulting program, called Library and Information Resources for the Northwest (LIRN):

seeks to provide the tools and conditions in which libraries in the Pacific Northwest can improve both the net store of information available and access to it through coordinated collection activity. LIRN will reduce the front end risks in trying new methods and new technologies in hopes of stimulating wide activity on the part of libraries. (Library and Information Resources of the Northwest 1985:1)

Regional wide collection management projects were not LIRN's objectives. Rather, the $3.5 million program undertook to provide the support for more organic units—united by geography, collections, missions, or other factors—which were expected to emerge in the Pacific Northwest (Haley and Ferguson 1986: 187). All types of libraries have been invited to participate, and collection development efforts are composed of three basic components. The program has three parts: (1) establishment of a regional resource-assessment process; (2) development of cost-effective delivery mechanisms; and (3) propagation of interinstitutional plans and agreements for ongoing resource development (Haley and Ferguson 1986: 187). Intensive training in a common methodology of collection assessment was an early priority, followed by the development of a computerized database, which would generate reports from the collection-assessment techniques. Finally, before LIRN ceases grant-funded operations, it will actively encourage collection-development activities among libraries that have completed the assessment (Forcier 1988: 43–45).

Training, Fred Meyer officials and the participants agreed, is important to the maintenance of effective cooperative efforts. The University of Washington Graduate School of Library and Information Science, along with Office of Management Studies' (OMS) personnel, instructed 28 trainers from five states in 1985. They in turn trained more than 230 librarians from 260 libraries in the use of the modified RLG conspectus. Once the collection assessments are completed, the resulting analysis will be made available to participants on-line. Development of the database is underway, as are plans to assess machine-readable portions of the database.

LIRN's efforts met with enthusiastic response. Over 230 libraries committed to completing collection assessment as a precursor to the development of resource-sharing arrangements in the Northwest. Involved were 97 academic libraries, 82 public libraries, and 55 special libraries. The assessments were added to the Pacific Northwest Conspectus database at the Oregon State Library as they were completed. The volume count of participating libraries ranged from six hundred to over two million volumes.

In order that all libraries would know the resources with which they were dealing, LIRN's first efforts concentrated on developing this assessment methodology. Essentially a revision of the RLG conspectus, modifications permitted the participation of even the smallest libraries. For example, the RLG lowest category of collecting activity was subdivided to permit even finer distinctions, and the language that defined the various levels was amplified to relate more clearly to public library collections. With the LIRN version, the conspectus is revised and is divided into 24 division levels, 500 category levels, and 3,500 subject levels. Librarians may elect to work from either an abridged category worksheet or a standard—and more detailed—subject worksheet (Forcier 1988: 43).

Local Activity

In order to complete the overview of resource-sharing activity, one example of a state model should suffice. The Network of Alabama Academic Libraries (NAAL) grew out of institutional initiatives and was nurtured by the protective benevolence of the state's higher education coordinating commission. For its first year, it sustained itself on voluntary contributions from its sixteen members, three of which are private institutions and all of which support graduate education. Subsequently it secured legislative funding, in some years obtaining more than one million dollars for its programs (Heath 1984: 5–9). Its initial programs are intended to achieve a uniquely single purpose: the development of a statewide machine readable database. Once achieved, available funds will be expended for coordinated collection development, the protocols for which are currently under development (Medina 1986: 69–75).

In addition to its all-out efforts to complete the machine-readable database, NAAL also funded activities designed to create additional collection management information using the AMIGOS software. The pilot project will use the education portion of the RLG conspectus. When this project is completed, the information will be used to coordinate collection-building efforts among the participants. In addition, NAAL members have endorsed and will begin to use collection-assessment techniques that identify collection levels for support of graduate study and research. The assessments will be used to strengthen individual collections to benefit statewide research holdings. Plans to place the results of that assessment on-line are as yet tentative.

Recognizing that effective document delivery is the characteristic of successful networks, NAAL has worked to establish a system that reimburses participants in the lending program on the basis of the intensity of participation and net lending activity. Members anticipate that NAAL programs to improve knowledge about the location of bibliographic information and promote resource sharing will decrease or eliminate traditional barriers to information access (Medina 1986: 71–75).

Other state efforts have also succeeded. Alaska has been working on coordinated collection development for about five years. Because of the low population density and the lack of library resources, all types of libraries have been involved. Organizational activities and collection analysis based on a modified RLG conspectus have characterized the early results (Stephens 1986: 173). Illinois has moved into cooperative collection development by building on the strong structure of resource sharing provided by the Library Circulation System (LCS), which includes twenty-six public and private academic libraries. As yet, the primary purpose is for resource sharing through interlibrary loan, but in recent years the Illinois Board of Higher Education has allocated modest funds for collection-development purposes and a collection analysis project has begun (LIRN 1985: 6–7).

In California, the University of California's nine campus system and Stanford participate in the Shared Purchase Program. The program had its origins in a legislative mandate to reduce higher education expenses and has been in operation for almost a decade. Each library contributes 3% of its materials budget. During FY (fiscal year) 1986, the shared program provided $800,000 to acquire materials that the participants felt should be shared because of high cost or low anticipated frequency of use. Purchase decisions are made jointly, and the library where the material will be stored is responsible for bibliographic and physical access (Buzzard 1986: 103–13).

CHARACTERISTICS OF SUCCESSFUL SYSTEMS

Up to this point, this chapter has reviewed some of the factors that have given rise to a new round of cooperative activity among libraries—chiefly in the area of resource sharing. Exemplary programs at various levels have also been reviewed. The purpose of this final section is to take another look at some of those undertakings and to examine the commonalities. Six common aspects of successful undertakings are discussed: (1) a shared starting point in the new automated environment that marks libraries in this decade; (2) generally stable funding sources in the programs' emergent years; (3) an effective governance structure; (4) clearly articulated policies regarding operations; (5) an elusive concept that may be best described as a sense of common purpose; and (6) a thorough process of assessment of the strengths and weaknesses of the resources to be shared. Each of these common elements is discussed below.

Automated Environment

To make this point requires little more than to recall the observation of DeGennaro that prior to the current avalanche of cooperative activity, lack of on-line computer and communications capabilities ensured that previous consortia would be largely ineffective. The dream of a shared database in which "collective strengths and resources can be managed and mobilized to serve the needs of researchers" was the vision that created the RLG (DeGennaro 1981: 1049). Similarly, it is a product of the cataloging utilities—automated databases that can be shared and analyzed—that is at the heart of the cooperative activity in the Pacific Northwest and in the Network of Alabama Academic Libraries. While speaking specifically of RLG, DeGennaro's vision of library cooperation in an automated environment is common to all three:

> In time, the separate collections of the member libraries will be viewed by users as a single large distributed collection to which they will gain efficient access via online systems

and the rapid delivery of requested items by electronic and other means as well as by personal visits. (DeGennaro 1981: 1049).

Similarly, in North Carolina, the TRLN cooperative was able to use its common membership in OCLC and SOLINET to advantage in the development of that important network. By ensuring that the three libraries would have access to each others' holdings in common format, TRLN cleared a large hurdle en route to developing its on-line network (Byrd et al. 1985: 72).

Funding

While each of the cooperative structures named above would deny any allegation of affluence, it is nevertheless true that RLG, LIRN, and NAAL generally had sufficient funds to meet organizational goals. To recall one masterful understatement, "There is no doubt that periodic, well-timed infusions of extraordinary funds are important for programs of coordinated collection development" (Hewitt 1986: 147). It has not been without a struggle, but each has been able to attract funds from local and external sources. NAAL, which began with modest dues contributed by its members, now enjoys a legislative allocation (Medina 1986). LIRN has had the enormous good fortune to attract the patronage of a major foundation, whose largesse has, in the words of the program officer, reduced "the front end risks inherent in trying new methods and new technologies in the hopes of stimulating wide activity on the part of libraries" (LIRN 1985: 1). Although RLG perhaps has had a rockier time of it, its funding base is also significant. In addition to the considerable annual dues, the collective prestige of its members has attracted significant foundation funding over the years from the likes of the Andrew Mellon Foundation and other national foundations (Shurkin 1982: 452–53). Others that have been mentioned peripherally share this characteristic. The Shared Purchase Program of the University of California system, for example, benefitted from a legislative mandate requiring that each library contribute a portion of library materials budgets to shared acquisitions. During FY 1985–86, the library directors of the nine participating campuses had $800,000 to administer (LIRN 1985: 5).

TRLN enjoyed the same reduction in "front-end risks" by securing external funding during the formative years. Higher Education Act (HEA) Title II-C funds permitted start-up and carried the organization through the first five years. The Reynolds Foundation also provided significant early support, as did the Carnegie and Rockefeller foundations. As the organization has matured, institutional budgets have been redirected, ensuring adequate revenue to operate TRLN efficiently (Byrd et al. 1985: 73; Hewitt 1986: 147).

Governance

Most of the structures presented earlier are strong organizations, operating under effective, formal guidelines that provide a structure for decision making, resource allocation, and conflict resolution. For many years, governance problems were probably the issues that retarded the development of cooperative activities. At every level during the early years, the necessary autonomy of individual libraries emerged as the primary concern. An objection frequently aired was institutional concern with the abandonment of local prerogatives accompanying agreements to buy and share resources in some pooled arrangements.

Largely because of these concerns, the early history of networks reveals a condition of voluntary participation where prerogatives were in fact rarely surrendered. Gradually, successful networks have demonstrated that some subordination of local autonomy to the general good is required if the cooperative is to be able to make a long-term commitment for the benefits of members (Galvin 1978: 7). Indeed, if there is an outstanding characteristic of the Network of Alabama Academic Libraries, it is the work that went into hammering out a governance structure that permitted sixteen universities to work together in uncharacteristic harmony. Indeed, the effectiveness with which these libraries work together is most unusual in a resource-constrained state where the executive director of the state higher education commission has described Alabama resource allocation as a "gang fight among 13 institutions" (Heath 1984: 10). The TRLN governance structure is equally effective, with the respective roles of the director, the coordinating committee, and the governing board carefully spelled out (Byrd et al. 1985: 74).

The Fred Meyer Trust and the LIRN Project understood that effective governance agreements were generally necessary for resource-sharing networks to function well. One of the early programs at LIRN was to encourage and assist in the drafting of collection-development agreements among groups of libraries in that region. There is no intention in LIRN to forge some supranetwork spanning the vast region of the Pacific Northwest. Rather the intent is that emerging groups will be determined by such criteria as common needs, size of libraries, and geography (LIRN 1985: p. 1).

Policy

Where the networks work well, there is generally a clear understanding by members of the policies that govern the operations of the network. Again, to review some of the examples I have discussed, the RLG fraternity has a rather clear understanding of shared collection responsibilities. It is probably unique among the organizations examined in this chapter in that the agreements among collection librarians are largely informal. TRLN has much the same history. Predating that new network is a long history of cooperation between Duke, the University of North Carolina, and North Carolina State. Indeed, with the help of external funds, the three institutions developed a joint library catalog in 1934 (Byrd et al. 1985: 71). Altogether different in origin, but perhaps even clearer, are the *Principles and Guidelines* promulgated by the OCLC Board. The guidelines regulate resource-sharing efforts among members in all instances where the utility's primary asset, its database, is to be shared among members and nonmembers. These guidelines remain controversial, and certainly lack unanimous support by the membership. However, they serve as the guiding principles of board and staff, and all membership activities involving cooperative use of the database must conform.

In contrast are those examples of cooperative ventures that evolved out of legislative mandate. The Network of Alabama Academic Libraries spent its formative years behind closed doors, agreeing on a set of ground rules to which all could adhere. In a remarkable display of consensus building, agreement was finally reached on a set of blueprints that could be supported by research libraries and smaller college libraries alike. Those guidelines have served to guide members through four years of operations with a tolerable degree of ambiguity and a high degree of consensus.

A similar situation seems to exist in California, another collection-development enterprise that emerged from governmental initiative. It is the general consensus of participating collection-development librarians that clearly understandable policies govern operations. Among the guidelines are: costs of acquisitions must exceed $1,500; the materials must be lendable (even if only from one rare book room to another); and not more than 15% of the funding may be spent for rare or archival materials (LIRN 1985: 4–5).

When selected leaders gathered in December 1985 in Portland, Oregon, to discuss various aspects of library cooperation as it related to resource sharing, they generally agreed that an effective cooperative collection agreement should be simple, unambiguous, and flexible. Toward that end, it should be sufficiently detailed to serve as a guide for the implementation and administration of the cooperative. Specific areas of agreement should include:

1. Clear reference to member obligations in terms of document delivery, hours of operation, information services, and access;
2. The extent of financial commitments or obligations;
3. Each participant's role in the governance of the organization;
4. Definition, where applicable, of primary collection responsibilities; and
5. Timeliness for all member and the organization itself for evaluation, review, and contractual renegotiation.

Most of the organizations whose success can be charted over time seem to share these characteristics (LIRN 1985: 11–14).

Common Purpose

More difficult to peg is another characteristic, an elusive concept of community and common purpose. A few years ago, I presented a small paper in Tennessee about a Union List of Serials effort then underway elsewhere in the Southeast.

Commenting at that time on the slow start-up of that project, its early criticism from a few, and its resounding subsequent success, I suggested that a cooperative must be stern in its expectations of membership. In the context of today's funding opportunities, too often membership in a cooperative is merely seen as a circuitous means of subverting or expropriating external funds to local purposes. The notion of cohesiveness of purpose would suggest that no consortium or cooperative venture should permit within its membership participants who either do not understand or do not support the principle of resource sharing. All-inclusiveness is not a key to the success of library cooperative ventures (Heath 1984).

Joe Hewitt suggests that cooperative efforts are more easily established when there is a certain parity or equality among participants. Recalling the similarities between Duke and the University of North Carolina, he questions whether other North Carolina institutions could contribute equally toward the goals of TRLN.

> I can think of only a few cases in North Carolina where a small library can collect systematically at a level that would be useful to the research libraries without seriously overbalancing the collections of the smaller library. (Hewitt 1986: 148).

RLG certainly reflects that closed-ranks sense of purpose, even while its members reserve the right to disagree among themselves. Most of the other examples covered in this chapter reflect a similar resolve. There are some key elements to this sense of purpose. Fraternity does not seem to be essential. While it is present in some groups, such as RLG, the diverse membership of the Pacific Northwest effort and the wide range in the types of colleges and universities represented in NAAL would suggest other factors must also be at work. Two aspects would seem to be present in most of these successful groups. First of all, there is group assurance of the principle of equity. In Alabama, where resource-allocation decisions among state universities have been characterized as a gang fight, NAAL is distinguished by the concept of mutual benefit. It is not necessary that all members benefit equally, merely that all benefit. There is a high degree of trust that grows out of the openness of the process and the effectiveness of the governance structure.

Secondly, it would appear that the leadership of key institutions and individuals plays a pivotal role. Analysis of the NAAL and LIRN examples reveals the critical role of individuals and institutions. During the formative year of NAAL, William Highfill of Auburn University and Elizabeth French of the state coordinating agency lent the force of their own personalities and the authority of their institutions to the forging of that undertaking. The former president of one of the universities, James Vickery, was influential among his colleagues and the legislature during those years. Likewise, the energizing model of Douglas Ferguson of LIRN was fundamental in getting that cooperative effort underway in the Pacific Northwest, while TRLN profited from the early advocacy of Joe Hewitt and others (Byrd et al. 1985: 73).

Assessment

Finally, while there are other variables that could be singled out and cataloged, it is apparent that the successful cooperative efforts have assessed—or are planning to assess—the outcomes of their ventures. The reverse also seems to be true. Where there have been problems with funding shared-collection development, for example, there has sometimes been no conspectus work beforehand, and the necessary knowledge of member collections has been lacking.

Sometimes the assessment has been rather cursory. The North Bay Cooperative Library System in California, for example, has concentrated on improving collection strength in those parts of the collection where there is high interlibrary-loan (ILL) demand. Through an analysis of ILL transactions, primary collecting responsibility has been assigned among participants in about ninety subject areas (LIRN 1985: 5). The primary language of assessment in libraries, however, has been the RLG *Conspectus*. It has been the means employed from Alaska to Alabama. It has been used as a device for computerized assessment of data tapes, and has been the tool of local assessment activities in countless libraries throughout the country. In most of these cases, classically illustrated by LIRN, assessment was preceded by careful training of staff in the techniques involved. It does not follow that elaborate protocols directing the precise collecting responsibilities of every consortium member are required. Studies abound that show that overlap among small- and medium-sized libraries is less than might be assumed. Whereas large research libraries might profitably agree on primary collecting responsibilities, a general knowledge of other institutions' collection strengths may be sufficient. Beyond a core of materials held by most, general guidelines based on the analysis of conspectus results could be sufficient to ensure the development of richly diverse collections in smaller and medium-sized libraries.

SUMMARY

In summary, the factors that seem to make library cooperation work include (1) an effective governance structure that enjoys the support of all concerned; (2) clearly understood policies that eliminate ambiguities and promote the efficient administration of the cooperative's work; (3) strong local commitment to the concepts, and direction and leadership at every level; (4) financial stability; (5) effective training programs for library staff; and (6) effective collection assessment using standard techniques (Ferguson 1985: 5). These characteristics apply to cooperation at any level: national, regional, or local. Furthermore, it is important to recall Walters' observation that any library is simultaneously a member of several consortia, many of them operating at entirely different levels.

Although detractors are quick to make the attempt, it is not yet possible to fully measure in dollar terms the costs and benefits of resource sharing and coordinated collection development. Increasingly, however, library leadership is advancing the persuasive argument that the returns are worth the long-term investment required. Across the nation, resource sharing agreements are being developed on the assumption that libraries can consider—at the same time—their local responsibilities and their contributions to a larger group with a common purpose. Without doubt these cooperative arrangements are here to stay. Mr. Downs would feel right at home.

REFERENCES

Avram, H. D. 1986. "The Linked Systems Project: Its Implications for Resource Sharing." *Library Resources & Technical Services* 30 (Jan.): 36–46.

Ballard, Thomas H. 1985. "Dogma Clouds the Facts." *American Libraries* 16 (April): 257–59.

Barker, Tommie Dora. 1936. *Libraries of the South: A Report on Developments, 1930–1935*. Chicago: American Library Association.

Beyers, C. 1983. "Surviving Its Goals: The Research Libraries Group." *Wilson Library Bulletin* 57 (March): 576–80.

Branin, Joseph J. 1986. "Issues in Cooperative Collection Development: The Promise and Frustration of Resource Sharing. In *Issues in Cooperative Collection Development*. SOLINET Occasional Papers. Edited by June Engle and Sue Medina, pp. 1–38. Atlanta, Ga.: Southeastern Library Network, Inc.

Buckland, Michael K., and Clifford A. Lynch. 1987. "The Linked Systems Protocol and the Future of Bibliographic Networks and Systems." *Information Technology and Libraries* 6 (June): 83.

Buzzard, M. L. 1986. "Cooperative Acquisitions with a System: The University of California Shared Purchase Program." In *Coordinating Cooperative Collection Development*. Edited by Walter Luquire, pp. 99–113. New York: Haworth Press.

Byrd, Gary D., Jinnie Y. Davis, William A. Gosling, and L. Russell Herman, Jr. 1985. "The Evolution of a Cooperative Online Network." *Library Journal* 110 (February 1): 71–77.

Cummings, Martin M. 1986. *The Economics of Research Libraries*. Washington, D.C.: Council on Library Resources.

DeGennaro, Richard M. 1980. "Resource Sharing in a Network Environment." *Library Journal* 104 (February 1): 353–55.

———. 1981. "Libraries and Networks in Transition: Problems and Prospects for the 1980's." *Library Journal* 106 (May 15): 1045–49.

Dowlin, Kenneth E. 1987. "Access to Information: A Human Right?" In *The Bowker Annual of Library and Book Trade Information*, 32d ed. Edited by Filomena Simora, pp. 64–67. New York: R. R. Bowker.

Farber, Evan. 1982. "Coping with Limited Budgets by Sharing Resources." *Briefings for Faculty and Administrators* 2 (May): 2–3.

Farrell, D. 1986. "The NCIP Option for Coordinated Collection Management." *Library Resources & Technical Services* 30 (January): 47–56.

Ferguson, Douglas K. 1985. "Coordinated Collection Development and the Pacific Northwest." Paper presented at the Collection Management and Development Institute, University of Washington, September 3–6, Seattle, Washington. Portland, Oreg.: Fred Meyer Charitable Trust.

Fletcher, Janet. 1983. ''Collection Development and Resource Sharing: A Major Institute on the Politics, Philosophy, and Prognosis of.'' *Library Journal* 108 (May1): 881.

Forcier, Peggy. 1988. ''Building Collections Together: The Pacific Northwest Conspectus.'' *Library Journal* 113, no. 7 (April 15): 43–45.

Gherman, Paul. 1987. ''Vision and Reality: The Research Libraries and Networking.'' *Journal of Library Administration* 8, no. 3–4 (Fall/Winter): 51–57.

Haley, A., and D. K. Ferguson. 1986. ''The Pacific Northwest Collection Assessment Project.'' In *Coordinating Cooperative Collection Development*. Edited by Walter Luquire, pp. 185–97. New York: Haworth Press.

Heath, Fred. 1984. ''Structuring a Limited Purpose Network: Problems and Prospects of the Network of Alabama Academic Libraries (NAAL).'' In *State Networking: Its Implications for Local and Regional Planning*. Papers presented at the SOLINET Annual Membership Meeting, May 11, 1984. Edited by Lisa Fox, pp. 4–11. Atlanta, Ga.: Southeastern Library Network, Inc.

———. 1984. ''Union Lists: Problems and Possibilities.'' Paper presented at the Tennessee Library Association. Memphis, Tenn., April 26. Unpublished paper.

Hewitt, J. A. 1986. ''Cooperative Collection Development Programs of the Triangle Research Libraries Network.'' In *Coordinating Cooperative Collection Development*. Edited by Walter Luquire, pp. 139–50. New York: Haworth Press.

Holicky, B. H. 1984. ''Collection Development vs. Resource Sharing: The View from the Small Academic Library.'' *Journal of Academic Librarianship* 10 (July): 146–47.

Jascik, Scott. 1986. ''Voters in 4 States Weigh Spending Cuts That Could Cut Funds for Higher Education.'' *The Chronicle of Higher Education* 33, no. 2 (September 2): 11.

Kantor, Paul B. 1985a. *Final Report On the Relation between Consortia, On-Line Services, and the Cost of Processing Monographs at Eight University Libraries*. Prepared for the Council on Library Resources. Cleveland, Ohio: Tantalus, Inc.

———. 1985b. ''The Relation Between Costs and Services in Academic Libraries.'' In *Financing Information Services: Problems, Changing Approaches, and New Opportunities for Academic and Research Libraries*. Edited by Peter Spyers-Duran and Thomas W. Mann, pp. 69–78. New Directions in Librarianship, no. 6. Westport, Conn.: Greenwood Press.

Kels, James J. F., Chairman, Elsevier Science Publishers, B.V., April 1988. Letter [to Librarians].

Library and Information Resources of the Northwest (LIRN). 1985. *Toward Coordinated Collection Agreements*. Two meetings of nationally recognized experts and Pacific Northwest librarians held in Portland, Oregon, on December 6–7 and 13–14, 1985. Sponsored by the LIRN Program of the Fred Meyer Charitable Trust.

Lowry, Charles B. 1988. ''The Cost of Cooperation in Academic and Research Libraries: An Issues Paper.'' Prepared as a discussion document for a mini-conference on the Cost of Cooperation in Academic and Research Libraries jointly sponsored by the University of North Texas, School of Library and Information Sciences and AMIGOS Bibliographic Council. Denton, Texas, May 11, 1988.

Martin, Susan K. 1982. ''RLG Update.'' *Library Issues: Briefings for Faculty and Administrators* 2, no. 5 (May): 5.

———. 1987. ''Technology and Cooperation: The Behaviors of Networking.'' *Library Journal* 112 (October 1): 42.

Medina, Sue O. 1986. "Cooperative Collection Management on a Statewide Basis." In *Issues in Cooperative Collection Development*. Paper presented at the SOLINET Resource Sharing and Networks Support Program, March 11, 1986. Edited by June L. Engle and Sue O. Medina, pp. 67–79. Atlanta, Ga.: Southeastern Library Network.

Melin, Nancy. 1986. "Cutting Edge (OCLC's New Online System)." *Wilson Library Bulletin* 61 (December): 38.

Mosher, P. H. 1986. "A National Scheme for Collaboration in Collection Development: The RLG-NCIP Effort." In *Coordinating Cooperative Collection Development*. Edited by Walter Luquire, pp. 21–35. New York: Haworth Press.

Online Computer Library Center (OCLC). 1987. *OCLC Annual Report 1986/87*. Dublin, Ohio: Online Computer Library Center.

"Opinion: Higher Education and Income Tax Reform: College's Views Are Assailed in 3 Newspapers." 1986. *Chronicle of Higher Education* 33, no. 2 (September 10): 38–39.

Segal, Joan S. 1987. "Networking and Resource Sharing in 1986: Facilitating Access to Information." In *The Bowker Annual of Library and Book Trade Information*, 32d ed. Edited by Filomena Simora, pp. 42–58. New York: R. R. Bowker Company.

Shera, Jesse. 1967. "Libraries against Machines." *Science* 157 (May 12): 746.

Shurkin, Joel. 1982. "The Rise and Fall of RLG: The Research Libraries Group Rides the Costliest Rollercoaster in Library Land." *American Libraries* (August): 450–55.

Stephens, Dennis. 1986. "A Stitch in Time: The Alaska Cooperative Collection Development Project." In *Coordinating Cooperative Collection Development*. Edited by Walter Luquire, pp. 173–84. New York: Haworth Press.

Structure and Governance of Library Networks. 1979. "Proceedings of the 1978 conference in Pittsburgh, Pa., co-sponsored by National Commission on Libraries and Information Science and University of Pittsburgh." Edited by A. Kent and T. J. Galvin. New York: M. Dekker.

Turner, Judith Ayler. 1986. "Scholars Weigh Library's Role in Collecting Computerized Research Data." *The Chronicle of Higher Education* 32 (July 16): 34.

Walters, Edward M. 1987. "The Issues and Needs of Local Library Consortia." *Journal of Library Administration* 8, no. 3–4 (Fall/Winter): 15–29.

White House Conference on Library and Information Services. 1979. *Information for the 1980's. Final Report of the White House Conference on Library and Information Services, 1979*. Washington, D.C.: U.S. Government Printing Office.

PART II

Personnel

5

Designing Jobs for Changing Libraries

Delmus E. Williams

It seems almost trite to point out that librarianship is now in the middle of one of the most dynamic periods in its history. Libraries have emerged over the last ten years from a period of calm to a condition where major changes are commonplace. This period of flux offers small- and medium-sized libraries a chance to develop their own destiny in a way that has not previously been possible. The challenge and the opportunity for managers of these libraries is to design their organization and to develop positions that will take advantage of the options that are becoming available to them and that can cope with the rapidity with which the library will be asked to change.

THE PROBLEM

The current environment in which libraries find themselves is putting a tremendous amount of pressure on them to change. A number of factors are combining to create this pressure. The first, and most obvious, relates to the various technologies that are now available to the library. Until recently, computers were affordable only through networks for limited uses (for example, OCLC) or to those libraries with ample budgets. The idea that a small library could afford a system that might cost $300,000 to $500,000 and its attendant staffing and maintenance costs has until lately been viewed as absurd, particularly by those who were not enamored with the idea that havens for books are being invaded by the age of the machine.

That is no longer the case. Decreases in the cost of magnetic storage and computing equipment and the increasing sophistication of small college computer centers have brought on-line systems within reach of more libraries. At the same time, regional networks that "broker" integrated library systems and the introduction of small computers with ever-expanding capabilities are bringing relatively sophisticated systems within the financial reach of almost any library. This trend is likely to continue, and it is likely to carry even the most reluctant librarians into automation.

Automation presents two kinds of problems for the library. Computers require that library staff members and those who manage them learn new skills that are foreign to their background and experience. In addition, librarianship is changing at a rate that outstrips conventional management techniques. Librarians have been encouraged to use planning processes that can take up to two years to complete in order to prepare for automation. These cannot provide timely solutions to librarians who are learning to amortize their computer equipment and software over a period of five years or less. Libraries have long been accustomed to buying books that will last for generations, and they have not yet proved their ability to move quickly enough to keep pace with the dramatic changes in the technologies that are breaking around them.

A more subtle but very real source of pressure that is forcing libraries to change is the demand for more services from patrons. This pressure is not new. Libraries are service organizations, and small libraries have been particularly good at compensating for their small collections with individual attention and specialized services. Libraries have always wanted to do more than they could afford to do, but users now are becoming more aware of the information services that can be made available to them, and demand is now being generated for relatively expensive services that once were the sole preserve of more affluent libraries. Demand has risen, and as a result virtually every library now offers on-line searching and bibliographic instruction, and more and more libraries are being called upon to develop audiovisual service programs, distribute computer software, upgrade interlibrary loan services, increase liaison and other outreach services to faculty, and facilitate access to their own library collections and to those of others for the students and staff members that they serve. Developing these services and tailoring them to local needs take money, expertise, and staff time.

Meanwhile, libraries of all sizes are being caught in a funding squeeze. The combination of the high cost of library materials, the need for labor to expand the service program of the library, and the limitations of university budgets make life difficult for those who are charged with finding resources to support the library. Funding levels for staffing, for maintaining the quality of the book collections, and for serial subscriptions are not keeping pace with inflation. The library administrator is being asked to make choices that reflect on the quality of collections and services whenever positions are refilled or whenever periodical invoices are renewed.

In addition, there have been major changes in the way that librarians and many new staff members look at themselves and at the services they are being asked to provide. Administrators can no longer count on being able to choose staff from a docile pool of librarians who will fit themselves into a traditional library program. Library schools have over the last twenty years found themselves in a position to recruit better educated students, many of whom bring with them higher expectations than did earlier generations of librarians. In response, library school curricula have changed. Library educators see themselves as leaders of the profession who are charged with introducing new ideas into library organizations. They expect to influence the future of libraries through their graduates while preparing students for a changing world. Information science is broadening. Schools are beginning to concentrate more on defining what constitutes the best practice for libraries and on identifying the future directions in which the profession might go rather than on teaching students current library practice.

The result has been very positive in that we are developing young librarians with perspectives and skills that were not previously taught. They are excited about new technologies and interested in introducing new services into the libraries in which they work. However, these people and their schooling still present some problems for library directors forced to operate within the context of conservative, cost-conscious institutions. Along with their idealism, new librarians can bring with them a higher regard for professional status than was previously present in the library, as well as a demand to participate fully in the determination of the directions library programs should take. Many of these people go to their first jobs with the assumption that futuristic views of the nature of libraries are universally shared by those who work in the field and that the desirability of introducing the newest technologies into libraries has been accepted everywhere.

Conflict is generated when newcomers to the profession encounter staff who are not particularly interested in seeing the libraries in which they work change. Many of the people working in libraries came to them as a refuge from a changing world. These people accept low pay in exchange for a work environment that is very stable. Many of them are very good at doing what traditional librarians do and find comfort in that fact. They understand cataloging, can select books that suit their clientele, and can find appropriate reference sources easily.

However, bringing new technologies and new ideas into organizations with a traditional work force can be threatening to those who work there. Ruth Person (1984) believes that without careful attention, automation can create a work atmosphere that is less pleasant for librarians and other library staff members. It may decrease the flexibility that individual workers have in determining what they do and how they do it, and thereby create jobs that are less satisfying. Moreover, in some cases, there is also a fear that library workers are being exposed to possible dangers and stresses from video display terminals. There are also those who resent the fact that they are no longer masters of all of the tools of their profession and feel uncomfortable that these new and radically different technologies are moving into their environment (Cohen and Cohen 1981). Many people have come to librarianship because of its stability and the value it placed on traditional values, and they are not comfortable with what they see coming into their environment. In fact, some librarians believe that the technology is deprofessionalizing librarianship, because automation is making information accessible to everyone without assistance (Nielsen 1980). In addition, many of the tasks that have required special skills valued by librarians (for example, the creation of specialized bibliographies) now can be done by downloading data from a central computer into microcomputer packages that can be mounted on virtually any home computer. Some library professionals are afraid that they face reduced status in society and perhaps a reduced labor market for their skills (Nielsen 1980).

ORGANIZATIONAL RESPONSES TO THE PROBLEM

As noted earlier, the concerns listed here are not new to libraries, and in larger organizations steps have been taken to cope with some of the challenges that have been presented. Some consolidation has taken place in the work force, and some organizations have changed the way that they cluster activities to try to cope with the new realities brought about by automation.

Most of these changes have consisted of minor organizational readjustments. New departments have been developed to handle automation, and organizational charts have been modified to reflect relationships between departments that have been altered as a result of the changing environment (for example, moving circulation to technical services). Positions have been created, eliminated, and moved as needed without dramatically altering the hierarchical nature of library organizations. In the final analysis, even organizations that view themselves as progressive are entering the 1990s with organizational charts that reflect positions developed in conformance with the principles of work simplification. Libraries are still attempting to break jobs into their smallest possible components, make them as repetitive as possible, minimize the amount of handling and transportation required in performing jobs, provide work conditions that focus primarily on efficiency, and maximize specialization (Kramer 1984).

Thomas Shaughnessy (1977) points out that modern complex organizations must change to conform to the needs of new technologies. In his words:

> If the new technology is simply superimposed, staff will inevitably become anxious, alienated, and perhaps incompetent. Organizations have to be redesigned both in structure and function . . . to use any new technology humanely and well. (p. 271)

However, both Shaughnessy and William Marsterson (1986) believe that libraries have resisted this requirement to change.

That is not to say that libraries have not begun to look at the future and to plan for it. Most library organizations and the structure of staff positions within them have been defined through organizational plans developed by managers in consultation with the library staff and faculty. In deference to the need for broad participation in decision making, committees and task forces have also been created to provide formal devices for communication between staff members and their managers. However, too often the results of these planning efforts are organizations that mirror those of like institutions rather than being adapted to local needs.

This approach creates special difficulties for smaller libraries as they try to adjust to changing times. Librarians working in smaller institutions have consistently felt that bigger libraries had much to teach them about management. As a profession, librarians have taken to disparaging stereotypes in which a single librarian sat behind a desk and selected, acquired, organized, and serviced collections. As a result, most small- or medium-sized libraries have taken their cues for organizing their operations from their larger cousins. In the name of bringing modern management practice to the library, even small libraries have substituted bifurcated systems with assistant directors for public and technical services and heads of one thing or another in hierarchies that conform to the ideals of bureaucratic management. The status that comes with titles of this sort and occasionally the higher salaries that accompany the titles have been valued as a substitute for having the resources to develop programming for the library.

The difficulty with applying some sort of reorganization to smaller libraries to help them cope with change is that the so-called functional divisions of labor that once seemed so appropriate for the library restrict its capacity to meet new demands on the resources that are available. Labor-saving devices can reduce the amount of time required to do specific kinds of work, but hierarchies are not always helpful when the library tries to reallocate those resources to other areas. When the library tries to recruit technical services personnel to work in public service areas or vice versa, or when it tries to develop special skills with reporting lines outside the hierarchy, managers always run the risk of violating the "chain of command" with all that this implies. Extraorganizational committee structures designed to facilitate organizational communication outside the hierarchy can add to the awkwardness of this kind of arrangement. In the five-to-ten-librarian library committee, members compete with line managers for authority. In essence, bureaucratic hierarchies that are designed to insure sameness and routinize tasks do not adapt to change particularly well. As Herbert White noted (1985), libraries that have organized scientifically to encourage specialization and that have assigned value to those specialties now find themselves with the task of developing new organizational values.

Take, for example, the operations of an automated cataloging department. It is not unusual for a cataloging unit to be able to produce records for twice as many books with OCLC as they could with catalog cards ordered from the Library of Congress. Since few libraries have been able to double their capacity to acquire materials, this eventually leads to some additional time for a variety of activities. Reallocation of resources might be a reasonable solution, but, at the same time, it is useful to limit the amount of time that individual workers spend with a computer terminal. Visual fatigue is a problem, and, as noted earlier, there is concern that extended exposure to them might be unhealthy. Consequently, it might be argued that terminal time should be limited to four or five hours a day and that the same number of individuals might be needed to catalog the same number of books. However, the jobs such as typing or filing that provided variety in cataloging and that might consume this additional time are no longer useful with a computerized or computer-produced catalog. As a result, the library is faced with either finding enough competent part-time workers to meet its needs, reassigning staff to other duties, or allowing the staff to follow Parkinson's Law and let work expand to meet the time available (Parkinson 1957). Too often the preference of the cataloging staff and the inattention of managers lead libraries to accept the last-mentioned course.

However, even when libraries have seen the difficulty of using hierarchical arrangements in small organizations, the solutions that are used focus on organizational schemes that impose unrealistic divisions in library activities. While collegiality is important in most university-related organizations, committee structures are often overdone, and mechanisms designed to facilitate communications can actually stymie them. At the same time, attempts at participatory management or the application of theories like matrix management have proven faulty, in part because of limitations in the theories, and in part because of faulty application.

Perhaps the most promising attempt to develop an organization that can cope with change is the approach taken at the University of Illinois. Over the last several years, the library there has worked to integrate its various functions so as to move professional librarians closer to their patrons. Professional library tasks have been distributed to the branch libraries to insure that maximum flexibility can be accomplished in the assignment of both direct service and support functions. Catalogers and collection specialists have been reassigned to service points, and cataloging, reference, and collection development are shared by these professionals and by the librarians who were previously involved only in direct service to patrons. At the same time, many of the tasks that could be routinized are coordinated in units that utilize large numbers of nonlibrarians (Gorman 1983a). The result has been a group of confederated libraries that have returned to the much maligned concept of the librarian who does a bit of everything. Gorman feels that this "multidimensional" approach is the best way for librarians to free themselves as creative professionals from the constraints of hierarchical organizations (Gorman 1983b).

The changes at Illinois are primarily designed to make better use of the library's professionals, but they are interesting nonetheless to small libraries in that they are a step back toward the one-person library. It must be noted, however, that this situation may be unusual. As John Cohn (1988) noted, responses to technology have only infrequently led to the implementation of this kind of plan. Robert Hurowitz and David R. McDonald (1982) agree with Cohn that the role of library units are more likely to expand beyond traditional departmental limits, but they also agree that organizational charts have yet to begin to reflect that fact.

JOB DESIGN AND CHANGE IN LIBRARIES

The key to success for smaller libraries is to break away from the lead offered by larger ones and to optimize the benefits of smallness by designing an organization that encourages library workers to act independently. Organizational theorists contend that the most flexible organizations are those where decisions are made close to the point of impact, and that good organizations involve staff at all levels in decision making. Small libraries tend to be more democratic in dealing with their staff than larger ones, and this can contribute to this ideal.

Managers in small libraries must identify talents among their staff that might go unrecognized in larger situations. They must be willing to use the resources that are available to them and to develop a flexibility in job design that has not always been present.

Small libraries must deal with unique problems in staffing their operations. The first is the relatively limited number of skills that can be expected from the professional staff. In the best of circumstances, libraries with professional staffs of five or ten librarians will only have real expertise in a few areas. Generally, they will at best have only one good cataloger, one person with an interest in automation, one person who can design and write brochures, and so on. Most of the staff will be good generalists with perhaps one or two side interests, and most of their time will be consumed doing the primary task for which they were hired. Keeping the library open seventy-five to one hundred hours per week tends to limit their ability to acquire and use new skills. As individual librarians leave organizations, they may take with them significant portions of the library program.

At the same time, smaller libraries tend to have talented pools of nonprofessional workers available to them. In college towns, there are generally a number of faculty spouses and others with good liberal educations who are attracted to work in libraries; and even in larger communities, there always seems to be a pool of educated people who are interested in library work. In a typical library, one might reasonably expect that half of the clerical and paraprofessional staff might have two or more years of college, and the majority of these will have college degrees. Some of these people will stay in the library for a year or two and then move on, but a remarkable number will stay in the library for a longer period. While these people are seldom compensated financially for their skills, most libraries have come to rely heavily on them for continuity and service delivery. The need for staffing service points frequently means that smaller libraries must train nonlibrarians to do many professional tasks. In addition, these organizations often have difficulty recruiting and keeping librarians who can catalog or who have expertise in automation, but frequently find talented nonlibrarians who have or can be taught these skills and who can do much to help maintain the library's program.

The implications of these staffing patterns are that the ideal small library organization must be developed around the specific skills that individuals bring to the library rather than trying to conform to some abstract model. The key point in organizing the operation cannot be an organizational chart that has been developed downward. Instead, libraries must begin by developing individual positions and then allowing an organizational structure to develop naturally as the need for coordination in the library becomes apparent.

This approach requires a very different approach to job design. Individual positions in the library must, at the point of hiring, be designed generally enough that new workers can work creatively while contributing to the specific needs of the area in which they work. As time passes, individual positions within the organization must be redesigned to accommodate the particular skills of those who hold them, compensate them for special skills, and develop a satisfying environment in which to work. Charles Martell (1984) contends that satisfying jobs are those that present those working in them with challenging work, that gain respect from their superiors, that are compatible with life beyond work, that contribute to society, that provide variety, that build self-esteem, and that have a future. All these traits are important motivators when increased productivity is needed. Martell suggests that the quality of life in an organization depends on the degree to which workers are challenged, have autonomy, are allowed to be creative, are provided an opportunity to learn, can participate, and are allowed to use skills and abilities.

Building an organization that includes jobs of this sort is very difficult. However, the newly automating small library is perhaps more suited to this approach than most organizations. Most of the production functions of the library are being replaced by labor-saving devices, and, as noted above, the distinctions between librarians and nonlibrarians are not well drawn. Pay differentials exist, as do differences in status in the university community, and this will not change. Library professionals are needed. They bring new ideas into the organization and can be hired with the certainty that they will bring specific skills to the organization. This factor will always be vital to the stability of the organization.

However, in changing libraries, librarians must look beyond being direct service professionals to roles in which they provide leadership and training for nonprofessional staff members. They must provide people who have been hired as members of the support staff with programs that will acculturate that individual, familiarize him or her with the role and mission of the library, and determine what special skills that person brings to the organization. That person's job must then be tailored to at least acknowledge the special contribution that he or she can make and to utilize his or her skills when possible. Certain baseline tasks will continue to be important to keep the library going, but most positions have enough flexibility to allow for creative task assignments, and most libraries leave enough things undone that tasks can be given to individuals without creating unneeded jobs. The library professionals in this kind of organization are called on to be facilitators and to operate as links to the larger world of librarianship.

To be effective, organizations that are built around the skills of their workers require substantial investments in training, designed to teach both the skills that are necessary to work in the organization and the values of the library. Few libraries have formal training programs, but successful ones develop channels that allow employees to develop the kinds of skills that the organization needs. In these programs all employees are treated as career employees. Money and time are expended from early in their career to insure that individual staff members understand what the library is about and what they can contribute to it. Departmental supervisors are encouraged to devote much of their time to on-the-job training. Professional development funds are available for junior librarians and for support staff to make them understand their importance to the organization and the importance that the library places on increasing their skill levels. Training should also be used to make transitions as organizations initiate new services or bring in new equipment, and retraining should be used to continually upgrade the skills of older employees as the library changes. Throughout the career of its employees, the organization must assume that the quality of its staff and their preparation for the tasks at hand are a direct reflection on the quality of the library and must do what it can to insure the success of everyone who works there. Money spent in this area is returned in commitment to the productivity, and it is always well spent (Peters 1987).

Organizations that expect to effectively utilize their staff must make a number of commitments to themselves and to that staff. First, they must commit to an almost continual process of redefining jobs as individuals mature in their positions and seek to move beyond them. Second, library managers must be willing to develop the communications systems in the library. Good information for decision making is hard to get, and is needed to develop the organization. Communicating the need to meet certain standards and objectives can be a difficult task. Many of the questions that must be asked and answered depend heavily on considerations of organizational values that are not always clearly articulated. Clear pictures of those values can seldom be obtained solely through formal communication channels. To get enough information to understand where the library is and where it is going, the manager must relate to the others who work in the library as colleagues in the truest sense of the word. While the manager must make it clear that he or she has the authority and responsibility to make decisions, that person also must serve as an example of what the library stands for. With this kind of trust, information about individual workers' values, concerns about their jobs, and other topics can be generated. As Smilor and Kuhn point out, the success of innovative organizations depends on the manager's ability to sense what changes are "necessary to obtain as viable and productive a future as possible. . . . It is the capacity to educate all members of the firm as well as the ability to learn from them as well as your customers and others.'' (1986: 169). Communication that will provide this insight requires high visibility within the organization and mutual trust between managers and staff members.

However, not all the roles played by the library director can be positive. Managers are the keepers of the goals of the organization, and it is their responsibility to define what constitutes an acceptable modification of a position. While it is critical that workers understand that their talents are valued, not all changes in position descriptions will contribute to the common good. Flexibility is encouraged, but the manager always must understand that it is his or her job to decide when individuals have strayed too far from the common purpose.

Small libraries have a tremendous advantage over their larger cousins in organizing this way. In small- to medium-sized libraries it is still possible for a director to see virtually every staff member daily. In this environment, the kind of ''management by wandering around'' favored by Tom Peters and Robert Waterman (1982) can be used to good effect in finding out the temper of the organization and its members. In this kind of situation many of the functions of the organization are handled by self-managing teams and the senior administrators manage more by example than by fiat (Peters 1987). As often as not, smaller libraries find themselves functioning with the kind of informality that has been described above either because they have never developed the hierarchy, or in spite of it.

One final note should be made about managing organizations of this sort. When one hopes to develop a structure based on intangibles like individual skills and values, it is much less ''safe'' than using hierarchical arrangements. Organization charts satisfy auditors and those who oversee libraries but do not understand them, and this can be useful. As Edward Shaw (1982) points out, varying from this model requires that managers take risks; if they are to succeed, they must have the courage to fail, and must, at the same time, be willing to accept failure on the part of those to whom they delegate authority. The thrust of an organization that encourages people to be all that they can be has to move away from a ''zero defects'' approach toward one in which the library is willing to accept some failures (indeed, Tom Peters says they must celebrate them) and then be prepared to control any damage that might occur as a result (Peters 1987). The attitude is, and should be, that if people try to do twice as much and accomplish only 80% of what is attempted, then they have still done 60% more than they might otherwise have accomplished.

The bottom line for smaller libraries is that their managers must follow their instincts in defining individual jobs and in organizing those positions. Consideration of various management theories should be made in the context of a solid understanding of the individual talents of those who will contribute to service delivery. The strength of the smaller library both as a place to work and as a source of information is its capacity to deal with matters in a very personal way. As those who must direct libraries strive to know more about management and to become better managers, they must be careful not to be too willing to compromise this strength. Small library organizations should be developed around the strength of its people, not in spite of them.

REFERENCES

Cohen, Elaine, and Aaron Cohen. 1981. *Automation, Space Management, and Productivity: A Guide for Libraries*. New York: Bowker.

Cohn, John M. 1988. "Integrating Public and Technical Services: Management Issues for Academic Libraries." In *The Smaller Academic Library: A Management Handbook*. Edited by Gerard B. McCabe, pp. 303–312. Westport, Conn: Greenwood Press.

Gorman, Michael. 1983a. "On Doing Away with Technical Services Departments." In *A Reader on Choosing an Automated Library System*. Edited by Joseph R. Matthews, pp. 221–23. Chicago: American Library Association.

———. 1983b. "Reorganization at the University of Illinois—Urbana/Champaign Library: A Case Study." *Journal of Academic Librarianship* 9: 223–25.

Hurowitz, Robert, and David R. McDonald. 1982. "Library Automation and Library Organization: An Analysis of Future Trends." In *Options for the 80s: Proceedings of the Second National Conference of the Association of College and Research Libraries*. Edited by Michael D. Kathman, pp. 613–20. Greenwich, Conn.: JAI Press.

Kramer, Lloyd A. 1984. "Increased Productivity: Work Simplification and Its Heirs." In *Austerity Management in Academic Libraries*. Edited by John F. Harvey and Peter Spyers-Duran, pp. 269–76. Metuchen, N.J.: Scarecrow.

Marsterson, William. 1986. *Information Technology and the Role of the Librarian*. London: Croom Helm.

Martell, Charles. 1984. "QWL Strategies: People Are the Castle, People Are the Walls, People Are the Moat." *Journal of Academic Librarianship* 10: 350–54.

Nielsen, Brian. 1980. "Online Bibliographic Searching and the Deprofessionalization of Librarianship." *Online Review* 4: 215–24.

Parkinson, C. Northcote. 1957. *Parkinson's Law*. Boston: Houghton, Mifflin.

Person, Ruth J. 1984. "Human Factors in Adopting Library Technology." Presentation in a session entitled "Training Issues in Changing Technology," sponsored by the Library Administration and Management Association (LAMA) Personnel Administration Section Staff Development Committee. Chicago: June 26, 1984.

Peters, Tom. 1987. *Thriving on Chaos*. New York: Knopf.

Peters, Tom, and Robert Waterman. 1982. *In Search of Excellence*. New York: Harper.

Shaughnessy, Thomas W. 1977. "Technology and Job Design in Libraries: A Sociotechnical Systems Approach." *Journal of Academic Librarianship* 3: 269–72.

Shaw, Edward. 1982. "The Courage to Fail." In *Library Leadership: Visualizing the Future*. Edited by Donald E. Riggs, pp. 53–65. Phoenix, Ariz.: Oryx.

Smilor, Raymond W., and Robert L. Kuhn, eds. 1986. *Managing Take-Off in Fast Growth Companies: Innovations in Entrepreneurial Firms*. New York: Praeger.

White, Herbert S. 1985. *Library Personnel Management*. White Plains, N.Y.: Knowledge Industry Publications.

6

Recruitment and Selection of College Librarians

Terrence Mech

Because college libraries are a direct reflection of the skills, abilities, and personalities of the unique individuals who work in them, the hiring of new personnel is a major decision. Personnel are the critical resource in any professional activity because the quality of work depends on the qualities of those hired. Professionals are not interchangeable. Professionals with equal capabilities and credentials will approach and solve the same problems in different ways. Given that an individual's work performance is usually consistent over time and that relatively few individuals are responsible for both the best and worst job performances, the importance of the hiring decision cannot be overemphasized (Shapero 1985: 1–2).

Evaluating and hiring candidates are not innate skills. They must be learned and practiced to be perfected. Success in hiring depends greatly on basic decisions made by the library, as well as on the education, training, and experiences of those doing the hiring. Hiring reflects a fundamental attitude towards employees. When a library hires, it enters into a relationship with an individual. A mistake in hiring affects not only the library, but an individual as well (Isacco and Smith 1985: 68). Hiring a librarian is not a simple case of adding personnel to the library. It is an exercise in public relations, investigation, writing, evaluation, and institutional politics that has potential legal ramifications (Higgins and Hollander 1987: 1). Unfortunately, few individuals have much experience with the hiring process. The following guidelines should be adapted to your library's situation. Because you can learn 80% of what you need to know about candidates before they interview on campus, this chapter will discuss the selection process only to the point of the on-campus interviews (Marchese and Lawrence 1987: 39).

THE SEARCH COMMITTEE

Once a decision has been made to fill a position, a number of decisions must be made that affect the entire process. Many of those decisions are or should be covered by institutional policy. How the position is to be filled and who is involved has a lot to do with how successful the institution will be in filling the position with the best available candidate. While a library may be in a hurry to make a selection, it is important to prevent problems by establishing some ground rules in the beginning.

In academe, hiring decisions are viewed as collegial decisions and not as the purview of a single administrator. A search committee, either formal or informal, provides administrators with the benefit of other opinions and facilitates a fair and open search, while providing legitimately interested constituencies a role in the selection process. With a search committee, personal agendas and ''individual biases can be identified and tempered through group discussion and consensus'' (Dewey 1987: 61).

Often the academic dean will ask the library director to begin the search process. Usually the committee chair is the immediate supervisor of the person to be hired. In a smaller library it is the library director, while in a larger library it may be the department head to which the new librarian reports. The search committee should consist of individuals who have a legitimate interest in the selection process: supervisors, peers, and colleagues within the library. Committee members should have good judgment, personal integrity, independence of view, and a genuine understanding of the library and college. In smaller libraries it may be more appropriate for support staff to serve formally on the search committee rather than simply to be asked for their reactions to the candidates. The committee should be large enough to do the work, but small enough to work effectively. Five or six members are enough for most search committees (Marchese and Lawrence 1987: 7).

Some individuals should not be part of a search committee. ''Avoid at all costs the appointment of known paranoids, gossips, and egotists'' (Marchese and Lawrence 1987: 7). Individuals with known prejudices who discriminate on the basis of age, sex, handicaps, personality, or race do more harm than good for the committee. Individuals who stand to gain politically by the selection of a potential ally should also be excluded from the search committee (Higgins and Hollander 1987: 11).

Once the committee has been assembled, it should meet with the institution's affirmative action and personnel officers to become familiar with institutional concerns, policies, and procedures in hiring. If the institution has a well-developed personnel department, a high level of assistance and counsel may be available to the committee throughout the selection process.

Committee members must remember that they are representing the institution. A clear understanding of equal opportunity and affirmative action procedures should prevent embarrassment or legal troubles. The committee must understand the scope of its charge and know who has the actual authority to offer the contract. Committee members must not operate on their own. To avoid problems, the mechanics of the search process should be clearly understood by all from the beginning. Clear procedures prevent the institution from being viewed as administratively inept. Fair and realistic procedures help preserve the individual dignity of both candidates and committee members.

Role of the Committee Chair and Contact Person

The success of the selection process depends a great deal on the skill and experience of the committee chair, who is responsible for seeing that all the preliminary planning is completed. Before the position is posted, the committee must have a complete job description and a consensus as to what the library and college want. It should determine the scope of the search (national, regional, or local) and identify the financial and personnel resources to support the selection and interview process.

The committee chair is responsible for monitoring the search process, convening committee meetings, developing a timetable, and maintaining all committee meeting minutes and documents. Frequently the chair also serves as the contact person for applicants. The contact person responds to and corresponds with applicants, arranges interviews, keeps applicants informed, maintains applicants' files, and assures that the equal employment and affirmative action procedures and policies are followed. The chair or contact person will require clerical assistance and a telephone with the capacity to place conference calls.

The committee chair is also responsible for preparing committee members to screen and interview candidates effectively. Time should be spent on the formation, ranking, and phrasing of interview questions that will yield the desired information. A common list of questions asked of all candidates provides some common points of reference and greater comparability. Because the selection process is a two-way process, the chair should see that candidates have sufficient information about the library, college, and community to make an informed decision.

The time needed to conduct a search is frequently underestimated. Waiting and delays are unavoidable. A properly conducted search will take months, even without unanticipated delays. It is important to have a realistic schedule and a committee chair who will not allow the committee to delay the process further by missing deadlines or getting bogged down by insisting on the ideal candidate. The ideal candidate is an abstraction, unknown in the real world: The best a committee can hope for is a good match between the needs of the institution and the resources and personality of an individual. Attention to the realities of the marketplace and the ability to get a good match between institution and individual could mean not having to fill the position again in the near future.

JOB ANALYSIS AND JOB DESCRIPTION

Before a library can hire, it must know what it needs. An analysis of the job and the development of a written job description provide the objective criteria from which to write the job advertisement, screen resumes, and interview candidates. The job analysis clarifies what the job entails and identifies the knowledge, skills, and abilities necessary to perform the job successfully. Over time, jobs evolve until they reflect the incumbent's skills and interest; thus, jobs may evolve into something different from what was originally intended. Changes in library priorities also make it necessary to review each position before it is filled.

A good job description conveys important information in a simple, clear, and concise manner. A two- to three-page job description allows everyone to have the same understanding of the position. The job title is followed by a job summary, a clear sentence or two defining the position's basic functions and major purpose. The job description also states the title of the immediate supervisor and identifies the lines of supervision, communication, or reporting channels, and expected contacts with others, both inside and outside the library and college. The authority delegated to the position and the boundaries of the position's responsibilities need to be defined.

The next section of the job description describes each of the major duties and responsibilities assigned to the position. However, in college libraries individuals have to understand that they may be called upon to perform the unexpected. As guidelines, job descriptions are not intended to preclude the occasional performance of miracles.

It is important to develop a clear picture of the job and its relationship to other positions. Talking with the incumbent and others can be very informative. Major duties and responsibilities should be identified and ranked in terms of importance to the position and importance to the library overall. Items should also be ranked in terms of how much time is actually spent on them. In reviewing the position, the library is developing a list of what it wants the position to accomplish.

Once the major duties and responsibilities have been described, the required knowledge, skills, and abilities necessary to perform the job can be identified. State these requirements in terms of functional skills and knowledge rather than in terms of specific educational credentials or experiences in specific types of libraries. This way qualified applicants are less likely to be overlooked and the institution has more protection against charges of discrimination in hiring (Isacco and Smith 1985: 71). Educational credentials themselves do not necessarily guarantee skills or knowledge. What is important is the applicant's ability and desire to learn and develop competencies, many which are unknown at the time of hiring (Dewey 1987: 35). Skills learned in any type of library are transferable.

When establishing the position requirements, distinguish between the minimum acceptable qualifications and preferred qualifications. Make a distinction between the skills and knowledge absolutely required to do the job and those that can be learned on the job. Realistic and objective requirements providc flexibility and allow for a larger potential applicant pool. If you cannot hire what you want, maybe you can develop potential candidates into what you need. Requirements that are artificially high or unnecessarily restrictive reduce the number of applications from which to select.

After the objective criteria and desired qualifications have been established, the more subjective, job-related personal characteristics can be identified. What are the characteristics and work habits of your most productive and successful personnel? What are the negatives of the job, and what sort of person would best be able to cope with them (Half 1985: 24)? What does it take to succeed within your library or college community? The ability to "get along" or work effectively with colleagues is more important in some positions than others. If desirable subjective, job-related personal characteristics are known in advance, it increases the possibility of a successful match between candidates and the library. When individuals do not work out, it is rarely because they lack credentials or technical skills. Rather, it is frequently because they lack motivation or the ability to blend into the work environment (Half 1985: 19). Match candidates to the environment, because the environment is not likely to change.

If the college requires additional abilities or personal commitments such as a commitment to the ideas of a liberal arts education or if a strong commitment to ideals of Christian education is essential, these should be clearly spelled out and communicated to potential applicants. However, "if you think you may be discriminating when you are drawing up job criteria, you probably are" (Half 1985: 29).

ADVERTISING

Advertisements are institutional resumes to potential applicants. They provide a quick perception of the institution. Like a good resume, the advertisement must quickly make a positive impression on potential applicants by highlighting the challenges, features, and benefits of the job. Applicants need to know what your job can do for them; in a competitive job market the advertisement must convince potential applicants that the position you offer is preferable to others. The advertisement should also make it as easy as possible for individuals to apply.

After the advertisement copy has been written, set it aside for a few days and review it. Because the advertisement must attract and convey a message in a short time, every word must count. Edit unnecessary words from the advertisement. Let others critique the advertisement before it goes out. The time and care taken to develop a quality advertisement improve your chances of attracting and hiring the right candidate.

The *Chronicle of Higher Education* and *College and Research Libraries News* are the most effective ways of reaching college librarians. The *Chronicle of Higher Education* may be the fastest way to get your notice before potential applicants. With most library publications you usually wait a month or more between receipt and publication of the advertisement. *American Libraries* and *Library Journal* carry advertisements for positions in all types of libraries. Public, medical, law, or corporate librarians are an unexploited source of qualified candidates.

The *Chronicle of Higher Education* and major library publications have a large circulation among potential applicants. By advertising in them, individuals "from both sexes and all racial, religious, ethnic, age groups and the handicapped have the same opportunity to see the advertisement and apply for the position" (Higgins and Hollander 1987: 23). Library schools, especially those serving your region, may be a source of potential applicants, particularly for entry-level positions. Local and regional newspapers, as well as telephone job lines, can sometimes be effective. No matter how well written, your advertisement is not going to be effective unless it is seen and read by a wide variety of potential applicants.

Developing the Advertisement

Advertisements should be concise and accurate. At a minimum, advertisements should contain a job description, qualifications expected, the name and address to whom applications are to be sent, and the date the review of applications will begin (Higgins and Hollander 1987: 38). The job title should clearly convey the nature of the job. If applicants cannot understand a job's title, they probably will not bother to apply for it (Dewey 1987: 31). Duties, including the less desirable ones; expectations such as committee work, publication, or weekend work; and any conditions of employment such as religious affiliation or expected commitment should be clearly spelled out.

The advertisement should distinguish between the minimum requirements and preferred qualifications. Preferred qualifications provide applicants with a good understanding of what the institution wants in a candidate. Preferences provide the library some flexibility and do not legally exclude applicants from consideration. The essential requirements (formal education, experience, and skills) should, however, be specific enough to discourage the unqualified from applying. Legally, a candidate who does not meet the minimum requirements cannot be hired without reopening the search with a new set of minimum requirements. A candidate who exceeds the minimum requirements can always be hired.

The nature of the position (faculty, tenure, administrative); length of contract; starting date; and salary and benefits should be clearly noted. If there is a minimum salary or range, state it. Phrases like "salary negotiable" or "salary commensurate with experience" only cause trouble and tend to mislead applicants. Specific salary information may attract "good people who are paid less, and save the time of others for whom the salary would not mean advancement" (Marchese and Lawrence 1987: 29).

A description of the library, library priorities, college, and community environment helps attract applicants. The advertisement must convey the challenge or opportunity the position provides that would make it worth while for individuals to relocate. Individuals faced with the task of voluntarily relocating are reluctant to move just anywhere; they want to work for a good school—in a good environment.

Finally, the advertisement should state to whom and where application materials are to be sent. Instead of using a deadline, indicate the date on which the review of applications will begin. A review date tells candidates when their resumes are expected and provides the committee some legal flexibility in the event of some promising late applications (Marchese and Lawrence 1987: 30). Occasionally it is difficult to determine whether an advertisement will attract a sufficient number of qualified applicants. In such cases the closing date might be stated as "applications will be received until the position is filled" (Higgins and Hollander 1987: 29).

Advertisements that are made brief to hold costs down, and that consequently omit essential information, may fail to attract the best applicants and result in the application and screening of many who would not apply if the proper information was provided (Higgins and Hollander 1987: 33). A small and poorly written advertisement is a bad reflection on the institution. Big block ads are easier to read and indicate that the institution cares enough about the position to invest money in a larger ad. If an institution cannot put forth a clear, concise, and informative advertisement, how can it hope to attract qualified applicants?

A good advertisement makes it relatively easy for qualified individuals to apply. In the beginning of the application process it is more efficient to request a cover letter and resume only. Later in the process, viable candidates can be asked for references and other supporting materials. The most qualified applicants may not be looking seriously for employment. Individuals who are happy in their current position but potentially are interested in making a career move should be encouraged to apply. These individuals are frequently unwilling to submit references until they are considered seriously (Higgins and Hollander 1987: 31). By allowing applicants to maintain the confidentiality of their candidacy, you may attract better applicants and avoid unnecessary embarrassment for applicants in their current positions.

If the institution feels it must request references early in the search process, applicants should provide the names, addresses, and telephone numbers of three to five individuals who know the applicant's background and qualifications. Written references sent early in the search process are worthless. By simplifying the process, libraries will find it easier to process the applications and correspond with the applicants.

RESPONDING TO APPLICANTS

To comply with the law, all applications should be recorded in a log to provide a history of each application. The log should contain the title of the position;

applicant's name; date the application was received and acknowledged; the results of each screening; and the date the applicant was notified of elimination from the process or date of the applicant's interview. Upon completion of the search, the application log should be sent to the college's affirmative action officer (Higgins and Hollander 1987: 39). Individual applications should be placed in a manila folder along with an application checklist and a resume evaluation form.

Each application should be answered, preferably within a week of receipt. With the availability of word processors and memory typewriters, acknowledgment letters should appear to be individually typed. Post cards or obvious form letters are unacceptable. Acknowledgment letters should state that the application has been received; when the review process will begin; the time frame for the selection process; and when applicants can expect information about their candidacy. The letter of acknowledgment is also used to provide applicants with an affirmative action form to complete and return. A stamped envelope addressed to the campus affirmative action officer is also enclosed.

Screening

On the appointed day, the initial screening of applications should begin. The initial screening is intended to eliminate from consideration all applicants who failed to provide the requested application materials or who did not possess the minimal qualifications listed in the advertisement. Applicants who fail to pass the initial screening should be notified with a polite letter as soon as possible.

The second screening is a qualitative screening for talent. Examine applications with care to assess the degree to which the applicant has met or exceeded the advertised criteria. To reduce bias and systematically evaluate applications against your established criteria, use some type of rating form. Each committee member should rate how well each applicant met each criterion on a scale of one (low) to five (high). Experts recommend that you do your rating "as much as possible at one point in time" to avoid impatient or inconsistent judgment (Marchese and Lawrence 1987: 33). Committee members should note an applicant's special strengths. Once the applications have been rated, it is necessary to review and discuss the top-rated candidates. Committee members may also suggest an interesting candidate about whom more should be known. It may be necessary to telephone these applicants to ask specific questions. In discussing candidates it is important to remember that "it is the committee's best judgment" and not the rating forms that moves candidates forward (Marchese and Lawrence 1987: 33).

By the end of the second review, you will have identified the serious candidates, individuals whom the committee feels fairly confident about but who must be investigated further. Unsuccessful applicants should be notified in a polite professional letter that their application was considered fully but that it is being considered no longer.

The purpose of the third screening is to reduce further your list of roughly six to eight top candidates. In selecting finalists, no single committee member can block or insist upon a given candidacy (Marchese and Lawrence 1987: 34). These top candidates should be contacted by telephone either by the committee chair or in a conference call with the search committee. Candidates who survive the telephone interview should have their references checked. Candidates who pass the reference check can be invited for an on-campus interview.

The Telephone Interview

Telephone interviews allow you to obtain relevant information on the candidate's experience, personality, motivation, character, and intellectual skills (Dewey 1987: 79). Telephone interviews also allow you to judge candidates without distractions such as dress, appearance, poise, mannerisms, and the like. However, telephone interviews eliminate or dramatically change certain interaction and communication such as body language, facial expressions, timing, and the free flow of conversation, which have important effects on the ultimate decision. While telephone interviews can be useful, they can also lead to erroneous impressions.

To make effective use of the telephone, carefully prepare a script and list of questions to be asked of all candidates. This provides a fair basis of comparison. Candidates are first called to set up a date for a telephone interview with the selection committee. It is not fair to you or the candidates to surprise them with a telephone interview at an inconvenient moment or place. Because the interview takes anywhere from thirty minutes to an hour, candidates may prefer to be called at home. At the agreed-on time and place, the committee chair places the conference call. Committee members are introduced before the committee chair begins the interview, so that the candidate knows who is listening. At the end of the prepared questions, the candidate and committee members may ask additional questions.

Candidates should be asked to describe themselves or asked how others (such as their references) would describe them. Conversations with candidates may also alert you to questions to be asked of references. At this time, candidates should be asked for permission to contact their references. As long as the questions are job-related, the telephone interview provides you with the opportunity to clarify candidate-supplied information and gain additional information without the cost of a campus interview. While the telephone interview does not replace the on-campus interview, it does allow you to make better use of the latter. How many candidates you invite for on-campus interviews depends on a number of things, including the number and quality of your finalists plus the amount of time and money you are willing to spend. Three or four candidates are about right for most searches, with three being an optimal number to bring to campus. This provides you with the ability to compare your best candidates at a reasonable expense (Marchese and Lawrence 1987: 39–40).

Rejection Letters

Once a negative decision has been made about a group of applicants, there is a tendency to get the unpleasant duty of informing them over with as quickly as possible. A word of caution: Very brief letters are perceived as a sign that the application was not considered carefully (Fielden and Dulek 1982: 43). The library community is not large. A library can acquire a lot of needless ill will by sending out insensitive or poorly written rejection letters.

Rejection letters should be as kind and courteous as possible without being misleading. They should also be presentable to the applicant's friends (Fielden and Dulek 1982: 42). Not all applicants hide their rejection letters. Your letter should begin and end with a courteous statement about the applicant's interest in working for your institution. The middle section contains the bad news. While applicants usually would like to know why they were rejected, it is best not to give specific reasons. An honest but general reason for rejection that does not insult applicants is better. "We were delighted with the overall strength of the candidates we considered even though that made the decision process difficult," implies that the applicant was one of many highly qualified candidates. This is a more positive statement than "There were many others more qualified than you" (Fielden and Dulek 1982: 43).

The rejection letter should focus on the applicant, not your institution. Restrict your use of "we" and "I" and maximize your use of "you" and "your." Do not overuse negative words like "sorry," "regret" or "unfortunately." You may be all of those things, but applicants will only believe so much (Fielden and Dulek 1982: 43–44). In writing the letter, be careful not to try to explain, give advice, or criticize. The letter should convey in a courteous and respectful manner that an offer of employment will not be extended to the applicant. Thank them for their time and efforts in applying, but tell them they are no longer being considered for the position.

Good rejection letters are difficult to write, but the extra effort that goes into a good letter is worth it. While an institution will only hire one applicant, it will have contact with several. How they are treated is just as important to the institution's good name as how the finalists are treated.

ANALYZING RESUMES AND COVER LETTERS

The academic resume, with an acknowledged etiquette unique to academe, is a highly stylized and formal document describing an individual's qualifications. Resumes are best used to gain a general impression of the applicant and to determine whether further consideration is warranted. To give each resume your full attention and maintain your perspective, read them a few at a time. Some individuals use resumes to sort candidates into categories as they read them: those in which they are definitely interested; those who could work out; and those whose resumes clearly indicate they are unqualified.

A word of caution: While the vast majority of individuals are honest, there are those who will attempt to shade the truth. A sure sign of misrepresentation "is the apparently deliberate creation of uncertainty or ambiguity." Watch for "omissions, abbreviations, peculiar wordings, and puzzling inclusions" (Vecchio 1984: 24–25).

The cover letter serves as a brief introduction to an applicant's resume and is as important as the resume itself. It is intended to entice the prospective employer into giving the applicant's resume extra consideration. Cover letters provide applicants with an opportunity to establish rapport and arouse a positive response. Cover letters are as diverse as the individuals who write them. They reveal, in subtle ways, information about the writer's communication skills. A cover letter can strengthen or weaken a resume by describing abilities, aspirations, and qualities that have no place in the resume but might help to obtain an interview.

Because the resume and cover letter are your first impressions, serious applicants will make every effort to make a good impression with a thorough and well-written resume. Applicants who fail to make a good impression have not learned some professional fundamentals. A good resume is difficult to write because it is an applicant's professional statement of self. Resumes should be concise yet long enough to provide a sense of who the applicants are and what they have to offer. Resume length will vary according to what an individual has to offer and the position applied for. A resume should be long enough to profile the applicant's salient qualifications, but short enough to avoid trivia. The absence of trivia reflects the applicant's perspective, sophistication, and experience.

In evaluating resumes, read not only what is written but also how it is written and presented. A resume's construction allows you to make judgments about an applicant's organizational skills, analytical ability, communication skills, and creativity. Resumes should be submitted on white or off-white 8 1/2 × 11 inch paper. Light beige, light gold, or very light shades of green or blue are acceptable alternatives. Even if the resume is error-free, a poor copy does not speak well of an applicant. An applicant who fails to communicate a professional image on paper is likely to perform poorly on the job (Davidson 1985: 68–69).

Beginning with the applicant's name, address, and telephone number, the resume should present information in a logical order. Resumes should contain only relevant professional and job-related information. Unless an applicant serves as an officer or board member, extensive listing of memberships may indicate that the individual is a "joiner" and not a "doer." "There is a fine line between an active, industrious person and an overbooked socialite" (Davidson 1985: 68–69). In hiring, the ability to perform the job competently comes before all other considerations. Much of the selection process is spent trying to determine the professional competence of applicants (Shapero 1985: 5).

Experience

Past experience and performance are the best indicators of an individual's capabilities and future performance. Because the experience portion of the resume is the most revealing, it should be read first (Half 1985: 65). Even applicants for entry-level positions should have a record of good work experience. Regardless of the level, field, or type of job, good work habits are transferable. Applicants whose responsibilities and accomplishments go beyond their normal job description, and applicants who are selective volunteers in community or professional associations usually possess a higher than average level of industriousness (Half 1985: 62–63).

The description of the applicant's work experience should include job title, name and address of the library or institutions, and a concise list of specific job duties and responsibilities (Dewey 1987: 65). Sophisticated applicants will list their work experience in reverse chronological order with their current or most recent position first. The chronology of positions will tell you something about the applicant's stability and career progression. The frequency of job changes is not as important as the reason the job changes were made (Half 1985: 64). Moving into a better situation is different from merely moving out of a bad situation.

The most important part of the work experience section is a brief description of the applicant's accomplishments in each position. This description allows applicants to show what they accomplished over and above the day-to-day routine. The applicant's experience should demonstrate initiative and the ability to organize, solve problems, meet challenges, and assume more responsible tasks. Phrases such as "knowledge of," "assisted with," or "had exposure to" may indicate that the applicant has little real experience (Half 1985: 64).

Quality of experience is more important than quantity. Several years of experience in one job may mean one year of experience repeated several times. An applicant's work experience should indicate growth, new duties, or special assignments. Three to five years in any position without a change of responsibilities does not suggest professional growth.

Each of the applicant's jobs should be reviewed in light of the position requirements and desired characteristics. The applicant's job responsibilities and accomplishments should be examined for evidence of functional and transferable skills, knowledge, and abilities. Do not draw conclusions based on stereotyped conceptions about job titles and types of institutions. Be careful not to read more into a resume than is already there. If a skill or experience is not listed on a resume, it generally means that the candidate lacks it.

When evaluating the resume and the applicant, examine the evidence carefully. While the ability to perform a job competently is primary, there are other important considerations. Applicants must demonstrate initiative. Much of what college librarians do is accomplished through independent work requiring self-direction and motivation. Applicants should also have the ability to enhance the overall performance of the library. In some cases "the potential effect of an individual on the group's performance" may be more important than professional competence (Shapero 1985: 6).

Education

The applicant's resume should tell you what degrees are held and date received, schools attended, and specialization of each degree. Where an applicant went to school is not as important as what the applicant accomplished while in school. Some applicants include a list of their continuing education activities. Applicants who continue to acquire and develop job-related skills are preferred to those who think their education stopped with their last degree. An applicant's potential for development and growth is important. Individuals who have maintained their skills are more likely to develop new skills in the face of a new challenge. In evaluating recent graduates for entry-level positions, search committees have used grade point averages, extracurricular activities, appearance, personality, personal goals, and the interviewer's intuition about the candidate. However, the evidence shows no reliable relationship between any of these and subsequent job performance (Shapero 1985: 26).

The resume is intended to provide enough biographical information to determine whether an individual meets the minimum formal requirements; provide indicators worth following up; and provide information that might be used to predict performance on the job. If an individual has succeeded in the past in a situation similar to the one being applied for, the individual will most likely do well in the future. Individual behavior is reliable over time, and past performance is the best predictor of future performance. The question is whether past situations are similar to those the individual will encounter in the future. The less variation between past and predicted situations, the easier it is to predict success (Shapero 1985: 11–12).

REFERENCE CHECKING

Effective reference checking is critical to determine a candidate's suitability. Know what you are looking for and know how to find it. Look for information about the candidate's job performance, personality, character, and ability to blend with the institutional culture (Deland 1983: 458). Checking references allows you to verify factual candidate-supplied information and develop a profile of the candidate's character, personality, and potential for success in the position. An assessment of the candidate's weak points, technical competence, and ability to work with others are matters of opinion. Because of the potential for legal problems, sensitive matters of opinion are best handled by conversation, preferably face to face but more realistically by telephone (LoPresto, Mitcham, and Ripley 1985: 9–10). Usually references are more candid over the telephone than on paper, particularly when specific questions are asked. The committee chair, perhaps with the assistance of one or two of the more experienced committee members, is responsible for checking references. When more than one individual is involved, it is important to coordinate telephone calls and share information.

Checking references is time-consuming and frequently frustrating, but valid reference information is the most reliable way of verifying impressions and candidate-supplied information. If the candidate is going to be working directly for you, do the reference checking yourself. Before checking references, it is very important to obtain the candidate's permission. Even with permission, some references, because of institutional policy, legal restrictions, or fear of trouble, will refuse or are reluctant to tell all they know about a candidate. It is important, therefore, to talk with as many former supervisors and colleagues as possible. Candidates naturally provide good references. Who a candidate uses or does not use for a reference reveals a great deal about a candidate (Deland 1983: 460). Former supervisors and individuals who have worked directly with the candidate are valuable references.

The most valuable information obtained from candidate-supplied references is access to other individuals who knew the candidate but were not listed as references. By seeking additional references you are seeking information from individuals who have no vested interest in protecting the candidate (Half 1985: 150). Moving beyond candidate-supplied references allows you to develop a more accurate, less favorably biased profile of the candidate (LoPresto, Mitcham, and Ripley 1985: 13). However, you must not jeopardize the candidate's current position by going on a ''fishing expedition'' and checking additional references without the candidate's permission. Candidates, unless they are finalists, may not want certain references contacted in order to protect delicate working relationships.

Checking references actually may require more skill than interviewing candidates. On the telephone there is no eye contact or body language to assist you. You must rely on your ears and listen closely for evasive answers and meaningful pauses. If a reference is willing to talk, questions should be direct and to the point. If answers need clarification, return to them later in the interview (LoPresto, Mitcham, and Ripley 1985: 13). Do not interrupt the reference. To get specific information, ask specific and well-developed questions of references. Information about job performance is difficult to check. Questions that require specific and quantifiable answers will be the most useful. When seeking information about a candidate's character or personality, direct questions work the best (Deland 1983: 460).

Make notes on every reference check. A uniform list of questions asked of all references will assist in conducting the interview and provide for consistency and comparability. References should be asked to comment on job-related criteria developed from the job analysis. ''Request only that information which is necessary for the recruitment process'' (LoPresto, Mitcham, and Ripley 1985: 15). It is also important to check the candidates' perceptions of what they have accomplished with their references' perception of their accomplishments. If questions arose from your telephone conversations with candidates, it may be appropriate to explore them with the references.

When talking with references, identify yourself and your institution, and state the reason for the call. Confirm that all information will be treated confidentially and explain the position for which the candidate is being considered (LoPresto, Mitcham, and Ripley 1985: 13). Begin your conversation in a neutral manner. "We are thinking of hiring Wesley Smith, and I would like to verify a few facts with you." Your initial questions should verify candidate-supplied information: title, dates of employment, and level of responsibilities. After verifying factual information, tactfully draw out the reference's impression of the candidate (Half 1985: 153–54). Establish the context in which the reference knew the candidate so you will know how to treat the information. Ask references for their overall assessment of quality and quantity of the candidate's work, major strengths and weaknesses, initiative, dependability, leadership, motivation, and the ability to get along with others. Concentrate on assessing the candidate's work performance and technical competence. Regardless of what you ask references, make sure you ask former supervisors, "Would you rehire?" Note how long it takes them to answer. If you sense hesitation, pursue the question tactfully and carefully (Half 1985: 155). Please remember that some references will avoid answering such "loaded questions." Another good question to ask is whether the reference thinks the candidate is a good candidate for the available position, and why or why not (LoPresto, Mitcham, and Ripley 1985: 12).

References are only part of the selection process, and should not be the only reason to accept or reject a candidate. When you get a negative report, do not jump to conclusions. A reference may have "an ax to grind." Make sure you double check it. References "who give a balanced account, listing a few problem areas along with the good points are probably the most credible source to be found" (Deland 1983: 463). If you discover substantial discrepancies between what the references and the candidate told you, simply drop the candidate from consideration. If you find discrepancies concerning a top candidate and the information is not overwhelmingly negative, give the candidate an opportunity to explain. (Do not, however, reveal the source of your information.) Ask for additional references who can verify the candidate's story (Half 1985: 156).

Reference checking is a time-consuming, intuitive, systematic, and demanding process in which a minimum of three to five references must be consulted to verify or determine a candidate's performance, competency, and the ability to work with others in the institution. Good reference checking takes time, effort, and skill, but it results in a better hiring decision in which employees are better suited to their job and job environment (Deland 1983: 463).

THE ON-CAMPUS INTERVIEW AND BEYOND

By the time you have selected candidates for the campus interview, you should know 80% of what you need to know about them (Marchese and Lawrence 1987: 39). However, there are things that only a face-to-face interview will reveal. The danger with the interview is that it is not always reliable. Because of that danger, interviews need to be prepared for in more depth than the remaining space in this chapter permits. While interviewing is almost an art form, there is a rich literature on interviewing available to search committees. Richard Fear's *The Evaluation Interview* and Bradford Smart's *Selection Interviewing* are two recommended titles. Remember that the interview is a two-way situation. Candidates are also checking out the job to see if it is right for them. When talking with candidates you are also trying to interest them in the job, because unless "the candidate wants the job, all the evaluation you do is irrelevant" (Marchese and Lawrence 1987: 44).

Once a candidate is hired and working in the library, it is important to provide a good orientation to the library and college community. You have invested considerably in your new librarian. Protect that investment with appropriate feedback and guidance during the probationary period and beyond. If, despite your best efforts, the candidate does not work out, it is important to terminate the relationship immediately.

The recruitment and selection of college librarians is not an easy task. While individual colleges and libraries will determine their own process, there are some basic guidelines. Stay within them: They will make the selection process much more effective.

REFERENCES

Davidson, Jeffrey P. 1985. "How to Read Between the Lines of a Resume." *The Practical Accountant* 18 (August): 68–69.

Deland, Rawle. 1983. "Reference Checking Methods." *Personnel Journal* 62 (June): 458–63.

Dewey, Barbara I. 1987. *Library Jobs: How to Fill Them, How to Find Them*. Phoenix, Ariz: Oryx Press.

Fear, Richard. 1984. *The Evaluation Interview*. New York: McGraw-Hill.

Fielden, John S., and Ronald Dulek. 1982. "What Rejection Letters Say about Your Company." *Business Horizons* 25 (September/October): 40–45.

Half, Robert. 1985. *Robert Half on Hiring*. New York: Crown Publishers.

Higgins, John M., and Patricia A. Hollander. 1987. *A Guide to Successful Searches for College Personnel: Policies, Procedures and Legal Issues*. Asheville, N.C.: College Administration Publications.

Isacco, Jeanne M., and Catherine Smith. 1985. "Hiring: A Common Sense Approach." *Journal of Library Administration* 6 (Summer): 67–81.

LoPresto, Robert L., David E. Mitcham, and David E. Ripley. 1985. *Reference Checking Handbook*. Alexandria, Va.: The American Society for Personnel Administration.

Marchese, Theodore J., and Jane F. Lawrence. 1987. *The Search Committee Handbook: A Guide To Recruiting Administrators*. Washington, D.C.: American Association for Higher Education.

Shapero, Albert. 1985. *Managing Professional People*. New York: The Free Press.

Smart, Bradford D. 1983. *Selection Interviewing: A Management Psychologists Recommended Approach*. New York: Wiley.

Vecchio, Robert P. 1984. "The Problem of Phony Resumes: How to Spot a Ringer among the Applicants." *Personnel* 61 (March-April): 22–27.

7

Staff Training

Gary A. Golden

Academic librarians strive to provide their patrons with efficient, quality services. We are not content with supplying the same services and products as we have in the past. Instead, we openly and eagerly embrace new technologies to make more information available in a timely fashion. We also use technology to make the quality of our everyday work better and our staffs more productive. To take advantage of the possibilities that these technologies offer implies having a well-trained staff. A short look at some of these innovations highlights this need.

Microcomputers have many functions within a library. Some of them include: word processing, spreadsheets, database creation, local area networks, computer-assisted instruction, and programming. Some libraries also search on-line databases via a microcomputer connection. Still others use micros for access to their on-line catalog or as vehicles for electronic mail networks within the campus environment. Information databases using CD-ROM or optical disc are fast becoming commonplace in even the smallest of academic libraries. What library does not already have or is not at least in the planning stages for an on-line catalog or circulation system? A current popular topic within the library literature is end-user searching of databases through Dialog or BRS Information Technologies. An even more current concern is how to use fax machines to obtain and send information instantaneously.

In addition to staff training for new technologies, management has an obligation to provide job development and enrichment. Personal job fulfillment and an employee's ability to do his or her job are important concerns of everyone within the library. This responsibility goes through all levels of the library: It extends from the director of library to department heads, and then to anyone who supervises a group of employees. The well-trained employee will help the organization meet and exceed its goals and objectives for both service and productivity. The objective of management becomes how to find the right method of reaching these goals and objectives.

A PROCESS FOR STAFF TRAINING AND DEVELOPMENT

There are several methods and procedures for training staff within libraries. One possible scenario might have the personnel department within the university conducting all the training. Some of this training might be general in nature and some specific to library applications. Another method might involve the library assuming responsibility for the training and development of professionals, while university personnel handles the support staff. However, the system found within many academic institutions has the personnel department responsible for the general campus introduction for new staff. The department also disseminates information on benefits and salaries. The actual training of library staff, from students to professionals, becomes the sole domain of the library.

It is probably better for the library to have the responsibility for training and development of library staff. After all, don't library staff know the most efficient manner to catalog a book or process a serial? Isn't it library administrators who establish the levels, quality, and types of public services? However, to do a good job of training and development for different types of jobs means having a plan of attack, a common training process for all jobs within a library.

This chapter will advance a five-level process for staff development within small academic libraries. This process is multifaceted in nature, and the levels are not mutually exclusive. The process evolves within the organization over time. There must be active and effective leadership by the library director and department heads. Open channels of communication between supervisors and employees are imperative. This process is also fluid and has the ability to change as the technology and library goals change. The levels of this process are:

1. Orientation;
2. Assessing needs and goals;
3. Planning developmental strategies;
4. Training; and
5. Performance feedback and reward.

Orientation

This is the critical first training step within any organization. You must get the new employee off to a good start. It is during the first few days and weeks that employees form attitudes towards their job, the library, and the supervisor. Therefore, a poor or limited orientation will lead to the development of poor attitudes.

A new employee arriving on the job is in an unfamiliar environment. Even if the employee had worked in a library before, this library is still new and has different goals and aspirations. The two critical areas for orientation are the subject matter covered and the length of time an orientation lasts.

The library needs to develop a checklist of items to cover in the orientation sessions. It is the supervisory staff who writes this list. If possible, it should be generic enough to use in other new employee orientations. This checklist includes things an employee needs to feel comfortable in new surroundings and to get ready to do the job. After orientation, the employee should understand the basics of the work situation and what the supervisor expects. Orientation does not include specifics on how to do a job or the production levels expected of each employee. Discussions should take place on items such as benefits, work hours, paperwork to request vacations, time cards, and other generic, everyday work things. A tour of the library and campus are also appropriate. Perhaps the new employee could sit in on a bibliographic instruction program for new students. The supervisor or personnel officer may introduce the employee to these items. In the smallest of libraries, the library director may even take on this responsibility.

There is no exact number of hours for orientation to last. It depends on the complexities of the library and campus. The key is to make the employee feel comfortable in their new surroundings. This will vary from employee to employee, but the supervisor should gauge when the proper level of orientation has been attained.

Assessing Needs and Goals

This second function in the development process begins the planning formulation stage. It sets the stage for a planned, systematic program. It is during this period when the supervisor determines what training is necessary to perform the specific job effectively. This is also the time when the employee articulates his or her career goals. In addition, one can also make a comparison between individual goals and organizational needs. If training is to succeed and the employee is to make a contribution to the library, individual goals and organization needs must be compatible.

It is the supervisor's task to determine what skills are necessary to do the job effectively. If a cataloging clerk uses a microcomputer to enter records, then the supervisor must know the skill level that person needs to successfully use a micro. This means the supervisor must detail the various operations of a job and be able to differentiate competency levels. More than just a job description is needed.

In addition, the supervisor must determine the career development plans of the employee. This is informational and will not change or guide an employee into a certain occupation. This involves discussions between supervisor and employee. This discussion attempts to get a feel for both who the employee is and where he or she hopes to be in the future. It also has the effect of opening the channels of communication between these two people. Career goals may and do change. However, the more accurate they are initially, the more useful they will be for planning developmental strategies. This is the next level in the training process.

What method should you use to reach these goals? Encourage each new employee to fill out an individual development plan. The supervisor and employee both complete the development plan. The appendix to this chapter presents an abbreviated individual development plan. If necessary, expand the planning form to include other items unique to a specific job or library. However, the form should not be longer than one page.

The planning form eases the process of needs and goals assessment. To effectively use this form, the supervisor should complete section one, ''Training Needs.'' List what you perceive as the major skill and knowledge requirements of the subordinate's job. You should also determine the subordinate's level of skill in each competency area. Finally, you should rank each area needing training by priority.

The employee completes section 1, 2, and 3 of the plan independently. Encourage the employee to put thoughtful effort into completing these sections. Be sure to discuss the fact that career objectives and goals can and do change over time. Emphasize that this form only serves as a starting point for discussions and action planning. It is not an inflexible document.

The developmental process begins during this first meeting. The supervisor should also explain how the development plan fits into the training process. The employee and supervisor then complete their sections of the form independently. After finishing, they meet to discuss and compare thoughts on training needs. A good method to follow is to have a third blank form available. Use this form to write down the agreed-upon decisions. Although completed by both, the supervisor has the most impact to the discussion on section 1, ''Training Needs.'' Ideally, the employee should feel that he or she has had a significant influence on the process of identifying developmental needs and priorities. However, the supervisor should be more directive in this area because training needs have a direct impact on job performance.

Planning Developmental Strategies

After determining training, development, and education needs, a plan can begin to take shape. Again, one can use the individual development planning form. The planning process follows the following steps:

1. Earmark the training, development, and education needs having the highest priority.
2. Describe in writing the performance standards that demonstrate the completion of each need. This is number 4, Developmental Objectives, on the form.
3. Discuss and define alternative methods of meeting each need. Select one or more methods that help the employee accomplish the developmental objective. This is number 5, Developmental Activities, on the form.
4. Set review dates.

The supervisor and employee, together, look at the priority of each need and focus on those with the highest priority. Before determining how much to take on, they should consider needs in relationship to work loads, budgets, and other contingencies. Let the employee take the lead in this discussion. If an employee initiates a decision, this will help bolster his or her commitment to the job.

Write the performance standards using behavioral objectives. It is too easy to say "Improve the writing skills on reports" as a measure of a performance standard. Can you measure this performance in, say, six months? Write specific behavioral objectives like: "Make no more than two grammatical errors in reports by October 1." This is a more specific goal, and is measurable and achievable. Having a general goal such as "Improve the writing skills on reports" can easily do harm to an employee because it is immeasurable.

The next-to-last consideration before training is to set review dates to go over the results of the developmental process. It is also a good time for an assessment of needs and goals to take place. Three to six months is a good target date for a training cycle. However, at intermittent dates the supervisor and employee should get together and check on the progress being made. A discussion can take place on any problems or questions. Even within a short period such as six months, both parties should be aware that needs and goals can change. There is the possibility that a comprehensive review and revision of the plans may be necessary.

After agreeing on and writing down the performance standards, the last step is to explore the various developmental activities. This is question 5 on the Individual Developmental Plan. It is time to set up the actual training program to achieve the desired results. The primary responsibility for setting up and overseeing this training rests with the supervisors.

Training

The formal training portion of the development process can have any number of variations. Included are on-the-job training, formal education, development programs, task assignments, and anything else to help employees do their job. You may use any one or a combination of all of these methods. Training runs from very formal to the informal. It can last from a few hours to several days or weeks, depending on the complexities of the job. Within the training context, there is always performance feedback and rewards for jobs well done. The following are some training methodologies available for small libraries.

On-the-job training (OJT) satisfies the most basic developmental needs of new employees. This training may consist of an experienced worker teaching a less experienced worker an advanced technique. It may be a group of staff members training each other in their duties. It can be a supervisor teaching job duties to a subordinate. On-the-job training usually takes place at or near the employer's work area. It is one-on-one or focuses on the small group.

There are some distinct advantages to using OJT rather than more formal developmental activities. Two of these advantages are that OJT allows for immediate feedback and there is little problem in transferring skills to the workplace. Since OJT takes place in what will be the employee's workplace, there is no need to simulate working conditions. There is little problem in transferring skills used in one situation, the classroom, to another, the job. Direct supervisor involvement in the training will further insure a successful transfer of knowledge and skills. A supervisor acting as an instructor is able to give a clear indication of his or her endorsement. Through observation and feedback, the supervisor can coach the employee. They can also determine if the learned skilled is applied and applied correctly.

The first thing a supervisor should do is to break down all the tasks of a job into their smallest parts. For example, inputting or updating cataloging records on an on-line utility like OCLC involves more than just typing on a keyboard. One may have to sign on, tag fields, check errors, and produce a record. Once broken into its smallest components, teaching a job can be done using the following four steps:

1. *Prepare*:
   Put the employee at ease.
   Briefly describe the task to find out what the employee already knows.
   Tell the employee why he or she needs to learn the skill—why it is important.
2. *Present*:
   Tell, show, and illustrate one important step at a time.
   Emphasize key points.
3. *Try out*:
   Have the employee try it and correct his or her errors.
   Have the employee explain key points as he or she begins to master the basics.
   Continue practice until mastering the skill.
4. *Follow-up*:
   Allow the employee to work on his or her own.
   Be available or have someone else available if the employee needs help.
   Check back frequently, encouraging the employee to ask questions.
   Gradually reduce frequency of follow-up.

These four steps will help transfer on-the-job taught skills from one employee to another. However, it is important to start with step one because many people have anxieties about learning something new. Many employees also have uncertainties about the purpose of the job training. Do not assume that an employee knows something. You should also not gear the training to too low a level. On-the-job training requires patience and good communication skills. It also requires a knowledge of the job and an understanding of the four-step process outlined above.

There are also some new methods available for on-the-job training. They revolve around microcomputers, videos, and interactive videodiscs or CD-ROMS. Using software like Hypertext and Windows, a library can easily develop an interactive program to use on a microcomputer. Through the use of questions and answers with prompts, you could develop a program for a new employee to use. For example, a program on how to do acquisitions on OCLC could be developed on a micro using this software. One could also develop programs for new students to train them in shelving, circulation procedures, or a host of other duties. This software can also be linked to a videodisc or CD-ROM so that you now have an interactive video. This means pictures or graphics to support your text. It will make a training program come alive and be that much more beneficial to the employee. These methods are still fairly new and may be too expensive for some libraries. However, you should be aware of what is happening in this field and be ready to take advantage of the potential of microcomputers and interactive videos.

Another technique for training employees is the use of a formal training, education, and development program. These can be library-sponsored courses, where an employee or outside person offers a formal program. For example, if someone on the staff has a certain language skill, he or she could offer a short introductory program for other employees. Private groups continually offer short seminars on library-specific items, microcomputers, word processing, telephone etiquette, and other subjects. For as little as $100 to $150 per employee, you could have them attend one of these seminars. Your book, serial, or on-line catalog vendors sometimes offer a course in the use of their systems. Universities and library schools offer another alternative for learning and training. A one- or two-day cataloging course could be a refresher program for an experienced worker and an introduction for new employees. An introductory course in cataloging at a library school could assist in the training of support staff. It is also a tool for the retraining of a professional. Associations, like the American Library Association, Medical Library Association, Library and Information Technology Association, and the Association of College and Research Libraries offer continuing education programs. They usually last from one-half day to two days. These offer the perfect opportunity to learn something new or could be a refresher and reinforce something previously learned. They are also an excellent and inexpensive way to introduce a new topic or technology.

Sending employees to formal training or education programs is an excellent way to help them obtain the skills and knowledge requirements previously identified in the assessing needs and goals stage. However, just because employees attend a program does not mean that they will actually learn new skills. It also does not mean that they can apply a new skill on the job. There are good and bad programs, and no one can guarantee a program's success. However, there are a few things that can help an employee transfer a new skill from the classroom to the job.

The supervisor must play an active role in helping to achieve this transfer of learning. Before the employee takes the course or participates in the program there are a few things the supervisor should do. He or she should show an interest in an employee's participation in a training program. A supervisor needs to express to an employee that he or she expects certain results from the program. The supervisor should be familiar with the course content and objectives. Discuss with the employees why they were selected for the course or why they signed up for it. Continue discussing your expectations from the course and how it relates to their job. Let the employees know you want them to concentrate on specific areas of the course. Finally, employees should be ready to discuss the course content and how they could apply this knowledge to their job. Throughout this discussion, the supervisor must give the impression that this is important to both the workers and to the library.

Since formal programs cost money and take employees away from work, you will want to maximize the return on this investment. In addition to a precourse discussion there should also be postcourse discussions. This can include asking the employees' opinion on the value of the course and how they will put this knowledge into action. Can anything they learned be taught to other members of the staff? Are they willing to do the teaching? A supervisor could provide actual job assignments that will allow the employees to apply what they have learned. You should also compliment them for progress made in applying what they learn. Schedule a follow-up later on to see if they are still applying what they learned. As the supervisor, you are in a good position to ensure an application of this learning to the job situation. If you do not do these things, chances are that the skills and knowledge gained will be lost. It is also possible that your investment in training will offer no results.

In addition to on-the-job and formal training there are two other possible learning opportunities. These are task assignments and a nonclassifiable group called "other." Within the other group are reading; visiting other individuals, departments, or organizations; and joining professional associations. Supervisors at all levels should be on the lookout for interesting articles that can help employees in their job. For example, an article on updating records in an on-line catalog may help people understand what they are doing when cataloging. A visit to a similar department in another library of comparable size might have the effect of showing employees something they could apply in their workplace. If nothing else, it shows them both the similarities and differences among libraries.

A learning opportunity within task assignments would be a supervisor giving an employee a new or challenging task. A good example is having the person plan a move or department reorganization. A job or task rotation within or between departments has the effect of broadening knowledge. One also gains a bigger picture of the library's operation from job rotation. Too often we permit people to work within the vacuum of their department and never allow them to see how their work impacts on other employees. Filling in for someone at a meeting or when that person goes on vacation has an effect similar to job rotation. Finally, allowing someone to serve on a committee or some other group project lets them learn and grow within a group setting. Any of these assignments may help the employee stretch current abilities or gain new skills and knowledge.

If development is to result from task assignments, it is essential to provide an atmosphere that encourages self-development. Do not be quick to penalize failure. Any challenge involves taking risk and therefore could fail. However, the supervisor must be willing to take this risk because he or she will also develop and grow through the process.

Performance Feedback

This final process in the staff development model is essential in the development of any skill. Remember when you learned to play golf, to bowl, or to do some other sport? You took the stroke or rolled the ball down the alley and saw the result. You then determined how well you had done. You either consciously or unconsciously realized you needed to continue your present pattern of behavior or, more likely, decided you needed to modify your behavior somewhat in order to improve. Feedback influenced your decision. In the previous example, the task itself gives the feedback. An observer, such as a coach or friend, could also be a source of feedback. Regardless of the source, feedback is necessary if performance is to improve.

Analyzing and improving job performance or assigned tasks is a major goal of performance feedback. This feedback can be formal or informal. Formal feedback is usually mandated by the organization through performance appraisal or performance evaluation. This serves the function of giving performance feedback to the employee, evaluating the employee's performance, and setting goals for improvement. There is usually a written evaluation or rating which is often communicated to higher levels of management. This type of feedback may affect the work situation when it determines pay raises or promotions. Formal feedback usually occurs quarterly or once or twice a year. This is in contrast to informal performance feedback, which is an ongoing process. Sometimes it may occur weekly, and other times it may happen several times a day.

Informal performance feedback is a regular and frequent occurrence. This is especially true for newer, less experienced employees. As employees mature on the job, the need for this type of feedback becomes less. For feedback to be effective, it should occur immediately after the employee's performance task. This is because the task will still be fresh in the employee's mind. Too often supervisors give feedback when something is wrong but not when a job was successful. A supervisor should be aware of the "negative imbalance" of only giving poor performance feedback. Giving positive feedback will remedy this imbalance.

However good performance appraisals are, there are still a couple of areas of concern. Formal appraisal discloses very little new information. This is because the supervisor, through informal feedback, should be constantly making the employee aware of where he or she stands. This includes detailing any corrective actions. If all of this were to happen at the formal stage, the employee would feel cheated and wonder why he or she wasn't told earlier. Another area of concern is with making the performance appraisal a discussion rather than a report. The session should be a discussion of the employee's performance, significant contributions, and needs for improvement. It should take place in an atmosphere of problem solving and cooperation by both parties.

To be successful, you should conduct performance appraisal within the context of a helping relationship between the supervisor and the employee. In addition, when doing this type of appraisal you should consider the following suggestions:

1. Give praise to reinforce good performance. Don't just give feedback on poor performance. Praise improvements too, even when they are not up to standard.
2. Ask the person to evaluate his or her performance before you do. Many times they will bring out the points you want to discuss. If people realize something on their own, the resulting discussions will become focused and two-way.
3. Ask the employee how they would improve their performance. Let the person try to figure out what can be done before you offer suggestions.
4. Primarily give feedback about the person's behavior or performance at work. Do not discuss personal qualities or out-of-the-office behavior.
5. When you must criticize, do it quietly, privately, and professionally. If possible, do not criticize when you are angry.
6. Be specific about the behavior or performance you want to discuss. General feedback often leaves the person wondering what to change.
7. Direct the feedback at behavior you want to change. You should also consider if the employee is already doing his or her best job. Is less than perfect behavior okay? Can you change working conditions more easily than the person's behavior?
8. Avoid words like: all, none, always, never, and invariably. They are too easily refuted.
9. Use the "we" approach. Share responsibility. For example: "How can we improve this process?"
10. Remember, the only person anyone can change is oneself. You cannot make someone else change. However, even though that person has the freedom not to change, he or she must accept the consequences of a decision not to change (i.e., your anger or punitive action).

Whenever giving employees feedback on their performance, the supervisor must be aware of the purposes behind this act. The end result of any praise or criticism is the improvement in an employee's work output. To be successful, however, you must always be cognizant of balancing the negative feedback with some positive feedback. The ten steps described above offer this balance.

CONCLUSION

The evolution and implementation of a staff training and development process does not occur overnight. It takes time, effort, and a commitment on the part of all staff members. It is especially important to have the front-line supervisory staff buy into this process early in the formative stage. This is because they are the integral link and will eventually determine the success or failure of your program. A supervisor who is energetic about staff development will pass this energy on to the employees. They, in turn, will be better employees and the library will benefit by having the highest quality services.

There are no tried and true methods for staff development that will work in every situation. Staffing levels, money, local situations, and your campus personnel office all affect a training program. You should be prepared to experiment with different types of programs based on the five-level process presented in this chapter. However, be aware that the foundation on which the experimental method is built guarantees that you will sometimes fail and have to start over. You have to be willing to accept this failure. You also must accept the fact that some things will not work in your specific library setting. If you are willing to do this, your chances of developing the best possible training program will increase greatly.

REFERENCES

Conroy, Barbara. 1978. *Library Staff Development and Continuing Education*. Littleton, Colo.: Libraries Unlimited.

Creth, Sheila D. 1986. *Effective On-the-Job Training*. Chicago: American Library Association.

Goldstein, Arnold P., and Melvin Sorcher. 1973. *Changing Supervisor Behavior*. New York: Pergamon Press.

Hammond, N. 1987. "Getting Started with Interactive Video." *Audiovisual Librarian* 13 (February): 38–45.

Prytherch, Roy, ed. 1986. *Handbook of Library Training Practices*. Hants, England: Gower.

APPENDIX: INDIVIDUAL DEVELOPMENT PLAN

1. Training Needs - These are the requirements needed for improving or maintaining satisfactory performance on the current job.

2. Major Skill/Knowledge Requirement — Degree of Proficiency

		High	Adequate	Low
a.				
b.				
c.				

3. Career Goals

a. Short term (within two years) Include education & development needs (e.g., requirements for performing satisfactorily in areas specified in 2).

b. Long term (2-5 years) Include education & development needs (e.g., requirements for performing satisfactorily in areas specified in 2).

4. Developmental Objectives (specific performances to show need has been met).

5. Developmental Activities (ways to prepare to meet developmental objectives).

6. Actual Results (date to check ______________)

Supervisor's Signature ______________

Employee's Signature ______________

Date ____________

8

Student Workers in the College Library

Evelyn Lyons

WHY COLLEGE LIBRARIES EMPLOY STUDENTS

The day-to-day operation of a library involves a large number of labor-intensive functions. Where dollars are scarce, and they usually are in small college libraries, it is not possible to hire enough full-time staff to handle all the routine activities. College libraries are also expected to maintain extensive hours of service. Staffing the building for sixteen hours—a typical college library "day"—can be prohibitively expensive. The small college library must have a source of cheap labor that is available for short, variable periods of time including the late hours cherished by the student clientele.

Right at hand the college librarian has a labor pool which is chronically in need of money and which has short, variable blocks of free time. Just as the student user values late hours in the library, the student worker is often willing to work until midnight. Students, then, are available and affordable.

The economic advantage to the library of employing students is clear, but this is a mutually advantageous transaction. Higher education is very expensive. The desire or the absolute necessity to earn part of their educational costs motivates students to seek employment. A job on campus offers the convenience of flexible hours, assignments that fit into an academic schedule, and a location that involves no extra transportation costs.

In the hierarchy of campus jobs, library work ranks rather high. It is far more desirable than dining hall or kitchen duty. The toughest on-campus competition for student workers that the library must face is from employment in the department of the student's major.

Serious competition for student workers may come from local businesses which usually offer a higher rate of pay than academic libraries. The college library may lose some of its potential workers. Fortunately there are many students who prefer to work on campus because they can integrate the job with their class schedules. They also appreciate an employer who understands the pressures of midterms and the exigencies of term papers. Foreign students are often more available to the library because the terms of student visas preclude employment in the outside economy (Sichel 1982: 38).

College libraries employ students because they are available, cheap, and able to do many of the varied tasks that must be accomplished if a library is to function. They staff service desks, file cards, reshelve books and other materials, type, and compute. When they have special talents they may arrange exhibits, letter signs, or set up statistical spread sheets. They fetch and carry, answer the phone, and help the staff keep in touch with the younger generation.

PROBLEMS IN EMPLOYING STUDENTS

Because the college library cannot do without them, it will devote time and energy to acquire a student labor force. The trade-off is that there are problems in working with students.

Libraries would prefer to recruit suitable individuals, train them, and have them ready to cover service desks and other assignments at the beginning of the semester. Most libraries can only approximate this ideal, even though staff members give student training first priority in the early weeks of the semester.

As much as possible libraries try to keep a cadre of workers from the previous year and to line up new students during the summer. The reality is that only after everyone is settled into their class schedules can the library fill all its vacancies.

Local practice will determine to some degree how the library identifies the pool of available students. The usual source is the financial aid office. On some campuses all student employees must be eligible for the College Work Study program. All funds for student salaries come from the federal government, and hiring practices are governed by strict eligibility rules. Since the regulations change nearly every year, the librarian must work closely with the financial aid office. The bottom line is that there is paperwork and that the library may not always be able to hire the candidates of its choice.

Other colleges may use a combination of College Work Study money and local contributions. In such cases the library has more latitude in whom it may hire, but the eligibility rules and paperwork do not go away.

It would be ideal if the college library had the time and resources to conduct a job search for each student position. In reality, the library management usually scrambles to fill vacant positions quickly from the available pool of students.

There are a number of strategies for improving the odds on recruiting suitable workers.

Libraries design employment application forms to elicit relevant information about the student. Questions asked should include class, major, previous library experience, and specific skills such as typing or word processing. Try to assess the English-language skill of foreign students.

The most important questions deal with hours available for work. It is useful to have the applicant fill out a class schedule and indicate willingness to work nights and weekends. Often it is schedule criteria that determine the selection of an individual for a specific position.

Since college librarians cannot afford the time to conduct in-depth job searches for their student workers, there will be a wide range of ability, motivation, and commitment among the students hired. This is something that all supervisors of student assistants must live with. There is a positive side to this high degree of student variability. Every year a few truly magnificent young people turn up, and the poor performers usually do not stay around.

The most persistent problem is lack of dependability. When students fail to report for desk duty, especially during evening and weekend hours, the very functioning of the library is seriously disrupted. The result is great inconvenience to the patrons and stress on the remaining staff.

The problems outlined above are neither inevitable nor insurmountable. The remaining sections of this chapter will deal with strategies for motivating students through orientation, training, evaluation, and good relationships with supervisors.

HIRING STUDENT ASSISTANTS

From among the pool of student applicants for jobs in the library, how does the librarian select and assign each applicant? The initial interview with the student applicant can be a crucial element in the selection process (Frank 1984: 53). Some libraries assign one individual to screen the students. This may be a support person, but it is preferable that a professional librarian be the staff member who represents the library as employer to the novice student worker. This librarian may make the assignment to the department or area of the library or a selection of perhaps three students may be sent to the supervisor for a final decision. In order for this system to work, the librarian who coordinates student employment must have a clear sense of the needs of each area of the library—exactly what hours must be covered and what special skills are required.

Information on the student hours budget is another necessary input if this process is to proceed rationally. The coordinator needs to know how many hours the library can afford to assign for the academic year and how many additional hours can be used during vacations and semester breaks. Since the number of hours available rarely matches the number desired by the library staff, efficient and equitable allocation is another essential task for the coordinator. This distribution may be based on past practice, but in the interests of efficiency and equity it is better to review with each area supervisor the minimum needs of the department. Once hours to cover essential service are allocated, the individual departments may present justification for hours to accomplish additional necessary work, to schedule extra help in service areas during times of peak demand, or to relieve staff members of routine or repetitive tasks.

If a special skill such as typing is required for a certain student position, the student may be required to take a skill test before assignment. Some departments may be looking for a student who has computer training or language-reading ability. This information should emerge from the application form.

ORIENTATION FOR NEW STUDENT ASSISTANTS

It is well to be aware when working with student assistants in an academic library that the job is not primary in the student's value system. The scholastic program, social life, activities including athletics, and, of course, the big career goals at the end of the rainbow are way ahead of the job in the library. At the library they are the lowliest employees—part-time and with limited assignments. "It is not surprising that they do not understand or are not committed to the library's goals" (Kathman and Kathman 1978: 118). Recognizing the limited allure of librarianship for most of the students they hire, academic librarians can nevertheless communicate a sense of purpose to these employees.

A well-conceived orientation program will help the student to understand the workings of the library and the role of part-time workers in the endeavor. It is the library's opportunity to present its goals, to define its activities, to describe departments of the library, and to introduce staff members. Orientation material should be presented to all new student employees—preferably in a meeting early in the semester. The library director should make the opening remarks and then introduce the staff. A little solemnity and the attention of the professional staff will go a long way toward giving the students a sense of their importance in the total functioning of the library. A tour of the building and orientation to the various departments of the library might follow the meeting.

Actual job training will be handled by each student's immediate supervisor. Orientation material includes information that applies to all workers. It is an opportunity to review the regulations and policies of the library in relation to its users and its employees. All essential regulations should also be outlined in written form and reviewed by every new assistant. All this necessary information may be presented in the form of a manual. There are some excellent examples of student assistant handbooks in Michael and Janet Kathman's *Managing Student Workers in College Libraries* (1986), enlivened with amusing line drawings.

At the orientation meeting the professional staff should try to give the students a sense of their role and its limits. Students should be very clear about the scope of the help they may offer patrons. Encourage a polite and helpful manner and a firm grasp of basic information about the library, but also convey the difference between simple requests for information and reference questions that require the intervention of the professional librarian. The orientation meeting gives the staff the opportunity to make its expectations regarding attendance and behavior very explicit. If possible, do it with a light touch. The essentials may be in the handbook, but hearing about it from real people will make the information seem more real.

Go over the mechanics of working in the library. If there is a time clock, explain its use. Tell the students when payday is and how long it takes to receive the first paycheck. Review the rules, dress code if any, and policies regarding socializing on the job, using the telephone, or wearing a walkman.

Round up as many of the staff as you can and have them at the meeting so that they can be introduced. Two weeks later when a staff member asks a student to take material to Ms. Johnson, the student may have some idea whom to look for. If there is a tour at the end of the session, the staff members could be introduced in their natural habitat.

TRAINING STUDENT WORKERS

When the new student assistant reports for work, training begins. It is most appropriate for the staff member who will be directly supervising the student to do the training. Most often it is support staff who work closely with students. The librarian in charge of the area should establish a friendly relationship with the student and perhaps offer some orientation to the goals of the department. The actual training in the details of the tasks will usually be handled by support staff.

In very small libraries or whenever student workers are in short supply, cross-training is a very effective strategy. If there is more than one service desk to cover, students may be trained to handle at least one other area. The supervisor's ability to shift student staff to the area of greatest need adds a degree of flexibility in assigning work.

We know that a successful employment experience on campus is a positive factor in student retention. Close relationships often develop between student assistants and their supervisors. Showing an interest in the student's life outside the library is an excellent way to develop loyalty and to give the student the opportunity to know a caring adult. Librarians can be role models, confessors, and advisors. While we do not hire students in order to recruit them into the profession, it can happen. Certainly, good personal relations with staff will help the student to identify with the goals of the library.

As important as personal warmth and interest in the student is the intellectual content of the training. Taking the time to explain the purpose of the job will convey an understanding of where the contribution of the student fits into the total structure of library service. Training must go beyond a detailed description of the tasks to be performed. The student needs to know why these tasks are important. Allow the student some latitude in structuring the assigned work.

Seek out the student's ideas on departmental procedures. Sometimes a fresh viewpoint produces creative solutions. I am not suggesting that student assistants become involved in policy discussions, but once in a while they should hear about issues that are being debated in the library.

If each department of the library has its own procedures manual, training time can be reduced. Of course, you will want to do more than simply hand the student a manual to read. However, the combination of oral instructions and a printed text is an effective way to convey the necessary task-related information. How many times instructions will need to be reviewed with the student and how closely the supervisor will need to check the student's work will vary. For most college students the best supervisory style is one that allows the student to organize the work and to proceed without frequent intervention.

Another element that will vary with the supervisor and the area of the library will be the interpretation of the rules governing schedules and absences from work. In no case should a supervisor accept unexcused absences, but obviously a cataloging assistant's schedule may be more flexible than that of a student who must cover a service desk. Whatever procedures the supervisor feels are appropriate for the area should be spelled out right at the beginning. Expectations should be clear and the consequences of not following the rules should be understood.

I do not want to belabor this point excessively, but years of observation of students at work in the library have convinced me that the quality of the supervision is the most critical factor in the successful performance of students. The essential features of good supervision are a friendly interest in the student, careful training for the assigned task, a clear and convincing statement of performance expectations, and a respect for the student's intellect and understanding.

EVALUATING STUDENT PERFORMANCE

Many library staff members find it difficult to criticize or reprimand student assistants. Too often inadequate behavior is allowed to continue when the right comment at the appropriate moment might clear up the problem. This is one of several reasons for developing a student assistant evaluation form. It is often easier to express criticism in writing, and a prepared form offers a relatively impersonal vehicle.

The student's immediate supervisor should fill out the evaluation, give it to the student to reflect on, and then discuss it in an informal meeting. The best time to evaluate a new employee is about four to six weeks into the semester. The student will have had time to learn the job, and persistent mistakes can no longer be ascribed to inexperience. A frank discussion of problems at this point may make the difference between a mediocre and a fine performance. The evaluation session will also give the supervisor the opportunity to praise the good aspects of the student's work. Reinforcing successful behavior is even more productive than criticism.

Although Sichel recommends a formal evaluation after two semesters, you may decide that it is unnecessary to continue to evaluate students who return to the library for several semesters or years (1982: 43). The evaluation process can be reinvoked whenever problems in work attitude or attendance occur. However, evaluations are essential at the end of a student's employment—at the time of graduation or leaving for another job. Frequently the college library receives a request for information about a former student assistant from a prospective employer. Sometimes a request comes in several years after the student has left the library. It is very gratifying to have a written record of the student's job performance so that the information that goes out from the library is accurate and fair to the student.

DISCIPLINING STUDENT ASSISTANTS

The library has rules governing student assistants and the students are informed about the rules. Supervisors must be consistent in applying the rules. If the manual says that students may not engage in extended conversations with patrons, then stop the conversation before it goes on too long, and do it with a smile. The student is acting naturally and spontaneously in wanting to socialize. The supervisor's role is to remind the young employee that this is a work situation.

The most frequent, serious, and exasperating discipline problem that occurs with student assistants is failure to report to work at a scheduled time. The library's policy in regard to absences and the need to find a substitute will have been spelled out in the manual and articulated in the orientation session and by the immediate supervior. When expectations are clear and the consequences of failure are understood, students usually conform to schedules. Libraries usually ask supervisors to deliver a warning in writing to the student the first time an unexcused absence occurs. Dismissal may follow a second occurrence. Do check with the dean of students or the financial aid office. There may be a campus-wide policy that covers dismissal of student employees.

REWARDING STUDENT ASSISTANTS

Student assistants—academic libraries cannot live without them and we have tried to show how we can live with them. In fact, experiences working with students in the library are mainly very positive. We may want to show our appreciation for the work that they do.

Where college regulations permit, differential pay scales are one very concrete way to express appreciation to a student who has done outstanding work over several semesters. Some libraries automatically increase the hourly wage for each semester or year that the student stays on the library payroll.

Another way to offer higher pay and honor exceptional students is to invite several to become "student supervisors." Choose faithful and very responsible individuals who have been with the library for several semesters to supervise the building and the other students at times when no member of the regular staff is on duty. In many libraries student supervisors open the building on weekends and keep things running smoothly for several hours before a reference librarian reports to work. They may also be placed in charge during late evening hours. It is, of course, appropriate for these students to receive higher wages.

All library staffs have occasional parties. Include students in some of the celebrations. Include them in the planning, too. Christmas is an ideal time to demonstrate good will toward students, who often take over the job of decorating the library with great energy. With the pressure of exams it is not always feasible to have a party, but punch and cookies in the workroom will be well received.

Most colleges have a number of endowed prizes or awards for students in various disciplines. Perhaps some friend of the library would endow an award for library service. Having something to compete for motivates many students and provides an incentive to continue working in the library in order to qualify.

Finally, even the best student workers leave the library: They graduate. Supervisors may wish to give some recognition to graduating seniors. It has been a rewarding relationship and we should acknowledge the value the library staff places on the contribution of students.

REFERENCES

Frank, Donald G. 1984. "Management of Student Assistants in a Public Services Setting of an Academic Library." *RQ* 24: 51–57.

Kathman, Michael D. and Janet McGurn Kathman. 1978. "Management Problems of Student Workers in Academic Libraries." *College and Research Libraries* 39: 118–22.

———. 1986. *Managing Student Workers in College Libraries*. Association of College and Research Libraries, College Library Packet Committee. Chicago: American Library Association.

Lyle, Guy R. 1974. "Student Assistants." *The Administration of the College Library*, pp. 164–69. New York: Wilson: 164–169.

Sichel, Beatrice. 1982. "Utilizing Student Assistants in Small Libraries." *Journal of Library Administration* 3: 35–45.

White, Emilie C. 1985. "Student Assistants in Academic Libraries: From Reluctance to Reliance." *Journal of Academic Librarianship* 11: 93–97.

PART III

Public Services

9

Circulation—The Workhorse

Mary Sellen

In the majority of small academic libraries, the circulation desk is the first point of contact for anyone entering the library. It has become the most labor-intensive department now that the Online Computer Library Center (OCLC) has come to the rescue of most cataloging departments. While every librarian seems to think the heart of the library ticks in their area of expertise, most patrons will tell you that the heart of the library, especially small academic ones, is the circulation department.

The work load at the circulation desk typically consists of at least the following, if not more: opening and closing the facility; checking in and out books; checking in and out reserve materials; processing overdues; processing reserves; acting as the central telephone point; and, as much as reference librarians will blanch at the idea, a secondary reference area. In the never-ending quest for the best utilization of money and manpower, such work as stack maintenance, serial control, student worker control, and computer assistance (when small labs are located in the library) are also coming under the circulation desk span of management.

Personnel requirements for such work are intriguing in the small academic environment. Physical environment can determine work quality and patterns. It is also an area in which written policies are essential and are referred to frequently. It is a rare small library that does not have at least one microcomputer, for which the software market has developed a smorgasbord selection of systems that directly impact on circulation services. The following comments on the above topics are offered to stimulate and perhaps change old ways of thinking about circulation in small academic libraries.

PERSONNEL

In large institutions there is no doubt that a professional librarian is needed to oversee the myriad workings of a large circulation operation. In smaller institutions the problem is not that clear. It is very difficult to assign a librarian the sole task of managing circulation when a typical small library staff just barely covers all the jobs that need to be done by a professional. However, the circulation department is very visible. When it does not work well, a campus-wide impression of total library mismanagement may result. Interaction with patrons, for example faculty and students unjustly charged for lost books, takes more than just minimal job training. This interaction many times means that the circulation person is interpreting policy and managing conflict, and is the first line of defense when a problem of any kind occurs anywhere in the facility. As micro technology and on-line circulation systems invade the circulation area, computer skills are also becoming a necessity for all staff members. This front-line staffing level ranges from the student worker to the professional, with all the staff level variations in between. To complicate the interaction further, since circulation is staffed for all the hours a library is open, there can be no telling what staff person the patron may encounter at any given time of the day. In other words, every person who must field patron questions and problems at the circulation desk must be well trained. The management problem is, who will oversee this training?

Not all professional librarians have the desire or the time to train circulation people well. It is a rare small academic library that can afford to have a professional doing only circulation. Working with clerical and student workers in a circulation desk situation can be as rigorous as teaching a course in basic rhetoric. Not only must all the procedures and policies be explained and taught, but follow-up and evaluation of work must be done on some kind of a regular schedule, as well as working with other departments, such as the business office, on campus. If this is not done, policy misinterpretation and loss of materials, could result, among other things.

Clerical workers rarely are expected to possess such management skills, as evidenced by their pay scales. Granted, they may do minimal supervision of student workers, but to expect them to train and evaluate student workers and also do their own work requires more than the clerical wages and training budget traditionally provides for in a library.

With the advent of the "paraprofessional" in library staffing, library administrators have been able to put better qualified people in areas in which neither professional nor clerical personnel are suitable. The circulation management position is a good example. Basic library knowledge is needed, and yet the theoretical training needed for other library areas is not necessary. Supervisional and management skills can be expected because the pay scale tends to be better than clerical categories, and yet the supervision and evaluation is overseen by a professional, and major decisions are not left to the circulation manager. It is a position in which initiative is critical and, because of the job category, should be expected.

Determining the number of people assigned to the circulation area will be determined by the circulation system used, physical layout, and hours of service. In general, one supervisor, three to five clerks, and student workers as needed should be assigned. True management skills come into play when the circulation staff can do the most work with the fewest number of people. Many circulation task analysis studies done at larger institutions have identified inefficient procedures and staffing patterns. Replicating and customizing these studies when a circulation department is larger than five people may be in order to make the best use of personnel.

THE PHYSICAL ENVIRONMENT

Because the circulation department has a key role in providing services, its physical arrangement must be thought out to ensure satisfactory work flow arrangements for the staff, and provide the proper security for the collection and accessibility for the patron. Actual square footage depends on the number of staff and volume count of the collection. With on-line systems or microcomputers at the desk, physical arrangement of the furniture becomes very important in terms of adequate power sources, security for the hardware, and accuracy of work in a highly public area. Manual systems are affected greatly by furniture arrangement behind a circulation desk as they take up even more space.

In many small libraries the circulation area is close to the main collection and study area, and noise factors are important. Much talking between patrons and staff goes on in this area aside from the noise of computer printers when present. Acoustic boxes for the printers should be routine equipment; sensitizing the staff to the volume of their voices is helpful also. As many impediments to noise such as lowered ceilings and panels separating this public area from study areas should be employed as judged helpful and practical. The placement of reserve materials is critical to their security. Staff must have access to them, yet public access must be highly controlled, normally through a closed stacks policy.

Placement of the service telephone is an important consideration. In a highly visible area, it might work as an unintended public phone, but if secluded, it may not allow the staff to interact efficiently with the patrons. The burden of answering telephone questions typically routed to the circulation desk, such as hours of service and referral to reference personnel, is eased by installing phone systems with prerecorded messages that answer the service questions and allow the phone patron to get to the reference person without the intermediary action of circulation.

POLICIES

Considering all the areas and functions in the library, the area where written policies have the most impact and are referred to with the most frequency is circulation. Who can borrow what and for how long must be spelled out and understood by the entire staff. In an academic library, interactions with the business office in the collection of fines is a preferred, if not common, practice. If policies and loan periods are not clearly defined, much confusion may result.

Balancing loan periods with staffing and collection size should be considered. If a loan period is short, overdues are generated more frequently and create more work. If a loan period is long, there may be problems of accurate tracking and student access to materials if the collection is not large. Shorter loan periods, however, allow more materials to circulate and satisfy more patron needs. In the past, faculty loan periods were long or entirely nebulous. Recent studies indicate that shorter loan periods and more accountability by faculty of the materials they check out are being instituted. Graduate students usually are allowed longer loan periods due to the nature of graduate studies, and the typical undergraduate loan period is three to four weeks. Many small institutions have uniform due dates to reduce the burden of generating overdues.

The dilemma of allowing people not immediately associated with the institution circulation privileges is very much an administrative decision. Local high school students are frequent users of academic institutions, especially when their teachers are recently out of graduate school. It is not only wonderful public relations to allow these potential college students the use of the institution's library materials, but it also can be used as a recruiting tool for the admissions staff. When considering colleges for their children, many parents take into account the library. Circulation policies must be sensitive to this fact. Admissions departments usually have good working relations with the local high schools. Working with them as much as possible on these policies will ensure cooperation even though the accountability of this type of patron makes the usual policy in-house use of materials only.

Alumni are another type of patron that must be served. While an institution most likely will extend borrowing privileges, other services such as interlibrary loans and computer searching must be handled with care. These services are costly and are better provided by a public library for those not directly involved in higher education.

In small institutions it is very easy to make exceptions to policies, but the more exceptions made, the less effective the policies become. Policies need to be well thought out and administered realistically yet firmly, with everyone knowing who makes exceptions and when. It is only in this way that circulation policies will be perceived as fair and acceptable to all patrons served.

AUTOMATED CIRCULATION SYSTEMS

Because of size, when prioritizing automation projects many libraries first grapple with OCLC and put circulation on the back burner, making do with in-house, primarily micro-based, circulation systems; and even then, only if money and staff interest are present. With microcomputers delivering 40 megabytes of storage and promising more for the future, micros most likely will become the automation choice of small institutions for circulation if the institution cannot afford the integrated packages that sometimes come with on-line catalogs.

There are two directions in which a library can go when automating circulation: design their own using an existing software language such as a version of DBase or Basic, or purchase prewritten software programs. Either way, it is a necessary and interesting exercise to think through the various permutations of the circulation process so that the end result is a system that will do what you want it to do.

Before writing or previewing any system, a number of questions require answers. By whom or how records will be input; what types of information should be readily accessible; how much information the system will have to support; where the system will be located; what information will be printed out; how menu-driven (giving the user prompts to proceed) will the system be; and who will be in charge of maintaining and backing up the system. Ideally a program will:

- Check out materials;
- Renew loans;
- Discharge materials;
- Place holds on materials checked out;
- Identify overdue materials;
- Issue recalls;
- Handle reserve circulation;
- Handle and prepare overdue notices; and
- Generate statistical reports.

These are just some ideas. Each institution will either expand or reduce the number of these suggested tasks.

Hardware considerations are the easiest decisions. For about $1,500, at present, anyone can buy a 40 megabyte microcomputer such as an Apple or IBM. Throw in about $300 to $500 more (depending on how sophisticated a system you want) for a printer and optical scanner, and the basic hardware for a circulation system can be readily had. Be aware that every year for the past three years hardware prices have dropped, and there is every indication that they will continue to go down. The decision to buy should be made when the interest and commitment of the staff is present—a crucial aspect of a small computerized circulation system, as the writing or selection of the software will be totally dependent on the people writing and working with it. If the staff is involved in these decisions as much as possible, people will not feel threatened. Allowing staff to acquire computer skills should be viewed as an added benefit to any position that improves a person's overall job skills.

Writing involves learning a computer language, flowcharting, prototyping (using a model program on a small number of records to see if the program really functions the way it is intended), and endless discussions with the staff members who will be using the system. The flexibility of an in-house program has no equal, and can be adapted no matter what changes occur in the circulation process. Be warned, however, that even if the library chooses to let a member of the computer science faculty or student write the program, the library's involvement in terms of input needs to be significant. Library literature is full of stories of unsuspecting librarians who thought a piece of circulation software could be developed with minimum input on their part only to be disappointed with the final program.

There are many software languages on the market that are suitable for writing programs for circulation. Circulation is a basic records management task, an application that lends itself to computer programs. Prices can range from $20 to $700. DBase is one of the easiest and most popular languages to use. At press time, DBase IV was coming to market. Although not cheap (at least $500), every successive version of DBase has not only been easier to use but more powerful—allowing the programmer to summarize and manipulate records in countless useful ways. One can write programs that will not only organize and index circulation records, but generate many varieties of reports and customize screens for input and output records. Taking the time to learn DBase gives one a valuable skill that goes far beyond knowing how to write and manipulate a circulation program.

There are numerous software packages libraries can purchase if the time and desire are not present to write a circulation program. Some integrated automated library packages promise circulation systems, but many times the on-line catalog part is such a huge undertaking that the circulation component is delayed dramatically if not left unimplemented in the large institutional setting. Very few small libraries, at this point, can afford the cataloging, let alone the circulation systems. There are packages for under $3,000, however, that run on micros yet can handle the volume of a small- to medium-sized library. Some of the recent ones are:

1. *CSL Library* (ISPN [International Standard Program Number] 12182–400), Chancery Software, Vancouver, British Columbia, Canada.
   Can track 30,000 books and up to 4,000 borrowers; can download from a main administrative system; has light pen and manual entry; can generate statistics; report formats can be customized; runs on Apple.
2. *Nonesuch Circulation System* (ISPN 66500–025), Ringgold Management Systems, Beaverton, Oregon.
   Two separate systems: Online—charging, discharging, holds, query; and Batch—overdues, statistical summaries; runs on IBM.
3. *On-line Circulation System* (ISPN 66368–400), Richmond Software Corp., Marietta, Georgia.
   Has barcode scanner on books and library cards; runs on Apple.

4. *Circulation Plus*, Follett Software, Crystal Lake, Illinois.
   Can handle 65,000 volumes and 15,000 patrons; runs on hard disc; has barcode scanner; can assign five different circulation periods; can be customized; runs on Apple or IBM.

There are many small programs designed for handling specific circulation tasks such as overdues. These systems can be modified and used as reserve tracking systems also. Some of the recent ones are:

1. *Library Helper ''Overdues''* (ISPN 74975–410), Southern Microsystems, Burlington, North Carolina.
2. *Overdue Books* (ISPN 66450–544), Right on Programs, Islip, New York.
3. *Overdue Collector* (ISPN 44575–300), Follett Software Co., Crystal Lake, Illinois.

The sources for publishing and pricing information on software are *The Software Catalog*, Elsevier, New York, published winter and summer; *Datapro Directory of Microcomputer Software*, Datapro Research Corporation, Delran, New Jersey; and *Library Software Review*. All are invaluable in keeping the user informed of new programs that are available, revised editions of existing programs, and revised prices for these programs.

The automation of circulation is an inevitable future for almost every library whether it be on a large or micro system. Hardware costs continue to drop and yet deliver greater efficiency; software and programming software packages are numerous, easy to use, and available in all price ranges; computer skills are basic and required in almost all positions in library work. Aside from all the above, circulation is records management—a task that is the original intent of the majority of business computer programs.

STATISTICS

The most important statistics of small libraries, the ones most influenced by the budget, are how much the facility is being used and what materials are most needed by the patrons. These come from the circulation department. Many a budget has risen and fallen based on what librarians do with these statistics. Collection evaluation to collection development, the weeding of materials, and the sociology of the library patron are all based on information gathered at the circulation desk.

Which statistics to gather will depend on the circulation manager and the library director. The number of books being checked out and the number of patrons using the facility are the most basic statistics for anyone to keep. Because circulation statistics can be broken down into many different ways, periodic reviews of what information is actually being kept should be done. The Office of Management Studies of the Association of Research Libraries published the monograph *Measuring the Book Circulation Use of a Small Academic Library*

Collection: A Manual in 1985. Its purpose is to "put into 'cookbook form' book collection use study methodology" for libraries doing planning (Trochim, Miller, and Trochim 1985: ii). This manual answers such questions as: How much data should be collected? How can this information be used? Who should be involved? It is a very useful method that gives the librarian a tested outline and beginning point for statistical collection from the data gathered at the circulation desk.

SUMMARY

In this age of technology and the management questions it creates in libraries, circulation challenges the creative small academic library administrator. It is one area where microcomputing is possible with small budgets and staff interest; where creative use of personnel can save time and money; where the image of the library becomes known to the public. Is it a workhorse? The answer is undoubtedly yes. The small academic library director who stays on top of microcomputing technology, trends in library personnel management, and the campus environment will be rewarded with a successful and rewarding department for the institution and the library.

REFERENCES

Burr, Robert. 1977. "Toward a General Theory of Circulation." *Occasional Papers; University of Illinois Graduate School of Library Science* no. 130, October.

DuBois, Henry. 1986. "From Leniency to Lockout: Circulation Policies at Forty-Three Academic Libraries." *College and Research Libraries News* 4: 698–702.

Farrington, Jean Walter. 1984. "Overdues and Academic Libraries: Matters of Access and Collection Control." *Library and Archival Security* 6: 67–75.

Reynolds, Dennis. 1985. *Library Automation: Issues and Applications*. New York: Bowker.

Trochim, Mary Kane, Arthur Miller, Jr., and William M. K. Trochim. 1985. *Measuring the Book Circulation Use of a Small Academic Library Collection: A Manual*. Washington, D.C.: Association of Research Libraries, Office of Management Studies.

Weaver-Meyers, Pat, and Kenneth W. Pearson. 1986. "Workflow Arrangements and Their Effect on Discharge Accuracy." *College and Research Libraries News* 4: 274–77.

10

Interlibrary Loan

Marilyn E. Miller and Patricia R. Guyette

Interlibrary loan (ILL) is one of the most dynamic areas of library service, and small academic libraries are finding themselves increasingly involved in interlibrary lending and borrowing activities. This chapter initially addresses various factors that have influenced and will continue to influence the growth rate in academic interlibrary loan activity. The remainder of the chapter presents considerations and suggestions for dealing with the practical daily operation of interlibrary lending and borrowing, and for coping with the new volume of this activity. It is assumed that the small academic library already has some form of interlibrary loan operation in place, and that the *Interlibrary Loan Practices Handbook* (Boucher 1984) is used as a continual reference source for basic general information in the ILL operation. Particular attention is given to use of the OCLC Interlibrary Loan Subsystem.

FACTORS AND GROWTH CHARACTERISTICS

Coupled with the availability of a vast number of publications is the fact that no library, no matter how well funded, can afford to purchase for its own collections all that its users will need. Interlibrary loan therefore becomes an indispensable and fundamental service for academic libraries. As such, it is developing as a major cooperative effort, being fostered by technological advances in the field of computers and by library networks. Though once seen primarily as repositories for the storage of collections, libraries are now viewed as places from which information is to be obtained. Emphasis on the need for access to and dissemination of information has encouraged developments in a number of areas. Interlibrary loan is an increasingly important and utilized component in the dissemination of information, and stems directly from developments in access.

Access to materials held by other libraries has evolved from finding tools in traditional printed format to computer output microform (COM) catalogs, and from there to shared circulation databases and then national bibliographic utility databases. The national databases have probably had the most pronounced effect on interlibrary loan activity. Access to information sources also has evolved, from quite limited traditional printed indexes to extensive and comprehensive computer-based literature-search services. The effect of computer-based literature searches on interlibrary loan activity was reported by Thomas Waldhart as usually being dependent on the specific situation (1985a: 218). The small academic library may well find that its access to information sources through computer-based literature-search services increases its interlibrary borrowing activity, especially for serial requests. Students today are highly computer literate, and they gravitate toward whatever information can be found using computers.

National Bibliographic Utilities

National bibliographic utility databases are having the greatest influence and impact on interlibrary loan activity. Initially useful as a comprehensive source for bibliographic verification of requests, the Union Catalog aspect also facilitates finding locations where requests may be sent. The integration of interlibrary loan system modules with bibliographic databases allows for the actual transmission of requests to specified locations.

Among the four major North American bibliographic utilities, each of which contains an automated interlibrary loan system module, the Online Computer Library Center's implementation in 1979 of its ILL module was especially significant. Waldhart found not only that from 1978–79 to 1980–81 academic libraries as a whole were experiencing an unusually rapid growth in overall interlibrary loan and in lending, but also that academic libraries of small or medium size were becoming more involved in ILL lending (1985a: 216). The small academic library whose holdings are in an on-line database accessible by other libraries will find itself increasingly receiving interlibrary lending requests even from libraries located outside the immediate state or region and from other than academic libraries. Data from the National Center for Education Statistics that Waldhart examined for the years 1974–74 through 1980–81 showed an average annual growth rate of 8.4% for lending, 5.6% for borrowing, and 7.4% for total ILL activities in academic libraries (1985a: 215).

Academic ILL Characteristics

There are a number of other interesting findings from Waldhart's review of existing research in ILL as it pertains to academic libraries (1985a: 220–24). Though the interaction of academic libraries with public and special libraries is quite complex, academic libraries have primarily been found to borrow and loan materials with other academic libraries. The form of material requested most frequently will be serials, but monographs are a close second. Materials requested tend to have been published within the past three years and are predominantly in English. Revision in the codes governing interlibrary loan activity in the last decade has had a visible effect on the ratio of student to faculty borrowers in academic libraries. With improved access to ILL being allowed, students have become the predominant users in academic libraries. While these findings are notable, it must be kept in mind that substantiating data is only as recent as the early 1980s. Since then there have been numerous advances in computer technology and considerable developments in library networks.

Library Networks

Any discussion of networking is incomplete without considerable mention being given to interlibrary loan. Susan K. Martin in her extensive writing on networking and networks has noted that the ILL network is one of the most common types of traditional networking (1986: 12). Libraries have formed consortia for some time, forming systems of some type to facilitate one or more goals they have in common. Interlibrary loan is the service most desired after that of sharing bibliographic records for cataloging.

The small academic library may have participated in such cooperative ILL networks either locally or regionally, with other academic libraries of similar size, or with other libraries having a similar specialization. In this traditional manner interlibrary lending and borrowing is a manual and time-consuming operation, with the means of communication being principally telephones, teletypewriters, and the U.S. mail. Libraries are currently witnessing a resurgence in telefacsimile machine usage. Telefacsimile has application both as a means of communication and as a means of document delivery. Its usage in the small library's ILL operation can be as an adjunct to the traditional manual environment in improving either or both the transit time for ILL requests and the transit time of the actual material.

During the past decade, on-line computerized networks have developed on national, regional, state, and local levels, with regional networks acting primarily as brokers for national OCLC services (Martin 1986: 175–237). Networks made up of libraries of one type have mainly given way to networks made up of many types of libraries. While regional multistate networks are usually privately funded, state multitype networks are publicly funded. The availability for participation in state multitype networks at reasonable cost opens up a wealth of resource-sharing opportunities for small academic libraries. The instantaneous communications that are possible in on-line networks supplant the various traditional means of communication for efficient, and at the same time growing, ILL operations in small academic libraries.

Stand-alone microcomputers and dial-access communication increasingly provide the mechanism for this participation. While prior to 1982 the small academic library had to participate as a full cataloging member in OCLC to have access to the OCLC Interlibrary Loan Subsystem, a "selective" status now allows active use of the OCLC ILL Subsystem through participation in an ILL group. The North Carolina Information Network is an example of a recently developed state multitype network through which small academic libraries in that state can now borrow and lend materials locally, statewide, and nationally via the OCLC ILL Subsystem. Having access to a national network's ILL subsystem is, or soon will be, a new opportunity for a number of small academic libraries.

Some academic libraries that have in the past utilized private vendor bibliographic services for cataloging or circulation may find an increased ability to communicate with other libraries utilizing the same vendor's bibliographic services for interlibrary lending and borrowing (Martin 1986: 169–70). Electronic mail functions can provide an avenue for communicating requests. A major drawback in private vendor interlibrary loan activity is the limitation in the number and type of libraries also using a particular vendor.

PERFORMANCE CONSIDERATIONS IN AN ILL OPERATION

As interlibrary loan borrowing and lending activity becomes a vital aspect of its library service, the small academic library will be confronted with the various elements of turnaround time vying for priority attention in the work site.

Waldhart describes turnaround time in five succinct areas: processing time by the borrowing library, transit time for requests, processing time by the lending library, transit time for materials, and, again, processing time by the borrowing library (1985b: 318).

The greatest amount of time spent in initial processing by the library as a borrower is in doing the necessary bibliographic verification, locating several libraries having the requested material, and then completing the required paperwork. The small academic library having access to a national bibliographic utility database and its interlibrary loan system component, whether through direct on-line or dial access, benefits in a number of ways. Particularly important are the automatic transfer of bibliographic information from a bibliographic database record to an ILL request form and the automatic transfer of a request to the subsequent locations indicated. This latter referral capability saves a small academic library countless hours of staff time as well as increasing the possibility for successful fulfillment and subsequent user satisfaction.

Utilization of the OCLC ILL Subsystem

This system is the most widely used today, and its correct usage is extremely important for effective and efficient ILL borrowing and lending. The new user of the system does have responsibility to be familiar with all aspects involved, as explained in OCLC's *Interlibrary Loan Training Manual* and its *User Manual*. While training workshops should be attended if possible, the training manual is geared to provide a self-instructional hands-on approach (OCLC: 1983). The following section focuses on certain aspects that warrant special attention.

The selection of the lender string is of crucial importance in filling out an ILL request form. In searching for an appropriate bibliographic record it may frequently be necessary to view several records, which will have different holding symbols attached. Since a charge is incurred for the holdings display of each bibliographic record, a printout or note should be made of at least ten locations, if available. Local and regional locations should be used first, and requests should be distributed to institutions in an equitable manner. The ILL Subsystem interfaces with the Union Listing (UL) component of the Serials Control Subsystem, thus making available summary or volume-specific information for serials. Though many libraries do not have their serials holdings listed yet, it is definitely worthwhile to consult what Union List groups are available and take advantage of any pertinent listings.

Some libraries require that their OCLC institution symbol be entered twice in succession in the lender string. A printout of the record entitled "Enter my symbol twice," retrievable by a title search (ENT,MY,SY,T), is useful for staff to consult. The record's listing should be reviewed periodically for printout updating. While the purpose of a location being entered twice is to allow additional time for answering the request, this time element should always be kept in mind when determining the lender string. When there are only one or two locations for a routine request, the extra time from imputting them two or three times may come in handy. The borrower is entitled to five insertions in the lender string for the price of producing the request, and this should be used to the library's advantage.

It can, however, be very dismaying to send a request to the only known location of the needed material and have the request finally reappear in the message file with the status "unfilled." While some libraries will use the "conditional" response to let the borrower know the reason (for example, missing, out on extended loan, or at the bindery), this was not the original intent of the conditional response, and many libraries now utilize the OCLC ILL Micro Enhancer software which mandates a straightforward yes or no response to batched requests. Thus, at this time, a standard ALA (American Library Association) request form sent by mail or telefacsimile usually provides the best means for securing a definite answer in a timely manner.

Familiarity with the individual lending policies of the institutions involved is, of course, very important when selecting potential lenders. The on-line OCLC

Name-Address Directory (NAD) is a primary source for staff to consult. ILL charges can be determined from these policy statements as well as pertinent information concerning loan periods, renewals, and noncirculating materials. Loose-leaf notebooks containing ILL policy information for institutions not found in NAD or in other sources should be maintained in the library's ILL office. An obvious, though often forgotten, activity is to keep one's own ILL policy information updated in NAD. The volume of interlibrary loans has increased so much nationally in recent years that many libraries are now charging for loaning books as well as for photocopying articles. Reciprocal agreements often exist on a local level to help alleviate this situation. Some libraries have set up coupon systems for payment with libraries that do not charge for loans to them, and some even ''advertise'' in their policy statements that they are open to agreements for free photocopy exchanges. It can be very beneficial to investigate the possibilities of various arrangements that may help cut costs or speed delivery time.

While accurate and complete filling out of work forms on the ILL Subsystem should be done according to the directions in the OCLC *User Manual* (1985: 2:3–22), the following are some helpful suggestions to note. Specific editions of a work or specific deadlines that a patron may have need to be stated in either the line so designated (''edition'' or ''needbefore date'') or in the ''borrowing notes'' line. Whenever more than one OCLC database record is involved in a request, these bibliographic record numbers need to be included in the field labeled ''verified.'' Photocopy requests present different problems, and attention must be paid to fields labeled ''maxcost'' and ''copyrt compliance.'' Without information supplied by the borrower in these fields, a request on the system may go unfilled. Borrowers additionally need to remember to place author and title information for photocopies of articles in the ''article'' line rather than using the ''author'' and ''title'' lines. Rush requests can be so noted, but should be asked for judiciously by borrowers. Utilization should be made respectively of the ''borrowing notes'' and ''lending notes'' lines to convey information that may be extremely helpful in clarifying an ILL request. The ability to have data for certain required or frequently used fields stored and then automatically transferred to ILL work forms and records is one a library should certainly take advantage of by creating and subsequently modifying as necessary its ''constant data'' record.

A lender must be accountable for paying attention to the information supplied on the ILL request. In checking one's message files regularly, staff members may want to use highlighting markers to spotlight specific details on printouts of incoming requests. ''No'' responses should be made by a library as soon as possible to allow requests to move on quickly to a possible affirmative answer instead of remaining in the message file for the four-day limit. If the lender has the possibility of later filling the request, a future date response is especially helpful to the borrower only having one or two locations left in the lender string. Lenders should take the initiative to deal with requests having incorrect citations.

By alerting the borrower to this situation, subsequent potential lenders will be saved much wasted time and effort.

"Shipped" dates and "returned" dates can be particularly problematic. Lending credit is received by OCLC participants at the time "shipped" data is entered. However, for the borrower this mailing date will only be as valuable as its accuracy. Mailing dates two to five days earlier than reality are deceiving, and further skew actual transit time for materials regardless of the method of delivery used. Entering "returned" dates needs to be an important step in the final processing activity by borrowers. Not only does accurate date information convey to the lender the expected receipt of its materials by whatever method of delivery is being used, but this return date also allows the lender to complete its records.

The storage of interlibrary loan records in the ILL Transaction File from time of request initiation until completion can be a useful reference for all libraries, whether borrowers or lenders. Chapter four of the OCLC *User Manual* specifies different search keys for retrieving records from this file (1985: 4:13–19). Two of these searches that are often overlooked can be extremely helpful: borrowing library and lending library search keys. In addition to finding information for those books that arrive without accompanying ILL forms but bear ownership stamps, the lists of what a particular library is currently borrowing or loaning can also be used to pinpoint patterns and disperse requests equitably at a given time.

For the small academic library, usage of the Interlibrary Loan Micro Enhancer (ILL ME) software package can save staff time significantly and free terminals for other work. Designed by OCLC to be used in conjunction with its ILL Subsystem, it allows many of the tedious, repetitive, and time-consuming on-line tasks to be batched and carried out automatically either during or after library hours. The ILL ME will automatically log on to the ILL on-line system at whatever time is specified, update records, and download and print records from one's Message Waiting File as specified (OCLC 1987: 6:1–24).

Staffing Considerations

For the small academic library, interlibrary loan is usually placed with the responsibilities of either the reference or circulation departments. The actual ILL staffing most likely consists of only one person, or perhaps two, with additional help from student assistants. While many library users discover their need for interlibrary loan through interaction with a reference librarian, and verification of requests to other libraries necessarily involves a multitude of standard reference works, the ILL operation is also a logical extension of circulation with its various circulation routines of borrowing and lending materials and dealing with overdue or lost ones, and its financial activities.

Wherever located, other staff in the department should be trained in the basic procedures for helping library users fill out ILL request forms and for dispensing

ILL materials received and ready for the user. This frees the actual ILL staff time-wise and allows for mobility in dealing with other aspects of the ILL operation. Additionally, interlibrary loan affords many opportunities for good public relations which are greatly enhanced if the services of initially receiving requests from users and providing user access to materials received are available any hours that the library is open. Incoming ILL materials ready for users can be kept on book trucks that are routed to circulation or reference desks at night and on weekends. A shelf system within the ILL office having materials arranged alphabetically by requestor's name, with a separate shelf or drawer for materials that must be used in the library, works well. Microfilm, in particular, is often returned to the ILL office when not being used by the requestor. Request forms can always be kept on hand at service points, and boxes or book truck sections can be designated specifically for placement of ILL materials returned from requestors.

Interlibrary loan is a constant meeting of deadlines, which need to be met even in the absence of the main staff person. Student assistants can be effectively utilized. Since incoming requests are supposed to be verified by the borrowing library, students should be able to search the card catalog, serials catalog, or on-line catalog, and then retrieve the material from the stacks. Problems, which undoubtedly will arise, need of course to be handled by the supervising staff person. Photocopying, an especially fast-growing activity in the ILL operation, can be done by student help. Proper packaging of materials for shipment and receipt processing of incoming materials are routines that students can handle. Depending on the number of students that may work in the ILL operation, it may be best to assign specific tasks to each one. When duties are shared it is wise to have students initial the work that they do in case follow-up questions are needed. Written instruction sheets that students can refer to at any time can help eliminate errors.

When the number of requests requires increased staffing, interlibrary loan lends itself to a logical division of borrowing and lending activities. The lending activities can usually be supervised by an assistant as the processing for such requests should be less problematic. Borrowing requests from users at the home institution, on the other hand, may range from "monographs" with all citation details clearly stated to illegible pleas of help for obscure and scantily documented sources of information. Staff working with interlibrary loan do become extremely familiar with the library's collection and its idiosyncracies. By the nature of the work, ILL staff may find problems involving cards missing from a catalog, incorrect cataloging, mutilated materials, serials never received, incorrect call numbers, and filing errors. While it may be tempting to proceed with one's specific task, it is always beneficial to take the time to follow through on any errors or problems encountered. Each time a mistake is brought to the appropriate person's attention and corrected, library users will have better access to needed information. ILL staff will at some point interact with every unit of the library, and good communication is essential.

Utility of Forms

Accurate record keeping, including statistics, is an essential aspect of an ILL operation, and thorough documentation needs to be planned for. Forms should be clear, concise, and, wherever possible, multifunctional. If as much pertinent information as possible can be included in statements on the form, ILL staff can often simply check the applicable portions. A form that is well constructed is a very effective and efficient means of communication, which can be personalized with the simple addition of a hand-written message. Whenever devising new forms or revising existing ones, it is helpful to acquire samples from ILL operations in other academic libraries. Evaluate the purposes of forms in use, and do not be afraid to experiment with different ways of setting up new forms.

Situations constantly recur where ILL requests cannot be processed or ordered and must be returned to the requestor. Forms attached to original requests that indicate by a simple check mark the respective situation do save time and effort. The problem of obtaining dissertations is a good example of the need for such a user response form. Virginia Boucher covers the topic of theses and dissertations well (1984: 73–86). Since obtaining dissertations can in reality be a complex endeavor, listing various options to which the requestor can respond is advantageous. An added convenience for the requestor is the attachment of a UMI (University Microfilms International) order form. Awareness should be exercised in creating user response forms to avoid building in unnecessary steps that may add to user frustration in obtaining the requested material.

With all ILL requests it is useful to send the requestor a written notification form regarding receipt of materials at the library. Telephone notification is time-consuming and often leads to third-party problems in message communication. The written form can clearly convey any charges to be paid, whether cash or checks are accepted, and how checks should be made out, all of which prepares the user for an expedient process when picking up the material. Most academic libraries pass on the cost of photocopied orders to the users. It is usually wise to stipulate that payment must be made before photocopying can be released. There will be situations when the cost of the photocopied material is not known upon receipt since many large academic libraries simply state "invoice to follow." It is best to bill the user in such cases rather than hold the photocopied material for what may be several weeks. As a lender of photocopied material, in turn, remember that sending the bill along with the material is desirable.

Another helpful form for borrowed ILL materials is a slip that the user signs and dates when picking up requested materials. It is impossible for any one person to remember or be involved in all ILL transactions, and knowing when and who indeed retrieved an item can be very useful. This is especially important if materials are available for pickup on nights and weekends from other than ILL staff. The slip can simply be clipped to the book cover and later attached to the ILL request forms.

More and more libraries are using some type of cover form or book sleeve on ILL books. This usually consists of a printed form on colored paper that is taped around the front cover of the ILL book. Essential items of information such as due date, user's name, any restrictions on use, and name and address of the library are usually featured on the form, as well as a statement that the cover is not to be removed. These covers can be used on either or both incoming and outgoing ILL materials. Not only do the covers highlight pertinent information in an immediate format, but more importantly they help eliminate the problem of ILL books ending up in the stacks of the borrowing library.

Since the type and ways of using forms do vary from library to library, it should be stressed to ILL staff and students that all forms that arrive with a package must be kept with that material. Forms may be found within as well as taped to the outside of the package, the latter often being labeled as packing slips or invoices. Close attention has to be paid to matching forms coming with the materials to forms on file in the ILL office. Due dates, restrictions, insurance, and packing instructions all need to be carefully noted.

Functionality of Files

Files make up the other part of the essential aspect of an ILL operation's record keeping. The important factors in setting up files are that they should serve a necessary purpose and facilitate quick retrieval of desired information in a logical and easily understood manner for those staff using them. Existing files should be evaluated to determine how easily they fulfill their respective functions. As with forms, the same advice can be given for files. Do not be afraid to experiment with different ways of organizing the interlibrary loan files. Existing setups may no longer be expedient for a particular operation. In a library environment where users constantly check the status of their requests, a pending file arranged by user name may be beneficial. The simplest method of arrangement is by date of request or ILL transaction number.

While individual institutions may have differing policies on record-retention schedules, copyright guidelines specify that records be kept by the requesting institution for three full years, and this is advisable for almost all ILL files. The need for a copyright file certainly exists for any ILL operation. One easy way for the smaller library to set up such a file is to simply make an extra printout of photocopy requests produced electronically and to use the pink copy of the standard ALA ILL form for photocopies requested by mail. The use of red tabs on forms, filed by title, after four requests have been placed for a particular title easily alerts staff to titles getting close to the ordering limit. Various software programs for charting copyright are now available and can be especially helpful for libraries with a predominance of serial requests. Though copyright law is extremely complex, a basic understanding is fundamental for all staff involved with interlibrary loan.

With the increased opportunity for using automated ILL systems, more libraries will be dealing with requests received electronically as well as with the standard ALA request forms. This can contribute to a proliferation of files. Computer requests have a number of processing steps with dates being input and/or monitored at each stage—pending, shipped, received, and returned dates. Since in the small academic library this terminal activity often takes place away from the ILL office, the use of small portable file boxes is very effective. Various request forms can be batched and filed by needed activity: all records needing a shipped date, all requests needing renewals, all requests to be searched, and so on. These forms can then be interfiled back in the appropriate files in the ILL office, often with the ALA request forms. For example, borrowed materials may be filed by due date whether the order was requested on-line or by mail. The important thing to keep in mind is that the entire ILL operation must remain flexible enough to deal with the change and growth that is taking place.

A file that comes into existence with the increased use of an automated ILL system is one for mailing labels. While a mailing label is usually attached to a request form received through the mail, this is, of course, impossible with on-line requests. It is therefore a good idea to exchange batches of mailing labels with libraries that are heavily used through the on-line system. When shipping requested loan materials, a label for the return of the items should always be included as well as specifications for insurance and packaging. Due to increasing insurance costs, many libraries selectively insure loaned materials rather than routinely doing so as in past years. Insulated mailing bags are being used more frequently, and are quite adequate if used sensibly. The need for accurate labeling, as for proper packaging, cannot be overly stressed to staff. Ramifications for not doing so range from needless delays for the user of the materials to the borrowing library having to pay the lending library for materials never received.

CONCLUDING REMARKS

The ever increasing need for not only having widespread access to bibliographic information but for actually disseminating that information through interlibrary borrowing and lending is evident today. Technological advances, making possible the present interlibrary loan systems as integrated modules of national bibliographic utility databases within the past ten years, are increasing the availability of these systems at reasonable cost for small academic libraries through a variety of networks.

Interlibrary loan is becoming an even more dynamic part of the small library's operations. For this growth in activity to be productive, there has to be a commitment to interlibrary lending and borrowing as part of the library's service mission. People, the staffing in the ILL operation, are the most vital component, as interlibrary loan remains foremost a cooperative effort that relies on the conscientiousness and good will of a great many individuals. Attending ILL meetings—making face-to-face contact with other ILL librarians, sharing problems, and exchanging ideas—is helpful in fostering smoother and more productive interlibrary loan activities on a daily basis.

REFERENCES

Boucher, Virginia. 1984. *Interlibrary Loan Practices Handbook*. Chicago: American Library Association.

Martin, Susan K. 1986. *Library Networks, 1986–87; Libraries in Partnership*. White Plains, N.Y.: Knowledge Industry Publications.

Online Computer Library Center, Inc. 1983. *Interlibrary Loan: Training Manual*. Dublin, Ohio: OCLC.

———. 1985. *Interlibrary Loan: User Manual*, 3d ed. Dublin, Ohio: OCLC.

———. 1987. *Interlibrary Loan: Micro Enhancer Manual*, 3d ed. Dublin, Ohio: OCLC.

Waldhart, Thomas J. 1985a. ''I. Patterns of Interlibrary Loan in the U.S.: A Review of Research.'' *Library and Information Science Research* 7: 209–29.

———. 1985b. ''Performance Evaluation of Interlibrary Loan in the United States: A Review of Research.'' *Library and Information Science Research* 7: 313–31.

11

Off-Campus Library Services

Nancy Courtney and Kathleen Tiller

Off-campus library services can be defined as an extension of normal library service for students and faculty of classes taught in sites physically separate from the college campus. These students are normally adults working full-time who are seeking further education and cannot conveniently attend classes on the main campus because they live or work too far away. Classes may be held at branch or satellite campuses affiliated with the main campus, community centers, local elementary or high schools, or almost any facility that can accommodate a class of adult learners. Such facilities may or may not be equipped with adequate resources to support college instruction. Prison inmates are another population often served by small colleges. Teleconference courses present other problems because often there is limited contact between teacher and student. Colleges must examine ways to provide the necessary support for extended services. A vital consideration is the library's role.

When taking on the responsibility of providing off-campus instructional activity, small colleges and universities should be aware of a number of assumptions. The purpose of the off-campus activity obviously must be in line with the college's educational mission. This mission implies that library service must be as available to off-campus faculty and students as it is to those who utilize the home campus. Access to the sponsoring institution's library services is as important as the knowledge of the availability of other libraries that off-campus students might use more conveniently. Access to library services necessarily involves quality bibliographic instruction that focuses more on research strategy and how to find materials than on what specific resources might be available in a particular library. Adequate library orientation in the form of tours, carefully prepared handouts, and on-site bibliographic instruction sessions insures that students can meet their information needs using any library to which they have access.

ACCESS TO MATERIALS AND SERVICES

Access to bibliographic tools, books, and journal articles is an important consideration in planning for off-campus library services. One method of providing access to materials is to make use of the libraries near the off-campus centers or students' homes. These may be public, community college, or other academic libraries. Use of these libraries has the advantage of convenience. Being nearby, they save precious time for students who may be several hours away from the home library. There are several disadvantages, however, to relying on local libraries to provide service to your students. First, they may be lacking in the quality and depth of their collections. Public libraries, especially, cannot be expected to have the resources necessary to support college-level education (Kascus and Aguilar 1988: 33). Second, there may be problems in students obtaining access to academic library collections where they are not enrolled. Third, the on-campus library has no involvement with collection development in the local libraries.

Utilizing the Local Library

Before beginning a program of off-campus services, or as new classes are added to an existing program, survey the materials and services available at the local libraries. What are the hours of the library? Are there adequate evening and weekend hours? In the cases of an academic or community college library, is the library open to the public? If so, are there restricted hours for use by the public? May people not affiliated with the college obtain borrowing privileges? What is the extent of the collection in the content areas of the off-campus classes? Is reference assistance available, and is it provided by a librarian? Is the reference collection adequate for your students' needs? What periodical indexes are available?

It may be possible to set up special arrangements with the local library to provide service to your off-campus students. Consider offering borrowing privileges to the local library's patrons in exchange for privileges for your patrons. Find out if the library would be willing to house a special reserve collection of books from your own library for use by your students (Slade 1985: 165–66).

On-Campus Library Materials

For reasons mentioned above, it is not desirable to rely completely on local libraries to meet the research needs of off-campus students. Regardless of any arrangements made with other libraries, the primary responsibility for providing service remains with the on-campus library. Reference assistance, circulation of books, and delivery of periodical articles are all necessary services that the library must provide.

In order for students to identify books in the library collection, they should have access to the library's catalog. Some libraries may be able to produce microfiche copies of the catalog that can be deposited in participating local libraries or distributed directly to the students. Libraries that have on-line catalogs with dial-up access ports might be able to work out an arrangement with local libraries having the necessary equipment to allow students to access the on-line catalog remotely (Johnson 1988: 255). Of course, students who have their own microcomputers and modems will be able to dial in to the catalog from their homes.

There are several possible answers to the problem of circulating books to off-campus students. Students may use the interlibrary loan services of their local public library, if they exist, but this is too time-consuming to serve as an adequate solution, as is sending materials through the mail. A very basic method is for the instructor to carry materials to the off-campus classes. These could be specific titles requested by the students or simply a set of appropriate books that the students could browse. The obvious disadvantages of this method are the limited amount of material that can be conveyed, the burden that is placed on the instructor, and the clerical problems of checking the books in and out. The on-campus library may also participate with other local libraries in an interlibrary delivery system, such as a van service, that could be used to deliver materials ordered by telephone. Of course, off-campus students should have the same in-person borrowing privileges that on-campus students enjoy.

Many libraries do not circulate periodicals and therefore limit their use by off-campus students. Another means of access must be provided so that off-campus students can make use of periodical articles. A photocopying service is one answer. Students can submit written requests for articles by mail to the on-campus library or send them via the instructor. Requests might also be made by telephone. The library should also handle interlibrary loan requests from off-campus students. Again, requests can be made by mail or telephone, and materials delivered by the method chosen for book delivery from the on-campus library.

Reference service is another area of access that needs to be addressed. Students will need help in developing search strategies and gaining access to bibliographic tools and on-line searches. Telephone contact with a reference librarian from the on-campus library is a valuable resource. If possible, the library should arrange to accept collect calls from off-campus students or provide a toll-free number for requests for reference assistance, computer searches, and photocopy and interlibrary loan requests (Johnson 1988: 254). On-line database searches can be performed by the on-campus librarian and sent to the students. Although many librarians feel it is necessary to have the student present during the search, this is not feasible for off-campus students. A telephone interview between the librarian and student combined with bibliographic instruction in on-line searches should be sufficient.

BIBLIOGRAPHIC INSTRUCTION

Successful utilization of the library's resources to satisfy information needs is dependent on the student's research skills. While on-campus students have access to the advice and expertise of instructors and reference librarians, off-campus students will be limited in the amount and quality of assistance they receive. Therefore it is essential that a sound bibliographic instruction component be built into any library's off-campus services. The most effective method would be an on-site visit by the librarian from the home campus. A successful on-site visit requires cooperation with the instructor and any other librarians from institutions that off-campus students might use.

The purpose of such a bibliographic session would be to train the students in research skills that are applicable to whatever library they may choose to visit. Time should be spent acquainting students with types of research tools such as statistical sources or indexes and abstracts, which they may not know exist or have had little experience using. Handouts from the on-campus library as well as those from cooperating libraries should be made available to students as early as possible. Along with the prepared handouts, explanations of any cooperating libraries' policies and practices should be included. The training in research skills should include traditional means of access to information such as printed indexes and abstracts as well as the more sophisticated electronic products such as on-line databases or CD-ROM technology.

In the case of searching a database on CD-ROM, students can be taught the basic concepts such as Boolean logic, methods for broadening or narrowing a topic, and the value of free-text searching. Even in cases where students will request that a librarian perform the search for them, such explanations can lead to the formulation of more clearly stated requests with a better chance for successful retrieval. Access to an on-campus library's on-line catalog via a modem at the off-campus site or the student's home may also have to be considered. Clear instructions and a demonstration of the catalog's capabilities can be accomplished by using any one of the liquid-crystal display plates currently on the market, along with an overhead projector and a personal computer. Where on-site visits by a librarian are not feasible, bibliographic instruction can be made available by means of a video recording or a newsletter.

PERSONNEL AND BUDGETARY CONSIDERATIONS

The success of the library's attempt to serve off-campus locations also involves financial and personnel considerations. The librarian chosen to handle off-campus service should be provided with enough flexibility to schedule visits to off-campus locations. Fellow librarians and staff should be well acquainted with the rationale, expectations, and procedures of an off-campus program so questions or requests can be handled properly. A secretary may need extra time to help prepare handouts and other librarians in the department may be requested to adjust schedules to cover the absence of the librarian visiting an off-campus location. Additional student workers may be necessary to handle the processing of document delivery if that is a component of the program. Some accounting and billing system will need to be worked out to provide efficient handling of photocopying and mailing costs. A department microcomputer with an appropriate database management package can be used to keep track of invoicing if necessary.

Decisions regarding librarians or additional staff, document delivery and attendant charges, and provision of reference service and sources are all budgetary considerations. If an off-campus site or a cooperating library is to be provided with reference tools, collection development policies can become an issue. Can the library budget handle duplication of materials so that the off-campus locations are adequately supplied, or will such centers be provided only with outdated materials? The basic assumption of equal access to library service is in question here. How much can off-campus students be expected to pay for having journal articles photocopied and sent to them? What part of the cost can the on-campus library absorb? Is the librarian who does off-campus instruction to be paid for time spent in that activity?

Several sources of funding for personnel, document delivery, and a reliable duplicate ''core'' reference collection are available. The budget of the home-campus library is the most obvious starting place. Whatever portion of the cost is not met by charging the patrons directly is simply handled as any other budgetary item. The continuing education department or a similar agency on campus might be asked to provide all or part of the necessary funding. Finally, the individual academic departments responsible for an off-campus class might be approached for monetary support.

According to the Association of College and Research Libraries (ACRL) Guidelines for Extended Campus Library Services, ''Changing patterns within higher education during the last few decades have placed broader demands on library resources and services'' (1982: 86). Planning is essential to meet the information needs of a quickly growing segment of library users. Such planning should include an appropriate needs assessment of the off-campus population under consideration, a written profile of those information needs, and a clear statement of program goals and objectives, as well as methods for measuring the success of the service.

REFERENCES

Association of College and Research Libraries (ACRL). 1982. ''Guidelines for Extended Campus Library Services.'' *College and Research Libraries News* 43: 86–88.

Johnson, Jean S. 1988. ''Off-Campus Library Services and the Smaller Academic Library.'' In *The Smaller Academic Library: A Management Handbook*. Edited by Gerard B. McCabe, pp. 249–56. New York: Greenwood Press.

Kascus, Marie, and William Aguilar. 1988. ''Providing Library Support to Off-Campus Programs.'' *College and Research Libraries* 49: 29–37.

Slade, Alexander L. 1985. ''Thirteen Key Ingredients in Off-Campus Library Services: A Canadian Perspective.'' In *Proceedings of the Off-Campus Library Services Conference II: Current Practices—Future Challenges*. Edited by Barton M. Lessin, pp. 163–83. Mount Pleasant, Mich.: Central Michigan University Press.

PART IV

Technical Services

12

Input and Output: Technical Services, 1989 and Beyond

Sheila A. Smyth

Technical Services departments in small academic libraries are continually challenged by technological advances affecting the college community. In the past, catalogers have faced cataloging new media items such as sound cassettes without guidelines. Simultaneously, faculty and students are anxiously waiting for these items. The advent of machine-readable data files, now called computer software, and compact discs, which are the new formats of the 1980s, have forced these librarians to adapt standard cataloging techniques to accommodate access to new media. Today librarians involved in all aspects of Technical Services find themselves using manual processing techniques, computer catalogues, Compact Disc–Read Only Memory (CD-ROM) authority files, and direct transmission of information. It is time for Technical Services staff to take a long, hard look at procedures. It is also time for increased communication between Technical Services and Public Services staff. The two need to become more involved with each other as the age of automation gains momentum: Each has much to offer the other.

Acquisition librarians procure materials, both print and nonprint, to meet the needs of the academic community. These librarians actively seek faculty input in the selection process so that the collection reflects the direction of the curriculum and to some extent meets the extracurricular needs of the community. Often *Choice* cards for a particular discipline are routed through a department. Reviews of materials may be photocopied and circulated to department chairs for routing to their faculty. This process encourages departments to order materials. Some institutions may request that all orders be routed through department chairs so that each department has a central control. If the department is a large one, the chair may appoint someone to act as a liaison between that department and the library. This person will meet with the acquisitions librarian to discuss the department's needs. Acquisition librarians may meet either with the department or its representative to encourage participation in the selection process. Another effective way of dealing with materials selection is to assign subject areas to the various librarians so that subject journals will be reviewed on a regular basis and recommendations made. Students can be encouraged to make recommendations through the use of a suggestion box.

Streamlining the acquisitions process is difficult in a manual system. Multiple-part order forms may be typed by a student worker. However, all work needs to be revised by a regular employee who has a critical eye for detail. All orders should be verified through *Books in Print* and other tools by an upper-level clerical person or the librarian. The checking process can be speeded up if one is able to use *Books in Print* on CD-ROM. The various copies of the order form need to be filed in the appropriate files. This filing may be done by a student and later checked by a paraprofessional. All expenditures have to be recorded manually. The use of a spreadsheet and a PC will simplify this process and ensure a greater degree of accuracy in controlling the budget. Some vendors such as Brodart and Baker & Taylor have automated services that alleviate some of the paperwork created in the above process. This is discussed in another chapter.

Simplification of acquisitions work is found in an automated system. Computers can generate orders and can be programmed to review files and automatically issue claim reports without human intervention. The initial search to determine whether a library has an item on a specific topic is much speedier and more accurate by computer than the traditional search of the card catalog. The librarian is essential to the smooth operation of any automated system. This person knows the collection and is trained to determine the quality of a specific title in relationship to the total collection as well as the institution's curricular needs. The accounting procedures are much tighter since the files are interrelated. Also, the librarian is aware of events outside the computer that will affect its procedures. Time released from filing and revising routines can be used more effectively to determine user needs. Automated circulation files allow an opportunity to study the use patrons make of the collection. Collection development can be refined as a result of knowing these use patterns. Once standard bibliographies are on-line, these tapes may be loaded into an on-line system, matches can be determined, and lists of nonverified titles can be generated. Professional judgment must be used to determine whether titles should be added to the collection. There are also opportunities for cooperative collection development when neighboring libraries that are on-line form a network.

The cataloging of the item describes the physical item, including author statement, title, publishing information, pagination, and size. Classification is the process whereby the subject location of an item is determined. Subject headings are also assigned at this time. Most libraries today use an outside source for the major portion of their cataloging.

Unit cards may be purchased from the Library of Congress (LC) for those libraries that lack access to the bibliographic utilities. Librarians review these cards and make adjustments so that the cards agree with the items in hand. Call numbers and subject headings will have to be typed on the unit cards. An electronic typewriter with memory may be used to type in call numbers on cards and labels. Student workers are an inexpensive labor source for these tasks. Books may be purchased from vendors who supply catalog cards (pretyped with call numbers and subject headings), which require verification against authority files by a student worker or clerical person who refers problems to the librarian. The librarian will review batch cards and materials before the items are sent to the shelf.

Cataloging in publication (CIP) can be photographed and then photocopied, edited, and again photocopied or hand duplicated. By this process one can create a set of unit cards, similar to those produced by the Library of Congress. It does require access to a photocopier which involves a slow-moving process and some mechanical dexterity on the staff's part. This process is time-consuming and not cost-effective for most small academic libraries. It is recommended for special items or rush materials. Unit card sets can also be typed into the memory of an electronic typewriter. Multiple unit cards can be created with a few key strokes. There is very little need for professional review once the initial copy has been reviewed. Personal computers with appropriate software packages for creating catalog cards are available. Access to a letter-quality printer is essential to guarantee quality cards. Student workers may be employed to cut costs. Often they work for short periods of time and bring fresh energy to routine tasks which become tedious when performed for seven or eight hours straight.

The bibliographic utilities such as OCLC provide an effective way to obtain prealphabetized catalog cards with call numbers, subject headings, and local information. In addition, an archival tape is created which creates a tape for a local system. National authority records are readily available on these databases to insure quality control. Time is saved and staff costs are cut when using a bibliographic utility. There are substantial membership and use costs, however. Each library needs to establish a balance between the national standards and the needs of local workers. Those persons involved with utilities have a responsibility to the profession to provide a quality catalog at the national level while maintaining cost-effectiveness within the local setting. Student workers, particularly in an institution committed to computer literacy, are interested in working on the computer and quickly learn the tasks. Students can search the database and locate records acceptable to the library. Professionals or high-level clericals can revise records for desired changes prior to inputting. Often a student may be trained to input into a specific format. Student skills are sharp and the error rates are lower since they are familiar with the vagaries of the format. Experienced paraprofessional staff can be trained to revise student inputting. Often the assigning of specific formats to individuals results in expert revision. This is particularly true in the small institution where a single librarian catalogs across formats. It is advisable to batch catalog-specific media types since it is easier to work in one format at a time.

Original cataloging is the most expensive route to take when cataloging an item. It is to be avoided since its costs in salary and accuracy are prohibitive. Some materials, such as locally produced materials or highly specialized items may require this sort of treatment. It may or may not be done on-line depending on the institution's resources, commitment to the national bibliographic file, and the content of the material.

The public catalog is the index to the collection. It is the end product of Technical Services and is the instrument that tells the user what materials are available on a subject and where they can be found. It may take the form of the traditional card catalogue, an on-line public access catalog (OPAC) or a computer-output microform (COM). Prealphabetized catalog cards are received from bibliographic utilities. This service enables cards to be filed in the public catalog faster than has traditionally been experienced by patrons. Usually, computer-generated cards have fewer errors. It is cost-effective to have students file cards that are revised by a senior clerical person or the librarian. It is best to assign the filing to one or two well-trained student workers. Filers should work for approximately one hour at a time.

An on-line system is an effective approach to streamlining access to the library's materials. As managers of information, the Technical Services staff is responsible for quality control of the bibliographic records for on-line systems. Errors that went unnoticed in the card catalog appear on a terminal. On-line systems also provide access points to those areas of the card catalog that were not indexed in the past, such as the content note and system requirements notes for computer software. Information needs to be standardized. This results in the creation and use of authority files. Authority files have not always been used in the smaller academic library, which is generally short-staffed. Time formerly assigned to manual tasks is now available to create quality bibliographic and authority records. Senior clerical people or highly skilled paraprofessionals can be used to clean up the database. Careful scrutiny of test databases enables the automation team to specifically design files for problems. Support staff or student workers can be used to correct some of the problems. In some instances, global changes are much more easily effected on-line. Additional subject and author/title headings for contents notes can be created easily in a local system.

In a card catalog or an on-line system, subject authority work is critical. Use of the bound edition of the *Library of Congress Subject Headings* is essential. The *Library of Congress Subject Headings Weekly Lists* keeps the search terminology up-to-date in the OPAC. Again, student workers can check current subject headings against these standard lists. This update is an ideal to be sought. In reality, however, a library may not have the staff or financial resources to exercise complete authority control in-house. An alternative is to determine which subject headings need immediate changes and correct them. The technology is being developed that will systematically convert subject headings to their most current form.

Local subject headings should be recorded and used when determining authority control. It is important to establish and use authority files whether one uses an on-line or a manual system, since the age of automation has certainly arrived. Authority control is the chief means to insure quality control in the database. Uniform language results that is essential for precision in patron subject and author searches. Major authority corrections should be done in late afternoon or before a weekend so system performance is not degraded.

The classification of materials is the process whereby call numbers reflect the subjects contained within them. This enables books and media items that deal with one particular subject to be shelved together in numerical order. Most academic libraries use either the Dewey Decimal Classification (DDC) or the Library of Congress Classification (LCC). A library should carefully consider any attempt to change from one classification scheme to another. Shelving needs during the interim period are a difficult affair to arrange. The library has to maintain two separate sets of shelves—one for the old classification scheme and one for the new one. Constant shifting takes place as one set contracts while the other expands. Additional staff is required. It is easier to do this on-line where programs can be developed to identify records with existing LCC or DDC call numbers. Barcoded items are helpful in the inventory process and generate labels automatically. It is best to undertake such a project during an intersession period or summer school. This is also an ideal time to set up an inventory. However, a professional librarian will need to monitor the process to determine the appropriate changes needed.

Librarians should be familiar with the curricular needs of students and faculty when classifying materials for the collection, since subject retrieval is an important issue. For example, the library must determine whether biographies and critical material will be classed with the subject's works. Similarly, does the library wish to class Spanish, French, or English fiction together as fiction, or in its respective language classification? Another question to be considered is whether media items will be classed in the same way as monographs. One may wish to place a dummy block on book shelves referring patrons to media locations if the two are housed separately. A library may need a unique call number depending on the patrons' desire to browse in the stacks. Often, faculty and students on the small liberal arts campus prefer this approach to the collections. A library may also decide to break out a specific collection with a special Cutter number arrangement or other numbering system when dealing with Shakespeare or Chaucer as author and subject.

The physical preparation of books for the shelf may be done in-house or purchased from the vendor. When purchased, the books appear in the library ready for shelving with the call number on the spine and pockets and cards in place. The library needs to apply ownership marks, security targets, and any uniquely determined information. Vendors, for the most part, are not capable of handling media or rush items. In-house processing uses student workers. Labels for book cards and spines produced on-line have fewer errors than typed labels. This process requires a letter-quality printer. Ownership marks may be embossed or stamped. Stamping books is more effective since pages are not damaged with perforations. Stamp the outer edges with a gentle rocking motion. Fan the pages of slimmer books, hold the fan and stamp. The library must choose carefully how it will apply ownership marks when dealing with rare materials and media items. Labels for computer software should be written before applying to the software. Use a soft-tipped or felt-tipped pen if it is necessary to write on a label attached to computer software. Security targets should not be used with software since the desensitizing process has an adverse affect on the stability of the software.

Book covers may be applied to preserve the life of the book binding. There are various adhesive-backed plastic products that can be used on paperbacks. More expensive and highly used paperbacks may be sent to the bindery as long as they are not rush or reserve materials. Imagination is needed when dealing with media items. Dialogue with the media staff is essential when making decisions about packaging media items for the shelf. There are plastic and cardboard containers for kits. Loose-leaf notebooks and plastic sleeves are available. Price is an important factor. It is important that a style manual be available to describe pasting, labeling, and covering procedures for all items. This manual will insure uniformity of procedures and fewer questions. It is very helpful to have a person not assigned to Technical Services review the manual for clarity.

All items should be checked before leaving Technical Services to make sure call numbers, author's name, title, and copy or volume information are correct. Security targets should not extend beyond the book's edges since otherwise a patron could get cut. A small set of manicure scissors may be used to clip the exposed target. This will not harm its effectiveness.

Repair and maintenance of the collection are Technical Services responsibilities. Books and media may be repaired in-house or a library may choose to purchase services. It is most effective to do minor repairs, such as mending torn pages, in-house. The use of glue guns to repair spine damage is also effective. If an effective communication process is worked out with circulation staff, materials can be identified for repair on a use basis. Judgment calls must be made as to whether a specific item can be fixed locally or needs to be sent to a bindery. Special media-repairing equipment is needed for media items. A splicing machine is needed to repair cassette tapes. Splicing of video tapes is relatively easy. Occasionally one may need to remount slides.

Maintenance of the public catalog involves communication between Public Services and Technical Services. Once an on-line catalog is up and running, the librarians need to determine the life expectancy of the card catalog. The choices run from removal of the card catalog to total maintenance of the existing catalog at the other extreme. Some libraries have chosen an in-between position, that is, a minimally maintained card catalog and total maintenance of an OPAC. In such a model, the traditional card catalog may serve as a backup until the technology provides a more satisfactory solution. Maintenance in a dual system requires shortcuts in the card catalog. Students may use white-out and a pen to neatly correct errors. Librarians may choose not to correct in the card catalog everything that they correct in the OPAC. Usually the guidelines for these decisions should be drawn up by professionals from both Public and Technical services. Authority control is essential in an on-line catalog. Librarians can no longer accept carte blanche what appears on the network. When doing series work, libraries will set local standards for designating what tag a series title will be assigned. Student workers can compare the MARC record with the local on-line authority files and then search the national authority file for differences (that is, make a printout). Librarians will want to review these printouts and make a final decision.

Another part of catalog maintenance is the area of withdrawals. Student workers can be trained to withdraw cards from the various paper catalogs. All work should be checked by a paraprofessional or a professional librarian. Withdrawal in an on-line catalog is much easier and speedier. Statistics should be recorded.

There are various alternatives open for retrospective conversion. It can be done in-house. The "quick and dirty" method is less expensive initially and employs student workers. Various levels of inputting are defined, requiring more sophisticated knowledge at each level. Items are tagged and identified for the appropriate level. This method results in cleanup work once the system is installed, but it does guarantee more local control. An alternative is to purchase the service. This method may involve using student workers and a personal computer or shipping the shelf list to a vendor.

Statistics can be kept manually or on-line depending on the capability of the on-line system. In addition, spreadsheets can be used so that statistics can be custom tailored to meet the library's needs. They are not difficult to use, and do streamline the process.

Technical Services units have changed with the advent of automation. A multifunctional personal computer can be used to access the national networks, local library system, and other campus systems. In addition it is available to the staff for creating local files, spreadsheets, and word processing. There are a variety of ways of accessing the national networks so that the library is not faced with dedicated costs. The networks are expanding their equipment so that librarians can purchase hardware locally. As institutions as a whole commit to the new technology, so too will the libraries. As OPACs replace the card catalog, Technical Services departments will be the first to see their typewriters replaced with terminals. During the process, work loads increase, and decisions are made, rethought, and remade. Eventually the routines fall into place, at least for a time.

REFERENCES

Allen, Geoffrey G. 1986. "Change in the Context of Library Management." *Journal of Academic Librarianship* 12 (July): 141–43.

Hahn, Harvey. 1986. *Technical Services in the Small Library*. Chicago: American Library Association.

Harrington, Sue Anne. 1986. "The Changing Environment in Technical Services." *Technical Services Quarterly* 4 (Winter): 7–20.

Horney, Karen L. 1985. "Quality Work, Quality Control in Technical Services." *Journal of Academic Librarianship* 11 (Sept.): 206–10.

Runkle, Martin. 1986. "Authority Control: A Library Director's View." *Journal of Academic Librarianship* 12 (July): 145–46.

Tauber, Maurice F. 1954. *Technical Services in Libraries*. New York: Columbia University Press.

13

Allocation Formulas: The Core of the Acquisition Process

David G. Schappert

The budget process in small academic libraries has two distinct components that demand very different skills. In the first, the director requests funds, sometimes abjectly, sometimes passionately, in some cases idealistically, but always with a careful eye to the political dynamics of the institution. No matter how difficult the struggle or how frustrating the result, most directors are comfortable with their role as advocate for the library. After consulting *Standards for College Libraries, 1986* (Association of College and Research Libraries 1986), they repeat the arguments heard everywhere: that compared to the standards the library has too few volumes and receives too small a portion of the education and general expenditures. The library always needs more money, and no matter how much it receives, the library can spend it all effectively and judiciously.

The second role is more problematic. Having been given final budget figures, and often not what is considered an adequate amount, it is now necessary to distribute those funds among academic disciplines. The petitioner is now the dispenser of largesse, and the choices the director makes will have serious implications not only for the quality of the collection, but also for the way in which the director is perceived by colleagues inside and outside the library. The choices that are made can only lead to three different outcomes: (1) parts of the collection are consciously given priority at the expense of others, (2) the collection is allowed to develop itself, as no control is attempted, or (3) all areas of the collection are emphasized fairly (McGrath, Huntsinger, and Barber 1969: 51–62).

Much of the problem is that an equal distribution of funds is not the answer. Needs of disciplines vary, so an equal distribution cannot be equitable, but how can one determine what is? One might even go so far as to argue that an appropriate division of funds is so unequal that only the members of the library staff can see the "big picture" and can determine what is fair by some combination of instinct and intuition.

The approach that demands the least amount of time might be to look at last year's allocations. After all, they were good enough last year; maybe they should only be adjusted to reflect the numbers of complaints that have been received, a sort of funding by decibel. Of course, no matter how well-intentioned the director, allocations made on the basis of tradition, complaints, or intuition are always subject to charges of partiality and arbitrariness. Even if the director has the wisdom of Solomon, when it is time to chop up the budget, no department chairs will step aside to preserve the integrity of the whole. For the purposes of this chapter, I will focus on situations in which departmental faculty play a predominant role in book selection, since this is the most potentially difficult and adversarial situation, and is not uncommon in small academic libraries.

One might argue that, in the absence of some quantifiable indicator of need, the decibel level of complaints is as accurate as any other. After all, funds are distributed on the basis of need, and the most direct expressions of need are book order requests and faculty complaints; these are much more noticeable and quantifiable than the students who don't find what they are looking for on the shelves. However, is there really a direct correlation between the needs of the population that the library serves and the way those needs are perceived by those who receive funding? The problem is that an allocation process starts with words (statements of need, standards, platitudes, or mountains of book requests) that must be translated into numbers (dollars). The premise behind an allocation fomula is that by manipulating numerical data, needs can be quantified, and this numerical expression of need can be readily translated into a percentage of the available budget. If needs cannot be quantified, an allocation formula cannot exist, but if needs can be accurately quantified, the allocation becomes mathematical and seems to acquire the simplicity and objectivity of arithmetic, putting a bit of the science back into library science.

The advantage most widely claimed for formulas is that they are fairer, since, if constructed correctly, they do not permit partiality to a particular group. It is philosophically correct to have an unbiased formula: it is more ethical. As Jasper Schad notes, the need for the perception of fairness is heightened by the scarcity of resources, which will require that sacrifices are made; by the complexities involved in making allocations, which heighten fears of negative outcomes; and by a lack of consensus about what objectives should be attained (1987: 479–86). The perception of fairness is really the issue here; we cannot pontificate about what is fair in some ideal realm, but must deal with what will be perceived in reality as most fair by all concerned. The fairest formula, if *perceived* as unfair, will never be approved or accepted. Schad lists three requirements for the perception of fairness; agreement must be reached on: (1) the principles that inform allocation decisions, (2) measures that are used in application of principles, and (3) the manner in which procedures are followed. Can these be accomplished without formulas? Possibly, but to articulate principles and procedures with rigor demands that very carefully chosen principles must exist. The director seems to have chosen yet a harder task: to emulate the rigor of mathematics without using numbers.

However, the main advantage of using formulas may be efficiency rather than philosophy. Obviously, if a formula leads to a fairer distribution of funds, it yields a more useful library collection and a happier group of users. However, it also speeds up the allocation process, since it removes the need for lengthy political debate. Once the necessary data has been collected, the allocations can be determined quickly. The sooner allocations are determined, the sooner faculty members or bibliographers can get a sense of how to prioritize book orders, the more likely it is that orders will be sent out before books go out of print, and the less likely that the Acquisitions and Cataloging departments will have large seasonal fluctuations in work load. Allocations not determined by formula may tend to fluctuate considerably from year to year as different disciplines are placated in sequence. Significant fluctuations might prevent a library from making use of approval plans. Once a formula has been approved, there should be at least a few years' respite from the annual budget struggles.

There are other benefits to formulas, in part because they deal with relative need rather than absolute need; that is, they determine that a particular department should get a certain percentage of the available funds. Under these circumstances, department chairs may be more anxious to support increases in the library book budget, since they know these increases will necessarily enhance their own level of the funding. Without a formula, chairs are more likely to spend their energy trying to expand their share of the library budget rather than lobbying to enlarge the size of the budget itself. Also, as budget revisions and reductions in the course of the year become more common, allocations given as percentages can be easily adjusted. On the other hand, if allocations were set by a more subjective and political process, it might be necessary to sit down with all the principals and refashion new deals.

Before choosing or developing a formula, it is necessary to determine who must approve its implementation. It may be a decision that can be made within the library, but often approval by an academic dean or a faculty library committee is necessary. Whatever individuals are concerned should be involved in the process from the outset. First they must be convinced that there should be a formula, and then they may wish to participate in its choice. Imposing the formula on people rather than allowing them to understand and participate in its creation removes the perception of fairness from the process.

Many formulas have been developed for different types of libraries, and it should only be necessary to modify one. Possibly the most famous and useful of allocation formulas was developed by William E. McGrath, Ralph C. Huntsinger, and Gary R. Barber (1969: 51–62). They identified twenty-two different variables concerning such issues as cost and numbers of books published, relative strength and funding by discipline in the past, faculty and faculty load, credit hours, enrollment, circulation, interlibrary loans, and citation analyses, to determine correlations between different factors. By examining their correlations, one can determine which factors seem to be connected and would only add redundancy to a formula, and which are independent and express something different and meaningful. In the formula they present (but do not prescribe for any particular environment) the three factors that appear are the number of books borrowed in a department divided by the total number of books taken out, the departmental enrollment as a fraction of total enrollment, and citations in theses from each department divided by total citations from all departments. Clearly this particular formula is not directly applicable to a small college environment, particularly given its use of citation analyses of graduate theses, but the article provides a very comprehensive view of the different variables to consider, as well as the skeleton of a formula in which to place them.

At the other extreme in terms of using variables is the Percentage Based Allocation. In this allocation formula, each discipline would receive the same percentage of the available library budget as it receives of the institution's instructional budget. As David Genaway points out, this method presupposes not only a rational and equitable division of funds by college and university administration, but also a strong correlation between a department's library intensiveness and its instructional and research budgets. Some of the major advantages that the author points out are that this distribution does respond quickly to changes in institutional priorities, and that it can be used on the school department or program level equally well. Since the formula does not depend on statistics concerning the use of books, it can be used across formats; individual departments can determine how to break down their funding between books, audiovisuals, periodicals, and so on. This allocation also may be seen as more equitable by many department heads or faculty (Genaway 1986: 287–92). I suppose that those who believe it an unfair distribution may be directed to those deans, presidents, or trustees whose leads you are following.

Genaway also points out the disadvantages of this method, including the severe changes in distribution of funds to which the implementation of the formula might lead, the inability in some private institutions to attain complete information about instructional and research budgets, the reliance on assumptions about the rationality of college budgets, and in correlation between instructional/research budgets and library budgets. I might add that even if the director found these assumptions to be reasonable, trying to convince others of their applicability might be so difficult as to prevent what Schad requires for the perception of fairness.

In another article, Genaway suggests a different approach to allocation formulas. He uses full-time equivalent student and faculty data, information that is readily available on campus, along with the relative library intensiveness of programs as expressed by the level of terminal degree offered, to determine how much funding should be given (Genaway 1986b: 293–306). There are many advantages to this formula, to which I cannot do justice in so short a space; however, if I were characterizing it, I could say it is a formula that, in general, sacrifices precision for ease of computation. While terminal degrees are important factors, and may be sufficient for one's purposes, the actual data of library use would give much more precise information on library intensiveness.

It is possible to develop a unique formula for one's own situation, and, the smaller the library, the more likely that the peculiarities of the situation will necessitate a special formula. In a research library, for example, we might give more credence to circulation data by subject because we can assume that there are at least marginally adequate materials on any subject, however arcane. In a small academic library, we will have to take into account the fact that, as institutional priorities change, there may be so few books in a particular subject that circulation data does not give good information. A new nursing program might start with only about a hundred books, especially if the library is not apprised of curricular changes in advance. The circulation of these materials cannot be matched against the circulation of thousands of history books. Whether taken as a percentage or an absolute number, the data will be skewed. In a small academic library, the numbers for relevant variables and the much smaller level of funding combine to demand an increased level of precision. Here are some factors to consider in the creation of a formula.

The best formula is one that quantifies need with the minimum number of variables, since each variable adds to the time and expense of data collection as well as the number of calculations that must be made to implement the formula. Each potential variable has to be judged by several different criteria. First, is the data readily available? Some automated library systems may be able to periodically turn out book circulation data by classification, but other institutions might need an individual to manually tally each transaction to attain this data.

Second, will this variable make your formula more reliable? A library might decide that in addition to using book circulation by subject as a variable, the number of circulating books that are used within the library and must be reshelved will also be counted. Many would argue, however, that it is moot whether this data is an expression of use, let alone an expression of need; and that the extra work involved in counting the items to reshelve would result in more data and more calculations but less accuracy. Interlibrary loan data raises the same sorts of problems. Clearly, interlibrary loan requests are an indicator of need, but without examining individual requests, it is not clear whether they indicate a serious weakness in the collection. It may instead be a situation where the materials needed are beyond the intended scope of the library's holdings.

Third, each variable must be judged not only on whether it seems to be a representation of need, but on how it will affect the formula from a purely mathematical standpoint. If the value of the variable will not vary from one case to another, it will have no impact on the final allocations. For instance, if part of the formula is the number of faculty, and each department has the same number of faculty, it serves no purpose to add this to the formula. On the other hand, if there is too much range between the different expressions of a variable, it might skew the data. This is particularly a problem when numbers are small, since a small numerical variance is a very large percentage difference. To use our faculty size example again, if the variables all have equal weight, two departments might have the same number of students, circulation transactions, and all the other variables you are considering, but if the first has four faculty members and the second has three, the variance in this one factor would mean that the first department would receive 33% more funding.

In some cases it might be necessary to weight your formula so that certain variables have less impact. Say that you determined at your institution that the number of books needing to be reshelved by subject was an indicator of need, but was not as important as actual circulation transactions. If you felt that the first variable was only half as important as the second, you might multiply the reshelved numbers by .5 and add them to the appropriate circulation figures.

The only way to test whether a formula is workable is to plug in numbers and see what happens. Using data from the previous year, see what the allocations would have looked like had you used the formula, also try out invented data. Do realistic numbers lead to realistic conclusions? Do unreasonable numbers lead to unreasonable conclusions? If not, your formula may flatten out allocations too much, and whatever happens, the distribution of funds will be relatively unchanged. Establish certain trends in your data and see if allocations change appropriately. If they do not, the formula will have to be reevaluated and retooled frequently, and you will be forced to argue each time that the old formula was fair, but that the new one is even fairer. This strategy might wear thin by the third or fourth change.

Even after a formula has been developed, other issues in its implementation must be addressed. If there are not separate budget lines for reference materials, binding, audiovisuals, and so on, how should these needs be accommodated? In a large university library, it might be possible to pay for all these items ''off the top'' of the materials budget. However, this is much more difficult in a smaller library. Buying all the audiovisuals requested might not be possible without using a disproportionate amount of the materials budget. It may be necessary to determine the maximum amount of the budget that should be spent in these different categories and then find some equitable way to make allocations to the various departments.

A related concern is how much funding should be set aside for the library itself. There are a variety of reasons why the library must keep some money, including the need to purchase general, cross-disciplinary materials, and to purchase materials in librarianship. It is also necessary to use library funds to respond to curricular changes, to help boost sections of the collection prior to accreditation, and to deal with past inequities. If the discretionary fund is too large a portion of the budget, or if the guidelines for its use are not clearly defined, it will become a political football of its own—a smaller version of the original allocation problem, as individuals come in to petition for discretionary funds to pursue their own agendas.

There are still other problems the library must address. If faculty members request the purchase of materials outside their disciplines, it does not seem fair that their department pay for them, yet the department responsible for collecting in that area may not wish to obtain those items. A general library fund might be the most appropriate way to pay for such materials.

Another example of this sort of problem is funding freshman research papers. As budgets shrink, faculty priorities are usually to order materials that service their majors (or, in the worst cases, their own advanced research). However, as students move away from traditional liberal arts majors, the need to write research papers is often reduced, and instead freshman research becomes a larger proportion of their total library use. These two factors combine to lessen expenditures for introductory materials at the same time that these materials are, relatively speaking, more important than ever. Freshman research papers are traditionally written for English classes, but their topics are often outside the realm of language and literature, the primary topics that English departments develop. Who should be responsible for funding these purchases? The most judicious answer is dependent on the type of allocation formula. If an allocation is based on circulation by classification, it is not reasonable for an English department to provide materials on a wide range of topics for freshman research, since they get no credit for the use of those items. Using their funds outside the *P* classification (or the 400s and 800s, as the case may be) would reduce the department's ability to expand the holdings in their own classifications. On the other hand, if credit hours taught is a key factor in budgeting, the English department receives the credit for teaching these courses and should also take responsibility for supporting them through library purchases.

If your library uses faculty to generate book requests, what should be done when a department does not spend all its allocation? The simple approach is to redirect the money to a department that requests more items than it has money for, thereby rewarding some requestors for their zeal and punishing others for their laxity. However, since the formula determines "need," isn't it the library's responsibility to make sure that approximately as much money as the formula suggests is expended on each discipline, even if the library staff has to identify the materials to buy?

The formulas themselves only determine how much money should be allocated to a particular department, and say nothing about how the qualitative needs of the department should be filled. A basic collection-development policy might be part of the library's mission statement, and could have guidelines about appropriate levels of support in terms of comprehensiveness, complexity of material, collecting materials in different languages, or refusing to purchase incunabula. However, it is also important that departments have their own policies for setting guidelines that will help in prioritizing orders and setting objectives. To some extent these guidelines should dovetail with the allocation formula; for instance, if some disciplines have graduate programs, their level of support will be different than departments without such programs, and this different level of need should be accounted for in the formula.

None of these are new problems, they are simply old problems that must be treated more systematically so that they do not undermine the basic fairness of the allocations. A formula provides a context to deal with these issues, and a basic rationale for resolving them. Formulas will not by themselves guarantee balanced collections, sufficient funding, or collegiality, but they will make the budget process less adversarial and arbitrary, and the acquisitions process more predictable and efficient.

REFERENCES

Association of College and Research Libraries. 1986. "Standards for College Libraries." *College & Research Libraries News* 47, no. 3 (March) 189–200.

Carpenter, Eric J. 1984. "Collection Development Policies: The Case For." *Library Acquisitions: Practice and Theory* 8: 43–45.

Cenzer, Pam. 1983. "Library/Faculty Relations in the Acquisitions and Collection Development Process." *Library Acquisitions: Practice and Theory* 7: 215–19.

Evans, Glyn T. 1978. "The Cost of Information about Library Acquisition Budgets." *Collection Management* 2, no. 1: 3–23.

Futas, Elizabeth. 1984. *Library Acquisition Policies and Procedures*, 2d ed. Phoenix, Ariz.: Oryx Press.

Genaway, David C. 1986a. "PBA: Percentage Based Allocation for Acquisitions." *Library Acquisitions: Practice and Theory* 10: 287–92.

———. 1986b. "The Q Formula: The Flexible Formula for Library Acquisitions in Relation to the FTE Driven Formula." *Library Acquisitions: Theory and Practice* 10: 293–306.

Hall, Blaine H. 1985. *Assessment Manual for College and University Libraries*. Phoenix, Ariz.: Oryz Press.

Hellenga, Robert R. 1984. "Departmental Acquisitions Policies for Small College Libraries." *Library Acquisitions: Practice and Theory* 3: 81–84.

Kevil, L. Hunter. 1985. "The Approval Plan of Smaller Scope." *Library Acquisitions: Practice and Theory* 9: 13–20.

Kohut, Joseph J., and John F. Walker. 1975. "Allocating the Book Budget: Equity and Economic Efficiency." *College and Research Libraries* 36 (September): 403–10.

McGrath, William E., Ralph C. Huntsinger, and Gary R. Barber. 1969. "An Allocation Formula Derived from a Factor Analysis of Academic Departments." *College and Research Libraries* 30 (January): 51–62.

Schad, Jasper G. 1987. "Fairness in Book Fund Allocation." *College and Research Libraries* 48 (November): 479–86.

Senghas, Dorothy C., and Edward A. Warro. 1982. "Book Allocations: The Key to a Plan for Collection Development." *Library Acquisitions: Practice and Theory* 6: 47–53.

Shirk, Gary M. 1984. "Allocation Formulas for Budgeting Library Materials: Science or Procedure." *Collection Management* 6, no. 3/4: 37–47.

14

Cataloging outside the Network

Lois N. Upham

The first order of business when utilizing a title such as ''Cataloging outside the Network'' must be to define terms and set parameters. ''Cataloging'' in this context means basically what it has traditionally meant: the creation of bibliographic records for materials held within a particular collection. These records are meant to provide access, normally through the use of some sort of catalog, to potential users of the collection. The term ''network'' means an on-line system that provides a bibliographic database from which users can extract, modify, and use records for their own purposes, and into which new records can be added. The operative term is ''on-line.'' By ''outside'' it is not implied that the organizations in question do not adhere to such accepted standards as the *Anglo-American Cataloguing Rules* (2d edition) or the MARC (Machine Readable Cataloging) formats. ''Outside,'' rather, indicates that an on-line linkage is not made to an on-line database supported by a network such as OCLC (the Online Computer Library Center) or RLIN (the Research Library Information Network).

Indeed, many small- to medium-sized libraries find it economically impossible to procure the monetary support necessary to participate in an on-line network. Until recently this normally meant that such libraries either had to procure their catalog records from a second party or do the cataloging themselves, or a combination of both. Some new developments in technology, however, have now provided smaller libraries with additional options.

The past five years have seen the coming of age of a technology that, although it has been in existence for a while, has just begun to make a significant impact on the way libraries do business. This technology is the compact disc or CD. Known initially as videodiscs (and currently sometimes as laser discs), the genre has progressed beyond just the video, and now compact discs are used for the reproduction of sound, images, or a combination of both.

The linking of compact disc players to microcomputers has made it possible to provide "on-line–like" services to people and organizations not capable—often for financial reasons—of participating in an actual on-line computer system. The particular application that will be discussed here will be that of using CD-based systems for cataloging purposes. This type of system is the most rapidly expanding technological alternative to the use of on-line systems for cataloging. It is not the only alternative, however. The option of using a microfiche-based system to create catalog records will also be discussed.

HOW DOES A CD SYSTEM WORK?

The Bibliofile system, created and marketed by the Library Corporation, was the first true compact disc–based cataloging system to come onto the market. This system has been followed by others, most notably Gaylord's Super Cat and General Research Corporation's LaserQuest. Because of the rapid growth in this area, a potential purchaser is advised to check for other products that may have come onto the market or been significantly improved since this chapter was written.

All the existing systems work in much the same way, although entrants into the marketing arena each try to offer more attractive options than their competition. It is best, before discussing differences, to begin by describing the basic way that all the CD-based systems work.

The Library of Congress (LC) file of MARC bibliographic records forms the base for all the compact disc cataloging systems currently being marketed. These records comprise what may be termed the master file. At least one system has added a significant number of additional records that have been contributed by their member institutions. Options for non-LC records, and the mechanism for including foreign titles and foreign language materials should be checked with each vendor. Users should normally expect, however, to have the option of accessing the entire file of LC-MARC records in all formats.

Each library will undoubtedly have a unique approach to the process of converting its current bibliographic file into machine-readable form. Some institutions may even be starting the process without the availability of a currently existing file. In any case, there will be certain steps to take regardless of individual variations.

Whether a person is working from a shelf list, an actual catalog, some other sort of file, or the pieces themselves, it will be necessary to match information that is supplied by the vendor against the master file. Many fields can be searched on CD files. A person can usually expect to be able to search by author, title, author and title, ISBN, ISSN, and LC card number. At least one vendor has, however, made the decision to heavily emphasize access by title, arguing that all materials have titles even if other access points such as author or standard number are missing.

After a search is transmitted to the system, it is normal to retrieve one or more records in response. If a single record is retrieved, it is examined by the operator to assure that it does indeed match the item searched, and it is then used—usually with at least some local additions or modifications—to produce catalog cards, download onto diskette, or both. Such local information as location, call number, volume and copy data, and so forth, can be added to the record that is retrieved from the master file.

Some libraries using the CD-based systems still do maintain a card catalog, and so continue to require cards. These can be produced from a printer attached to the microcomputer on which the search is being done. Almost universally, however, these institutions are ultimately anticipating changing to a computer-based catalog. To this end, even when cards are produced, records are downloaded to a diskette. The records so saved then can form the basis for such a new catalog.

If more than one record is retrieved in response to a search, the operator has to examine each one to determine which if any matches the item in question. There are several reasons why seemingly duplicate records may be in the master file. Different editions, such as deluxe, large print, revised, and so on, require separate records. Editions in different languages and from different countries also merit separate records. The same work in different formats, such as print and microfilm, will also have individual records. It is the responsibility of the searcher to ascertain which of the records found will actually be used by the particular institution. Despite the fact that multiple responses to a search may occur, sometimes none of them actually matches the item being searched. Careful attention must be given to the examination and choosing of correct bibliographic records.

Even when one record is chosen by the searcher, it is sometimes necessary to modify it—beyond just adding site-specific information—to meet local needs. Things such as subject headings or notes may need to be added or augmented to meet the requirements of a library's patrons. Such additions can be accomplished before records are downloaded or cards are produced.

Each institution can expect that some percentage of items held will not be reflected by an existing MARC record, even one that must be modified for local use. In such instances, it will be necessary to create an original bibliographic record. Each of the vendors has a routine for creating a new MARC record. These routines vary from vendor to vendor, with each affording some unique features. Depending on the number of items expected to require original cataloging, a prospective buyer should carefully evaluate this record-creation feature and weigh it appropriately among the custom features of each system.

Normally it can be expected that each vendor will allow a degree of local customization with regard to tags that always display on a work form, the number of tags for fields such as notes or subject headings that display, and so on. It is even possible for certain pieces of information to be inserted automatically when a work form is displayed.

When a library is in the initial creation phase of a computer-based catalog, each search is a new search. That is, since there are no previously created machine-readable records, each search can be made only against the master file. At the end of the first pass through a previously existing catalog or through the collection, the diskettes containing the downloaded and newly created records are sent to the vendor for conversion onto compact discs, magnetic tapes, or both.

While it may at first seem redundant to make both a CD copy and a magnetic tape copy of the same file, there are actually good reasons to consider this option. The CD copy will undoubtedly form the basis of the public catalog. It is not currently possible, however, to merge this copy with any other file—yours or anyone else's. Thus, if there is any possibility that participation in cooperative arrangements may lie in the future, you will find that a magnetic tape version of previously created MARC records will greatly facilitate the development of any type of merged bibliographic file. If the acquisition of both a CD and a tape version of the same file is not possible, it is of the utmost importance to request the return of the floppy diskettes containing the converted records when the CD version is completed. Having access to the diskettes will allow the freedom to merge files if it becomes desirable to do so at any time in the future.

Following the initial creation of a library's catalog on compact disc, there is the ongoing necessity to keep it up to date. This activity can entail such activities as adding new records as well as revising or deleting old ones. Approaches to this updating vary, and more options are likely to be developed. The thing that should be kept in mind, however, is that, until vendors begin to utilize a compact disc system that allows the user to write new information directly onto it, a CD file resembles such formats as microform or book in that, unless it is reproduced completely to include all changes, there will be the necessity to look in more than one place in order to discover exactly what is in the full file.

Vendors vary on the amount they charge for remastering a file, and some even vary according to the number of records that are being processed. In the latter case, per-record price reductions are usually given for larger files. The amount charged will tend to control how frequently a library can have a new master created. When evaluating systems, this variation should be considered carefully with regard to its effect upon future currentness and completeness of the purchaser's file.

If a library using a CD-based cataloging system still is maintaining a card catalog and downloading to diskette the records retrieved from the CD or created by the institution itself, it will be necessary to be able to identify items that have already been cataloged on the system when new materials are handled. Usually this will be apparent from the cards in the catalog, but until the full effectiveness of the system is achieved by accessing the converted records through computer-based access, there will be the danger of reconverting records that have already been added to the file.

VENDOR VARIATIONS

As has been stated, all CD-based cataloging systems have many things in common, but there are variations from vendor to vendor. All vendors, of course, hope to convince potential customers that their system is better than the others.

There are indeed some very impressive features exhibited by various systems. These include, among others, the "compare" function on Gaylord's Super Cat system, the user-contributed records and non–LC MARC records on the General Research Corporation (GRC)'s LaserQuest system, and the continuing attractive pricing of the Library Corporation's Bibliofile. Gaylord's "compare" function facilitates the comparing of records when multiple responses are indicated for a search. The augmented database of GRC can help users avoid the creation of records for older materials that have already been cataloged by other users at the same facility, and provides access to records contributed by the National Library of Canada. Of course, pricing is an important factor for any potential buyer, and the Library Corporation remains a formidable competitor in this area.

An article by Norman Desmarais entitled "Laserbases for Library Technical Services" includes a section on cataloging. In addition to the three systems mentioned above, several other less-known systems are also mentioned—some of which were in the development stage in 1987. It must, therefore, be stressed that before a decision to purchase a system is reached, a thorough study of the existing possibilities should be undertaken. It might indeed be worthwhile to retain the services of a consultant for a day or two to assist with the initial evaluation and final choice.

A MICROFORM-BASED OPTION

Although compact disc–based systems are the best-known alternative outside the network to either having a second party provide a library's cataloging or to doing the cataloging in-house, there is at least one successful microform-based option that a library may want to consider. This option is MITINET (pronounced Mighty-net) and is marketed by Information Transform, Inc.

This system works in much the same way as the CD-based systems. The difference is that instead of working with a compact disc reader attached to a microcomputer, the searcher works with a set of LC-MARC microfiche records and an Apple II, IBM PC, or other IBM PC-compatible microcomputer. (In some locations, Union Catalog data may additionally be provided in CD format.) When a match is found on the fiche, a unique number—which includes a "check digit" to assure accuracy—is keyed into the computer. Local call number and copy information is then added. This information is stored on floppy diskettes and then forwarded for processing to Brodart. Various products can be produced according to the user's specifications. Union Catalogs can also be created.

The option to modify existing LC-MARC records does not really exist in this system, although it is undoubtedly possible to set up specifications regarding inclusion and exclusion or consistent modification of fields for Brodart to follow when processing an institution's records. If, however, a library wishes to extensively modify a record or cannot find a satisfactory record, a program called MITINET/marc has been created to allow the creation of a new record. The program is a type of "expert" system, leading the operator through the entire process with a minimum of complexity. The basic knowledge of the MARC system required to successfully operate this program is minimal.

Although MITINET may not offer as many special features and options as the CD-based systems, the low cost and relative ease of use make it worthy of consideration when evaluating options for cataloging outside the network. Readers wanting more information about this system can read "MITINET/retro: Retrospective Conversion on an Apple" and "An Expert System for Novice MARC Catalogers," both by Hank Epstein.

A FURTHER OPTION

There is one more option available to libraries wishing to catalog outside the network. This option consists of leasing a compact disc file of cataloging records as well as whatever equipment that might be necessary to access and download to diskette records selected from the CD file. Compact disc files are currently available for lease from organizations as diverse as Gaylord and SOLINET (Southeastern Library Network). Purists may argue that leasing from SOLINET is not cataloging *outside* the network, but it should be noted that libraries need not become members of the network to lease the file. Nonmembers are, however, required to pay more for the service than are members. The problem with a lease arrangement is, of course, the updating. Once a library has converted existing files to machine-readable form through the use of the leased file, a mechanism should be put in place to insure that the currentness of information is maintained. Unless the file is to be leased at regular intervals, a program or system capable of producing MARC records must be available to allow the addition of new information. If such capability is available, the lease option might be feasible.

THE FUTURE

One thing that can be said about the opportunities available to libraries that do not wish to ally themselves with a network for the purpose of obtaining catalog records, is that the future promises even greater options. Without compromising on standards such as *AACR2* (Anglo-American Cataloging Rules, 2nd edition) and MARC (Machine Readable Cataloging) format requirements, libraries with smaller collections and limited budgets will be able to choose from an expanding array of options available to create computer-based systems. An additional advantage to these systems will be the fact that not only will they fill local needs, but they can also be shared with other institutions and consortia to promote resource sharing and assist in collection-development activities.

The key to taking advantage of developments is to stay apprised of new and evolving systems by reading the current literature; attending meetings, workshops, and exhibits; conferring with colleagues; and when faced with actual decisions about options, utilizing a competent consultant. A librarian must accept the responsibility associated with the identification and use of appropriate new technology. This can, however, be an exciting as well as a challenging task. If the challenge is not accepted, viable opportunities may pass by while staff continue to struggle with outdated and ineffective methods of performing such common library tasks as cataloging "without benefit of the network."

REFERENCES

Desmarais, Norman. 1987. "Laserbases for Library Technical Services." *Optical Information Systems* 7 (January/February): 57–61.

Epstein, Hank. 1983. "MITINET/retro: Retrospective Conversion on an Apple." *Information Technology and Libraries* 2 (June): 166–73.

———. 1987. "An Expert System for Novice MARC Catalogers." *Wilson Library Bulletin* 62 (November): 33–36.

15

Preservation Programs in Small Academic Libraries

Cheryl Terrass Naslund

Preservation of library materials, the action taken to anticipate, prevent, retard, or stop deterioration, has become a mainstream activity in many large research libraries and needs to become one in many more small academic libraries. A significant portion of the books printed between 1850 and 1900 are not expected to survive this century in usable condition largely owing to the highly acidic nature of the materials used in their manufacture. Preservation of library collections can no longer be limited to the conservation of a few rare and unique items, but instead must focus on maintaining sizable collections in usable condition. Much basic information on preservation and the establishment of preservation-planning programs has been developed in large research libraries. Small academic libraries should not be deterred by this, but instead should utilize and adapt this information to meet their own needs. For a compendium of information on preservation in a single volume, consult the *Preservation Planning Program Resource Notebook* published by the Association of Research Libraries.

Preservation of a library's assets represents protection of an expensive and precious investment. More often than is generally realized, small academic libraries hold the only known copy of a given work in usable, or preservable, condition. An attainable goal that most libraries can meet affordably lies in the creation of a preservation program aimed at maintaining library materials in usable condition. Despite the immense magnitude and scope of the preservation problem, and the accompanying sense of paralysis in the face of so great a task, leaders in the preservation field have identified much that can be done to improve the situation with available resources regardless of library size. Aggressive preservation of incoming materials alone, from this day forward, would do much to alleviate future problems in library preservation. This chapter highlights the more affordable aspects of preservation programs aimed at optimizing the future condition of library materials. Whether you handle books on a regular basis, make decisions about access, coordinate continuing education programs, or manage the budget, preservation is part of your job and responsibility. If librarians are to protect their precious investment, they must accept responsibility for their collections and take immediate action to insure preservation.

The key to understanding the preservation problem is to understand its causes. Causes of deterioration of library materials include (1) the chemical, physical, and biological deterioration of paper; (2) use of destructive materials in book manufacture; (3) poor binding practices; (4) lack of temperature and humidity control with resulting fluctuations; (5) exposure to light; (6) effects of air pollution; (7) ravage by mold, mildew, insects, and rodents; (8) heavy use; and (9) the improper handling and repair practices of library staff and users.

ORGANIZATION OF A PRESERVATION PROGRAM

The success of any program requires the following: (1) keen observation of the current situation; (2) thoughtful analysis of the problem; (3) identification of potential solutions; (4) commonsense evaluation of viable solutions; (5) implementation of an organized program; (6) follow-through in all aspects of the endeavor; and last but by no means least, (7) strong administrative support.

The shortage of trained professionals in the preservation field is insufficient reason to avoid setting up a preservation program in even the smallest academic library. The organization of a preservation planning committee whose members are selected thoughtfully and representatively from each department within the library has many advantages. Committee members serve as avenues of communication for each area of the library, coordinating the gathering of information and disseminating information as needed throughout the library. Their direct participation leads to ownership of the program and strengthens a library-wide commitment to preservation. Some libraries can afford a preservation professional, but even this person must enlist the assistance of all library departments.

Once the team has gathered, it should begin the important task of planning a preservation program by outlining long- and short-term goals and objectives. Timed, realistic, and measurable goals serve to delineate progress and maintain the momentum of the program. The preservation planning committee is charged with surveying the problem, defining the needs, and establishing a plan in writing. A step-by-step approach, breaking the whole into pieces, is necessary to avoid the overwhelming sense of paralysis that can occur in the face of major long-term projects. A proactive approach to preservation is necessary to avoid crisis management at a later date under the worst of conditions. Standing committees can be appointed as needed to implement the plan generated. The small academic library may find it useful to have a preservation planning committee, a preservation action committee, and a disaster planning and preparedness committee. As funds permit, a preservation office staffed by a professional preservation administrator may be created. The preservation committee or officer should report directly to the highest level of administration owing to the library-wide nature of the problem and the need for strong administrative support.

From an administrative standpoint, the committee should be charged with the following functions: (1) coordinate all preservation activities; (2) develop a timetable for implementation of the program; (3) insure continued administrative support; (4) prepare and organize a collection of materials on preservation for staff and patron use; (5) establish and update a library-wide statement on preservation policy; (6) incorporate preservation-policy concerns into collection-development statements; (7) incorporate an allocation for materials needed for preservation into the annual budget; (8) support, in all areas of the library, the hiring of persons with preservation knowledge or a willingness to participate in a preservation program; and (9) insure consistency and effectiveness in the implementation of the program. The size and complexity of the preservation issue frequently generates frustration and despair. It is important to remember, however, that any big problem must be tackled one step at a time, and that small successes are indeed major contributions to the whole. The timetable should realistically balance the needs of the collection with the available resources of the institution. It is important to remember that, while some goals will require financing and therefore planning along budget cycles, many are easily accomplished for little or no money. All committee recommendations should be specific, and should include as much ordering and cost information as possible in order to assist the library administration in their overall evaluation and implementation. Each of the following areas of concern should be discussed, and all options considered.

PRESERVATION ISSUES

Preservation programs should involve attention to nine major areas: (1) the library's physical environment; (2) disaster planning and prevention; (3) materials selection and commercial library binding practices; (4) a book repair and treatment program; (5) housekeeping, shelving, and handling practices; (6) information reformatting, including microfilming, photocopying, optical disc, and so on; (7) staff and user education; (8) cooperative preservation and the sharing of resources with other libraries; and (9) funding sources. Conservation activities, usually the physical treatment required to maintain or return an item to usable condition, are also a significant part of a comprehensive preservation program. Each library must prioritize preservation components to achieve a program balanced to meet the needs of their own collection.

Physical Environment

The physical environment, including temperature and humidity control, is the single most important factor in the preservation of library materials, but it is usually the most difficult to remedy. Chemical reactions that result in paper deterioration accelerate with increased temperature. High humidity increases the likelihood of mold growth. Building temperatures should be maintained at the lowest comfortable level, and the optimum range for humidity is 50 to 70% RH (relative humidity). Because fluctuations in temperature and humidity levels are even more damaging than consistently elevated temperatures or extreme humidity, libraries should be considered for careful monitoring on an individual basis. Air conditioning may pose additional local problems due to moisture condensation, and should be monitored closely. Routine monitoring of environmental conditions also provides important data to back grant proposals and budget requests for needed improvements.

Cumulative exposure to light, most notably in the ultraviolet range, also results in the structural deterioration of paper. Sunlight and fluorescent lighting emit ultraviolet light in large amounts, while incandescent bulbs emit very small quantities. Lower wattage bulbs, ultraviolet light sleeves, and ultraviolet window coatings reduce the intensity of the light, and light timers can control the length of exposure. Display cases are sources of dramatically increased light exposure, resulting in significant damage to photographs, inks, and watercolors within a very few months. Whenever possible, cases should be equipped with on-off switches, and materials should be rotated frequently.

A library's physical environment should be of paramount importance in planning for the construction of new facilities. Today, any library director who undertakes the construction of even the smallest library or addition without substantial regard for environmental concerns consistent with current preservation knowledge is guilty of gross negligence. The hiring of a qualified preservation consultant during the design phase can provide long-term returns that far outweigh the expense.

Disaster Planning and Prevention

Disasters require crisis management of enormous proportion, and are extremely expensive in terms of materials, money, and effort. A disaster plan should be prepared for every library. The staff time required for the preparation of such a plan is inexpensive insurance. Disasters strike without warning, and speed is of the essence in the proper handling of the catastrophe. In the absence of formal disaster plans, shock takes over and frequently results in aimless, if not damaging, efforts. For this reason, procedures to be implemented in case of disaster should be laid out carefully ahead of time, and should be fully understood by all personnel. Disaster plans should be written down and should contain an easy-to-follow outline of steps to be taken. They need to be revised continually to reflect changes in location of materials and personnel, building renovations, staff turnover, supply lists, supplies on hand, and so on. To insure preparedness, disaster drills should be held on an annual basis or as needed. Drills allow library staff and patrons to become familiar with the written routines and often result in substantial improvements to the disaster plan.

Overall responsibility for the handling of a disaster should be assigned to one individual with a backup chain of command sufficiently long to insure that a trained and responsible person will always be available. Contact telephone numbers should be readily available and up-to-date for related services including the utility company, electrician, janitorial service, insurance company, and so on. Sources of professional assistance outside the library should be identified for each type of potential disaster.

When planning for disaster and other preservation needs, there are many sources of assistance, including a number of regional conservation centers throughout the country and the Library of Congress National Preservation Program Office in Washington, D.C. Most of these agencies have general written information and consultants to answer specific questions. In addition, disaster plans are available from a number of libraries upon request.

A well-designed disaster plan deals first with the safety of patrons and staff and subsequently with rescue and recovery techniques for the collection materials. Possible disasters include: fire, water and flood damage, loss of air conditioning, loss of humidity controls, computer failure, and theft. The card catalog has the most expensive replacement ratio per cubic inch, a point that should not be overlooked in planning. Computerized catalogs pose different but no less important issues, and backup mechanisms are essential.

Knowledge of a building's history, including its age and past disasters, can provide valuable information in preventing future disasters. Building layouts including location of power boxes, fire extinguishers, and alarms, should be available at several locations both within and outside the library. Fire detection and prevention equipment, including smoke alarms, heat sensors, and fire extinguishers, should be installed strategically, and requires regular testing to be effective. Sprinkler systems should be designed in such a way that equipment malfunctions that cause water leakage do not create crisis situations. All heating, water, air conditioning, and security or alarm systems should be maintained routinely. Any equipment parts that require frequent replacement or those that must be ordered in advance should be stocked. Some libraries will want to consider service contracts. Housekeeping chores including the emptying of waste cans should be performed regularly and with an eye for potential hazards. The library should be thoroughly inspected on a regular basis by the fire chief.

Librarians alone can determine individual library strengths and which materials are unique or most valuable to a given user group. In the case of serious or widespread disaster, it becomes important to know which materials warrant maximum effort. Materials are identified by location, but categories requiring special treatment (such as art books with coated paper, photographs, and so on) should be readily identifiable, as should materials of extreme value and unique copies.

Disasters do happen even to the most well prepared, and to further minimize loss, it is important to update insurance contracts regularly. A good disaster plan may help lower insurance rates. Thorough and immediate follow-up on needed corrective action will also prevent or minimize disaster.

Material and Binding Considerations

Librarians who make routine selection and binding decisions can make significant progress toward protecting the collection through (1) the selection of acid-free paper, noted by the infinity symbol (∞); (2) the use of acid-free processing materials including adhesives; (3) the selection of appropriate bindings for the expected use and retention of a volume; and (4) requiring commercial binderies to take sound preservation measures. Most binderies will do so if their contract requires it, but generally do not volunteer this service or do it routinely. Selection of a particular binding type depends on how and how frequently a book is used, any distinctive physical characteristics such as foldouts or loose material, its expected retention period, and its intrinsic value to the collection. Library staff should retain control over the binding decision, and should expect a commercial bindery to be able to use a variety of binding styles. Bindery practices to be encouraged include (1) never trimming the edges of a book; (2) not cutting the spine; (3) retaining the original sewing whenever possible; (4) using durable, stable materials, such as acid-free endpapers; (5) saving original covers, labels, bookplates, or other items of special interest even when not specifically requested; and (6) calling the library staff with questions about materials or procedures rather than taking the shortcut approach. Commercial and in-house binding practices should be critically evaluated in accordance with American Library Association guidelines.

Book Repair Program

All libraries repair books to some extent. R. J. Milevski and L. Nainis note that book repair and treatment programs are preventive in nature and should stress making minor repairs to avoid the need for major ones (1987). A few dollars spent on book repair can save significantly on the library's binding budget. The preservation committee should establish criteria for the selection of materials for repair and, in consultation with a trained conservator, should provide general procedural guidelines for in-house repairs. Repair programs should promote the use of archivally sound supplies throughout the library. Unfortunately, today even new bindings are often too weak to withstand normal library use, thereby necessitating repair before they go on the shelf. Techniques should be easily and completely reversible and appropriate for the volume in question. Some techniques, such as mylar encapsulation or boxing, serve to stabilize the piece until proper repairs can be developed or performed.

Book repair programs generally focus on performing large quantities of routine treatments. Ideally, a systematic review of all items in the collection should be performed at least once every few years. Written retention guidelines, included in an overall collection development policy, frequently serve as the basis for identifying books for routine repair; the input of collection development staff is critical to the evaluation of material for nonroutine treatments. The collection development librarian is responsible for determining the historical and bibliographic significance of a volume being considered for restoration. A professional conservator cannot determine the value of the work in the context of the library collection, and by the ethics of the profession will treat each item as a treasure if not instructed otherwise. The conservator should provide a written price estimate for the work to be performed, and any material leaving the library for restoration should be insured.

Housekeeping, Shelving, and Handling Practices

A library that is clean and neat encourages users to use it with respect. Food and drink should be prohibited except in designated areas away from where books are used, stored, and processed. An annual cleaning program including book dusting should be established in all sections of the library, but must be carried out by carefully trained personnel if it is to do more good than harm. Shelving should provide proper support for the books. If at all possible, large volumes should be shelved separately from smaller volumes. Only bookends specifically designed to prevent damage to materials should be used.

While it would be difficult to train every library user in the proper handling of books, staff use accounts for much of the handling, and all library staff should be taught the proper technique for removing and replacing a book on the shelf. Books should be removed by pushing the two adjacent volumes back and then grabbing the book at the center of the spine (as opposed to grabbing the book by the top of the spine and thereby tearing it). Circulation staff should provide plastic bags to patrons for transporting library books when it is raining or snowing. All bookdrops should be eliminated permanently as they are the cause of significant damage to many volumes.

Photocopying of materials by individual users causes marked damage. Proper photocopying techniques can be posted at the copy machines. Fragile and oversize materials should be copied only as absolutely necessary by the library staff. When replacing photocopy machines, care should be taken to select those that are least damaging to materials.

Alternative Formats and Reformatting

The preservation committee should develop systematic procedures for coping with materials identified as unusable. The decision to restore, reformat, or replace a volume depends on the value of the item to the collection. The level of use, the condition of the item, its value as an artifact, and its content all contribute to its value within the collection.

A multitude of treatment choices for an unusable volume are available as detailed below (DeCandido 1979). It is also important to realize that the failure to make any decision is a decision in itself.

1. Do nothing: a default option, not appropriate for valuable materials;
2. Discard: sell, exchange, or give volume to another institution that can preserve it;
3. Store: useless for access, but it can buy limited time;
4. Rebind: acceptable if not rare or historically significant;
5. Replace: purchase reprint or photocopy on acid-free paper for content—when purchasing out-of-print copy, check condition carefully, as it may be no better than original;
6. Reproduce: microfilm, optical disc, and so on—size and permanence are advantageous, but access and quality, especially color, may be impaired; space savings may be a significant asset;
7. Protect: protective covers including boxes, boards, portfolios, or encapsulation buy time; or
8. Restore or repair: expensive and time-consuming.

Restoration of materials is a major expense that should only be undertaken in an organized manner in cooperation with other institutions so that duplication of effort is avoided.

Preservation Education

Education in preservation issues of all library staff and patrons is an ambitious but essential goal of the preservation committee. Appropriate information on various preservation topics should be circulated to all staff including shelvers and processing and circulation staff. Too often information reaches only those who are responsible overall for a given issue, and in a field like preservation, where most staff members handle books, this is not enough. Staff training should include technical demonstrations, audiovisual presentations, and workshops as appropriate and necessary. Both practical and theoretical aspects of preservation should be covered. Many of the regional and state conservation facilities have materials available for loan including presentations on the care and handling of books, loading of book trucks, cleaning of books, and so forth. Preservation information sessions including instruction on the proper handling of books should constitute a piece of the initial training program for all new staff and student assistants. Professional development for selected personnel should be encouraged and funded. Attendance at conferences, visits to other institutions, and participation in preservation activities at the local, regional, and national levels provide important avenues for keeping up with new developments in the field.

Preservation education for users is relatively inexpensive. Library patrons, the largest users of the collection, should be encouraged to learn about the proper care and handling of books. This is easily accomplished through orientation programs for students and other library users and by aggressive public relations on the part of the library. Exhibit space can be used for interesting preservation displays, some of which are available for loan from the Library of Congress National Preservation Office. Bookmarks can carry preservation reminders as can plastic bags for transporting books in inclement weather.

Cooperative Preservation

The preservation planning committee should consider the feasibility of participating in cooperative preservation efforts at the national, regional, and local levels. The National Preservation Program Office at the Library of Congress provides information and assistance to the library community through the following activities: a preservation reference service; an audiovisual loan program; a publications program including a newsletter, *National Preservation News*, and a preservation leaflet series and monographs; a workshop and lecture program; an intern education program in conservation and preservation administration; and a cooperative microfilming program. The Society for American Archivists sponsors basic and advanced archival conservation programs. Cooperative regional preservation centers offer tremendous support in light of tight financial resources, the volume of materials requiring treatment, the highly technical nature of some procedures, and the shortage of trained conservators. The Northeast Document Conservation Center (NEDCC), formerly the only regional conservation center in the United States, has served as a model for the development of several new centers and provides a host of technical and educational services.

Preservation consultants can also provide expertise, and the preservation committee should maintain a list of persons and facilities providing such services. Because libraries may require a wide variety of specialized preservation techniques for repair and restoration, it is important to identify skilled persons qualified to meet the library's needs. In a field in which no national accreditation standards exist at the present time, demonstrated capability, written qualifications, and recommendations should be evaluated carefully. Local historical societies and specialized libraries also provide communities with additional sources of expertise.

Cooperative programs, however, cannot meet all preservation needs within the library, and they should supplement rather than substitute for in-house preservation programs.

Preservation Funding Sources

Funds are available for preservation from a variety of sources. Clear documentation of need is the most common basis for assigning such funds. Potential local, regional, and national sources of funding should be identified by the preservation committee. Frequently, grant funds may be applied to the initial establishment of a preservation program, and can often close the financial gap pending internal budget requests for preservation monies. The potential of interested community groups should not be overlooked. Library friends groups and genealogical and historical societies may be particularly interested in the preservation of certain rare or local materials. University and college development offices may also provide assistance in locating additional sources of funding. Finally, some states have passed preservation initiatives to encourage program development, and in some cases have even allocated funding.

CONCLUSION

The information, guidelines, and considerations presented provide a basic framework on which to build a comprehensive preservation program. Many of these suggestions can be implemented in a small academic library at little or no expense in that they only require adjustments in materials used, reassignment of a limited amount of staff time, or an awareness of proper preservation practices. Because certain recommendations will require months or even years of planning and budgeting, it is important to begin immediately if we are to rescue our prized treasures before they can no longer be salvaged. Faced with an obstacle of astounding proportions, we must work together and hasten one step at a time to overcome it.

REFERENCES

Association of Research Libraries. 1987. *Preservation Planning Program Resource Notebook*. Washington, D.C.: Office of Management Studies.

DeCandido, R. 1979. ''Preserving Our Library Materials: Preservation Treatments Available to Librarians.'' *Library Scene* 8: 4–6.

DeCandido, R., and G. A. DeCandido. 1985. ''Micropreservation: Conserving the Small Library.'' *Library Resources and Technical Services* 29, no. 2, 150–60.

Milevski, R. J., and L. Nainis. 1987. ''Implementing a Book Repair and Treatment Program.'' *Library Resources and Technical Services* 31 (April): 159–76.

Morrow, C. C., with G. Walker. 1983. *The Preservation Challenge: A Guide to Conserving Library Materials*. White Plains, N.Y.: Knowledge Industry Publications.

Patterson, R. H. 1979. ''Organizing for Conservation: A Model Charge to a Conservation Committee.'' *Library Journal* 104 (May 15): 1116–19.

Winkle, B. 1985. ''A Guide for Small Libraries: Preservation on a Shoestring.'' *American Libraries* 16 (December): 778–79.

PART V

Technology

16

Microcomputers in Libraries: Planning for Effective Use

Deborah Barreau

The development of the microchip, resulting in affordable, powerful technology, is bringing change to the information field. Many newsletters, indexes, and databases formerly accessible only in print are available in machine-readable form. Electronic mail, electronic publishing, and other computer-generated data are new forms of information that present new problems of storage, organization, and access. Libraries, with a traditional mission to store, organize, and make information freely accessible, will find a challenge in trying to fulfill this mission in a society that is fast becoming electronically sophisticated.

Automated library services are perceived to be an asset to colleges and universities competing for students and funds, but many smaller academic institutions lack the resources to computerize despite pressure to do so. Pressures come from administrators who want their campuses and libraries to be perceived as progressive, from those students and faculty who appreciate the gains in more convenient access to library services, and from librarians who anticipate improvements in services. The result is increased purchasing of computers and computerized systems for library use. Some academic institutions have completely embraced the new technology, wiring campuses to connect students and faculty to large networks for information sharing, including on-line access to the bibliographic records of the library catalogs (Moran, Suprenant, and Taylor 1987). Advertisements for library systems and articles with guidelines for selection pervade the literature, yet most systems, particularly those that offer integrated functions for circulation, cataloging, and so on, are unaffordable for the small academic library. Software prices alone for integrated library systems on a mainframe or minicomputer may cost as much as $80,000 to $100,000 with additional annual maintenance fees, and this price does not include the costs of hardware purchase, installation, and service.

The microcomputer is the least expensive and most promising option for small libraries with a goal toward automation, and is therefore the focus of this chapter; however, purchasing a micro is not always the correct choice for solving a problem or improving a service. Libraries must take an active role in automation choices to guarantee continued quality of service while rising to meet new demands, and small libraries with limited human and financial resources must plan carefully to avoid costly mistakes.

This chapter is for the manager or the selection team considering the purchase of a computer for the first time or upgrading systems already owned. The first section examines the potential for microcomputers in a library setting. It is followed by suggestions for how to plan for computerization, guidelines for selecting systems, and sources for assistance in the selection process.

MICROCOMPUTERS IN LIBRARIES

What Are Microcomputers?

Computers are usually grouped into three categories: mainframes, minicomputers, and microcomputers. The mainframes, the largest and most expensive category, require a trained staff for management and support of the system, and housing in a specially designed, climate-controlled environment. Mainframes support many users, offer access to a wide range of peripherals, and allow multiple tasks and programs to operate simultaneously. Minicomputers are the middle range of computers in size, power, and price. Microcomputers, the smallest, slowest, and cheapest category of computers, exceed the capability of the mainframes of a few years ago, and there is such a fine line between the categories that the most powerful microcomputers are hardly distinguishable from minicomputers.

All computers, regardless of size, support five general functions: (1) to allow the input of information; (2) to store information; (3) to process information; (4) to control the information; and (5) to output information in some form (Costa and Costa 1986: 33). The microcomputer has the advantage of being able to perform these functions within a single workstation which is relatively inexpensive, easy to use, and requires little maintenance. Microcomputers may accept input from a terminal keyboard, a program loaded into memory, data sorted in a file, a barcode reader, or another device. Information is stored temporarily during program execution in the computer's volatile random access memory (RAM), and more permanently on less expensive, nonvolatile magnetic tape, discs (floppy, micro-floppy, or fixed), or devices such as "write once read many" compact discs. Information is processed by the microprocessors that determine the computer's power and design. Information output is routed to a screen, printer, disc, or other device. Information is controlled by the computer's operating system—software that defines the working environment for the applications programs.

Microcomputer technology is a highly dynamic field. It is estimated that generational turnaround in the design of microcomputer systems takes place about every six months, meaning that the system purchased today will be old technology in a year's time (Kesner and Jones 1984: 25–32). Careful choices must be made to select systems that meet the library's current needs but also provide the flexibility to take advantage of technological advances as they develop.

Microcomputers are priced from a few hundred dollars to as much as $20,000 for some of the larger, multiuser systems. They range in size from small laptop to large desktop models. The capability of the micros varies greatly dependent on the particular microprocessor installed, the amount of internal random access memory (RAM) available, the word size (the amount of data the computer can address at one time), and the number and variety of peripherals that the microcomputer can support. Peripherals usually require special interface boards or cables, and many are designed for a specific computer architecture and will work on that brand of computer only.

The computer hardware is useless without software, the programs that make it possible to create the specific applications for such activities as budgeting, maintaining and analyzing statistics, writing letters, publishing newsletters, searching databases, and requesting items through interlibrary loan. Software development has not kept up with hardware technology, and most existing operating systems and applications packages fail to take advantage of the full power of such microprocessors as Intel's 80386.

Software is relatively computer-specific, and is designed for a particular operating system in a particular hardware environment, so programs that run on an IBM system, for example, will not run on incompatible computer architecture such as the Apple II. This is often true for data generated as a result of these programs as well, though there are ways of transferring and sharing data among different systems.

Microcomputer Use in Libraries

Libraries are using microcomputers successfully for management tasks such as budgeting and word processing; for public service tasks such as circulation, on-line searching, and interlibrary loan; and for technical service tasks such as acquisitions, cataloging, and serials control (Woods and Pope 1983: 45–63). There are even some small special libraries and school libraries that have integrated library systems on a microcomputer.

Microcomputers are placed in libraries for many reasons. Computers enhance the image of the library and the librarians, giving an impression that the library is progressive and technologically advanced. This has been reason enough for many librarians to purchase microcomputers, yet sometimes these machines are underused or used ineffectively because of misconceptions about what computers can do.

One common misconception is that microcomputers offer an affordable option for an integrated library system for small academic libraries that cannot hope to bid on mainframe or minicomputer-based systems. Though optical disc technology holds future promise, microcomputers are still an insufficient alternative for manipulating large bibliographic records in all but the smallest collections (Kesner and Jones 1984: 131). Micros have been used a little more successfully to automate the functions that make use of brief records such as circulation, acquisitions, or serials control, but these systems are costly and may prove inadequate as the library's automation needs change and efforts are made to integrate functions (Boss 1985: 657–59).

Another misconception is that if an application *can* be automated, it *should* be. Assessment of the tasks involved in automating a function must include the financial, human, and physical resources required to accomplish the process, evaluated in terms of gains in staff productivity and in service to patrons. Processes that operate smoothly may not require automation.

New users often expect the computer to perform simple tasks automatically, not realizing that proper software, hardware, and training are required to produce the specific applications desired (Walton 1983: 52). When this happens, computers sit idle for months because staff members are not sure what to do with them.

It is important for librarians and staff to be involved in the selection of computers for the library, as they are most familiar with the library's mission and goals. Knowledge of the problems and services that are being considered for automation as well as knowledge of the capability of computer hardware and software are required for a successful automation program. Realistic goals and careful guidelines for an implementation program that includes training, technical support, and regular access to the computer and to personnel with computer expertise will stimulate appropriate use of the system.

PLANNING FOR MICROS: NEEDS ANALYSIS

Recent cutbacks in public funding of social and educational programs have forced colleges and universities to review programs and establish strategies for maximizing resources. Many administrators are adopting a goal-oriented "strategic-planning" approach to program revision and development. This approach requires careful analysis of the environment and resources of the institution, evaluation and revision of goals and objectives, and development of strategies and systems to achieve those goals. Libraries can benefit from strategic-planning methods as departments must compete for funds, and those programs that are most important to the institution's goals will most likely be funded

(Moran 1985: 290). Planning within the library must therefore take the institution's goals into consideration as well as the library's objectives.

Library use patterns are already being affected by the use of computers. This is reflected in changes in interlibrary loan requests and periodical use patterns brought about by installation of micro systems with access to indexes such as the *Reader's Guide to Periodical Literature* on CD-ROM; and very likely this trend will continue. Libraries faced with increasing pressure to provide on-line access to collections will be competing with the computer center and other departments for resources to fund and maintain systems. Librarians must prove that money allocated to their programs will be well spent, and this requires careful analysis of programs and services to ensure actions that will yield the greatest efficiency.

Determine Needs and Set Goals

Kesner and Jones suggest that the planning process should begin with a needs assessment to determine the library's objectives by defining the services and procedures performed in the library and setting goals and priorities for the future based on that analysis (1984: 55–59, 81). Analysis of programs and services should take the future into consideration as well as current practices, not only to anticipate growth, but also to set goals for improving performance (Duke and Hirshon 1986: 199).

Identify Processes Ripe for Automation

The needs analysis will identify any processes that may be ripe for automation, and further analysis will determine if computers are an appropriate alternative for the situation. Processes that are conducive to automation are those that involve repetitive tasks, require accuracy, make use of the same data frequently, and must be performed within a specified time. However, other factors must be considered such as the availability and training of staff for the job and the costs of automating the function.

A library may set a priority to focus on improving circulation processing, for example—getting overdue notices out more quickly, moving patrons through check-out lines more efficiently, improving accuracy, and returning items to the shelf faster. Automated circulation offers an attractive solution for improved service, but it is initially expensive and labor-intensive. Without adequate funding and staffing, it is not feasible, and there may be ways to improve the manual system significantly and postpone automation until the resources can be found. Careful analysis of a process and redesigning procedures to make them more efficient are valuable activities to precede automation. Programs and procedures that are badly designed will function no better through automation.

Select a Team to Identify the Hardware and Software Requirements

The importance of planning cannot be overemphasized. Once the environment is analyzed, the needs are defined, and the priorities are arranged, there will be a clear understanding of which processes should be automated. The next step is to identify the specific requirements of the system to be purchased, and this is best performed by a team of individuals who understand the goals and complexities of the tasks being automated and who have enough skill in using micros to be able to read and analyze documentation and recognize system features and capabilities (Hannigan 1985: 341).

Microcomputers are more complicated to use than typewriters and copiers; they require more training and skill. The team must know the job the computer is to perform and who the users will be in order to make decisions and formulate adequate policies for acquisition and use. Knowledge of the nature of the data and amount of data to be processed is also an important consideration.

The software will be selected first as it is more specific to the application desired, unless hardware already owned by the library is to be used. There are a number of checklists available to assist individuals in identifying the software requirements for different applications (Burton and Petrie 1986: 195–96; Costa and Costa 1986: 299–315). Features of word processors will vary significantly from database-management systems or spreadsheets, so it is a good idea to list the functional requirements before the search for the right program begins.

SELECTION OF HARDWARE AND SOFTWARE

Software

Some knowledge of computers is necessary to understand software capability, but listing the features required for a particular application demands the library staff's thorough understanding of the tasks to be performed and the outcome desired. Sources previously mentioned offer specific checklists and guidelines for selecting a product (Burton and Petrie 1986; Costa and Costa 1986). Most recommend a strategy that includes listing the requirements for the system, selecting three or four products that meet the specifications, testing those products, and making a selection. If software cannot be found to fulfill the requirements, it can be developed locally or commissioned; however, tailor-made systems will be expensive and will take time to develop (Burton and Petrie 1986: 185–86).

Listing the Requirements of the Software

There are several things to keep in mind when developing a list of required features, including: (1) who the users will be and what their needs are; (2) the size and number of files the system will be processing and the expected growth of the files; (3) the level of complexity of the system being automated; and (4) the desired output for the system. Cost is a consideration too, though probably not as much for software as for hardware. Microcomputer software costs can vary by a few hundred dollars, but to buy a package that lacks an important feature in order to save a few dollars will prove to be no savings at all.

Knowing who the users are will help define the general features and type of user interface needed for the system. A system that will be used by many different individuals may require more protection mechanisms, a simple menu-driven interface with an advanced on-line help facility, and simple mnemonic key-stroke command combinations that facilitate learning the system. Systems that will be used by a few highly trained individuals need not be so user-friendly, but may require more detailed printed documentation and more advanced features.

Most software packages list a maximum file size and a maximum number of files that can be open at one time. Knowing the number of records in a planned database, the length of the average and largest documents to be word-processed, or the maximum number of items to be included in a spreadsheet is essential for selection of adequate software. An estimation of the growth rate of the files over a five-year period must be included in consideration of the file size the software must handle.

Listing the processes that will be performed upon the data—sorting, merging, calculating, printing, and so on—and knowing the additional storage requirements for the data generated from these processes will aid in identifying the right package. Identification of the specific operations the system is to perform ensures the selection of a package at the proper level of complexity for those operations. If the goal of automation is to produce a printed alphabetical list of patrons for the purpose of mailing labels, then a simple, inexpensive, menu-driven software program may be adequate. However, if a more complicated system is desired to allow the file to be searched, to produce lists according to variable conditions, or to automatically update records, then a more powerful program will be needed. While it is safe to assume that needs will change, it is wrong to assume that the most powerful, expensive, and complex system is the one to buy for every application.

Output capability, the variety and quality of reports and other documents that may be generated by the software, is an important feature. If output must be of excellent quality, the software should support different printers, provide graphics, and offer different layout options. If it is variety of output that is important, then different formats, sytle sheets, report forms, and so on, must be among the software features, and should be relatively easy to produce, save, and modify.

Selecting the Product

Once the desired features have been listed, the selection team can identify three or four packages that meet the criteria and evaluate them. Evaluation includes reading the documentation and experimenting with the software on a computer to check performance; that is, how efficiently the software performs the identified features. Often it is not possible to test the system within the library before purchase. When this happens, the team must rely on journals that report on software performance and on the experience of other users.

The evaluating team will need to note the number of steps required to execute the feature, the speed and response time of the software in executing the task, and the quality of the results. It is advisable to look for additional features beyond those specified, and for safety features that guard against such disasters as accidental deletions. Consistency in command structure and program behavior at all levels of operation are other desirable features.

A final feature to consider is the operating system and hardware environment for which the software is designed. If the choices have been narrowed to packages that are very similar and one operates efficiently only on a powerful, specialized $10,000 system while the other operates efficiently on a variety of micros in the $2,000 to $5,000 range, then the decision may be clear.

Hardware

The hardware decision is easier to make once the software is chosen. A list of hardware requirements that conform to the software specifications will provide guidelines for hardware selection. Selection will depend on the minimum amount of random access memory required for the software to operate efficiently, the amount of storage required for the software and the data that will be generated and used by the program, the speed and processing power required to handle the data, and the peripherals required to operate the software (graphics board, barcode readers, plotters, modems, printers, and so on) (Burton and Petrie 1986: 199–200). Of course, the hardware must support the operating system for which the software is designed.

There are two schools of thought regarding hardware selection: (1) those that recommend buying a known, tested name brand of computer likely to be in business for a long time, and (2) those that recommend buying the cheapest model and brand available that will do the job. Though this author is prejudiced toward the former school (which is branded by some as "cowardly" and "unimaginative"), those with the time and resources to do the necessary research and willing to take a risk can save hundreds of dollars by following the latter strategy.

The likelihood of compatibility problems increases with the complexity of the hardware, particularly if systems have been assembled from different vendors. If the selected software has graphics capability, it is important to know the type of graphics it supports, as standards vary for adapter cards, monitors, and other peripherals. Incompatibility problems are not uncommon, and they sometimes cannot be fixed without additional expense, exchanges, and frustration. Buying a complete system from an established vendor will cost more—sometimes a lot more—but the problems and delays of incompatible software and hardware usually can be avoided.

As for performance, the name brand is no guarantee of superiority, so the equipment should be tested for the particular software applications, especially when response time is a crucial factor. Installing co-processors or accelerator boards are affordable alternatives worth investigating to improve system response, but care must be taken to ensure compatibility.

Probably the most important consideration in purchasing hardware is not the brand, but the dealer and the level of support and warranties offered on the equipment. Repair delays can cripple a library dependent on a computer, and a local dealer who will guarantee a rapid turnaround time or offer a loaner while repairs are made may be worth the extra cost.

Mail-order companies offer low prices, and many offer warranties and telephone support to assist with problems, but they are more risky than buying from a local dealer, particularly if you know little about computers and software. However, if adding a hard disc, a graphics card, or a math co-processor to a computer the library already owns is all that is needed to make a system compatible with new software, mail order may be the best alternative.

Libraries often are required to select a vendor through bidding. In this case, the system specifications must be highly detailed, including performance requirements, software compatibility needs, desired level of maintenance, a list of peripherals, minimum memory configuration, operating system, and so forth, yet they must allow enough flexibility to take advantage of dealer packages that offer a faster processor or a hard disc with greater capacity than may be specified.

Sources

The most comprehensive source of information on hardware and software are the vendor advertisements and reviews (Burton and Petrie 1986: 183–84). Brochures can be obtained directly from vendors, and the reviews, product announcements, and results of performance tests can be found in a number of computer journals. *InfoWorld*, *BYTE*, and *PC Magazine* are among the better sources. There are specialized journals for almost every leading brand of computer, and each contains helpful information about software and hardware, including benchmark tests and performance comparisons.

Regular software reviews and columns dealing with computers appear in *Library Journal* and *Wilson Library Bulletin*, and information of particular relevance to libraries is included in specialized periodicals such as *Library Software Review*, *Small Computers in Libraries*, *Library Technology Reports*, and *Microcomputers for Information Management*. Computer books and software directories can also be helpful, particularly those that are updated frequently. Reviews can be found through manual indexes or through one of the on-line databases such as *Microcomputer Index*, *Microcomputer Software & Hardware Guide*, *Computer Database*, and *Online Microcomputer Software Guide and Directory*, all accessible through DIALOG or BRS Information Technologies.

Other valuable sources of information are local computer dealers, and workshops, demonstrations, and computer fairs, which are offered at shopping malls, universities, and other locations. Attending conferences where equipment will be demonstrated and displayed and taking courses on how to use computers are beneficial.

One of the most valuable resources for product information are the formal and informal networks of people who use computers. This may include everyone from personal friends and contacts in other libraries who are successfully using systems to computer clubs, library computer-users groups, and electronic bulletin boards and news groups. The electronic sources are quite helpful—almost every problem posted is a problem that someone else has had and has solved. These news groups offer programming tips, warn of "bugs" in software, and share free software from the public domain.

One example of a successful library computer-users group is in North Carolina. The Microcomputer Users Group for Libraries in North Carolina (MUGLNC) has offered camps and workshops to train librarians to use computers and to help libraries manage computer projects more positively (Smith and Burgin 1984: 61–62). MUGLNC has cosponsored a colloquium ("Managing the New Technology: The Impact of Automation upon Libraries") with the School of Information and Library Science at the University of North Carolina at Chapel Hill to discuss issues relevant to library automation. These groups are easy to form, affordable (annual membership in MUGLNC is $5), and helpful to librarians in every type of library.

CONCLUSION

Libraries are benefitting from computer technology. Large collections are becoming more manageable and more accessible, processes are more accurate and efficient, and services are improved in libraries where computers are being used well. Smaller academic libraries are beginning to share in the benefits of computers largely because of affordable microcomputer technology, but there are libraries where the computers have failed to live up to expectations, where micros sit unused or underused, and fail to perform well the functions for which they were acquired. Libraries with restricted budgets cannot afford such costly waste.

Librarians must carefully evaluate programs and services, and set goals and priorities before determining which processes are ripe for automation. Strategies for selecting proper software and hardware for the chosen application will ensure the purchase of a workable system, but the planning process does not stop with acquisition. Librarians must be as dedicated to the maintenance and support of the system as the acquisition process if automation is to succeed. The commitment must be a commitment in terms of staff and facilities as well as financial resources, and failure to take this into account may result in other valuable programs being neglected. Libraries accountable for expenses and in competition with other departments for funds cannot profit by neglecting any programs.

Careful planning is the key to the success of any program. In the case of computers in libraries, the payoff will be a library that is as progressive in providing service and fulfilling its mission as its technology makes it appear to be.

REFERENCES

Boss, Richard W. 1985. "Microcomputers in Libraries: The Quiet Revolution." *Wilson Library Bulletin* 59: 653–60.

Burton, Paul F., and J. Howard Petrie. 1986. *The Librarian's Guide to Microcomputers for Information Management*. New York: Van Nostrand Reinhold.

Costa, Betty, and Marie Costa. 1986. *A Micro Handbook for Small Libraries and Media Centers*, 2d ed. Englewood, Colo.: Libraries Unlimited.

Duke, John, and Arnold Hirshon. 1986. "Policies for Microcomputers in Libraries: An Administrative Model." *Information Technology and Libraries* 5: 193–203.

Hannigan, J. A. 1985. "The Evaluation of Microcomputer Software." *Library Trends* 33: 327–48.

Kesner, Richard M., and Clifton H. Jones. 1984. *Microcomputer Applications in Libraries: A Management Tool for the 1980s and Beyond*. London: Aldwych Press.

Moran, Barbara B. 1985. "Strategic Planning in Higher Education." *College and Research Libraries News* 46: 288–90.

Moran, Barbara B., Thomas T. Suprenant, and Merrily E. Taylor. 1987. "The Electronic Campus: The Impact of the Scholar's Workstation Project." *College and Research Libraries* 48: 5–16.

Smith, Duncan, and Robert Burgin. 1984. "Micros in the Carolinas." *Public Libraries* 23: 61–62.

Walton, Robert A. 1983. *Microcomputers: A Planning and Implementation Guide for Libraries and Information Professionals*. Phoenix, Ariz.: Oryx Press.

Woods, Lawrence A., and Nolan F. Pope. 1983. *Librarian's Guide to Microcomputer Technology and Applications*. White Plains, N.Y.: Knowledge Industry Publications.

17

Microcomputer Personal Productivity Software

David R. Dowell

Academic library computerization is occurring on three levels as the end of the 1980s approaches:

1. Automation of department-wide files;
2. Creation of electronic databases that can be used directly by the entire campus; and
3. Provision of personal productivity tools.

The first level, generally called library automation, became widespread in academic libraries in the early 1970s. On some campuses it manifested itself as a circulation system, on some as an automated acquisitions system, and on some as a machine-generated list of serial holdings. The most venturesome systems tried to do all the above. For the most part, these early systems operated in batch mode to print book orders, update lists of items checked out, update the status of fund accounts, and do similar tasks once daily (generally at night) or even less frequently.

The retrospective conversion of bibliographic records for circulation systems, combined with the automated cataloging of new acquisitions, paved the way for the on-line public access catalogs that became common in the 1980s. Increasingly, the on-line public access catalogs displayed circulation status and often interfaced with the catalogs of other institutions to provide information about the collections of other libraries. No longer did the patron need to go to the library to find if an item existed, to determine whether it was checked out, or even to check it out. Thus the users of the library databases could be anywhere on the campus computer network or even connected only by a dial-up link.

It is the third area of library computerization that is the focus of this chapter—that of personal productivity software commonly used on personal computers. The 1980s have been the decade of stand-alone personal computers in academe. Leading-edge institutions indicate that the 1990s will be the decade of tying these stand alone workstations into local area networks (LANS) and other methods of connectivity. Although the workstations discussed in this chapter would not meet the technical definitions for the high-powered CAD/CAM applications of a Sun engineering workstation, in the library they serve the same purpose. They provide librarians with access to all the databases and personal productivity software necessary to perform their work. For instance, such a station might provide word processing, spreadsheets, database management, desk organizers (which provide calendars, ''to-do lists,'' telephone lists, address directories, and calculators), and file managers, as well as access to the library's on-line catalog, circulation status files, on-order files, acquisitions funds files, serials check-in files, bindery files, want files, electronic mail, and commercial databases such as Dialog, BRS, and so on.

The purpose of this chapter is to help librarians assemble the tools that will become the building blocks of such a workstation. As long as the components are put together thoughtfully, there is no reason to wait and buy the entire station at one time. This chapter will emphasize the necessary software, although some comments will also be made concerning hardware.

The most important decision in purchasing hardware is to ensure that it will run the necessary software. Unfortunately, many people acquire a personal computer and then look for software to run on it. In the process they may unduly constrain their options for software, they may purchase more computing power than they need, or they may purchase computers that are otherwise inappropriate.

STANDARDIZATION

Most colleges and universities have attempted to standardize using one or two types of personal computers. Librarians, particularly if they are relative novices in the personal computer arena, would be well advised to stay with any standards that may be emerging on the campus. IBM or IBM-compatible computers clearly are in the lead. Macintosh is the only other microcomputer with wide acceptance in academe at present. The Apple II series has had incredible market penetration at the elementary and secondary education level, but has made hardly a ripple in the higher education market. Unless the academic library has a major role identity with elementary- or secondary-school teacher training, it should be advised to stay away from the Apple II. In general the library would do well to restrict its hardware choices to IBM-compatible computers or the Macintosh.

In the author's experience, IBM-compatible personal computers have proved to be equally as reliable as IBM nameplate personal computers. In most cases the compatibles are faster, and they certainly cost less. For the true compatibles, maintenance is usually easy to find. In general, personal computers often fail during the first few days as a result of defective parts, faulty assembly, or damage in shipment. At that time the computer is still under warranty. Once the initial problems, if any, are behind you, the computers should be fairly reliable for at least two or three years, when some of the parts may start to wear out. Dust, smoke, other pollutants, and irregular electricity also can create problems. Disc drives, particularly hard drives, do not tolerate jolts well. The read/write heads of hard discs should be removed from the disc surface with a *Ship* or *Park* utility any time the computer is going to be moved even a short distance.

Libraries in which the library itself or its parent institution has made a serious commitment to be on the "leading edge" of the application of information technology will not need to restrict themselves to IBM, IBM-compatible, and Macintosh computers. In such situations, experimentation with hardware and software beyond the tried and true is considered to be a virtue unto itself. Librarians who operate in such an environment may not need to read this chapter. At the other end of the spectrum, librarians at institutions that consider personal computers to be "scarce resources" or "necessary evils," will find themselves in a position to exercise more of a leadership role in defining what the campus standard should be. At the very least, they may be left to establish their microcomputing policies on their own without a lot of role models to follow. It is primarily for this latter group that this chapter is addressed.

Standardization of software is equally as important as standardization of hardware. Many institutions have chosen the software that they will support. This "support" may mean that no other software may be purchased with institutional funds, although this extreme is very rare. The support may be in the form of negotiating "site licenses" or volume discounts. In other cases, the support may be in the form of training and trouble shooting when problems occur.

In instances where the campus has not adopted such standards, it may be in the interest of the library to develop its own. In the author's library, a word-processing package, a spreadsheet package, a database program, and a desk management package have been chosen as the officially supported programs. Other competing packages will be purchased only after compelling documentation is provided that the standard equipment will not adequately serve the purpose. Librarians are not prohibited from using other programs. However, training and trouble shooting will not be provided for nonofficial programs. As a result, most of the staff use the "official" programs, but one or two librarians use an unofficial word-processing or database package. When it is necessary to provide a machine-readable version of a document or database, it is the responsibility of those librarians to be able to transfer their files into the standard format or to take the standard format and transfer it for their own use.

TRAINING

Lack of access to personal computers and lack of training in the use of personal-computer software seem to be the major hindrances to librarians taking advantage of the power of personal productivity software. The first factor is rather obvious. They do not have adequate access to the software and a personal computer on which to run it. Experience shows that full advantage will not be made of the power of microcomputers unless they are available at the convenience of the professional. When personal computers must be shared or scheduled, they are used only when absolutely necessary. It becomes a hassle and is inefficient to arrange a librarian's schedule to match the availability of the computer. Sometimes this is the only way that a library can begin to use the personal productivity power of microcomputers. However, it is too easy to forget that the real objective in introducing personal computers is to increase the effectiveness of the people in the organization. Therefore, managers should not lose sight of the ultimate goal. That goal should be to schedule the $2,000 personal computers at the convenience of the $30,000-a-year librarians rather than to schedule the librarians at the convenience of the personal computer.

In addition, much office tension and stress is often generated in departments that are in the process of adopting personal computing. Latent jealousies and other tensions can be brought to the fore when professionals must compete for access to personal computers.

A second hindrance to rapid adoption of personal productivity software is that most librarians have a well-developed work ethic. Librarians are reluctant to spend work time learning how to use a new software package. To them it seems that personal experimentation or even reading a software manual is "playing" when there is work to be done. This is one of the reasons why librarians who have personal computers at home have a learning curve that is at least three to five times that of other librarians. At home it is "OK to play," and they are willing to invest the time to learn.

Therefore, administrators who wish to accelerate the use of personal computers by their staffs should explore every avenue to encourage librarians to acquire computers that can be used at home. Many colleges and universities have negotiated discounted prices for hardware and software; and these purchase plans are often available to staff interested in having computers at home. Some institutions as well as some companies have sold older computers to staff when upgrades are purchased for the office.

If more permanent arrangements fail, provision of a lap-top or other transportable computer to be taken home on a temporary basis will pay dividends in a number of ways. First, librarians will have the leisure to experiment without feeling guilty that they should be working. Second, projects will get done for which there was never enough time at work. In addition, once individuals experience the advantages of having a computer at home, they will become much more motivated to acquire one on a permanent basis. In any case, the productivity of the librarian will be increased.

Librarians do not think that it is playing if they are sent to a formal training session to learn how to use personal computer software. In fact, many of them seem to think that management has a responsibility to provide such training opportunities before they should be expected to use a new technology. Experience seems to indicate that formal instruction is not the most effective method to learn such skills. My wife is often paid $50 an hour to go to an office to train secretaries and other workers one-on-one after they have completed a two- or three-day off-site training program on popular office productivity software at fairly expensive tuition. People seem to learn best how to use microcomputers in their own environment while they are accomplishing a task that they are committed to completing.

Two distinct archetypes of learning behavior occur when librarians set out to learn a new software program. The first type uses the manual as a reference book, and the second uses it as a text.

The first type installs the software and immediately tries to get it to run. Representatives of this type only consult the manual when they are unable to accomplish what they are attempting. They consult the on-line help screens before the printed documentation. These individuals are less interested in the total capabilities of the software than in accomplishing some specific activity.

The second type will read the manual before trying to load the software. They may not read it cover to cover, but they will at least skim it. The manual will not necessarily make a lot of sense to them, but at least they will get a systematic overview of the capabilities of the entire package—assuming that the documentation is moderately comprehensible. Only then will they load the software and attempt to use it.

Which learning behavior is best? I would not dare to attempt an answer to that question. I am an example of the first type, and my wife is an example of the second. When each of us sets out to learn the same software, each learns things that the other does not. Then we are able to complement each other's knowledge. It is hoped that there is a random distribution of these learning behaviors in your library.

I have found the following system to work well with either type of learning behavior. Each librarian who is interested in learning a new piece of software is encouraged to think of a project that would make good use of that program. When such a project has been identified, a mentor is found who is willing to sit with the novice for twenty or thirty minutes as the librarian actually starts to use the software. Those librarians who use manuals as textbooks probably will wish to do extensive reading prior to this session. Usually within thirty minutes the librarian can learn the basic commands that are necessary to make significant progress on this first project. Emphasis is placed on making progress with that specific project, not on learning every nuance of the software. After the initial session, the mentor will need to be accessible to answer questions. However, most librarians will be able to make at least limited use of the new program within the first half hour. By the end of the first session, the novices will have completed some work, thereby satisfying their work ethic. This doubles the positive reinforcement. Something new will have been learned, and some work will have been accomplished.

WORD PROCESSORS

By far the most important single type of personal productivity software is word processing. This is generally the first microcomputer application that librarians attempt; and many of them have yet to progress beyond this point. However, word processing by itself, if used extensively, can easily justify an investment in a microcomputer.

> Few other aspects of personal computing arouse as much passion as word processing. Rarely do you see people getting worked up over the merits of the latest spreadsheet program. But mention your favorite word processor to a group of computer users and watch the fur fly. (Brogan 1988)

> If personal computer software is a jungle, then word processing and word-related products undoubtedly constitute its thickest and possibly most hazardous part. Truly, you can buy a word processor for $50 or a best seller for $500 and *never notice the difference*. (Glossbrenner 1984: 299)

If you are purchasing the software only to handle personal correspondence, memos, and some internal documents, the $50 package may be perfectly adequate. However, if you are selecting a word processor to become the library or campus standard, you would be much better served by selecting a more versatile product. Many checklists of features desirable in word processors exist. I will not attempt to repeat any of them here. However, if you have difficulty finding such assistance, Glossbrenner's *How to Buy Software*, although slightly dated, has not yet been replicated.

No word-processing software should be considered unless it has the capability of reading-in a DOS text file (sometimes called an ASCII file). It should also be able to output any file as a DOS text file. This is the minimum level of compatibility that should be considered even when purchasing a very inexpensive program. If this capability exists, then it will be possible to transport texts from one word-processing program to another without having to type them a second time. At this level of compatibility, the words can be moved. However, the spacing, underlining, boldfacing, footnoting, and other special characteristics may be lost or garbled. It will be possible, although perhaps inconvenient, to share documents with those using other programs; and it will be possible for librarians to upgrade to another word-processing program and still have access to the hours of work that went into the creation of the documents that were written with the old program.

A far better level of compatibility can be had by purchasing a word-processing package that includes a conversion program. At the very least, this conversion program should convert text, along with most common format commands, both to and from at least one of the major word-processing programs such as WordPerfect, WordStar, MultiMate, and so forth. Once a document has been converted into one of these latter formats, it can be reconverted from the major format to another less standard format if the receiver of the document has a similar conversion program that works with the destination word-processing program. Of course, all these steps can be eliminated if you are using the same word-processing program as the one being used by those with whom you will be exchanging documents.

SPREADSHEETS

Spreadsheet programs, particularly VisiCalc, are given credit for having launched the personal computer revolution. Their applications for librarians are infinite. As the Prudential Insurance ad on television says: "If you can dream it, you can do it." This phrase is true for all kinds of personal computer software, but it is particularly true for spreadsheets. Whole books have been written on library applications for spreadsheets.

Basically, a spreadsheet should be used when numbers need to be added, subtracted, or used in some other calculation. It is particularly useful in situations where figures are frequently updated. This is because the spreadsheet can be set up so that it automatically recalculates all row and column totals or recalculates the result of some other formula when any of the numbers within it are updated. It is also very useful in "what if" planning. What if everyone's salary were raised? What if journal prices went up 12%, or 15%? Planning assumptions can be changed with a few key strokes, and all the totals will be recalculated automatically.

Of course the most obvious applications are for budgeting and for monthly statistics of transactions. It is very easy to set up a template to keep track of vacation and sick-leave records for library employees. Accruals can be posted automatically for each time period, and only leave time used must be added. The result can be printed out periodically for the employees and their supervisors.

When choosing a spreadsheet program, the same concerns with standardization apply. Lotus 1–2–3 has a market dominance among spreadsheets that no word-processing program enjoys. It is not necessarily the best spreadsheet, but it is clearly a standard. Compatibility with Lotus 1–2–3 is definitely a most important consideration in choosing a spreadsheet. Compatibility means being able to move both the original spreadsheets and any associated graphs from one package to another and being able to adjust the raw numbers and the graphs after the document is in the new program. A number of spreadsheets such as SuperCalc are just as good as Lotus 1–2–3. Actually, in this category of spreadsheet, the best is the one with the most recent release. Each adds the features that the other added in its most recent release, and then adds a few more. Either one of these spreadsheets will satisfy the needs of most librarians.

There are both more and less powerful spreadsheets that will meet the needs of some librarians. A new class of spreadsheets is now being designed to take advantage of the 386 chip. If you do not know what a 386 chip is, you probably do not need one of this new category of spreadsheet. Basically, the original IBM

PC used a 8086 chip as its processor. The IBM AT and AT-compatibles use an 80286 (that is, a 286) chip. The 386 is just the next most powerful step up in the evolutionary process. At this writing it appears that these new programs will be a revolutionary step rather than an evolutionary step in spreadsheets. However, only the power users who use very large spreadsheets will really need them, at least for the near future.

The other end of the spectrum is where many more librarians currently can be found. Librarians, who occasionally process numbers in a spreadsheet, may find all the power they need in some of the spreadsheets written to be used with some of the more popular word-processing packages. For example, librarians who are currently familiar with the commands of WordPerfect and occasionally need to use a spreadsheet, would be well advised to try PlanPerfect. Many of the basic commands are identical, and this should shorten the learning curve needed to become productive in a spreadsheet. However, a librarian who is already familiar with a more powerful spreadsheet such as Lotus 1–2–3 or SuperCalc probably would not be satisfied in moving to a somewhat limited spreadsheet such as PlanPerfect. Each has its niche in libraries. If one selects programs with care, the resulting files can be moved from one program to another as it becomes necessary to do so.

DATABASES

Librarians should be familiar with databases. Library catalogs have long been some of the most complex databases in existence. More recently, commercial electronic databases have become a prominent feature of information services. Database software for personal computers such as dBase can be used to create smaller databases that have most of the same properties of the databases mentioned above. They can be bibliographic (for example, journal want lists or bibliographies), mailing lists, supply inventories, client research interests, and so on. The entries can be indexed by any field. Boolean searches can be conducted. Again, the claim that "If you can dream it, you can do it" applies almost literally.

DESK ORGANIZERS

Desktop organizers are bundled packages of utility programs that can help librarians organize their time and their desktops. Such packages typically include a calendar, a calculator, an address book, and a list of telephone numbers. Side Kick and WordPerfect Library are examples of such groups of programs. Usually most of these programs are active in the memory of the computer. This allows them to be activated while the librarian is in the midst of running other programs. For example, if you are in the middle of a long word-processing document and you need to consult a calculator or schedule a meeting on your calendar, you can go to the calculator (or calendar) without having to save the document you are processing. After you have finished dealing with your interruption, you can return directly to the point in the document where you were processing. Some of the calendars have "to-do lists" which allow you to make a list of tasks to be performed on specific days. These lists can be very unforgiving. If you do not complete the tasks (and tell the computer that you did so), the task will automatically be moved to your list of priorities for the next day.

PROJECT MANAGEMENT

In many ways project management does for a project what a desktop organizer does for the time of a librarian. It asks for data about each stage or each component of a project. Then it indicates when each step must be initiated if all the parts are going to come together to complete the project in the minimum amount of time. Usually the costs of the project are budgeted for and reconciled as well. This software is definitely worth investigating if the library is initiating significant renovation, automation, or projects of similar complexity.

GRAPHICS

Many librarians are already familiar with simple graphics programs such as Print Shop or News Room Pro. These packages are useful in producing banners, signs, and other documents that draw from extensive libraries of predesigned graphic icons to enliven text documents. This is one area where the Macintosh has built its reputation. Although software for IBM-type personal computers has considerably narrowed the gap, librarians who have an extensive need to produce graphic images may be well advised to investigate the capabilities of the Mac.

DESKTOP PUBLISHING

More complex page-layout techniques will be required as librarians begin to realize the full capacity of desktop publishing. The integration of text and graphics will both challenge the ingenuity of the librarians and allow an integration of many of the various pieces of software discussed above. Because of its graphics handling capability, the Macintosh has a significant role to play in desktop publishing. The advantage of IBM-compatible software in other areas allows IBM to be competitive as well.

PRESENTATION

Presentation software, such as Show Partner and Storyboard, is similar to desktop publishing, but the end product is different. It is used to create presentations that can be stored on a computer disc. In addition to slides to be used to supplement a speech, the software allows reports to be distributed on a disc. This is particularly useful if graphic information needs to be conveyed. Demonstrations and interactive tutorials can be created. Even animation and sound can be incorporated.

Storyboard is the closest to a standard of compatibility for the exchange of icon files, both commercially produced and those created by the individual. Therefore, it is important that the package you buy can convert individual pictures to and from Storyboard. Unfortunately, the IBM package, of which Storyboard is a part, may not have some of the features offered by some of its competitors.

STATISTICS

Statistics software is available for personal computers. Versions of the mainframe mainstays, SPSS and SAS, are available, as well as packages designed specifically for microcomputers. If you are familiar with statistical analysis in the mainframe environment, you may wish to stay with the micro version of the same product. Otherwise, many other options exist, generally at a more modest price.

As more and more librarians become involved in research, this capability will become more prevalent. In addition, the tables and charts that can be prepared with such packages make them ideal to arrange data for management reports.

CONNECTIVITY

In some ways the personal computer revolution has come full circle. The speed with which the revolution spread was a testimony to the need for individuals to be able to control computing rather than letting computing control them. Clerical functions were made more productive by the early mainframe-based automation efforts. However, the mainframe was such an expensive resource that people had to be scheduled to maximize the productivity of the machine rather than the machine being scheduled to maximize the productivity of the individual.

Stand-alone microcomputers brought control of computing to the individual professional. For a while that was sufficient. Now, however, many of us realize that the full potential of the microcomputer revolution will not be realized unless we connect the stand-alone workstations to each other and to the mainframe. If the 1980s have been the decade of the stand-alone personal computer, the 1990s promise to be the decade in which we connect them together in local area networks (LANs). The next step will be to connect the LANs to campus networks connected to national networks, which in turn are connected to international networks.

Electronic mail will become a more natural part of life in the library environment. Information that is now shared only via a "Nike Network" (that is, a person running from one computer to another carrying data on a floppy disc) will be accessible instantly via an electronic network. One example of the potential for enhancement in productivity is the ability to call up simultaneously the electronic calendars of several librarians. This will greatly simplify the task of identifying possible meeting times. In addition, we will gain more efficiency as we become more proficient in downloading and reusing information from large databases such as Online Computer Library Center (OCLC), Research Libraries Information Network (RLIN), DIALOG, and the new Compact Disc—Read Only Memory (CD-ROM) products. From a single workstation we will have access to all the above, plus the library's own on-line files such as the catalog, the serials holdings file, the on-order file, the payment files, the circulation files, and so on, as well as all the personal productivity tools discussed above.

The full potential for such networking will not be realized in this century. We will have electronic mail; however, the capability to transmit video, voice, and data simultaneously will come much slower. In all our progress toward capabilities such as connectivity and large file servers, we must make sure we do not relinquish control of personal computing and allow the network managers to become as powerful as were the mainframe managers of the 1970s. We must remember that the networks exist to facilitate the personal productivity of professionals.

All of this offers much potential for librarians as we develop the workstations that will allow us to play an important role in an information society. On our campuses we must provide the information services and library resources that will enrich the curriculum for students and will make teachers and researchers more effective in their information-gathering activities.

PUTTING IT ALL TOGETHER

Personal productivity software for microcomputers is an excellent example of the whole being more than the sum of its parts. For example, it would be difficult to code data for statistical analysis directly into a program such as SPSS. However, it is relatively easy to enter the data into a database system such as dBase or a spreadsheet program such as SuperCalc. The data file can then be output into a DOS text file which can be read by SPSS. Tables created by SPSS can then be inserted into a word-processing document in WordPerfect or into a presentation being assembled in Show Partner. The possibilities are endless. The librarian's microcomputer tool kit needs to contain many instruments. Real productivity is knowing how to choose the right tool to do the job at hand.

Three phases are generally accepted as necessary before the full benefits of any new technology are realized:

1. First, we use a new technology to do faster what we are already doing.
2. Next, we find new things to do.
3. Finally, the technology changes our lifestyle.

In our adoption of microcomputer software into libraries, most of us are now somewhere in phase 1 or phase 2. Word processing has allowed us to create documents faster than we were previously able. Spreadsheets have allowed us to balance our budgets faster than before. We now have ways to improve our oral presentations. We are starting to find entirely new things. It is too early to ascertain how all this will change our work- and lifestyle.

REFERENCES

Brogan, D. ''An Ambitious Addition to Word Processing.'' *Chicago Tribune*, Sept. 4, 1988, sec. 7, p. 5.

Glossbrenner, A. 1984. *How to Buy Software: The Master Guide to Picking the Right Program*. New York: St. Martin's Press.

18

CD-ROM in a Small- to Medium-Sized Academic Library

Deon Knickerbocker

Information and its control or access has become big business. The ''information explosion,'' coupled with innovations in computer and related technologies, has made information available as never before in history. In fact, ''knowledge, once seen as a national treasure, property of all for the furtherance of our society and democracy, is now defined as information, a commodity, which can be bought, sold, and owned'' (Herther 1987: 56). Libraries, which have long considered themselves caretakers and repositories of knowledge, are now in the position of having to decide how best to handle all the new means of access to information. After all, information stored is of no use unless it is retrievable. ''A record, if it is to be useful . . . must be continuously extended, it must be stored, and above all it must be consulted'' (Bush 1986: 5). How are librarians to consult all the records now available? There are several options: among them are print sources, on-line services, and CD-ROMS. I propose in this chapter to discuss aspects of CD-ROM (Compact disc—read only memory) technology, which may be of interest to librarians, particularly those in a small- to medium-sized academic library.

Librarians are accustomed to dealing with information. For years information was available in print form only, and it was an awesome and often frustrating task to delve through reams of paper and acres of books to find what was needed. When on-line searching capabilities came along, libraries were early and eager subscribers. Suddenly a personal computer and a telephone line were all the equipment necessary for access to immense databases of information. On-line searching seemed like the answer to many problems. It provided current, extensive access to information in many fields. Unfortunately, it has its drawbacks. One difficulty is that one needs training in order to take effective and economical advantage of the service. Access is limited to those with the training, generally librarians. The need for training not only limits searching capabilities, but it also means that valuable professional time must be spent on each search. That time means cost, another drawback. A user is charged for all the time spent searching on-line. Different databases have different cost structures, but all of them can result in considerable expense for a complex search.

The expense involved has led to debate on free versus fee information. Should librarians be in the business of selling access to information? Generally speaking, librarians said no, but they were left with the problem of too little money and a great demand for expensive services. It is conceivable that the expense involved would mean that only industry and government would be able to afford access. Arguments raged about whether we could allow an "information elite" to develop, and about what could be done to ensure ready availability of access to information by the nonwealthy. This debate continues, and will continue as long as access to information remains an expensive process.

Access seemed destined to remain expensive until recently, when CD-ROMs were introduced. The information storage capacity and ease of access made possible by these little discs has the potential to change the way we view information access.

CD-ROM technology grew out of the compact disc audio market in the early 1980s as its potential as a medium for the distribution of large quantities of digital data became clear. Timing was important in this development; CD technology had to coincide with the general availability of personal computers to make it at all viable. Leonard Laub points out that in late 1984, after the PC market had begun to stabilize, several brands of CD-ROM drives were unveiled as prototypes. It was not until 1985 that commercial drives and subsystems were released, along with the first wave of CD-ROM databases (1986: 53).

CD-ROMs are in many ways a remarkable medium for the storage of information. They are durable, compact, and hold an incredible amount of information. Made of a polycarbonate material coated with a layer each of aluminum and plastic acrylic, a disc is virtually indestructible. The top transparent, acrylic layer prevents scratching and retards wear. Data is stored on the disc as a spiral track of microscopic pits. Judith Roth explains that CD-ROM drives read the information contained on the disc by focusing low-powered laser beams on the microscopic pits. An optical unit measures the pits' reflectivity back as a binary signal that can be read by a computer (1986: 8).

A single 4.72-inch disc stores 550 megabytes of data, the equivalent of 1,500 floppy discs, or 250,000 pages. Any piece of information on the disc can be located within a few seconds. Compact discs permit random access, with the capability of indexing every single word in a database. The potential is enormous, but there are problems.

One major problem is lack of standardization. Physical recording standards that specify the number of data blocks on a disc, their length, the location of codes, and so on, are fairly well established by two manufacturers, N. V. Phillips and Sony Corp. Logical standards of how information files are organized and reported to the computer are not well established. Basic logical disc standards have been proposed, however, by a group of people calling themselves the High Sierra Group (HSG). Although these standards are not universal or official, they are a step in the right direction, and should be considered when purchasing a CD-ROM system. They are expected to become an American national standard. To that end, librarians have become involved in the National Information Standards Organization (NISO), which is working on developing standards for CD-ROM data file structure. This CD-ROM committee hopes to help expedite the interchangeability of future technology. The lack of official standardization means that some software will only operate with very specific hardware, and vice versa. Such difficulties as these will have to be reconciled before the industry can be truly accessible and successful. Most users cannot afford separate hardware for each CD-ROM product they may wish to purchase. This is particularly true of most libraries, which function on limited budgets at best.

There are many CD-ROM products on the market today with specific applications to libraries. In fact, as reported by Carol Tenopir, in June 1987 there were over 100 different CD products for the library market (1987: 62). Before a librarian decides which of these products would best suit the needs of the particular library and its patrons, he or she must determine if CD-ROM as a medium would be suitable. When the same or similar material is available in different formats, purchasing decisions may be difficult. For example, ERIC (Educational Resources Information Center) documents are currently available in three formats: print, on-line, and CD-ROM. Academic libraries will already have access to ERIC documents via print sources. The great advantages of print indexes are that they are already available and paid for, and many more than one patron can use them simultaneously. When I say they are paid for, I mean just that. The library owns the material and keeps it even if it should decide to cancel its subscription. Print indexes are not, however, necessarily current. Their indexing is, in fact, often six months behind.

The ERIC file is also available on-line from BRS and Dialog to name just two sources. A major advantage of on-line searching is currency. Both search systems (BRS and Dialog) update their ERIC database monthly. Another advantage to on-line searching as opposed to print indexes is the ability to do complex searches using Boolean search techniques. By using linking terms such as "and," "or," and "not," the searcher can search indexes in ways that are not available using print sources. One can search for material dealing with relationships between two, three, or more disparate terms. For example, one can check on the relationship between stress and intonational patterns in adult speech. The ability to perform complex searches opens up new opportunities for research.

CD-ROM is a third alternative to print and on-line sources. CD-ROM delivers much information in a compact, durable form, but the initial cost can be fairly high. In 1989 the complete starter set for ERIC on Silverplatter was $1,200, which includes a quarterly subscription and archival set of two discs but does not include hardware. In the second year, the cost drops to $650. Additional copies of the annual subscription are $250 each, again excluding hardware, which can add $4,500 to the total cost. Once again, it is a one-user-per-workstation situation, with each workstation taking space and money.

CD-ROM, however, varies from on-line searching in that with minimal instruction patrons can use the system, and they can take as long as necessary to complete their search because there is no on-line charge. Once the system is in place, searches are basically free. To look at it another way, the original price is fixed, so the more the service is used, the lower the average cost per use. In a typical academic library, ERIC searches are in great demand. When one considers the cost of doing numerous on-line searches as compared to the same number of CD-ROM searches, there may be a distinct advantage to CD-ROM. If a library has kept a record of on-line expenses in various databases, it should not be too difficult to determine the difference.

It is thought by some that "CDROM technology . . . offers a new method of information delivery which will eliminate the elitism of online information delivery and allow all library patrons to access databases which were heretofore only available through the online terminal . . . at a fixed cost" (Pooley 1986: 40). Boolean searching is available on CD-ROM as it is on-line. In fact, the storage capacity of these discs is such that it is often possible to index every word of an article or report and so insure retrieval that is vastly superior to a print source.

CD-ROMs may complement or substitute for print or on-line sources in certain instances, depending on the needs and resources of a particular library. A library may decide to maintain a subscription to a print index and have CD-ROM and on-line access as well. The print index is a permanent fixture, and remains valuable for searches of a simple nature. The CD-ROM then can be used to good advantage with more complex searches, without incurring the expense associated with on-line searching.

Following is a list of some of the products now available on CD-ROM that may be of interest in an academic library. The list is not exhaustive since new products are being developed all the time. Some of these databases are available from more than one source. I will only list one source, since my purpose primarily is to show the range of databases available, not the number of producers.

1. *LISA on Silverplatter*
   Library and Information Science Abstracts from 1969–1986, with annual updates. Publishers suggest that it be offered as a supplement to, rather than a replacement for, the printed service. A 20% discount on the purchase of the printed source is offered when CD-ROM is obtained.
2. *Medline on Silverplatter*
   The entire MEDLINE database of the National Library of Medicine, updated quarterly.

3. *ERIC on Silverplatter*
   Resources in Education (RIE) and Current Index to Journals in Education (CIJE), with quarterly updates.
4. *PsychLIT on Silverplatter*
   Citations on psychology and behavioral sciences, updated quarterly.
5. *Sociofile on Silverplatter*
   Contents of the world's journals in sociology since 1974, updated semiannually.
6. *NTIS on Silverplatter*
   Citations to government-sponsored research and development reports, produced by the National Technical Information Service, updated quarterly.
7. *AGRICOLA on Silverplatter*
   Publications relating to all aspects of agriculture, updated quarterly.
8. *PAIS on CD-ROM*
   Entries from *PAIS Bulletin* and *PAIS Foreign Language Index* from 1972–82, updated quarterly.
9. *Code of Federal Regulations and Federal Register*
   1985–86, updated annually.
10. *Compact Disclosure*
    Corporate profiles for more than 10,000 public companies, updated quarterly.
11. *Books in Print Plus* and *Ulrich's Plus*
    Material from the print sources on CD-ROM, updated quarterly.
12. *BIBLIOFILE*
    Complete English-language MARC catalog file, all titles from 1965, plus popular titles since 1900, updated quarterly.
13. *Grolier Electronic Encyclopedia*
    A 20-volume encyclopedia on CD-ROM; full text of the *Academic American Encyclopedia*.
14. *Wilsondisc*
    There are currently twelve databases available, each on a separate disc, updated quarterly. Starting dates range from 1982–1984. The databases included are:

    Applied Science and Technology index

    Art index

    Biography index

    Business Periodicals index

    Cumulative Book index

    Education index

    General Science index

    Humanities index

    Index to Legal Periodicals

Library Literature

Reader's Guide to Periodical Literature

Social Sciences index

Please consult the publishers for current prices on all CD-ROM products.

There are other databases available on CD-ROM, and many more will undoubtedly become available as the demand increases. The ones I have listed will be of particular interest to academic libraries, but others will be very specialized, dealing perhaps with cancer research or environmental problems. It will be up to the library or business to decide which databases best suit the needs of their patrons.

Obviously, there are a wide variety of subject areas already covered on CD-ROM. There is also a considerable difference in the cost, so each database must be considered separately. The librarian should keep in mind that CD-ROM may not be a simple replacement for a print or on-line medium but may rather serve as a supplement to frequently used databases. "It is a whole new medium with enough differences from existing media to require a reexamination of appropriate products and markets" (Meyer 1986: 468).

Librarians in a small- to medium-sized library will have a fairly accurate idea which indexes are most heavily used by their patrons and themselves. They also should, if they do on-line searching, have a very good idea of how much money they are spending for those searches in any given database. Such knowledge will serve them well when they attempt to decide which if any databases to obtain on CD-ROM.

To return to the earlier example of ERIC, an academic library may well decide that it would be advantageous to have this database in three forms: print, on-line, and CD-ROM. By the same token, a hospital library may decide the same about MEDLINE. Print sources are very handy for several patrons to use at once. On-line data searching is best for truly up-to-date information. CD-ROM provides access to complex search strategies without the exorbitant cost of an on-line search. It can also be helpful and cost-efficient to work out a search strategy on CD-ROM, and when it is perfected, to go on-line with the same strategy for more current information. This approach means that the searcher can work with various terms and combinations thereof on the CD-ROM and see what retrieves the most pertinent information. Occasionally experimentation with terms and combinations will take some time. Once the search strategy is determined, it is fairly simple to duplicate the search on-line and the time-consuming, costly part of the process is greatly reduced.

So far I have primarily discussed indexes and other avenues of access to information and how they adapt to CD-ROM. There is also discussion and speculation in the literature about the possible benefits of storing archival materials and runs of periodicals on CD-ROM. Space is becoming a critical problem for many libraries. They are finding it difficult to absorb new books, much less store long runs of periodicals. Great masses of new material are fighting for space with older but nevertheless valuable sources of information. Libraries have increasingly turned to microfilm in an effort to conserve space and still maintain access to materials. Unfortunately, microfilm has its drawbacks. It is rather fragile, a reel of microfilm does not hold a great amount of material, and people do not like to use it. CD-ROM as an alternative is appealing because it is virtually indestructible, it makes possible the storage of hundreds of thousands of pages in a very small space, and people enjoy using it because it is connected to a PC and a printer.

Dave Biesel lists some advantages of putting a continuous sequence of a journal on a CD-ROM disc. He says that it saves valuable shelf space for books and serials that should not be on a CD-ROM disc, and it can aid in the preservation of material that, in some cases, is rapidly deteriorating. Periodical holdings in CD-ROM also can allow greater flexibility in interlibrary loan if you have several copies of the disc to circulate, and it would be possible for students or instructors to check out the complete file of a journal in this way. Students or instructors can even buy the complete file if they so wish (Biesel 1986: 211).

The practicality of Biesel's last points depends to a great extent on how many discs are sold. As with any market, availability and demand influence the price of the product. The factor of supply and demand is further reinforced with CD-ROMs by the economic facts of production. The major expense in producing a CD-ROM is the development of the master disc, which can cost over $30,000. Once it is developed, however, individual copies are quite inexpensive to produce. Therefore, the more copies are sold, the more copies are amortized against the original cost of production, so the lower the price per copy. It would obviously be to the consumer's advantage to have CD-ROM technology become immensely popular. Not only would the price per disc drop, but an established market would mean that more producers would be presenting material on CD-ROM, thus increasing the variety of databases and indexes.

Keeping all these points in mind, it is obvious that there are many things to be considered before a library purchases CD-ROMs. Given some budget flexibility, it is very tempting to jump on the bandwagon and embrace CD-ROMs as a marvelous new avenue to information storage and retrieval. It is important, though, to keep in mind that there will be special requirements that must be met in order to receive maximum benefits. Anticipated use must be heavy enough to justify the prices of software and hardware. The scope and immediacy of information needs in the particular database must be considered. On-line searching capabilities should perhaps also be available if truly current information is required. The number of people who may require access to the material at the same time should be calculated. For many databases, print access will also be necessary, or even vital. Ideally, the equipment should be available to answer quick reference questions, so it should be put where it can be easily used. Security of the computer, the CD-ROM drive, and the CD-ROM discs must be considered. It is possible to lock up the computer and the CD-ROM drive, and leave only the screen, keyboard, and printer open to public access. If the library decides on public access, location of the equipment may be a problem. "CD-ROM is not currently a replacement for other existing forms of computer memory. It fulfills different requirements. As a low-cost, high-capacity, mass data distribution medium, it opens new prospects" (Murphy 1985: 24). It should be carefully considered by each individual library. Once a library has decided to purchase CD-ROM, it is then in the best interest of the library to take an active interest in the industry and promote it whenever possible to insure that it reaches its full potential.

With a fairly new technology like CD-ROM, its direction is still somewhat undecided. Because of their nature, libraries are in a good position to help determine the future development of CD-ROM products. Carol Tenopir feels that "the library market is strong because it has a base of installed CD drives and many libraries are eager to try out new information technologies" (Tenopir 1987: 62). There are already CD products on the market for cataloging support, on-line public access catalogs, collection development, and reference support. Of these four areas, reference support currently enjoys the largest number of products, probably because many databases had already been developed for on-line searching and consequently were already available in machine-readable form. It is important that librarians give thought to ways in which CD-ROM could benefit them and their patrons, and make their wishes known to publishers. Because of the nature of their work and experience, there is good reason for librarians' thoughts on these issues to be taken seriously. They are, after all, society's experts on information storage and retrieval, and are also quite likely to be the heaviest users of the technology.

Nancy Melin draws some apt conclusions about the library and CD-ROM. In spite of its perceived limitations, CD-ROM offers great potential for library use. Some of its particular advantages are as follows. Databases on CD-ROM may be searched repeatedly, even on a 24-hour basis, with the distinct advantage of actually increasing the cost-benefit ratio. No telecommunications charges or connect charges are incurred; the user may search at leisure; and the librarian need not be a search intermediary in order to reduce costs. CD-ROM databases offer the possibility of simultaneous multiuser access, eliminating the problem of duplicating important and frequently used materials. CD-ROM is an excellent storage medium, as it reduces the amount of space required to house vast amounts of materials. CD-ROM may be effectively used to preserve rare or fragile items even as it makes it possible for countless users to have access to them (Melin 1986: 516).

We always come back to the fact that decisions on CD-ROM technology must be made on an individual basis by each library and with regard to each database. "The decision to purchase CD-ROM databases requires a commitment from librarians to adapt to a new technology, to approach bibliographic instruction from a new perspective, and to stay abreast of developments in a rapidly changing field" (Graves 1987: 393). It also requires a decision on the part of individual libraries about whether this new technology is appropriate for their needs and their patrons at this time. Even if the answer is no, librarians should be aware of the possibilities should circumstances change.

REFERENCES

Biesel, Dave. 1986. "Old Books—New Technologies." *The Reference Librarian* 15 (Fall): 209–15.

Bush, Vannevar. 1986. "As We May Think." In *CD ROM: The New Papyrus*. Edited by Steve Lambert and Suzanne Ropiequet, pp. 3–20. Redmond, Wash.: Microsoft.

Graves, Gail T. 1987. "Planning for CD-ROM in the Reference Department." *College and Research Libraries News* 48 (July/August): 393–400.

Herther, Nancy K. 1987. "CD-ROM and Information Dissemination: An Update." *Online* 11 (March): 56–63.

Laub, Leonard. 1986. "What is CD-ROM?" In *CD ROM: The New Papyrus*. Edited by Steve Lambert and Suzanne Ropiequet, pp. 53–60. Redmond, Wash.: Microsoft.

Melin, Nancy. 1986. "The New Alexandria." In *CD ROM: The New Papyrus*. Edited by Steve Lambert and Suzanne Ropiequet, pp. 509–16. Redmond, Wash.: Microsoft.

Meyer, Rick. 1986. "From Online to Ondisc." In *CD ROM: The New Papyrus*. Edited by Steve Lambert and Suzanne Ropiequet, pp. 467–81. Redmond, Wash.: Microsoft.

Murphy, Brower. 1985. "CD-ROM and Libraries." *Library Hi-Tech* 3, no. 10: 21–26.

Pooley, Christopher G. 1986. "Silverplatter Brings CDROM to the Reference Desk." *Database* 10 (August): 40–42.

Roth, Judith Paris, ed. 1986. *Essential Guide to CDROM*. Westport, Conn.: Meckler.

Tenopir, Carol. 1987. "Publications on CD-ROM." *Library Journal* 112 (Sept. 15): 62–63.

19

Electronic Book Ordering

Barbara B. Hunsberger

One of the primary concerns for all libraries in the 1980s (including university, college, public, special, or school libraries) is the automation of various library functions. Limited only by imagination and funding, libraries are utilizing computers from simple microcomputers for word processing to complex mainframes for complete integrated systems.

The potential for automating book acquisitions has been under discussion since the early 1960s. The size and cost of the hardware thirty years ago, however, prohibited most libraries from seriously considering the use of computers. There are two major reasons for the earlier lack of systems offered by networks or vendors. First, acquisitions procedures are much more complicated than might be determined at first glance. Various types of procedures are necessary because not all materials are acquired in the same manner. Second, there is a great deal of variance among the different purchasing procedures and requirements established at the local level over which the library staff has little or no control. Circulation and cataloging policies and procedures were largely within the control of the library staff, which led to circulation and cataloging functions having higher priorities in most institutions (Bierman 1980: 171). The resultant lack of software and high cost of hardware delayed the automation of acquisitions functions for most libraries until the 1980s.

Today all sizes and types of computers are available and within the budgetary means of most libraries. Software development led by vendors of automated library systems, both commercial and noncommercial, and by book wholesalers with in-house computer systems, have put electronic book ordering within the financial possibility of most libraries, regardless of size or budget. The options for electronic book ordering range from in-house development, which is very expensive, to offerings from bibliographic utilities such as the Online Computer Library Center (OCLC) Acquisitions Subsystem, stand-alone integrated library automation systems like the Northwestern Online Total Integrated System (NOTIS), and software programs from individual book wholesalers (Boss 1984: 40–41).

Various academic libraries developed in-house automation procedures as early as the late 1950s. The early systems "tended to be order/receipt control systems or funds accounting systems. Only a few combined these systems" (Boss 1984: 42). By the mid–1960s, more extensive automation methods were developed in-house by many large academic libraries. Many of these systems were able "to control the various aspects of ordering: producing purchase orders; issuing open order reports; printing in-process reports; and summarizing expenditures by purchase order, vendor, unit of the library or requestor" (Boss 1984: 43). Richard Boss further states that the greatest drawback was that the systems operated in batch mode and the output was solely in hard-copy form at fixed intervals.

Although many acquisitions functions were automated by the 1970s, the majority of the systems were not comprehensive due to the technical and financial limitations on the libraries that developed them (Boss 1984: 44). In the 1970s, several book vendors supplied comprehensive systems to run on local computer systems, and by late 1981, "approximately one out of five libraries with annual acquisitions budgets of more than $200,000 were using an automated acquisitions system" (Boss 1984: 44–45).

During this same period, bibliographic utilities were also developing comprehensive automated acquisitions systems. By late 1981, twenty libraries were using the OCLC system, while more than thirty other libraries had placed orders for it (Boss 1984: 45). Other bibliographic utilities were also offering comprehensive systems to their members or had them under development.

The attractive feature of a utility-based acquisitions system, such as the one developed by OCLC, is the database upon which the entire system was built. The OCLC "database, which includes the Library of Congress Cataloging in Publication (CIP), has proved to be an excellent resource for bibliographic verification prior to ordering" (Ra 1985: 84). The OCLC system provides for electronic ordering to numerous vendors and publishers. The process for placing orders is simple and efficient. The title to be ordered is searched for in the bibliographic database and appears automatically on an order work form. Then, various items of information are added such as the vendor, fund to be charged, number of copies, destination, and so on (Ra 1985: 85). Equipment costs for the utility systems are nonexistent if the library is already a member of the cataloging system, but a basic fee is charged for each title ordered. Each library must evaluate these ongoing costs to determine whether such systems are cost effective for them.

By the 1980s the technological advances made in microcomputers had resulted in lowered costs of hardware along with substantial increases in speed and memory capacity. Software development kept pace with the hardware advances, which resulted in a proliferation of microcomputers in schools, homes, and businesses nationwide. Furthermore, much of the software was designed for the novice computer user or individuals with no background in computer programming. Book vendors were also updating their own computer systems, and by the mid–1980s they began offering inexpensive electronic access to their company databases for the ordering of library books.

This brief historical overview discusses the progress made in the general area of automating library acquisitions over the past thirty years. However, the purpose of this chapter is to limit the discussion to electronic book ordering and not to encompass the entire realm of library acquisitions. Electronic book ordering means that a library places orders directly from an in-house computer via telephone communication to the computer of a book wholesaler or vendor.

The first question to ask is not whether a library can automate acquisitions functions, because almost any library can, but whether a library *should* automate acquisitions. What are the motivating factors for a small academic library to automate book-ordering functions? Certainly the trend in libraries has not been to ever-larger budgets. In fact, when comparing costs for books and serials, many libraries have increased the percentage of the budget spend for serials at the expense of the percentage spent for books. The addition of new technologies such as on-line database searching and CD-ROM products has also come at the expense of the book budget in many institutions. Therefore, if there is less money for books, why do more and more small libraries see a necessity for the automation of book-ordering functions?

Richard Boss indicates a number of motivating factors common to many institutions that choose the option to automate acquisitions. ''Common motivations include:

1. Reducing ordering backlogs
2. Reducing acquisitions costs
3. Containing acquisitions costs
4. Speeding order writing and/or receipt of materials
5. Improving funds control
6. Expanding a single function automated system into an integrated system
7. Improving management information
8. Achieving compatibility with resource sharing partners
9. Committing the library to the use of new technology'' (Boss 1984: 45).

Boss further emphasizes that whatever the reason for automating, the library administration must be honest with itself, even if a study should suggest that automation of a particular function is not necessary (Boss 1984: 45).

In order to have interactive electronic ordering between libraries and book vendors, there must also be motivating factors in the book trade industry for the automation of various functions. Sharon Bonk states that "it is observable from services and products offered and bookseller internal order processing systems that their concerns are decreased order turnaround time, lower per-item costs of processing, and increased volume of business with static or decreased staff" (Bonk 1983: 21). During the 1980s, several booksellers and book vendors have developed methods of electronic ordering and are offering these services to libraries, some at no cost. The larger vendors are interested in supplying electronic services to libraries as long as the product does not have to be unique to a specific institution.

Motivating factors for electronic book ordering do exist for libraries, and software programs have been developed by book vendors that make electronic ordering feasible. Several of the larger vendors provide the software programs at no charge. The Baker & Taylor Company was one of the first to offer an automated acquisitions system to libraries with its BATAB system in 1969. BATAB was a batch software package designed to run on a local mainframe computer. Over the years, Baker & Taylor has developed a simplified electronic ordering device called BaTaPhone. The BaTaPhone system is a hand-held terminal that allows the operator to input the order number, quantity, and International Standard Book Number (ISBN) into the system. The terminal can hold just over 400 ISBN numbers. The back of the BaTaPhone terminal is a modem to which the operator attaches a telephone receiver and transmits the order via a toll-free number to the Baker & Taylor computer. Verbal confirmation of receipt of the order is received by the operator upon successful transmission. Within approximately three days, Baker & Taylor mails the library a written confirmation either with or without multiple order forms. When the BaTaPhone system was inaugurated in 1984, the cost for the system without multiple order forms was $275 and with the forms was $50 additional.

In 1986, Baker & Taylor offered new acquisitions services designed to run on several different personal computers. The BaTaSYSTEMS acquisitions software and services included three components: order, search and order, and acquisitions. The order component is an electronic book-ordering software program for personal computers that allows book orders to be keyed in by ISBN number for toll-free transmission to Baker & Taylor. Bibliographic data is then transmitted back to the library for on-site printing of multiple order forms and confirmation reports. The hardware necessary for this electronic ordering package is an IBM, APPLE, or TRS–80 personal computer with a single disc drive and 64K RAM, or compatible machines. Additional required hardware is a 1,200-baud modem and a printer with a minimum 80-column capacity. The introductory cost for the order portion of the system was $325 in 1986. Multiple-part order forms cost extra. By 1987, Baker & Taylor no longer charged the basic fee for the electronic ordering software. At the present time, confirmation lists can be printed on-line within approximately fifteen minutes of placement of the order, and the first shipment of books is received within five days.

The other two components of the acquisitions system require per-hour connect charges. The full acquisitions systems, which includes electronic book ordering, invoice transmission, local automated fund accounting, and management reports, also requires a personal computer with a hard disc.

Other booksellers such as Midwest Library Services, Blackwell North America, and Ingram Library Services also offer various options for electronic book ordering and additional acquisitions services. Costs vary depending on the level of service requested by the library. Several of the larger book vendors offer electronic ordering at no cost in the same way as the Baker & Taylor Company.

Small academic library administrators must consider several factors when considering the implementation of a vendor-based electronic ordering system. Librarians should analyze the costs of their current systems, whether manual or automated, and determine whether electronic ordering would result in savings of time and personnel costs (Bonk 1983: 24). In addition, serious consideration should be given to the present capabilities of booksellers for receiving orders on-line and the specific plans the individual booksellers have for the future (Bonk 1983: 24).

Equipment costs certainly will need to be evaluated carefully if the library lacks a personal computer capable of running the vendor's particular system. In considering equipment costs, however, librarians need to realize that the microcomputers in question can be used for shared functions such as word-processing and spreadsheets. Small academic libraries will not be using the system continuously throughout the day, and therefore the computer can be used for other functions or even shared with another department within the library.

If the library already uses one major vendor, does changing to electronic book ordering mean changing vendors? Will electronic ordering relieve an overburdened staff from typing order lists and multiple order forms? Does it mean looking for a new vendor, or does the good service of the present vendor override any consideration of automation? How much will electronic ordering require staff to batch work and change procedures? What is the most important factor to consider when choosing a vendor? These questions must be considered and answered to determine whether electronic book ordering will provide an efficient and fast method of acquiring library book materials.

The fact that a number of booksellers have entered into electronic book ordering indicates that sufficient customers (libraries) are interested in the service to make the development of the software profitable. In an era of reduced budgets and often reduced library support staffs, electronic book ordering allows a library to automate this particular function of acquisitions for relatively little cost. The computer training necessary to implement electronic book ordering is relatively simple and usually requires no outlay of training funds. After the initial outlay of funds for the equipment, the annual costs for maintaining many of the vendor-based electronic ordering systems is little or none.

An electronic ordering system that allows for the transmission of confirmation reports to be received on-line by the library saves time by the elimination of typing book lists and mailing an order to the book vendor. One hurdle in this procedure may be the institution's local purchasing authorities, since this method of ordering bypasses the purchasing department's approval for these book orders. As long as librarians can maintain satisfactory security for the authorization of order placement, purchasing officials should be able to accept electronic book ordering as an acceptable alternative method for ordering library materials. Since vendors require some kind of access code for the placement of orders, security should not present a problem for most institutions.

In conclusion, electronic book ordering can provide a small academic library with an efficient and cost-effective means of ordering library books. Staff time for the placement and typing of orders is reduced, as is turnaround time for the receipt of orders, and the initial outlay for equipment is low when compared to most automated systems. Some changes in ordering procedures may be required depending upon the vendor chosen; but the savings in staff time and the increased speed in delivery of materials will far outweigh any small inconveniences resulting from the change in procedures.

REFERENCES

Bierman, Kenneth J. 1980. "Vendor Systems and On-line Ordering." *Journal of Library Automation* 13 (September): 170–81.

Bonk, Sharon C. 1983. "Integrating Library and Book Trade Automation." *Information Technology and Libraries* 2 (March): 18–25.

Boss, Richard W. 1984. "Issues in Automating Acquisitions." In *Issues in Library Management*. White Plains, N.Y.: Knowledge Industry Publications, Inc.

Ra, Marsha H. 1985. "The OCLC Acquisitions Subsystem at the City College Library: An Appraisal." *Library Acquisitions: Theory and Practice* 9: 83–92.

20

Integrating New Services and Technology into the Library

Ronnie C. Swanner and Sallieann C. Swanner

Why should small academic libraries be involved with cable television, communications satellites, and other forms of media? The primary reason is to increase access to information. Few if any librarians would disagree that libraries are rapidly changing. Today's library provides much more than just books. The library's primary service should be to provide information and not documents. Computerized databases and audiovisual materials as well as printed library materials are valuable sources of information, and should be included in all academic libraries. Machines and the information they contain, not books, are becoming the library. To speak of a modern academic library today implies the extensive use of computers, videotape players, and laser discs. Libraries have finally entered the era of machines.

This chapter deals with technology and its impact on academic libraries. The goal is to identify the relevant technology for small academic libraries, to discuss the potential, as well as the advantages and disadvantages of each, and to describe the role that each will play in the future of academic libraries. The driving force behind the development of new programs and systems should not be simply the allure of new technology. Rather, libraries should continue to base their decisions about new ventures into telecommunications on the educational problems they are addressing. CD-ROM will not be discussed because it is included in another chapter.

The use of the computer and telecommunications by librarians to access databases outside the library is a very important and far-reaching development. In fact, it has changed the way that one views a "library," the "collection," and a "librarian." Immediate access to outside databases has broken down the barriers of space needs and resource budgets, and has brought us closer to the reality that access to information, not materials, is what libraries are all about. This chapter will discuss different methods of delivering information to the user through electronic technology.

FACSIMILE TECHNOLOGY

Facsimile is the technology that permits the transmission of documents or computer-generated images over telephone lines and their reconstruction as paper copies at another site. The concept of facsimile or fax dates from the nineteenth century, although practical applications did not develop until the 1920s. Since that time, newspaper publishers, police departments, military installations, and meteorological stations have widely used facsimile to transmit documents. Facsimile systems began to gain general use in the late 1950s. However, most libraries did not consider using a fax machine until the 1960s or early 1970s. At that time, facsimile transfer had to compete with the TWX and telex devices that many libraries already had for rapid document transfer.

The facsimile has the major advantage of not requiring the retyping of the document by a skilled operator. Fax systems require little operator training and will accept documents with both text and graphics. Despite these major advantages, facsimile systems gained little acceptance because the equipment proved to be unreliable, slow, and incapable of consistently satisfactory output, and the cost per page was quite high. During the 1960s and 1970s, a number of libraries began experimenting with fax machines primarily for use with interlibrary loan requests. Most of the experiments proved to be a disappointment for the reasons mentioned above, and many libraries eventually abandoned their fax machines. However, by the early 1980s facsimile technology had made significant improvements in equipment reliability, copy quality, transmission speed, and equipment compatibility. Today most medium to large businesses and government agencies have one or more facsimile transceivers. Still, many librarians who either had or heard of bad experiences with the older fax machines are reluctant to try the newer technology, and facsimile remains underutilized in libraries today. As the demand for high-speed document delivery intensifies, users of online bibliographic searching and other forms of automation will require expanded and improved interlibrary loans. Collaboration on joint projects with deadlines, such as grant writing, is also much more feasible when drafts can be exchanged on a daily basis among libraries. Facsimile once offered the promise of solving the library's document delivery problem, but until now has never met that expectation. With the vastly improved technology and the rapidly escalating costs of books and periodicals, facsimile should be reconsidered as an option for smaller academic libraries.

Today's machines are fast: Transmission time is as short as fifteen seconds per page, and they produce copies with 200 lines of resolution, which is twice the quality of the 1960s machines. While the cost per page of the older machines was often cited as a problem, the new machines have greatly reduced these costs. One study conducted over a period of one year in the state of Washington produced an average cost per page for the twenty participating libraries at $.36 (Moore 1988: 59).

Since it is necessary to have a fax machine at both the sending and receiving library, it is very important to know which other libraries have fax machines. At least two directories have become available. *Telefacsimile Sites in Libraries in the United States & Canada,* which is in its third edition, lists nearly 700 library fax numbers and such additional information as contact person, voice-phone number, and type of equipment. Compiled by C. Lee Jones, it is available at $18 from: CBR Consulting Services, Inc., P.O. Box 248, Buchanan Dam, Tex. 78609–0248. *The Official Faxsimile Users' Directory*, published in 1986 by FDP Associates in New York, lists approximately 400 libraries in alphabetical listings and an index under "Educational, Cultural, and Social Services." The price is $55, and orders may be addressed to 461 Park Ave. South, New York, N.Y. 10016.

The costs of transmissions sent during the evenings, when telephone rates are lower, is presently competitive with first-class postage rates, and facsimile transmission is much faster and more reliable. A high-quality machine such as the Harris/3M model 2110 or the Cannon 350 cost less than $2,500 to purchase. These machines can also be rented or leased for as little as $100 per month. Facsimile machines will likely be a very important tool in smaller academic libraries in the future.

PACKET SWITCHING

"Packets" are data units of 130 characters. Communications systems in which a series of computers are connected and used to move packets of information from one location to another are known as "packet switches."

Packet switching takes advantage of the fact that data communication users rarely utilize the entire capacity of a communication line. A packet switch provides users with a path to a computer within a network but does not necessarily provide a dedicated path. The path or line is shared among all the users who are connected to the network. Each user in the network is connected to other locations or nodes in the network by a series of trunk lines. These lines or paths are shared among all network members, who connect to one node directly or indirectly to other locations in the network through that node. The ability to control line sharing allows data exchange at less expensive rates than by dedicated lines. The fact that any of several paths between users can be used to transfer information also makes packet networks highly reliable.

PACKET RADIO NETWORKS

Packet radio represents a marriage between digital radio transmission and packet-switching techniques. Instead of transmitting packets across telephone wires or other types of point-to-point links, each participating location in a packet radio network can exchange packets across a radio channel. Although other methods of transmission can be used, the most common carrier for packet radio networks is through the Instructional Fixed Television Service (IFTS). IFTS is a set of 22 channels set aside for higher education and regulated by the FCC. These channels are assigned within the frequency range of 2.5 to 2.686 GHZ. These radio frequencies utilize microwave links which are essentially line-of-sight paths (a straight line with no visible obstructions in the path), and therefore the transmitting towers are usually situated on hills or tall buildings to minimize interference. The microwave links are usually placed no more than thirty miles apart because the curvature of the earth causes the signal to go into space at greater distances. As with other radio signals, atmospheric conditions affect the transmission of microwave signals. Therefore, any packet radio network must take distance, terrain, and atmospheric conditions into consideration when designing such a system. It may be necessary to design some locations as repeaters for other locations. However, this is easy to do since any location can either receive or transmit at any given time.

The development of low-cost, low-power, and reliable microwave equipment has brought this technology within consideration for many types of applications. When transmission volume is high and distances exceed twenty-five miles, packet radio networks utilizing microwave systems are usually less expensive than telecommunications options that require special cables. The construction cost for a microwave system is very high ($50,000 per microwave location), and is probably not practical for most libraries unless the transaction level will be quite high. However, in most locations, space on existing microwave systems can be obtained at a reasonable cost. In many areas, fire departments, television stations, police departments, railroad companies, or other public and private companies operate a system, and since a single microwave transmission can carry up to 1,800 voice channels, most systems operate at less than their maximum capacity. Therefore, libraries could lease space on existing systems at a fraction of the installation cost for a new system.

Packet switching can also utilize other types of communications systems, including the telephone lines and cable television systems. One existing network has even used shortwave radios as their communications link between libraries. Packet radio networks will likely play an important role in future communications for small academic libraries.

VIDEOTEXT

Videotext is text and graphic information that is transmitted by either telephone lines or cable television, or broadcast through the air waves. The information is usually received over standard television sets; however, some systems require that the television set be adapted to display the signal. A keypad is used to interact with the system. Videotext systems were one of the first experiments with two-way data communication. Neither the concept nor the technology of videotext is new. In the United States, experiments utilizing videotext technology were conducted as early as 1948. However, the British were the first to actually use the system in the early 1970s as a means of providing captioning services for the deaf. Other similar experiments took place in France in the early 1970s and in Canada in the later 1970s. The British Post Office (BPO) currently operates a system called Prestel which offers subscribers access to more than 450 information-providers. These information-providers provide databases and information services through the Prestel system. The British Library and several library associations provide information on Prestel. However, specific items cannot be requested or checked out through the system. Some publishers like Macmillan use Prestel to list new titles of books. Today, a number of videotext systems are in operation throughout the United States. However, they are mostly still in the experimental stage. Sears, Roebuck & Company in San Francisco plans to offer a catalog ordering service through a videotext service in late–1988.

Videotext can be used for instruction, news services, financial reports, electronic banking, and electronic mail. While the concept and technology are not new, the costs for these services have only recently dropped to a level that is affordable. Lower cost and increased availability make videotext a source of information that should not be overlooked by small academic libraries. However, it is likely that its primary value may actually have been its role as a pioneering format that opened up possibilities for future communication systems.

CABLE TELEVISION

When most of us think of cable television we think about access to many channels for our home television set. Few realize that cable television can provide libraries with an inexpensive distribution system for database searching and information files such as library holdings as well as audio and visual programs. While most television cables are one-way, two-way communication is possible through these cable systems. This two-way capability vastly increases the potential of the system, and the interactivity enhances the system's instructional and informational usefulness.

Many businesses and government organizations utilize cable television lines for various purposes, such as credit card and check verification and security systems. These organizations make use of an existing cable network and simply rent a part of the "cable space" or "band width" on which they transmit and receive data. Band width represents a certain percentage of the total amount of information capacity of the cable network. Many local companies do not utilize their full cable capabilities and are willing to sell cable space. One large county library system in Oregon, the Washington County Cooperative Library Service, utilizes the local cable television system as the communications system for their shared automated library system. The only hardware difference for using the cable system instead of telephone lines is the modem on the terminal. Instead of a modem that transmits a signal in the audible range, which is needed for telephone lines, the modem transmits an inaudible radio frequency (RF) signal. This RF signal is transmitted through the cable system and received by modems that are designed to receive a particular frequency.

The advantages of cable television telecommunications include:

- High-speed (9,600-baud) and high-quality signals;
- Rapid response times;
- Low operational costs;
- Local network maintenance; and
- Ease of adding new locations to the system.

The disadvantages of cable television telecommunications include:

- High start-up costs; and
- Instability of cable company ownership.

Cable television offers many opportunities to libraries as a low-cost distribution system for information, and in locations where cable television systems exist, those possibilities should not be overlooked by the small academic library.

OPTICAL DISC TECHNOLOGY

Optical disc technology utilizes a laser beam focused on pits impressed into the plastic surface of a round disc which is spun at a high speed. There are currently three types of optical disc products on the market: compact audio disc, video disc, and CD-ROM or Compact Disc–Read Only Memory. In spite of the tremendous potential of optical-disc technology, the acceptance of this format has been very slow.

The primary advantages of optical discs are:

- High picture and sound quality;
- High resistance to damage;
- Long life of the disc;
- Easy and rapid searching; and
- High storage capacity.

Compact Audio Disc

The compact audio disc was the first form of this technology to be accepted by the general public. Compact disc development has been largely due to the joint efforts of the Phillips Company in the Netherlands and Sony in Japan. Optical technology, developed by Phillips, merged with Sony's error-correction techniques to create the compact disc format. While Phillips first proposed the system in 1974, Phillips and Sony did not reach an agreement to collaborate until 1979, and the Compact Disc Audio System was announced one year later. However, the system was not introduced into the United States until 1983. Since that time it has become the dominant audio format. Its phenomenal sales during this five-year period has made it the most successful electronic product ever introduced. Today, CD sales have pushed ahead of LP record sales, and if the trend continues (and there seems to be no reason why it will not) LP records will go the way of the 45s. We would strongly urge small academic libraries to begin the switch to compact audio disc as quickly as is feasible.

Video Disc

For more than ten years, video disc has promised to be the ideal playback format for video materials. While the potential still exists for the video disc, the reality of the situation is that video disc will have a difficult time in replacing VHS half-inch videotape, which has saturated both the home and library markets.

The greatest use of video disc has been made by the training and education communities, where the full potential of video disc can be utilized. The commercial video players have a built-in microprocessor that can provide random access, by frame number, to any point of the disc. When the video disc is combined with a microcomputer, the interactive nature of the disc becomes even more apparent. With the computer controlling the video disc player, the user can branch through an instructional program while switching between images generated by the computer and the disc. The ability to interact with the user depending on answers to specific questions has made the video disc seem like the ideal teaching and learning tool. While the potential exists, the limited availability of commercially produced discs and the high costs of producing one's own discs have greatly limited the use of this technology.

A number of companies have experimented with the use of video disc as a type of picture book. Sears, Roebuck and Company put their catalog on video disc and added moving images and sound to add impact to the product. Arete Publications has produced a video disc version of its *Academic American Encyclopedia*. Rather than being a video recording of the original publication, it combines visual information with music, sound effects, and spoken words in a way that is not possible with the conventional printed book.

While most people agree that the potential for the use of video disc is great, most experiments have had mixed results. Video disc is a technology whose time has not yet arrived. At this time, small academic libraries should not invest in video disc technology. Nonetheless, the future may still be bright for video disc.

COMMUNICATION SATELLITES

Communication via satellites is undoubtedly revolutionizing information distribution. Satellites can transmit and receive voice, data, and images independently or simultaneously between any points on earth at lighting speed (one-tenth of a second per page) and at costs that are independent of the distances involved.

There are two basic components to a satellite communications system. The first is the satellite, which is placed in a circular orbit in the plane of the equator at an altitude of 22,300 miles. The satellite's speed is set to match the earth's rotational speed, so that the satellite appears to be stationary. Such satellites are said to be in geostationary or geosynchronous orbit. The second component is an earth station, which is composed of a satellite dish and the associated transmit/receiver equipment. The earth station can be designed to receive and transmit or to only receive signals.

The most common and least expensive system is a receive only or TVRO (Television Receive Only) system. These TVRO systems are usually designed to only receive geosynchronous satellites. Satellites in this belt most frequently transmit on frequencies in the "C" and "KU" band. These letter designations are arbitrarily assigned to a specific range of frequencies. "KU" band transmissions are affected by heavy rainstorms, while "C" band transmission are not affected by rain. This is important to take into consideration if one will be transmitting signals to a satellite. Libraries that are considering installing a satellite system should purchase a system that is at least capable of receiving both these bands.

Satellite receiving systems are rapidly dropping in cost. The standard home satellite dish system can be purchased for as little as $695. However, a college or university should not purchase such a unit. An institution should purchase a ten-foot black mesh dish such as the Winegard with Ecosphere Tracker 8 electronics. This complete system will cost about $2,500, but will provide high-quality performance and years of reliable service. However, more sophisticated and expensive systems are required to receive such signals as Soviet Union television broadcasts since the Soviet satellites are not in geosynchronous but rather in an elliptical orbit. Because the satellite is actually moving around the earth, a series of four equally spaced satellites, each transmitting for six hours, is required to maintain a constant signal. The system used to track and decode this signal is much more complex and expensive. A system of this type costs between $10,000 and $15,000. However, most of the systems that will track elliptical satellites will also track geosynchronous satellites, thereby eliminating the need to have two systems, unless of course one wishes to receive more than one signal at a time.

Potential Library Use of Satellites

- Delivery of documents in real time via facsimile transmitters (interlibrary loan);
- Searching of bibliographic and numeric databases;

- Searching of automated catalogs;
- Remote browsing using slow-scan television;
- Distribution of cataloging information; and
- Continuing education for faculty and staff.

During the spring of 1988, the students in an international relations course at Tufts University in Boston and students in a similar class at Moscow State University in the Soviet Union participated in a history-making event utilizing satellite technology. The classrooms in the United States and the Soviet Union were linked together by satellite, and students and faculty discussed the history of nuclear weapons on live television. This was the first time that satellite technology had been used to link classrooms in the United States and the Soviet Union. This teleconference symbolizes the growing interest among many American universities in using technology to help exchange ideas and information with foreign universities. Most experts agree that this type of communication will be commonplace in the near future. Today the cost of this type of communication is still very expensive—each two-hour teleconference cost Tufts $30,000—but cost will undoubtedly drop significantly as technology improves (DeLoughry 1988).

CONCLUSION

The next decade will certainly see the increased use of technology in small academic libraries. Computers, optical discs, facsimile machines, and satellite communications will become an integral part of most library operations. The 1990s will be an exciting time for libraries, but one must be ready for many technological changes.

REFERENCES

DeLoughry, Thomas J. "Interest Rises in Satellite Links to Foreign Colleges; Tufts, Moscow State Offer Class by Teleconference." *The Chronicle of Higher Education*, April 6, 1988, pp. A–11–12.

Dowlin, Kenneth E. 1984. *The Electronic Library: The Promise and the Process*. New York: Neal-Schuman.

Hills, Philip J. 1982. *Trends in Information Transfer*. Westport, Conn.: Greenwood Press.

King, Donald W., et al. 1981. *Telecommunications and Libraries: A Primer for Librarians and Information Managers*. White Plains, N.Y.: Knowledge Industry Publications.

Lancaster, F. W. 1982. *Libraries and Librarians in an Age of Electronics*. Arlington, Va.: Information Resources.

Lawrence, David M. 1988. "Satellite Transmission for Voice, Text Data, and Video." In *The Smaller Academic Library*. Edited by Gerard B. McCabe, pp. 275–79. New York: Greenwood Press, 1988.

Moore, Mary Y. 1988. "Fax it to Me: A Library Love Affair." *American Libraries* 19: 57–64.

Riggs, Donald E. 1982. *Library Leadership: Visualizing the Future*. Phoenix, Ariz.: Oryx.

Saffady, William. 1985. *Video-based Information Systems*. Chicago: American Library Association.

PART VI

Material Selection

21

Selecting Monographs in a Small Academic Library

Barbara Jones

In the 1980s, the library press has documented the challenge to large research libraries to build and preserve their collections in the face of inflation, dollar devaluation, brittle books, and higher education's financial and political crisis. Small academic libraries, too, have unique obstacles to overcome in their environment. Regardless of collection size or circumstance, the best way to approach the monograph selection process is as one activity in a comprehensive collection management strategy. The Association of Research Libraries' Office of Management Studies uses a fivefold breakdown of these strategic functions: organization, budget, collection assessment, preservation, and resource sharing.

In the first place, what is a monograph? For the purposes of this chapter, it is an item that is a complete physical, bibliographic, and financial entity—in contrast to a serial, which continues publication indefinitely. Because the monograph is usually a one-time, discrete purchase (with the exception of a monographic series), the selection, ordering, receiving, processing, and physical maintenance differs in some respects from the serials work flow.

While costs for monographs have not risen as sharply as those for serials, problems remain. Monographs are often the ''victims'' of serials cost encroachment within the budget. It is not unusual to hear of a monograph-serial ratio of 30–70 in a materials budget; a decade ago it would have been closer to 50–50.

ORGANIZATION

In smaller academic libraries, collection management functions tend to be decentralized and spread among many library staff and teaching faculty members.

It is typical to find each librarian responsible for selection in at least one subject or curricular area, in addition to a technical or public services assignment. Furthermore, preservation and disaster planning is often the work of a committee. James Cogswell's recent organizational analysis of six workable collection-management models is most helpful in evaluating the effectiveness of the above approach (1987). He diagrams each model and evaluates it on a scale of "more effective," "neutral," and "effective" for eight collection-management functions. He moves all the way from model "A"—an assistant director for collection management with a staff of bibliographers—to "F"—the library director as collection management authority with fiscal oversight, each librarian as a selector, and no committees. Cogswell does not recommend "F" because he thinks it is difficult for the library director to facilitate all the decentralized functions, and because there is no policy-making body. Nonetheless, this model is often chosen by smaller libraries that cannot afford to maintain an exclusive cadre of bibliographers.

Cogswell's model "C" is a viable middle-ground alternative for the smaller library. A collection management coordinator reports to the library director as an administrative staff position with rank equivalent to department heads. This coordinator has no personal staff, but chairs a council of subject selectors. These subject selectors include the bibliographic function as part of their other duties, as catalogers or reference librarians for example. The director is still involved in setting priority and direction for collection management, but is not the direct implementor.

One of the advantages of the above and similar models is that widespread involvement and commitment to collection management reinforces its high priority and makes it possible for all librarians to have direct contact with teaching faculty. Also, because computerized library systems have already begun to blur the lines among departments, this is yet another shared function that can mobilize a library staff to meet a common goal. Diverse input into the selection process helps ensure a diverse general collection.

This same advantage of diverse, decentralized participation can cause problems. If none of the librarians perceive collection-management responsibility as a priority, book selection can go on the "back burner" of the list of responsibilities. Implementing this change can be stressful to an already hard-working staff. Lynne Gamble's article offers a helpful account of the change process in a small California academic library (1986), while Bonita Bryant's discussion sets forth a formula for measuring book selection work load (1986).

The following is a suggested way to implement collection management as a campus-wide responsibility. First, the library director must establish collection management as a high priority within the library and on campus. This can be done during strategic planning sessions or budget hearings. The concept must be explained to the library and central administration, all of whom will need to weigh staffing and financial commitment. The library director must not assume that the library staff and central administration understand the collection-management concept. It is relatively new to the profession and, in fact, was only recently added to library school curriculum.

The evaluation process and job description for subject selectors must make it clear that subject selection is an important part of their duties. The council of selectors serves not only as a policy-making body, but also as a forum for sharing problems and ironing out work flow in the new system.

Second, the importance of collection management must be communicated to the campus. The library should try to obtain a seat on the campus-wide curricular-planning body. It is important that the library speak up and place a price tag on new programs requiring significant investment in library resources. Teaching faculty may feel threatened by library intervention that could smother curricular innovation. They must be persuaded that library input is critical to the success of their new courses or programs. If an appropriate dollar figure can be documented, it is easier to request a budgetary adjustment for a new program.

In working out a teaching-faculty liaison program, it is important that the librarians take the initiative. For example, the physical sciences subject selector could ask to be on the agenda for a chemistry department meeting. This gives the librarian an opportunity for dialogue about new areas of study, trends in the discipline, and faculty research interests.

One of the challenges on a small campus is meeting needs of a faculty whose research interests might well go beyond the purview of a small academic collection. Prospective faculty candidates should get a realistic sense of the library's services and collections during the campus interview. The library can be used to recruit good faculty if library staff can participate in the candidate's visit. The candidate will appreciate this honest assessment, which need not be negative. Often a small library more than makes up for its limited collection through prompt, personal service. A small library can describe the depth of the monographic holdings in one subject area, for example, and then discuss interlibrary loan and van service to nearby research libraries. Some free photocopying and on-line database searching could be offered as a further incentive.

Library "friends" and other campus groups can be used effectively within the collection-management structure. Alumni can be involved in "adopt-a-book" campaigns, or specific university colleges can challenge each other to fill in subject-area gaps. The senior class might make a library donation as their class gift. Monographs are especially suitable one-time purchases in the above cases.

In these days of scarce financial resources, it is crucial that the collection building process be a planned process. Institutional officials often view library collections as "bottomless pits." Statistical collection assessment, using a popular PC spreadsheet package, is useful for budget justification.

Collection-management organization can be set forth in a strategic plan, with goals clearly articulated by the library administration. It can be reinforced and updated through regular library conference attendance or locally organized educational programs. Within such a framework, a planned selection of monographs can be achieved.

BUDGET

Maintaining the monograph budget is a challenge because several current factors threaten to erode it.

Automation

The pressure to automate holdings in small libraries is justifiably great because of the possibility of electronic linkage to larger collections. Resource sharing as a product of this connectivity is certainly a commendable goal. Computerized library systems are a popular purchase with faculty, students, and administration; justifying the need and projecting the finances is often easier to accomplish for on-line catalogs than for books. Library administrators should strive to prevent an either-or situation.

The "Bottomless Pit" Perception

It is all too easy to assume that libraries will always have books. Surprisingly, many academic officials have no idea how sharply monograph costs have risen. To some administrators, the book budget may seem like an area that can be "raided" from time to time and paid back in later years. The collection-management officer should be able to prepare a regular, concise report for campus administration. It could include such items as: inflation rate for domestic and foreign monographs; comparison of the dollar to foreign currencies; projected cost for supporting a new interdisciplinary program; and rate of increase in interlibrary loan requests. The accompanying narrative should explain the significance of the statistics.

Skyrocketing Costs of Periodicals

Because periodicals are costly and a continuing financial obligation, it is common practice to pay for them first and apply the remainder of the budget to monographs. However, it is no longer practical to delay monograph purchases, because titles are back-listed more quickly now than in the past. Some specialized materials, in art for example, may be totally unavailable in a very short time.

New Types of Information Products and Services

If bibliographic utility products and services, such as on-line databases, are part of the materials budget, it becomes increasingly difficult to hold the line on monograph purchases. CD-ROM, telefacsimile transmission, and campus information networks will also compete for limited materials dollars.

Book Maintenance

Books carry with thcm such maintcnancc costs as binding and rcpair. Whilc a paperback purchase may seem like a bargain, rising binding costs must be factored in along with other preservation considerations.

Solutions to the preceding five problems are complex and require strategic planning, data gathering, and educating the campus about the high costs of purchasing, processing, and maintaining book collections.

The library director should seriously consider establishing the materials budget as a fixed line item, if it is not already. The director or collection-management officer should be able to justify the dollar amount and any requested increases using inflation and other meaningful statistics as well as local curricular needs. If at all possible, library automation costs should be in a separate line.

The dilemma of subject versus format deserves careful study. The new information formats, services, and technologies may well have the same value to the collection as printed books. However, they should be evaluated carefully because of possible added hardware costs and space requirements. One solution is to assign each subject selector all formats, including periodicals—and possibly subject-related databases. Selectors can then monitor trends by subject field, so that differing monograph-serial-database ratios, in chemistry and history for example, can be identified and justified. When the selectors' council meets, participants can report on trends and recommend policy changes to the library director. Reference sources relating to a variety of subject areas can be discussed in this forum as well.

The allocations within the materials budget can be accomplished via very complex formulas or by informal negotiation among subject selectors with eventual review and approval by the library administration. The money can be allocated by Library of Congress (LC) or Dewey classification, subject, priority systems, or even by academic department. Using the LC or other classification system is ''tidy'' because it can be tied to conspectus building or accreditation team lists. The disadvantage is that such a system can become too rigid. As increasing numbers of programs are interdisciplinary, LC class does not define an academic program very accurately.

Funds can be allocated by subject. In a small library this can be quite successful, since a small group of subject selectors meeting informally can ensure that areas shared by departments do not fall through the cracks. A subject list can be compiled with the help of Library of Congress classification or subject headings, the college catalog course listing, or lists of majors in academic departments. Regular consultations with academic departments can help librarians to get a sense of new trends in various fields. However, the subject selector should also be prepared to balance a collection to some degree if a particular academic department does not cover certain areas. Though this system is flexible, it can be more time-consuming while defining subject areas into which purchases fall.

A priority system is another proven method for small academic institutions. Priorities can be established within subject areas, or one can deal with one undivided chunk of money. Faculty or subject selectors assign priorities to every request. For example, "1" could be "absolutely necessary for current curriculum"; "2" could be "nice but can wait for the next academic year"; and "3," "must wait for budget increase." The understanding would be that there would be sufficient funds to purchase all of priority "1." Priority "3s" are kept in a desiderata file. The middle category requires careful perusal by the subject selectors. If there is money left, certain priority "2" materials could be chosen for purchase to achieve fair balance among subject areas.

One potential but not insurmountable problem with this system is that it can become reactive rather than proactive. The selectors should be actively selecting, reading reviews, and surveying the field at all times; not simply responding to teaching faculty requests. Otherwise this system can skew the purchasing toward the larger or more aggressive departments, who submit more purchase requests. On the other hand, now that libraries no longer aim for comprehensiveness, on-demand systems merit some investigation. If the library, for example, is involved in a consortium that has assigned collection responsibilities, then a collection favoring an institution's strengths enhances the consortium.

Money can be allocated by academic department. In fact, in some institutions library funds are allocated directly to the academic department. Such assignment can be problematic because it makes interdisciplinary purchasing difficult. It also has the potential of politicizing the selection process and takes from the library the flexibility to redistribute funds. The advantage is that the teaching faculty get very involved in the process and can be welcome partners to pressure the academic administration for more book dollars. A disadvantage is that the teaching faculty might not distinguish individual research requests from classroom needs, and some purchases may be of limited use.

There are a variety of formulas available for consideration. Mary Scudder's recent article explains the use of one for small academic institutions (1987). It is based on the premise of teaching faculty collaboration by department in order to arrive at figures based on availability (counting annual *Choice* reviews by subject or department), cost, enrollment, and library use.

Formulas can be a problem, regardless of the components. In this case, enrollment can be a very misleading variable because large sections of required courses compete with small graduate programs or independent study seminars. Interdisciplinary courses or general education sequences often defy assignment to a department. If used improperly, the book-cost variable could "penalize" the hard sciences. Finally, the factor of library use is very hard to discern, particularly in periodical-intensive disciplines where readers browse and circulation records do not reflect use.

One model that seems to work well in small libraries is the following, which combines some of the above:

1. Determine at the beginning of the fiscal year a benchmark monograph-serial ratio. This can be done by subject, the overall budget, or other breakdowns. Librarians establish a point at which the ratio needs to be examined. New technologies and services can be included.
2. Negotiate allocations at two levels. First, the subject selectors can meet and recommend their needs based on previously established formulas, priority systems, or other criteria agreed upon by all. Then the library administration can make the final determination. The administration might hold a certain amount in reserve—for subject balance, and for the unexpected. It is important at this planning stage to anticipate curricular change. Ideally there should be a policy in the campus-wide curriculum review process to provide start-up funds for new programs. Other potential funding sources are grants for new programs or projects taken on by such groups as the Friends—purchase of expensive sets, for example.
3. Discuss, in a general way, what is requested but not purchased in a given year. Do any patterns emerge? Are teaching faculty submitting requests inappropriate to the library's current collecting policies? What is the impact of CD-ROM databases, and rising periodical costs? What kinds of resource-sharing opportunities could ease the budgetary pressure? Such a discussion is invaluable for formulating future directions for collection management in a library.

ASSESSMENT

Assessment is a critical tool for evaluating a collection's strengths and weaknesses, and for establishing and justifying monograph expenditure levels. The University of Notre Dame Libraries included a collection-assessment component as part of their Collection Analysis Project (CAP) for the ARL Office of Management Studies. They tried a variety of assessment techniques. Their final report is a valuable summary of the strengths and weaknesses of each method, and helps clarify the problem of the user-oriented approach.

Standard Bibliography

One traditional method especially appropriate for a small academic library is the application of a standard bibliography to the library's holdings. *Books for College Libraries* (American Library Association) is a good example. Citation studies from journals and a variety of sources are more complex to construct and thus more time-consuming. However, for a limited or new subject area, a librarian can get a "handle" on the field through citations in a few key articles.

Faculty Interviews

The teaching faculty can be an invaluable source of information on new publications or subject areas. A librarian attending a department or college meeting can determine new emphases in the local curriculum. At Notre Dame, the librarians tied local subject interests to the Library of Congress classification and then sampled the shelf list. In the sciences, publication date would be a key factor in such a sample.

Availability Studies

This approach is user-oriented. Users can be interviewed to discover their rate of success in finding desired material on the shelves. This kind of study not only targets "thin" areas of a collection, but also identifies problems users have in accessing the collection. From such a study can come ideas for user orientation, public catalog revisions, or a new system of signs.

PRESERVATION: MONOGRAPH MAINTENANCE STRATEGY

For years the brittle book problem publicized in the 1970s was viewed as an issue for large academic research libraries alone. Certainly when one views the award-winning documentary "Slow Fires" (1987), the scale of the book deterioration problem at such institutions as New York Public Library is dramatic and monumental. However, as the decade progressed, small academic libraries began to tie preservation to an economic premise: It is less expensive to preserve even an item that is not rare than it is to replace it. Thus, preservation became an issue of inventory maintenance for all types and sizes of libraries. At that point, many libraries added book preservation as a program priority and charged a staff member or committee with the task.

Small academic libraries' general and special collections are, indeed, subject to the same physical stresses found in a large library: damage to book spines due to photocopying, "disasters," and the polluted air or fluctuating temperature and humidity in the stacks. Preservation is discussed in more detail in another chapter. It is mentioned here because it is a vital component in any collection-management plan.

RESOURCE SHARING

In some respects, the last segment of this chapter is the most significant of all in the monograph selection process—yet often the most disregarded. It is simply impossible to fill all legitimate monograph purchase requests in any library, much less a small one. As Paul Mosher stated at a 1985 conference on cooperative collection development, "The myth of the self-sufficient collection is dead" (Luquire 1986 : 26). Collections are, for better or worse, becoming increasingly client-centered rather than collection-centered. This situation will continue as books prices increase along with the growth in the amount published and the rising demand for faculty research and publication.

Administratively, it is helpful to consider access to resources outside one's own library as a significant part of any collection development scheme, and as a relief to the dilemma described above. Small libraries often feel reluctant to enter into resource-sharing arrangements, because they feel that as a net borrower they are a drain on the system. My experience in at least one interlibrary loan consortium shows that this is not always the case. Libraries tend to borrow regionally, and not always from the biggest library. Also, a small academic library can often provide faster turnaround due to less backlog and more personalized service. For a small, specialized library, the in-depth contribution in even a few fields will probably be invaluable to a consortium's well-being.

One caution is the danger of depending too heavily on other libraries. A library must be very certain about accreditation obligations. Also, college and university administration must realize that consortia do not mean the demise of the book budget. The Minnesota MINITEX library network criteria for participation offers as a guideline the suggestion that 95% of library needs should be met at the institutional level. This type of guideline encourages the development of a core of material at the local level to respond to a high percentage of normal clientele needs.

How does a librarian decide what to borrow and what to purchase? The following elements need to be considered; some are client-centered and some collection-centered:

- Has the monograph been frequently requested through ILL by many different local users?
- Does the monograph support local curriculum, or is it an item likely to be of interest for only one highly specialized project?
- Does the monograph support local commitment to a cooperative purchasing agreement or conspectus?
- Is the monograph likely to be designated with noncirculating status (a reference item, for example), and thus difficult to obtain through interlibrary loan?

Another way to make the purchase decision is to analyze all the kinds of resource-sharing arrangements. Interlibrary loan is the oldest. It has now been joined by even bolder steps—shared purchasing agreements and conspectus building. Furthermore, all resource-sharing arrangements have been enhanced by old and new technologies: computers, CD-ROM, telefacsimile transmission, and electronic publishing.

The state of Iowa has an interlibrary loan system that can grow with demand and new technology. While it is by no means fully developed, it is a good model for study because smaller academic libraries are active participants in the system. The Iowa Locator is a Union Catalog of holdings of over 400 libraries geographically distributed throughout the state. This information can be found by searching on the compact disc with a microcomputer. Recently, a second edition of the Locator was made available; information can be transferred directly into the Iowa Computer Assisted Network (ICAN), Iowa's microcomputer-based interlibrary loan system. Resource sharing will be the next step, since the next Locator edition will allow local or regional library consortia to display their holdings as a group. This edition will be updated every three months.

One of the important steps beyond interlibrary loan, and the "backbone" of cooperative collection development, has been the building of a conspectus. Here the role of small academic libraries should not be underestimated, particularly if there is some highly esoteric, specialized field covered in depth. One might be surprised, for example, to find a strong Romanian literature collection at the University of Northern Iowa, but a series of fortunate circumstances have placed it there. In conspectus building, a group of libraries assign and accept responsibility for purchasing within certain subject areas, and at a certain collection depth. In the 1985 Illinois conference proceedings, *Coordinating Cooperative Collection Development: A National Perspective*, several notable models are documented (Luquire 1986). The Pacific Northwest Collection Assessment Project is a particularly interesting model, because it defines a role for the smaller academic library.

Finally, after all the talk about new technologies, a very old one is still a possibility: motor vehicles. Many small libraries have had to implement policies that they cannot support individual faculty research unrelated to the curriculum. Instead, they may offer van service to nearby research libraries. This kind of service, along with an active ILL program and electronic links to other academic institutions, can be used to recruit faculty who might be reluctant to locate far from a research library.

BOOK SELECTION AND INTELLECTUAL FREEDOM

As budgets continue to tighten and publishing continues to grow, there is an understandable tendency to respond solely to user demand. Furthermore, as was stated previously, no library can be comprehensive or self-sufficient anymore. There are at least two dangers in this trend. First, for the shelf-browser, a subject area in the stacks may no longer represent diverse points of view on a subject, especially if an academic department has a particular approach. It is important for the subject selector to be aware of that tendency and to fill in the gaps, if even to a limited extent. Second, if the library responds to user demand rather than the subject area of the collection itself, there might be a tendency to succumb to pressure not to purchase certain controversial materials for the collection. Academic librarians need to be well-versed on the Council on Library Resources and American Library Association statements on access and the freedom to read. They also need to know their state's confidentiality and privacy legislation so that all users, including foreign students, are afforded their legal rights to privacy in what they read, study, or check out.

REFERENCES

Bryant, Bonita. 1986. ''Allocation of Human Resources for Collection Development.'' *Library Resources and Technical Services* 30 (April/June): 149–62. Provides formulas for realistic division of selection responsibilities among librarians.

Cogswell, James A. 1987. ''The Organization of Collection Management Functions in Academic Research Libraries.'' *The Journal of Academic Librarianship* 13 (November): 268–76. Offers several helpful models along with the strengths and weaknesses of each.

Gamble, Lynne. 1986. ''Assessing Collection Development Organization in a Small Academic Library.'' In *Energies for Transition: Proceedings of the Fourth National Conference of the Association of College and Research Libraries*. Edited by Danuta A. Nitecki, pp. 82–85. Chicago: ACRL. How one library reevaluated and changed their procedures and policies.

Luquire, Wilson, ed. 1986. *Coordinating Cooperative Collection Development: A National Perspective*. Proceedings of a Conference in Chicago, April 1–2, 1985. Sponsored by the Eastern Illinois University and the Illinois Board of Higher Education. New York: The Haworth Press. Covers the major U.S. cooperative programs and documents the role of automation in conspectus building and other projects.

Millson-Martula, Christopher. 1985. ''The Effectiveness of Book Selection Agents in a Small Academic Library.'' *College and Research Libraries* 46 (November): 504–10. A model showing librarians and teaching faculty sharing responsibility for materials selection.

Scudder, Mary C. 1987. ''Using *Choice* in an Allocation Formula in a Small Academic Library.'' *Choice* 24 (June): 1506–11. How to work with teaching faculty to develop an equitable allocation system based on *Choice* reviews.

Slow Fires: On the Preservation of the Human Record. 1987. 16mm and video. Color. Producer/Director Terry Sanders. Santa Monica, American Film Foundation.

Thomas, Lawrence. 1987. ''Tradition and Expertise in Academic Library Collection Development.'' *College and Research Libraries* 48 (November): 487–93. Philosophical issues related to the teaching faculty and librarian roles in the traditional academic model.

University of Notre Dame, University Libraries Task Force on Collection Assessment. 1981. ''Collection Analysis Project—Final Report.'' Notre Dame, Ind., June 10.

22

Guidelines for Periodical Acquisition and Budget Control: An Overview of Selection and Deselection in the Small Academic Library

Jamie Webster Hastreiter

CURRENT SITUATION

Periodical costs are currently the most volatile part of the library budget, and librarians have had to monitor price increases closely because of the dramatic impact they have had on budgets. In 1987, the U.S. Periodical Index far surpassed the Consumer Price Index (CPI), with prices increasing at more than five times the rate of U.S. inflation. In 1986 they rose about two to three times the inflation rate. The average journal cost in 1978 was $27.58, the average cost is now $71.41 (Knapp and Lenzini 1987: 40, 43). These are horrifying statistics.

The publishing climate in which these increases appear has been discussed at length in the professional literature. The sheer volume of titles published in the last fifteen years presents a problem to libraries attempting to provide suitable coverage in each discipline. The reasons for this explosion of information are many. The term "twigging" has come into being to denote the branching of a field until one arrives at the smallest publishable unit. Faculty members operating under a "publish-or-perish" system of advancement exacerbate the growth of journal titles. Individuals needing to build their reputations often rework research into several articles which may be sent to various periodicals.

Faced with an abundance of submitted papers, publishers often have increased the size or frequency of their journals while correspondingly raising subscription prices. One science publisher has been notorious for its practice of adding supplemental volumes during the year as a means of responding to the overwhelming number of papers. While librarians may applaud the publishers' desire to make the results of scientific research available in the most timely manner possible, it means they must deal with unexpected bills in mid-year. As these extra volumes are numbered sequentially, there is no opportunity for librarians to decide whether to purchase them. This is just one example of why it is necessary to be aware of the business practices followed by publishers. By recognizing which publishers are likely to present problems, librarians can make necessary adjustments in budget projections.

The practice of "twigging" has also led to a proliferation of new titles. While it is the publishers who must bear the start-up costs and support the publications until the numbers of subscriptions allow the periodicals to become self-sufficient, it is the librarians that must attempt to find the money in an already overburdened periodical budget to purchase new titles in expanding fields of knowledge.

Other factors impacting on periodical costs include foreign publisher takeovers and differential pricing systems. Much American research is being printed abroad by multinational publishers. The reduced buying power of the dollar and the discriminatory pricing system to U.S. libraries are among other factors accounting for rising costs. Differential pricing systems whereby libraries are charged an institutional rather than an individual membership rate have become accepted practice. The result is that libraries often end up subsidizing personal subscriptions. All these factors have pushed yearly periodical increases well above the inflation rate, while libraries have generally received budget increases based on the CPI. This means that many libraries are no longer receiving sufficient funds to meet their needs and have to resort to drastic measures. Even those libraries that have received special additional funds to maintain subscriptions are only postponing the inevitable. Supplemental funds will need to be increased each year, taking money from other needed areas, until the library takes action. The problem will not resolve itself.

Small colleges are not alone in facing this problem. Many large research libraries have reported having to cancel subscriptions to remain within their budgets. Stanford and Cornell predicted $600,000 shortfalls in their materials budgets ("Falling Dollar" 1987: 317–18). Studies at Louisiana State University, Clemson University, and the University of Michigan showed that a very few publishers, accounting for a small percentage of titles, are responsible for a large share of the cost increases. Elsevier, Springer-Verlag, and Pergamon "accounted for 43 percent of Louisiana State University's increased expenditures for journal subscriptions in 1987. These three supplied only 2.5 percent of all paid subscriptions but received 20 percent of all serial expenditures" (Hamaker 1987: 3). Studies at Eckerd College had similar results.

Some steps are being taken. The Association of Research Libraries released a "Statement on Discriminatory Journal Pricing" decrying the fact that libraries in the United States and Canada are being charged much higher rates than libraries in other countries. The statement concludes that the "sole purpose of these practices is to maximize profits"; they are not based on actual costs to publishers (1986: 4). Librarians are becoming more vocal about the inequities that are having such a negative impact on the services they are able to offer. They are becoming more informed about publishers' business practices and are sharing this information. Periodicals such as *Library Issues: Briefings for Faculty and Administrators* publish charts tracing the buying power of the dollar so that librarians can keep abreast of economic conditions and make more accurate budget projections. Faculty and administrators are recognizing that hard choices must be made, and that their involvement and cooperation is vital if improvement is to be seen, not only on campus but also in the outside academic community.

Positive results may come from this crisis in the periodical area. Librarians are being forced to communicate with their academic colleagues to educate them about the severity of the problems that must be faced. Studies are being initiated at more colleges to develop documentation on which to base decisions. Policy statements and guidelines are being drafted to provide a framework for the selection and maintenance of materials. The question of ownership versus access is being raised again, which may stimulate further cooperation between libraries on a formal or informal basis. All this may ultimately result in better service to patrons through the development of cost-effective periodical departments.

ACQUISITIONS

New publications and changes in curriculum and faculty often lead to requests for additional periodicals. Even if a library is in the enviable position of being able to purchase all its requests, it is still wise to have a procedure for handling requests, and this process should be known to all faculty members.

A survey of college libraries conducted by Jamie Webster Hastreiter, Larry Hardesty, and David Henderson shows that most journals are requested by faculty members and approved by the library director and serials librarian. Thirty-nine percent of the respondents required that faculty fill out a request form. Although a large majority (83%) of the respondent libraries did not have a collection-development policy for periodicals, most libraries (80%) did provide guidelines to be considered for any subscription (Hastreiter, Hardesty, and Henderson 1987: 7).

While a majority of respondent libraries did not have a periodical collection policy, such a document may prove very helpful in dealing with the current publishing crisis. A collection-development or management policy stating the goals of the periodical collection provides a good basis for selection and deselection of titles. To achieve widespread acceptance of such a document it is best to have faculty sponsorship such as a Faculty Library Committee might provide. A major issue that needs to be addressed is what person or body should have final authority for the acquisition and deselection of journals. It is important that a statement on deselection be included to explain what measures will be used and what procedures will be followed before a journal is dropped. The policy should also address the question of materials for faculty research. If such titles are to be purchased, one needs to determine the priority they should receive in comparison to curriculum-related journals. Furthermore, it should take into consideration accreditation requirements for various disciplines that specify a minimum number of journals to be held. This need for policy is also discussed in chapter 23.

Requiring faculty members who wish to purchase new journals to submit a request form encourages a more judicious selection process by asking that they evaluate each request on the basis of set criteria. Along with the request form, the librarians should distribute guidelines enumerating the requirements they feel make a journal successful at their institution. The following criteria might be considered for inclusion in such a statement. Of major concern should be the sophistication and diversity of the student body. Small undergraduate institutions will want to gear their journals to the particular demands of the curriculum and the reading level of the students. Access to a title through indexes and abstract services is vital, and inclusion in one of the more popular indexes encourages the greatest use. Faculty should be reminded that students rely on indexes, and tend not to browse in journals unless such a process is part of an assignment. The language of the publication must be considered along with the question of suitability, as foreign-language journals are unlikely to receive heavy use. The number of students who would be likely to use the journal or the number of courses it would supplement should be a consideration. Cost, availability in the local area, and reputation and longevity of the publication can be listed as qualifications for purchase. Each library can establish priorities for the above categories to suit the needs of their institution.

The request form itself should ask for title, a description of how the faculty member envisions using the journal in courses, whether it duplicates or supercedes titles already held, if other titles might be dropped should the journal be acquired, and in what format the material should be stored. An advertisement or sample copy may be required for review. Once this information is provided, the librarians will then need to determine where (or if) the journal is indexed or abstracted, its cost, whether it is available at other local libraries, and if it has been recommended by some authority such as *Magazines for Libraries* or *Choice*. The library may also want to check interlibrary loan records to see if the journal has been requested frequently. Citation studies of student papers or researching citation indexes might provide further justification for purchase.

In evaluating requests, some colleges have developed a point or ranking system using criteria such as those listed above. For example, the University of Evansville has a weighted system that awards points based on the amount of indexing, the number of interlibrary loan requests, the expected level of demand (faculty, student, and so forth), the impact on program support, cost, and miscellaneous factors such as format or local availability. By multiplying the points in each category by a weighting factor and totaling the result, the library arrives at a score. Each journal request can then be numerically ranked and compared. The weighting factor is subjective, and each library can assign priorities to each category on the basis of its importance to the institution (Miller and Guilfoyle 1986: 15–17).

Maintaining files of approved request forms, or otherwise keeping track of who ordered a title, can aid in the deselection process. Such a file will enable the librarian to identify and contact the proper discipline when the requestor leaves the college to see if the journal is still considered necessary. If a course for which the journal was purchased is discontinued, the requestor can be asked to determine if the title will still be useful in related courses or if it could be dropped.

BUDGET ALLOCATION

The respondents to the survey indicated that very few libraries used formulas to allocate periodical funds. Those libraries that used formulas based them on enrollment, level of courses taught, number of faculty, and average industry costs. Even those libraries that did not apply a precise budget formula replied that they considered these same criteria in responding to requests for new periodicals (Hastreiter, Hardesty, and Henderson 1987: 7).

Formulas are readily available in the literature for the allocation of the book budget, but formulas are less prevalent and much less successful in dealing with the periodical budget. Book funds can be reduced or increased each year as variations in departments occur. When funds are expended, ordering of books ceases until the next fiscal year. With journals, however, a long-term commitment is involved. A library cannot logically subscribe to a journal for alternate years or as funds permit. A periodical budget cannot fluctuate wildly in response to yearly variations in enrollment or number of faculty in a department.

To apply a formula to a new periodical collection is a relatively easy matter, and indeed should be part of the initial planning whether formal or informal. However, few librarians are in the position of designing a collection from scratch. When working with an existing subscription list, evaluation on the basis of the above criteria in an effort to bring equitability to the periodicals collection and budget is the major thrust. Negotiation with faculty to achieve this process requires diplomacy, tact, and persistance. Requirements can be applied to the purchase of any new titles so as to maintain what is determined to be the proper balance of funds for the institution. Over a period of years, an existing collection can be molded to reflect a formula, but to try to achieve this state in a year or two would create chaos and faculty uproar.

Those colleges wishing to institute a formula will find Jasper G. Schad's comments on the need for the perception of fairness in allocations as important for periodical as for book collections. People may favor a budget formula because it appears to be the fairest method of allocating funds even though there are practical limits to such a method. Insufficient funds can foster a competitive approach to allocation formulas, and campus politics often can exacerbate this condition. Consequently, it is important in creating a formula for periodicals that all parties agree on the principles and procedures used in the allocation (1987).

Some libraries have developed alternative policies that allow them to respond to journal requests. Colleges may allow disciplines to subscribe to journals using funds from their book allocation for a specified period of years (Hastreiter, Hardesty, and Henderson 1987: 8). In this way, disciplines are forced to make a value determination that a journal is important enough on which to spend their monograph allocation. This method offers the advantage of not having to use the periodical account to support this cost for a set number of years. During this time, the librarians can plan more effectively for future budget years, and they can document the need and use of this journal.

Franklin & Marshall has a "drop-to-add" policy. It states that

> A new subscription can be initiated by formally denoting title(s) of approximately equal cost that may be cancelled. However, no more than one (1) subscription will be placed for any one (1) subscription to be cancelled. (Hastreiter, Hardesty, and Henderson 1987: 107)

On a special form for periodical substitution, faculty are asked to give a brief rationale for the title to be added and for the title or titles to be dropped. The library expresses the caveat of taking care not to cancel titles "which contribute to the basic coverage of a quality liberal arts library" (Hastreiter, Hardesty, and Henderson 1987: 107). By using a substitution method, the college remains within budget while still being able to respond to the faculty's need for new journals.

EVALUATION OF TITLES

As mentioned earlier, policy statements should include provisions for deselection as well as acquisition. To achieve this end, there must be some criteria for evaluation of holdings. The library should have procedures that allow it to provide data on the use and importance of titles.

Texas A & M University approached the subject by setting up a procedure to identify unused and little used journals. Staff members attached a label to each issue, and as journals were reshelved after use a hatch mark was made on the label. If materials were out of order on the shelf, a hatch mark was given for assumed use. Information about titles that were not used was recorded when materials were pulled for binding. The librarians looked at nine variables from these results, among which were frequency, cost, length of run held by the library, indexing, and language of the journal. The study allowed the library to make statistical comparisons of various parts of the collection, which proved helpful in working with faculty to evaluate titles and identify possible candidates for cancellation (Alldredge 1983: 62–64).

Eckerd College has also maintained use figures since 1982. Any issue being reshelved, or any issue found out of place on the shelf, is recorded with a hatch mark on a card for that title. If, as at Eckerd, space dictates a need to place volumes in storage or on microfilm, it is possible, by identifying the year of publication when recording hatch marks on the card, to provide statistics on the cutoff dates at which use declines.

To forestall those professors who claim that the use figures are incorrect because they and their students read journals and replace them properly on the shelf, it is possible to insert slips of paper at specific pages in volumes so that if the journal is opened the slips will fall out or be displaced. At the end of the year, library staff can tally use as indicated by the missing slips. Yet another method for handling faculty distrust of use figures is to place questioned titles in a closed area so that issues must be requested. New titles in particular may be treated this way if proven use is necessary to justify subscription renewals. Detractors of this approach may claim that use is inhibited because students do not want to bother requesting a journal from a closed area even if there is no time delay in receiving it. The experience at Eckerd, however, indicates that if a journal is important, it will in fact be used.

A more informal indicator of use employs an unobtrusive measure that has been labeled the "dust factor." Professors may not feel this is reliable, but librarians have a sense of what journals are being read, and by checking the dust on otherwise pristine volumes they can confirm this instinct.

While use is a consideration in deselecting materials, the librarian must also evaluate the significance of the title in question. Checking the ranking of journals in citation indexes, surveying faculty and students, and referring to a recommended source such as *Magazines for Libraries* are typical methods.

Maintaining use figures and researching titles is a tedious process that serves no one unless the librarian is able to use the data to effect some change. It is up to the librarian to see that the information is used as a basis of discussion with professors to negotiate the cancelling of unused titles, trading unused titles for journals that may better suit student needs, or assisting in devising assignments that encourage students to consult these unused titles. To assist in the argument for deselection, the librarian may choose to prepare tables showing cost per use for those journals that are seldom or never used. This figure can be calculated easily by dividing the subscription price by the number of uses during the subscription year. The more years for which this information is available, the more reliable the final figure. Depending on the receptiveness of the campus climate, the librarian may wish to publish the titles of the most highly used journals, the most infrequently used, and those that are not used at all. In presenting this information in meetings with faculty, the librarian may suggest alternative methods of securing materials, such as recommending the use of interlibrary loan, full-text database searching, document delivery, or availability at a local library as cost-effective alternatives to ownership.

MAINTENANCE

The survey of small college libraries conducted by the author showed that a small majority of the respondents had automated some portion of their periodical operation, with cataloging, holdings lists, and check in and claims being the most prevalent procedures to be automated (Hastreiter, Hardesty, and Henderson 1987: 12). Use of manual check-in methods is still prevalent in many college libraries where the number of periodicals does not warrant an automated system or where funds to initiate an automated system have not been forthcoming. Automation can be labor-saving from both the clerical and the professional point of view, but cost, downtime, training time, and start-up time are issues that need to be addressed by libraries deciding whether to automate.

Librarians should shop around to determine not only which jobbers give the best discount or handle the greatest number of journals in the most efficient manner, but also which agency has the periodical management package that best suits their library's needs. Many vendors now provide a variety of on-line services. Using a personal computer, subscribers can have access to the information in a vendor's databank on thousands of journals. Each vendor has its own system tailored to its qualifications and using its own particular access points. In general though, EBSCO, Faxon, Read-More and others offer their clients title information, publisher addresses, order forms, and on-line claiming procedures. By choosing a particular operation, the librarian can search a journal by title, vendor code, subject, publisher, or date of first issue. Each function is designed to let the library proceed through the form with a minimum of effort and time. Learning to operate such systems is generally very simple as vendors provide manuals and training.

On some systems, on-line check-in of journals can be accomplished by use of a barcode reader or by typing in a title or code. A screen for the title is called up and the library worker needs only a keystroke or two to record receipt of an issue. If an issue has been missed, it can be claimed with minimum effort at this time. The system can also be set up to claim issues automatically for items not received by an expected date or to print a potential claim list for review prior to being claimed automatically.

Even if the library does not use the on-line services, numerous reports are available from vendors when the library's account is in the vendor's database. Historical price reports on each title are helpful in charting the cost of a journal so that the library can project for the next budget year. If the librarian is interested in knowing where titles are indexed, vendors can supply listings by index or title. Once the library provides the vendor with an assigned code or HEGIS (Higher Education General Information Survey) number for each subscription, reports can be arranged by subject if that would be more beneficial to the library.

Reports on the subscriptions supplied by each publisher can aid librarians in evaluating publishers' service by reviewing the number of claims or rate increases for problem titles. These are only a few of the possible reports available. Whatever the need, librarians should check with their vendor to see if a customized report can be prepared.

Stand-alone systems such as Checkmate, INNOVACQ, and NOTIS also allow the library to automate check-in and claiming procedures. Fields can be programmed with expected arrival dates so that systems can automatically print and batch claims. If periodicals are cataloged, call number labels can be printed for each issue received as they are being checked in. Routing slips can be generated for those issues that circulate to certain departments or individuals. Additional services can be added so that personalized listings of journals to be reviewed by faculty can be generated. They can also be used to remind librarians of titles for which the tables of contents need to be reproduced and distributed to interested readers.

For many librarians the main reasons to automate include the ease in making changes, the ability to produce multiple copies of holdings lists, the portability of these printed holdings lists as opposed to visible files, and the ability to manipulate data to generate various reports. In addition, networking becomes more workable, even for those with stand-alone systems, when a library is able to easily share its holdings list with neighboring libraries.

Many librarians have taken the initial steps toward automation of the serials area using a combination of systems: Cataloging is done on OCLC, ordering and claiming may be accomplished on a vendor's system, an in-house budgeting system might use a spreadsheet package, and generating multiple holdings lists might be done on the college computer. What is really needed, however, is to take the final step toward an integrated system that automates circulation, cataloging, binding, acquisitions, and serials. The interdependence of library departments is stressed in such a system. Cataloging information on a new title is immediately available to the patron, data on what issues have been received and what volumes are at the bindery can be retrieved instantly from the periodicals department, and the reference and public services staff have access to continually updated information for assisting patrons. Service is improved by being able to quickly and efficiently identify the status of materials being requested by a patron.

CONCLUSION

The periodical area of an academic library has always had its unique frustrations. Journals cease, restart, change title, switch frequency, change size, and increase in price; and they may do all these things in the space of one year. To a collection that already demands vigilance and meticulous record keeping has been added the problem of skyrocketing price increases. Now more than ever librarians must be aware of their environment and plan for their options. In order to deal with growing numbers of titles, rising costs, and shrinking budgets, librarians must begin laying the groundwork today. Faculty and administrators should be informed of the problems facing the library and be aware of the various remedies available so they can cooperate in preparing policy and selection statements that clearly reflect the library's priorities.

The librarian should establish an evaluation procedure, initiate use studies, and be ready to provide documentation to aid in selection and deselection decisions. To help with this, the librarian should take advantage of the automated services available to the library through vendors, or other systems. This is likely also to make the periodicals area more cost-efficient. Utilization of price reports aids in budget control. Being vocal to publishers, vendors, and academic colleagues about the problems facing the journal collection insures that the librarian will not be alone in facing these issues. This is a time of upheaval for periodical librarians, but it can also be a period of opportunity to affect worthwhile changes.

REFERENCES

Alldredge, Noreen S. 1983. "The Non-Use of Periodicals: A Study." *Serials Librarian* 7 (Summer): 61–64.

Association of Research Libraries. 1986. "ARL Statement on Discriminatory Journal Pricing." *Library Issues: Briefings for Faculty and Administrators* 6 (July): 4.

Dougherty, Richard M., and Nancy E. Barr. 1988. "Paying the Piper: ARL Libraries Respond to Skyrocketing Journal Subscription Prices." *Journal of Academic Librarianship* 14 (March): 4–9.

"Falling Dollar Imperils Research Collections." 1987. *American Libraries* 18 (May): 317–18.

Hamaker, Charles. 1987. "Impact of Higher Journal Prices and Dollar Devaluation on U.S. Academic Libraries." *Library Issues: Briefings for Faculty and Administrators* 8 (September): 2–3.

Hastreiter, Jamie Webster, Larry Hardesty, and David Henderson. 1987. *Periodicals for College Libraries* (*CLIP* Note no. 8). Chicago: ALA/ACRL.

Knapp, Leslie, and Rebecca T. Lenzini. 1987. "Price Index for 1987: U.S. Periodicals." *Library Journal* 112 (April 15): 39–44.

Miller, Ruth H., and Marvin D. Guilfoyle. 1986. "Computer Assisted Periodicals Selection: Structuring the Subjective." *Serials Librarian* 10 (Spring): 9–22.

Schad, Jasper G. 1987. "Fairness in Book Fund Allocation." *College and Research Libraries* 48 (November): 479–86.

23

Faculty and Librarian Participation in Selecting Journals for a Small Academic Library

Charmaine B. Tomczyk

In a small academic community, faculty involvement in journal-collection development is imperative. Their subject expertise, knowledge of the curriculum, and overall use of the library for their classroom preparation or individual research are valuable assets to consider for a successful journal-selection process. Librarians must inform the faculty of the library's selection processes and collection policies on a regular basis to reinforce the vital role faculty play in selecting appropriate materials.

THE PERIODICALS MARKET

The choices for new periodical subscriptions are increasing steadily. Some 70,800 periodical titles divided into 542 subject areas are included in the 1987–88 edition of *Ulrich's International Periodicals Directory*. They are selected from the Bowker International Serials database of 139,700 entries, to which approximately 1,500 brand new or new-to-Bowker titles are added quarterly. That is about 6,000 or a 9% increase per year. These titles are produced by 59,000 publishers from 197 countries worldwide. Bowker's quarterly updates to its serials database include approximately 1,000 title changes and cessations in each issue. Not only are more new journals coming onto the scene, but more are merging, splitting and ceasing, and then beginning anew. Katz's introduction in *Magazines for Libraries* notes the process of choosing sixty-five hundred titles from sixty-five thousand possibilities. John Lubans (1987) recently told *American Libraries* that over one million serials have begun and ceased since the appearance of the first newspaper in 1609. Given these numbers, it is no surprise that deciding which new subscription titles to buy for your library is an arduous task based simply on the sheer numbers available.

This chapter will deal with a subset of serials, namely journals, which are defined as publications appearing in parts and not monographic series or annuals. The terms "periodicals" and "journals" may be used interchangeably in this chapter.

A PERIODICALS COLLECTION-DEVELOPMENT POLICY

This plethora of periodical titles can be quickly reduced for purchase considerations by consulting your collection-development policy. You say you don't have a written periodical-collection development policy? You're not alone. According to a CLIP (College Library Information Packet) Note survey conducted in 1986, over 83% of the 118 respondents said they did not have such a policy in their libraries, even though the library literature hails it as sine qua non (Hastreiter, Hardesty, and Henderson 1987: 7). Of the libraries that did have a policy, most were written by a committee of librarians or the periodicals librarian. (Only one library's document was written by a faculty library committee.) The study, however, did reveal written guidelines for selection that were available as an acquisitions tool from a majority of the libraries surveyed. While these guidelines are an alternative, they are not a substitute for a policy. When the tough decisions regarding journals need to be made, the established policy, not the guidelines, will be your defense. A written policy "lends credibility to, and a consistent frame of reference for, the librarian's action" (McReynolds 1984: 76). If you lack a periodical collection-development policy, consider drafting one as your top exigency. The results of the Clip Note study mentioned above provide ten sample periodical collection-development policies ranging from one paragraph to three pages, all from colleges of varying sizes.

Components of the Policy

Drafting a periodicals collection-development policy is the process that will set the scene for all your journal selections. Some basic components of your policy should be:

1. The purpose of the periodicals collection in relation to the college's curriculum and/or research;
2. Methods of evaluation—how to judge quality;
3. Criteria and their weights for selection of new titles for the collection;
4. A regular timetable to reevaluate the periodicals holdings for additions and deletions;

5. Retention decisions, including format for and extent of backfiles; and
6. Restating the library's gift policy as it relates to journals.

Other considerations may be a statement on financial responsibilities and priorities for journal costs, dispositions of paper issues and backfiles, detailed procedures for regular review of holdings, duplicate subscriptions, special co-operative agreements with area libraries, and purchases for recreational reading or community interest. The cornerstone of your journal-selection operations is the collection-development policy. Your daily procedures for selection are based on the policy. Small college libraries may not feel the need for such a structured process, but on the contrary, because of the fewer choices available due to financial constraints and the pressing individual attention paid to patrons of smaller colleges, specific criteria and evaluation are needed to reduce the subjectivity of selection, as well as to allow for expedient and judicious selection.

COLLECTION SUCCESS

College Goals

The primary mission of most small college libraries is to support the undergraduate curriculum. Therefore, the bulk of the journal collection should satisfy the needs of the undergraduate students in completing their course assignments. This also means keeping abreast of new courses and programs. Keeping the student satisfaction level high requires continual information gathering at various levels. The first information source is the faculty committee that approves new courses. Ideally, a librarian should be an active, vocal member of this committee to insure that library resources and funding are considered when new courses or new programs and majors are added. Even if a librarian is not or can not be a member, nearly all faculty committees allow guests. If this is not possible, the librarian should keep abreast of agendas and actions by reading the minutes of the committee. The new course approval form at the University of South Carolina–Coastal Carolina College (USC-Coastal), for example, includes a section on library usage and materials needed for this course. This requires the instructors of the proposed course to review the library's holdings in that area. (It could be their first serious perusal of the periodicals collection.) It is also helpful to add a line for a librarian's signature to approve the assessment of needs as valid. It is an early opportunity to identify gaps in the periodicals collection and to recommend additional funds for needed resources. Granted, it is a recommendation only, but a request approved by a faculty committee should carry more weight than a single request from a lone librarian. While this political process may vary from college to college, an opportunity to publicize the need for more library funds should not be set aside. The process should alert teaching faculty to the importance of assessing library materials for their courses and inform librarians of forthcoming information needs.

Reference Connection

Another source of information for gauging the periodical collection's success in fulfilling curriculum needs is the reference office. Based on the question and concerns lodged at the information desk, are students finding what they need? Of course the process starts with your bibliographic instruction (BI) program. It allows suggestions and feedback for student assignments, especially if problems in finding enough journal information may be evident. It should be the librarians' roles to promote the use of the journal collection to both faculty and students. The instructor may assign the paper, but it is often the librarian who can predict how well the student may succeed based on the library's holdings. More about faculty-librarian liaison work for collection development will be discussed later.

Interlibrary Loan Activity

Reviewing and analyzing interlibrary loan (ILL) activity is another source for measuring the success of the periodicals collection. Many libraries adhere strictly to the copyright guidelines suggested for ILL procedures by the National Commission on New Technological Uses of Copyrighted Works (CONTU). As stated in their final report in 1979, no more than five photocopy requests from the same journal title can be honored within one year. Otherwise, it is recommended that the borrowing library consider purchasing the title. It does not appear unreasonable to monitor repeated requests for the same journal title over a year and to give serious consideration to purchase of microfilm format or current subscriptions if continued use is predictable. Other journal services exist, such as purchase of individual issues from Universal Serials and Book Exchange, Inc. (USBE) in Washington, D.C., or purchase of individual articles from University Microfilms International's (UMI) Article Copy Service or the Original Article Text Service (OATS) of the Institute for Scientific Information (ISI). These last two services handle the copyright royalties for thousands of journal titles. Use studies provide valuable hard data to support either continuing or cancelling a subscription, but with the exception of ILL activity, use studies do little to assist in selecting new journals for the collection. With the purpose of the library's periodical collection firmly implanted, librarians need to make judgments based on the college's curriculum and anticipated library use. Does the cost of subscribing and maintaining a new journal title in-house outweigh the cost and time delays of ILL?

EVALUATING NEW PERIODICALS

Selecting new journal titles is always somewhat of a gamble. Marcia Tuttle identifies a unique problem in evaluating serials versus books in that you cannot view the former in its entirety (1985:40–44). One issue's contents can not guarantee satisfaction with future issues. Only when the publication ceases can its meritorious contributions truly be assessed. For this reason, Tuttle feels reviewers tend to exclude serials. Nonetheless, good sources of serial reviews do exist.

Review Sources

Now in its 5th edition, Katz's *Magazines for Libraries* is a good general source for a variety of subject areas. Annotations are derived from recommendations of over 100 subject specialists who are listed with their addresses at the start of each subject section. Basic lists of periodicals are also given for each subject section by audience level, for example, academic. Evan I. Farber's *Classified List of Periodicals for the College Library* is another worthy source. The evaluative comments are brief, but they do provide a good beginning. *Choice* magazine's monthly columns entitled "Periodicals for College Libraries" are good evaluative sources, although they cover new journals whose value still needs the test of longevity. *Library Journal* also has a column on new periodicals that is edited by Katz. *Serials Review* provides lengthy reviews of new journals. Also, several subject lists are available, such as the Mathematical Association of America's *Basic Library List for Four-Year Colleges* (1976), and the *Current Periodical Publications in Baker Library* (Harvard Business School). Several other bibliographies of journals by subject can be found in the literature, but keep in mind that duplicating or emulating these lists of journals may not suit your library's unique profile of curricular-support needs.

Even with a review, newly published journals are difficult to evaluate. The reputation of the publisher is sometimes a clue to a journal's lasting value and level of content. The publisher's reputation for quality should never be overlooked. Journals from some publishers that are notoriously high-priced or known for irregular publication schedules should be closely reviewed in relation to other selection criteria. However, even good ventures fall by the wayside, and the library may be left with a few good issues or years of an un-indexed, ceased journal title. Checking *Ulrich's* for a title's circulation statistics can be an indication of the journal's financial stability and longevity. Verifying the journal's bibliographic information includes watching for indications of instability. Has the title and its content changed frequently over its history? Does it have a regular publication frequency? I do not suggest exclusion of "irregular" publications, but I do urge librarians to be wary of those that have suspended publication more than once over a short period of time. Read the publishers' flyers on the journal. Even though these are marketing tools, they will target the subject content and intended audience of the journal. Always review a sample issue to confirm the flyer's description and to see firsthand the quality of the issue. Granted, one issue may not be representative of future issues. (It may actually be their best effort, expended only for the premiere issue.) Most of us would not consider purchase of any product sight unseen. Given the time, effort, money, and space that must be devoted to adding one new journal title, it is imperative to inspect the merchandise before investing.

CORE LISTS

A core list of journals should be one that satisfies about 90% of patrons' needs. Attempts have been made to compile core lists of selected subject areas. The evaluative instruments used to measure which journals are essential have varied with different studies, and their value has been moot. Donna Goehner's core lists results were based on 178 survey results of checklists from faculty who were recommended by the library directors of their institutions (1984: 23–38). Six core lists, including art, literature, history, psychology, mathematics, and physics, are appended to the study. While this methodology succeeds in using the subject expertise of faculty reviewers, it fails to test the value of these lists to satisfy students' needs. Robert Rose offers a core list of business periodicals based on a combination of tools; namely indexes, databases, and citation analyses (1983: 77–82). The methodology is more balanced than Goehner's, but the citation analyses of scholarly publications is not suitable for an undergraduate collection. Still, Rose's results show that the highest percentage of core titles were included in the *Business Periodicals Index*, and this index most closely adhered to the core. Clearly, the *Business Periodicals Index* is a mainstay for undergraduate use. The literature offers other lists, but be skeptical both of the tools and methodologies employed to compile these lists and, in particular, of how they may relate to your library's purpose.

The Resources and Technical Services Division (RTSD) of the American Library Association established an ad hoc committee in 1981 to study the feasibility of creating dynamic lists of core serials. According to the committee's chairperson, Suzanne Striedieck, the group is still researching quantitative indicators to justify the feasibility of core lists (telephone conversation with the author, 1988). As library literature has proven, citation studies are a clear indication of the journals that are used most heavily for scholarly research. Unfortunately, this data does not greatly assist small college libraries in search of evidence of use by undergraduates.

Another approach pursued by the RTSD committee is gathering the number of subscriptions held with vendors such as Faxon or EBSCO. Their serials' databases allow for easy manipulation; however, their databases are not comprehensive lists representative of a universal list of serials. Possibilities might be forthcoming in using OCLC to derive lists based on holdings, but until more sophisticated tools are available to manipulate comprehensive subject journal holdings, the feasibility of drafting universal core lists may not be possible. The

RTSD committee continues its investigations, and libraries look forward to their final report, which promises, as noted in the group's initial charge, to include suggestions concerning the utility of these proposed lists.

Bradford's law concerns the distribution of journal articles. In nearly any scientific field it has found that a small number of the journals publish a large percentage of cited articles. What the Bradford formula does to measure the usefulness of journal articles, the measuring of the number of subscriptions placed with vendors does likewise for journal titles. It identifies the "popular" journal titles by volume of subscriptions, an indication of the journals that are presumed most valuable. The presumption must be that each library's subscription has been evaluated and deemed an important subscription to the collection. Given the amount of activity in journal evaluations and cancellation projects in recent years, and the shrinking materials budgets, it seems reasonable to assume that college periodical collections have been more firmly cemented now and are less apt to fluctuate greatly.

CRITERIA FOR SELECTION

The major criteria for evaluating journals for an undergraduate college are:

1. Support of the curriculum;
2. Indexing;
3. ILL activity;
4. Reviews;
5. Potential use; and
6. Cost.

Indexing

Indexed journals are guaranteed greater use by the undergraduate. Indexing is usually the most important factor in selecting a new journal. The Undergraduate Libraries Discussion Group of the Association of College and Research Libraries (ACRL) proposed a model statement for the mission of a university undergraduate library. "The undergraduate library's collection of periodical reference material will concentrate on the more standard and interdisciplinary periodical indexes, since these are most heavily used by undergraduates; the periodicals collection should emphasize the titles covered by these indexes" (ACRL 1987: 194). *Ulrich's* or subscription agents' catalogs can be consulted to ascertain whether a title is indexed and where, but studies and personal experience have cast doubts on their accuracy. While the subject content of a new journal may seem to fit the curriculum, it may be too new to be indexed. To verify that a journal is indexed, check the index itself. Journal titles are often dropped or added to indexes after their listings in other bibliographic sources.

Reviews

Journal reviews are available in *Choice*, *Serials Review*, and *Library Journal*, but keep the reviewers and their background and place of employment in perspective. A reviewer from a large university library may consider a new journal on James Joyce, for example, a must for academic libraries, but your college's curriculum may not have even an entire course on Joyce to justify its purchase. While some of the reviewers in these sources are tough critics and all are good writers, they are not necessarily librarians. Their focus may be different from what you need to know about a journal.

Costs

Evaluating the cost of the journal depends in part on the size of your serials budget and how it is allocated. The periodicals budget is usually a single budget item, not formula-driven, and is generally controlled by the library. This control is a crucial device in securing the proper balance in the journal collection. Instances of relinquishing control to faculty departments have been disastrous. After many years of budget cuts and journal cancellation projects, one midwestern university formed a faculty senate ad hoc committee to develop a new approach to library materials allocations (Goehner 1985: 181–84). Sixty percent of funds available for library materials were allocated to academic departments, where the final decisions on purchases were made. Many previously cancelled journals were reinstated, and book purchases were forfeited for the acquisition of journal backfiles. At one point, an average of approximately 77% of allocations went to periodical subscriptions. In some disciplines it was higher, such as biology at 92%. The lesson learned was: do not relinquish control of library monies to academic departments.

Librarians are faced with static budgets and rising journal costs. To sidestep the tendency to shift more materials funds to the periodicals column (as the faculty above did), librarians tend to tighten their belts. In our true character of thrift, we begin cancelling journal titles. In addition, some libraries require a cancellation before a new title can be added. At some point, this becomes unproductive. Initially, if the periodicals collection has not been reviewed for years, the "cancel one—add one" philosophy may work to eliminate the unused titles, but eventually you will be undermining the core collection of journals to take a chance on a new title. Faculty may see no end to the need for more and more journals, but the undergraduate students' needs will be satisfied with a finite number of quality journals in an on-site collection, supplemented with some ILL. Class assignments do not seem to change dramatically from year to year. Overall there is no question that some disciplines use more journals than books, so let the mix of the journal and book collections reflect this reasonably.

Table 1
Extra Journal Funding for New Majors or New Faculty

When a new major is added, how frequently is the library given extra funds to purchase needed journals?

100%	75-99%	50-74%	25-49%	1-24%	0%
2(1.7%)	9(7.7%)	7(5.9%)	2(1.75%)	26(22.0)	72(61.0%)

How frequently is special provision made in the periodical budget for the needs of new faculty to buy the periodicals they want?

100%	75-99%	50-74%	25-49%	1-24%	0%
1(0.8%)	5(4.2%)	5(4.2%)	5(4.2%)	34(28.8%)	68(57.6%)

Source: Reprinted with permission of the American Library Association, excerpt taken from *ACRL Clip Note #8*; copyright © 1987 by ALA.

THE JOURNAL BUDGET

In Hastreiter, Hardesty, and Henderson's 1986 study (1987: 6), a majority of libraries indicated that no additional funds were budgeted for new majors or new faculty (see table 1). This is sometimes a difficult problem to address since new or junior faculty needs may not always be considered a high priority by the administration. However, if new faculty are hired for their expertise in a particular area that is new to the curriculum, and if they are encouraged by the administration to establish this new program or course, then their request for funding new library journals may get a more attentive administrative audience than the library's usual annual request for more funds. Keeping in touch with the faculty is paramount. A comprehensive orientation program for new faculty is a good beginning for introducing the faculty to their role as selectors and for the library to select potential library advocates and liaisons.

Allocation Formulas

Hastreiter et al's study of 118 college libraries showed 50 libraries, or 42.2%, allocate their periodicals funds by discipline or department; but very few of these (9, or 7.6%) use an allocation formula (1987: 7). Instead, they consider the following factors most heavily: (1) enrollment in a curriculum; (2) level of courses taught; (3) number of faculty in a discipline; and (4) average industry cost by subject area. I presume that without a formula, the distribution is largely based on past allocations and, therefore, is too subjective. These factors can be compared across disciplines with the compilation of some firm numbers from the admissions or academic affairs offices on campus, and then a weighted formula can be applied. I am not suggesting a sterile analysis of numbers to derive a final departmental budget allocation. These numbers alone should not dictate comparable library size by discipline. Certainly other variable factors, such as projected library use and library-related assignments, should be çonsidered to readjust some final totals. The more objective the approach to budget allocations, the more convinced the faculty will be of an equitable distribution throughout the departments.

The USC-Coastal library begins its yearly departmental allocations with a formula, but reviews the final outcome for adjustments where the need appears valid. Statistics are gathered from other college offices regarding:

1. Number of courses per discipline (excluding independent study courses and labs);
2. Number of FTE (full-time equivalent) faculty (half-time or quarter-time faculty are added to the nearest whole number);
3. Number of student credit hours per department;
4. Circulation statistics per discipline (using LC classification); and
5. Average cost of book per discipline (using the most current *Bowker Annual*'s U.S. College Book Prices statistics).

A computer program, developed at USC-Aiken campus, has been revised by USC-Coastal library to include the last factor, average cost of a book. From each departmental allocation the library deducts, off the top, the subscription costs for journals in that field. The library continues to reserve a separate periodicals budget for subscriptions to general titles, such as multidisciplinary titles and browsing or recreational titles. The library also reserves a budget for all ongoing microfilm and binding. Requests for backfile runs are paid with the departmental allocations. To avoid a journal spending spree by faculty, the library limits journal expenditures to one-third of the respective allocations. Exceptions may be made for journal-intensive disciplines, upwards to 50%. Still, the library has the final decision on all new journal subscriptions, and the departments are constantly reminded that the funds are library monies provided for their purchase recommendations.

THE JOURNAL REQUEST FORM

The form should ask all the pertinent questions to gather information in support of your criteria for evaluating journals (see appendix). In the absence of such a form, or even in conjunction with it, guidelines should be provided to faculty for journal selection. The requestors are responsible for providing information on how this title would meet the objectives or priorities of their departments, and in particular, which courses it would support in terms of assisting students with their assignments. The faculty should understand the library's policy on adding specialized journals that would support their own research.

This request form requires the requestors to add their signatures. The requirement of a second signature from the dean or department chair is a valuable checkpoint for a second faculty opinion, and a means of controlling fair distribution of limited journal funds among the various areas within the department. The dean or chair's main interest may be monetary, a means of monitoring expenditures. The equally important purpose of this signature is the opportunity for the dean or chair to evaluate the merits of the request against the objectives of the department's curricula. Here, as throughout the selection process, the faculty's input must be concisely marked and their role clearly communicated.

Liaison Work

Not every faculty member may be well-versed in the library's journal holdings in his or her area. The requestor should be encouraged to review the library's holdings before submitting a new subscription request. Ultimately, it is the library's responsibility to analyze how a new title will fit into the collection. Scrutiny should be given to duplication of materials by similar titles and balance of the collection in relation to other subject areas vis-à-vis FTE enrollment, majors, and library use.

Some controversy ensues over who knows best what materials students need: the instructor or the librarian? Some profess that the instructor is responsible for identifying what an educated student in a particular subject area should know, and hence what assignments are made. The librarian observes and instructs the students in their research, and hence knows what information may be lacking in the collection for their needs. For a small college library, the fact is that both sides are needed. No one person can judge the strengths and weaknesses of an entire collection, nor know the breadth and depth of an entire discipline. A cooperative team approach is the best use of available time and human resources. Communicating this collaborative effort, its goals, and its inner workings to each participant is the first step.

Begin with identifying faculty members who appreciate and show an interest in the library. Find at least one library advocate in each department. This is not to say that recruiting or proselytizing is off-limits, but the above approach is the preferred path given one's time restraints and other duties. Usually the disinterested faculty are also those who do not get involved in a supportive or controversial way with the library anyway. Their other activities take precedence. Retention of faculty representatives may also become a problem. Try to avoid selection of only junior faculty who are usually ''volunteered'' for the job. With their other new duties, burnout may result in them either resigning their post too soon or neglecting their library role. Seek stability for faculty selection. The reward will be more consistent growth and development.

Setting up meetings is preferable to memos. Establishing a rapport with faculty one-on-one or in departmental meetings will encourage faculty to become involved in collection development and understand the library's mission. Request that you be regularly added to the agenda for the annual or semester departmental meetings. This helps the faculty to see the development of the library's journal collection as part of their role on campus. Get on the agenda for new faculty orientation so that new faculty can be introduced to library policies and procedures early.

A sure method of involving faculty with important library issues is to convince their administrators that it is valuable work that is worthy of rewards. Serving as a faculty liaison to the library or serving on the library committee should be viewed as meritorious service to the college. Such accomplishments should carry weight on annual evaluations, with tenure and promotion criteria and, therefore, should be linked to monetary rewards. This status is not easy to attain, especially if librarians do not have faculty status or rank, thereby making the teaching faculty their peers. Highlighting the library as an integral part of the educational process is paramount.

The axiom of the library being the heart of the university is more a platitude than a reality. The importance of the library for helping the college accomplish its goal successfully should be stated continually. It is more than a support service, as some accreditation bodies would think. It may be one area where the quality of students' education can be evaluated, as William J. Bennett, former U.S. secretary of education, has seen the national trend lean toward measured assessment for a quality education.

It is academically, politically, and functionally sound to include the library director on the chancellor's cabinet, dean's council, or whatever name is given to the team of administrative advisers to the academic dean and chancellor. Library issues will have the opportunity to receive the attention they deserve by the administration, who will, hopefully, pass down these issues to their faculty with a sense of import. The exposure should be a two-way process, allowing the library to partake of, and contribute to, broader college issues that affect the library and its collection.

CRITERIA WEIGHTS

Once the journal request form is received by the library, the periodicals librarian should review it for completeness. This includes verifying the bibliographic citations in an appropriate source, confirming indexing, adding more than one review and their sources, checking the content and frequency of the college courses it purports to support, attaching the library's current journal holdings in that subject, adding ILL and circulation statistics (if available), and examining a sample issue (preferably more than one if possible).

The review process can take different paths. All the librarians and the library committee may be involved in these recommendations, which could be a means of curtailing an abundance of requests that could drain the budget. However, there is an inherent danger in including too many reviewers. Time expended and lags often cause delayed and inconclusive results. The periodicals librarian may singularly route a recommendation to the library director for final approval, but this process might be too brief and subjective. While the reviewers may vary among libraries as deemed by their organizational structures or traditions, the process itself should strive for maximum objectivity. One method of achieving this is by weighting the accepted criteria for selection.

Each factor of the criteria can have an attribute value based on its importance as accepted locally. Program support, for example, would generally have a greater value than cost. Individual libraries can determine which factors fit their purpose best. To indicate these variances, a weight is given to each category. Assignment of maximum points for each category is determined by the individual library to reflect its unique preferences. While the points and weighting values are subjective and largely based on past performance of other titles, it tends to focus attention on the more important and measurable factors for subscribing. As seen in Table 2, the University of Evansville in Indiana calculates the category score and then multiplies it by the weighting factor to arrive at a total weighted category score, that can then be ranked numerically with others (Miller and Guilfoyle 1986: 21).

Journals that would not fare well with this system would be recreational journals or local interest journals that may not be indexed nor support the curriculum, but are useful for their browsing appeal. If the indexing factor is a weighty one, librarians must regularly evaluate their index collections and then select and cancel with an eye towards the impact of these decisions on the journal collection. Also, for colleges that give some support to faculty research (especially for those that may be affiliated with a local institute, for example), additional means of evaluation should be employed. Still, for the bulk of the journal collection, these numerical scores prove helpful for preliminary ranking. Once tried and tested locally, they may also be used to identify core lists of journals within the existing collection.

REEVALUATION

As noted in the components of a collection-development policy, a regularly scheduled reevaluation process should be established. All too often it is an administrative edict to cut back on journal spending that forces librarians to evaluate the collection. The reevaluation process should be ongoing and not a onetime project to reduce costs when journal dollar costs, and not value, may be the primary decision-maker. Depending on the extent of the reevaluation process and the number of participants, the timetable may range anywhere from annually to four years for a small academic library. The Evansville model above can serve as a reevaluation form.

Faculty Input

Some libraries may survey the faculty to ascertain their priority rankings of journals in their subject areas. A grading scale of defined qualifiers such as

Table 2
Journal Subscription Factors

UNIVERSITY OF EVANSVILLE
JOURNAL SUBSCRIPTION FACTORS

I. INDEXING (8 or 5/2 points) WEIGHT: 1.5
- 1. Primary indexing: ASTI/BPI/CIJE/CINAHL/CLI EDI/HUMI/PSYCH/SSI/USPSD
- 2. Secondary indexing available of U.E.
- 3. Multiple indexing

II. INTERLIBRARY LOAN (5 or 10 points) WEIGHT: 1.0
- 1. 5-8 requests in the last yr. from multiple requestors
- 2. >8 requests in the last yr. from multiple requestors

III. REVIEW/ CORE LIST/ BIBLIOGRAPHY (4/3/3 points) WEIGHT: 1.5
- 1. Strong review
- 2. Indication of appropriateness for U.E.
- 3. Currency of review or list

IV. DEMAND (4/4/2 points) WEIGHT: 1.0
- 1. Faculty
- 2. Librarian
- 3. Student or other patron

V. PROGRAM SUPPORT (4/3/3 points) WEIGHT: 2.0
- 1. Substantial number of students or courses/programs supported
- 2. Periodical use by these courses/programs is high
- 3. Relative strength of current periodical holdings for courses/programs is low

VI. COST (4 or 0/3/3 points) WEIGHT: 1.0
- 1. < $75
- 2. $75 +
- 3. Amount Spent for all subscriptions for this department or area (vs. other areas) is low in relation to need and use
- 4. Amount spent for subscriptions (vs. books) for this department or area is low in relation to need and use

VII. MISCELLANEOUS FACTORS (3/3/1/3 points) WEIGHT: .5
- 1. Format appropriate
- 2. Not available locally
- 3. Publisher reputation sound
- 4. Published longer than one year (an acceptable risk)

Source: Ruth H. Miller and Marvin Guilfoyle. 1986. "Computer Assisted Periodicals Selection: Structuring the Subjective." *Serials Librarian* 10, no. 3 (Spring): 15. Reprinted with the permission of Haworth Press, 10 Alice St., Binghamton, NY 13904.

1 = essential, 2 = important, 3 = useful, and 4 = marginal, can be provided based on the selection criteria plus added emphases on use. However, this method is subjective and faculty tend to rank their personal favorites high even though they may not directly support the undergraduate curriculum. Results can show diverse preferences among faculty within the same department. Unless the faculty member is conscientious enough to visit the library and actually review all pertinent titles, their memories may be apt to fail them.

Use Studies

Use studies are the main tool for judging retention of journal titles. Methods vary from adding colored dots on journals as reshelved to stapling use statistics sheets inside paper issues, and from simply tallying journals left on tables or carrels (coined the "sweep" method) to monitoring direct observation. Journal counts might include not only those found on tables and carrels but also these found misshelved. One University of Chicago use study concealed ballpoint pens in sample volumes, telling the finders that if they completed the short questionnaire enclosed they could keep the pen. The questionnaire asked for their collegiate status and the reason for using the journal, among other things. Even if the questionnaire was not completed, the missing pen was considered evidence of use. Questionnaires can also be distributed at the entrance of the library, but unless the form is short and the patron is asked to complete it right there in front of you, follow-up on participation is nearly impossible. It is disheartening to find multiple copies in trash receptacles throughout the library. Prank results compiled by group efforts are also likely. If journals circulate, use statistics become less of a special project. Some use studies remove selected titles from display so that patrons must ask for them. Also, librarians must remember that statistics may be diminished by the length of holdings. A new title with only one year backfile will get less use than one with fifteen years. This variable must be kept in mind when compiling statistics. Likewise, journals at the bindery become exempt from use. You might be able to reduce your binding shipments during the use study, but ceasing shipments, especially for several months, is not advisable from the binding department's point of view.

A 1983 study conducted by Johanna Ross at the University of California-Davis used direct observation to record browsers' activities for both books and journals at sample times and places. The data showed that of the 6.7 mean number of volumes removed from the shelves by the observed patron, 5.5 of these were replaced. This is evidence of one of the major flaws in unobserved-use study methods. While these methodologies are not without flaws, their numerical results can assist in journal reevaluations.

Another problem with the use study is preparing patrons for it. Their cooperation with not reshelving journals is crucial. This patron preparation factor is difficult to gauge. On the one hand, prior notification alerts regular patrons to resist their habit to reshelve. On the other hand, it alerts others to falsely inflate use of their favorite journal to boost statistics, thereby decreasing the risk of its cancellation. In the University of Chicago study, it is possible that students removed additional volumes from the shelves only in search of another gift pen.

Use study results can be misleading in that they measure what has been used and not what should be used. Many undergraduates' experiences are false starts in library research. There is no way to distinguish a valuable, authentic use of an item from an incorrect choice as Ross' results confirm. Some studies are conducted for only a few weeks in the fall semester, or for the spring semester only, perhaps because more staff time cannot be expended. These limited time frames may overlook important library use trends or patterns. For example, some library-intensive courses are taught only once per year, the timing of term paper deadlines can also be a pivotal point in collecting use data. A full year of data gathering is a better approach. Thereafter, regular intervals of use analyses should be conducted.

No matter which method is used to gather use statistics, the results are valuable measures to consider along with the other criteria used for journal selection to produce a cumulative assessment. While use studies expend valuable staff time, cost money for additional supplies, and may temporarily inconvenience patrons, the expense of continuing to subscribe, bind, microfilm, and store unused journals is greater. More specialized and more expensive serials are naturally reducing the rate of per article use by our patrons. Libraries are spending more money only to achieve diminishing returns. Reevaluation is crucial to limiting the size of a periodicals collection, and use analyses are the means of determining the essential titles.

BACKFILES

Use studies can also indicate the value of backfiles. Many undergraduate assignments require current information. The latest five years of a title are probably used the most. Rosalee McReynolds estimates from use study findings at Loyola University that journal holdings in the areas of physics, chemistry, and medicine of fifteen years back, and twenty-five years back for botany and zoology, are considered generous backfiles (1984: 79). She estimates adequate backfiles for educational methodology, social work or experimental psychology as fifteen years, and for political science and anthropology as thirty to forty years. However, she notes that the important work and findings of this vintage should now be available in monographic format. McReynolds' recommendations cover only part of the scientific literature. It seems that the areas of literature and history would enjoy much longer backfiles, to be determined by local needs and use study data. Now that accreditation agencies are leaning toward evaluating the quality of the collection and not just the quantity, libraries should look more seriously at evaluating their backfiles of dead titles for deletion.

MICROFILM

University Microfilms International (UMI) provides over 16,000 periodical titles and 7,000 newspaper titles in microfilm or microfiche formats. Most of the titles that would be owned by a small college library would probably be available from this source. Still, the first step in deciding whether to purchase a microformat is to verify availability. The purchase of some titles is restricted only to those who currently subscribe to the paper issues. UMI identifies these in their catalog.

The obvious advantages to microformat over binding are space efficiency, especially if you can splice several reels together, and eliminating the need to replace missing paper issues, unless you decide to bind incomplete volumes. Except for art journals that have reproductions; journals with lots of illustrations, such as *Life*; and journals with graphs, maps, and minute statistical data where quick comparisons between pages are necessary, microfilm is the preferred format. Color microfilm is available, but its cost is still too high for most small library budgets. Many scholars and students, particularly those in English and history, still prefer to work with a bound volume. Valid complaints of eye strain from long reading sessions of microfilm or poor-quality equipment can reduce the use of the journal and the patrons' levels of satisfaction. Whenever possible, preferences for bound volumes should be honored, but lack of space and vandalism may necessitate microformats. The librarians should ultimately decide on the format and extent of the backfile.

COOPERATIVE BUYING AGREEMENTS

Local or regional agreements among libraries to purchase certain journals is sometimes a valid approach to relieve rising journal prices and strained serials budgets. Its success depends on the types of journals involved, the reciprocity of the agreements, and the turnaround time for lending and borrowing materials. Graduate-level or research journals are good candidates for cooperative buying, since their costs are generally high and their potential users tend to be graduate students or faculty who can generally afford to wait longer for materials than undergraduates, who need information more quickly for short-term assignments. For small college libraries it is a matter of geographical proximity to similar libraries with comparable needs. A nearby large university library may glean minimal benefits from resource sharing with a small college library. An agreement that is more mutually beneficial will be more fruitful. For any small college journal collection with little fat to trim, cooperative buying titles are likely to be primary or core titles of high on-site demand. Efficient document delivery is a vital ingredient to successful resource sharing. Unless off-site materials can be made available promptly, patrons' needs will be neglected. With the right mix of libraries, journals, and good ILL performance, cooperative buying agreements can serve the respective libraries as well as their patrons.

SUMMARY

Journal selection must adhere to a collection development policy. Regular reevaluations of the collection must also be scheduled with the policy in hand, along with use statistics and knowledge of new courses and majors on campus. Liaison work with faculty should incorporate all means of communication to alert faculty of their role and responsibility in selection and the proper procedures and guidelines for their recommendations. Assisting faculty with their journal needs while keeping them abreast of the library's various journal problems will reduce surprise complaints about the collection as well as increasing faculty support when needed for funding, self-studies, or accreditation reviews.

Frequent contact with the administration to assertively communicate the budgetary requirements of the journal collection is a necessity. Reciprocal borrowing agreements and other resource-sharing ventures regarding journals can be sought to enhance patrons' accessibility to journals beyond the core collection. The budget and faculty demands often dictate change for journal holdings, but librarians' knowledge of their collections and their patrons, and librarians' abilities to communicate these to their constituencies determine the extent and type of change.

REFERENCES

Association of College and Research Libraries. Undergraduate Librarians Discussion Group. 1987. "The Mission of a University Undergraduate Library: Model Statement." *College & Research Libraries News* 48: 542–44.

Farber, Evan I. 1972. *Classified List of Periodicals for the College Library*. 5th ed. Westwood, Mass.: F. W. Faxon Co.

Goehner, Donna M. 1984. "Core Lists of Periodicals Selected by Faculty Reviewers." *Technical Services Quarterly* 1, no. 4:17–38.

Harvard Business School. Baker Library. 1986/87. *Current Periodical Publications in Baker Library*. Boston: Harvard Business School.

Hastreiter, Jamie Webster, Larry Hardesty, and David Henderson. 1987. *Periodicals in College Libraries*. (CLIP Note no. 8). Chicago: American Library Association, Association of College and Research Libraries.

Katz, William A. 1982. *Magazines for Libraries*: 4th ed. New York: Bowker.

Lubans, John. 1987. "Scholars and Serials." *American Libraries* 18: 180–82.

Mathematical Association of America. Committee on the Undergraduate Program in Mathematics. 1976. *Basic Library List for Four-Year Colleges*. 2nd ed. Berkeley: The Association.

McReynolds, Rosalee. 1984. "Limiting a Periodicals Collection in a College Library." *Serials Librarian* 9 (Winter) : 75–81.

Miller, Ruth H., and Marvin C. Guilfoyle. 1986. "Computer Assisted Periodicals Selection: Structuring the Subjective." *Serials Librarian* 10: 9–22.

Rose, Robert F. 1983. "Identifying a Core Collection of Business Periodicals for Academic Libraries." *Collection Management* 5, no. 1/2: 73–87.

Ross, Johanna C. 1983. "Observations of Browsing Behavior in an Academic Library." *College & Research Libraries* 44 (July): 269–76.

Stagg, Deborah Bolton. 1985. "Serials in a Small College Library." *Library Resources and Technical Services* 29: 139–44.

Striedieck, Suzanne. Telephone interview with author. February 25, 1988.

Tuttle, Marcia. 1985. Magazine Fulfillment Centers: What They Are, How They Operate, and What We Can Do About Them. *Library Acquisitions* 9: 41–49.

Ulrich's International Periodicals Directory, 1987/88. New York: Bowker.

APPENDIX: JOURNAL REQUEST FORM

University of South Carolina
Coastal Carolina College

Kimbel Library
Conway, SC 29526

JOURNAL REQUEST FORM

Title:____

A. Major Factors for Subscribing:

1. Indicate subject matter of journal____________________

____

2. Why is this subject appropriate to the collection? Does it fill a gap? What does this title provide that others already owned do not?

____

____

3. Which courses would it support?

DEPT.	COURSE NUMBER	COURSE TITLE
________	____________	____________________
________	____________	____________________
________	____________	____________________

4. In which indexes can this title be accessed? (Consult librarians if not known)

____

B. Other Factors:

Cite reviews, language, reading level, publisher, and cost.

____

____

Please attach a sample copy of the title and/or a brochure from the publisher. Return completed form with sample to ________________.

____
Signature of requestor(s)

____
Signature of School Dean or Assistant Dean

24

Microform Periodicals

Jeanne E. Boyle

Microforms are used widely by libraries of all sizes and types, and library users are generally more comfortable with microforms today then they have been at any time previously. In spite of this, many library users are still disappointed when they find that "their" periodical is available only in microform. The challenge microforms present to libraries has been well-summarized by Francis Spreitzer:

> The value of the ever-increasing amount of information published in microform today can be realized only if libraries make their collections truly available. This means providing well-designed and carefully maintained equipment in clean, attractive, well-organized facilities. It means staffing those facilities with well-trained and enthusiastic people. It means making information about the microform collection available through the library's bibliographic records, conveniently located publishers' indexes, and guides prepared in-house for staff and library users. Libraries managing their collections in this way report greatly increased use of and appreciation for microforms. (American Library Association 1985: 47)

Since most small academic libraries use microforms for the backruns of periodicals (namely newspapers and journals), this chapter will provide an operational view of the selection, access, and service considerations that periodicals in microform require. For information on storage and preservation, equipment selection and maintenance, and facilities, the reader is referred to the references listed at the end of the chapter.

POLICIES AND PROCEDURES

A library collecting microforms should have a policy statement that describes why microforms are collected and how they are selected. Procedures about how microforms are acquired, maintained, and serviced should be developed; and microforms should be included in all other relevant library policies, such as circulation and photocopying.

PERSONNEL

Because the attitudes of those working with microforms directly affects user attitudes, staff should be selected on the basis of their enthusiasm for microforms. A strong public-service concern and an interest in training are essential. Technical abilities and the willingness to learn technical procedures are needed. Some manual dexterity is essential.

One person should be appointed to be in charge of the microform service. In a very small operation, this person could also be the head of periodicals. The library with an extensive collection of other materials in microform should appoint a separate head of microforms. Within library organizations, this person commonly reports to either the director of the library or the director's assistants. The microforms specialist must have a strong commitment to both public and technical services. Staff should be allotted to the microforms service with at least the same generosity as they are allotted to other library services. The microforms service may, in fact, require a larger commitment of staff because of greater public service and technical needs.

Depending on the size of the operation, the microforms specialist either performs the total responsibilities of the position or trains other staff or student workers to do so. These responsibilities include reference service for the collection, collection development, retrieval and refiling of microforms, checking in and processing of new materials, assistance with machines, basic equipment maintenance, arranging for repairs, training librarians and staff, and publicizing the collection. Although the specialist may not work full-time with microforms, the library's investment in its collections and equipment is advanced by giving the specialist the opportunity to attend courses, workshops, and conferences about microforms, and the chance to visit other libraries.

A procedures manual that would be the basis for staff training should be developed. Procedures could be included for each responsibility enumerated above. The manual could also include information on the bibliographic records that describe microforms, a floor plan, copies of library-developed publications on microforms, equipment manuals, emergency procedures, routine personnel procedures, and a library-wide telephone list.

COLLECTING MICROFORMS

Libraries purchase microforms primarily for reasons of space and economy. Microforms also provide increased security and preservation for valuable collections.

Periodicals may be obtained in microform in lieu of binding paper copies, in lieu of paper subscriptions to little-used titles, as a major one-time purchase to replace older volumes, or for enrichment of a collection by the addition of retrospective volumes. Newspapers are purchased in microform because the paper on which they are printed deteriorates rapidly. Saffady describes the most popular reason for ongoing microform acquisition of journals:

> A number of libraries leave paper copies of scholarly journals and other periodicals unbound at the end of the volume year and acquire permanent shelf copies on film or fiche from a micropublisher. Following a predetermined period of most active reference—typically one or two years after receipt of the last volume issue—the paper copies are discarded, leaving the microform backfile to satisfy continuing, but presumably diminished, use requirements. This approach to the management of the periodicals collection offers two potential advantages: backfile integrity and economy. (1985: 5)

Since only a very few micropublishers allow a reduced cost when subscriptions are entered for both the paper and microform editions, the cost of the microform subscription must be offset by the elimination of binding costs. To determine and compare these costs, Folcarelli suggests using average subscription and binding costs:

> The average cost of a subscription from University Microfilms International is \$13.46, so to purchase 50 titles in microform, the library must budget about \$673. To determine binding costs, the formula is: titles × volume yield per title × (the sum of the binding cost + library binding preparation cost), or:
>
> $$50 \times 1.5 \times (6.50 + 4.25) = 806.25$$
>
> In this example, microfilm saves the library \$133.25 per year. (1982: 64)

While usually put in a budget line separate from the materials or book budget, the costs of microform space, equipment, supplies, and personnel must be included when the overall budget is prepared. These costs are all too often underestimated. One-time costs should be separated from continuing costs, although one-time equipment costs are more palatably presented if they are amortized over the life of their availability.

Unless all journal titles are retained in microform, a policy must be devised for deciding which titles will be converted. The most heavily used titles may be selected to gain increased availability. Titles with detailed engineering drawings or medical illustrations, or publications where color is important may be skipped.

All titles treated in a certain index may be considered, and the index could then be housed with the microforms. Missing, damaged, or mutilated volumes may be purchased individually, but it is usually more economical for the library and better for user access if whole runs are acquired immediately. Inflation keeps costs on the rise, and it is likely that other volumes in a run are also deteriorating (Folcarelli, Tannenbaum, and Ferragano 1982: 72).

Sets of retrospective periodical volumes in such special subject areas as ethnic cultures or the underground press could be a major new support offered and publicized by the library.

TYPES OF MICROFORMS

The proper selection of microforms requires technical considerations beyond the usual collection-development review of content and price. Characteristics that should be identified include format and size, type of film, image type, reduction ratio, and packaging.

Periodicals are usually available in 35mm or 16mm microfilm or microfiche. The sequential arrangement of microfilm makes it more suited for periodicals than microfiche, although microfiche should be considered for heavily used current titles. A microfilm reel containing an entire volume of a periodical limits the use of that volume to only one person at any one time. With microfiche, however, each issue of a journal volume can be used separately. When compared to microfilm, microfiche is harder to keep in order and is more easily mislaid or stolen. Micropublishers normally charge the original volume price for replacement microfilm, but microfiche issues can usually be replaced individually for a nominal fee. It is easier to keep microfilm in order, while microfiche certainly requires staff time to keep in order. Users find it easier to place fiche into readers than to thread microfilm, but in so doing they may leave behind fingerprints that can obstruct the image. If the library is interested in providing a duplication service, microfiche duplicators are available at reasonable prices. Microfilm remains the most popular format for library journal collections.

There is disagreement within the microforms community about whether 35mm or 16mm microfilm is the size of choice. 35mm is certainly more commonly found in libraries. With a larger image area, 35mm film is necessary for large-format materials such as newspapers, so that an entire newspaper page fits on one frame of the microfilm. It may also be necessary for scientific journals with detailed diagrams and formulas using tiny subscripts. In terms of storage capacity and equipment availability, 16mm has definite advantages. It takes about half the storage space to house the same number of reels of 16mm as 35mm. In addition, Boss notes that there are many more 16mm readers and reader-printers available because it is the size used by business (1981: 32–33). Critics maintain that the small frame size of 16mm microfilm results in poor readability and reproduction.

Silver halide, diazo, and vesicular are the three types of film in wide use.

While silver halide is the only film to meet archival standards, its archival potential exists only if it is stored and handled using rather exacting regimens which would be difficult in a busy small academic library. Silver is also considerably more expensive than the other types and is not necessary for the provision of good microform service. Both diazo and vesicular have very good abrasion resistance, with diazo being a little tougher and a good choice for heavily used titles. While they differ in their sensitivities, all microforms should be protected from extremes of light and temperature. Both diazo and vesicular are available in several color shades. Black or blue-black are better for making copies, while blue is easier on the eye for reading (Boss 1981: 36).

The choice of microform might also be made on the basis of image type (polarity), and reader-printer availability. If more reading than copying is anticipated, or if photographic images are to be viewed, the library may wish to specify positive film. The dark background of negative film, on the other hand, has the advantage of reducing eye fatigue because less light is projected onto the viewing screen, lessening screen glare and eliminating magnification of dust on the film. The library with a reader-printer that makes copies in reverse image could choose a negative polarity because copies can be made in the more familiar positive image.

Reduction ratios of new selections should be compatible with equipment on hand or new lenses may have to be purchased. Common ratios used are 18 × for newspapers, 24 × for most journals and monographs, and 42 × for computer output microfiche.

The frustration a user can experience when trying to thread a microfilm machine is alleviated if reels are packaged in cartridges or cassettes. Cartridges, which are available for 16mm microfilm, also reduce damage from manual handling of the microfilm. Cartridges are generally made to be compatible with only one manufacturer's equipment and are not interchangeable, although recent development of an American National Standards Institute (ANSI) standard cartridge may alleviate that problem if it comes into wide acceptance. Since users also have problems with the use of cartridges, the added expense of cartridges may not be worthwhile. Cassettes have never become terribly popular and are offered by very few manufacturers.

ACQUISITION AND PROCESSING

Once the library has selected the titles to be received in microform, a reputable micropublisher should be chosen. Catalogs can be obtained from several micropublishers, and the library title list can be compared. Micropublishers will often search a title list and give a quotation. This can save the library a tremendous amount of work and provides timely cost information.

A comprehensive list of microform offerings which includes periodical listings is the annual *Guide to Microforms in Print* (Westport, Conn., Meckler Publishing Corp.). This cumulative listing of microform titles available from some 400 micropublishers includes pertinent purchasing information. Journal entries are listed by title unless issued by a government agency or sponsoring society, association, or so forth. Newspaper entries are by title followed by city and state or country. There is a companion *Subject Guide to Microforms in Print*.

Along with considering availability and price, Saffady cautions that contractual considerations are an important part of the acquisition process (1985: 138). The library should review guarantees and discounts offered, compare time payment plans, confirm the availability of replacements, and come to an agreement on the release schedule for current microfiche issues and year-end or volume-end microfilm reels. Various discount programs are offered, including price reductions for trade-in of hard-copy volumes. Free reading or storage equipment may be available when orders of a certain dollar amount are placed. There should be an agreement that defective microforms will be replaced as discovered since some time may elapse before defects are found.

Once the vendor is selected, it is time to issue the order. The American Library Association gives a succinct list of the items that should be included in a microform order: bibliographic description of the original work or name of the collection, vendor identification, format, reduction ratio, number of units (reels, fiche, cartridges, and so on), film type (silver halide, diazo, or vesicular), polarity, price, billing and shipping instructions, purchase order number, number of copies ordered, date of order, and nature of guides or catalog copy (1985: 7).

New microforms should be inspected immediately upon receipt and before invoices are processed. All elements of the order should be verified, and a preliminary evaluation of the quality of the microform and any accompanying materials should be made. There are many technical writings that detail what makes a good microform, but library workers do not have to become technicians to know what is acceptable. A competent inspection of incoming materials might include checking the following: purchase order and packing slip, reel and fiche packages and labels, leaders and trailers on reels (should be about 20 inches), headings on fiche, whether reels are wound correctly, number and sequence of fiche, bowing (width) or curling (length), clarity and suitability of eye-legible target frames, and legibility of microform segments (Folcarelli, Tannenbaum, and Ferragano 1982: 98). Any item that is not acceptable should be returned at once.

Additional processing could include correcting any minor deficiencies noted on the preliminary inspection, such as rewinding a reel that was wound backwards or placing fiche in acid-free envelopes. The American Library Association recommends that ownership marks be placed on all packages and film leaders with perforation or a film-marking pen (1985: 30). Rubber bands on microfilm reels should be replaced with acid-free button-and-tie wrappers because the sulfur in rubber bands is harmful to the film. If several fiche are contained in one envelope, an acid-free paper behind the first fiche will make the header easier to read.

Processing supplies are available from the regular library supply houses, and may be purchased in bulk.

Microform periodicals should be checked in on the library serial record in the same manner as papercopy periodicals. If microform is regularly received in lieu of binding, it is desirable that separate check-in records be maintained for the paper and microform versions and that they be immediately distinguishable from each other. In a flat file, for example, different colored check-in cards could be used or different colored plastic tabs could be inserted under the edge of the card holder. The record for the paper copy should indicate how long the paper version is retained and be kept current as to what issues have been discarded. If only an occasional backrun is purchased, the microform may be added to the existing papercopy card, but its format, extent, and location should be clearly noted.

ACCESS

Microform users must be able to find out what the library owns and where it is located. This must not be harder to do for microforms than for any other library material if microforms are to gain acceptance. It is therefore recommended that microforms be given the same bibliographic treatment as papercopy materials. In this time of open stack access, it is further recommended that users have open access to microform collections, although the library may wish to specify that staff do all the refiling.

Microform periodicals should be located in a centralized collection near the papercopy periodicals collection, whether these are bound backruns or only current issues. A very small microform collection might be dispersed throughout the regular collections. The advantages of this system for access are obvious, but the disadvantages in terms of service must be considered carefully. While the user will be able to locate the microform titles in the same way as other titles, the availability of appropriate reading equipment and staff assistance would be more complex. Provision of a proper storage environment would be extremely difficult. If papercopy periodicals are classified, time would have to be spent also classifying the microform versions.

Various recommendations for cataloging level are made in the library literature. In the end, libraries are only able to do what can be managed. It should be borne in mind, however, that for periodical collections the primary access points needed are title and subject. Papercopy indexes and reel guides also require access by author or compiler. All records should indicate location.

Classification and arrangement by Library of Congress or Dewey call numbers may provide familiarity to users, but the effect is otherwise wasted since microforms are not browsable in the same way as paper copies. In addition, most libraries house microforms separately from their papercopy collections. Microform periodicals must be arranged first of all by format—microfilm or microfiche—because the practicalities of storage require it. Within each format, it is common for libraries to arrange microform periodical collections alphabetically by title. If a classification scheme is used, it should follow the arrangement in the simplest possible way. The only classification required with a title arrangement, for example, is a format-specific location symbol such as "FILM" or "FICHE."

Some libraries develop more complex arrangements and correspondingly more complex classification schemes. Libraries that arrange microforms by format and consecutive numbers, for example, may use title and item numbers in addition to the format symbol. Microfilm reel 11 in the seventh title acquired would be found at MFM/7/11. An advantage to this system is that major expansion is confined to one part of the collection, while a disadvantage is that users must refer to a bibliographic record of some sort in order to locate the titles they need. Libraries that try to provide shelf- or drawer-specific location information for their users on bibliographic records inevitably develop record maintenance problems as collections are shifted. Such a scheme is not recommended. Whatever classification is adopted, the classification assigned should be written on each microfilm box and leader and on each microfiche envelope. Cabinets and shelves should be labeled to match.

The same access method should be used for microform periodicals as for their paper counterparts. This could take the form of a card file, on-line catalog terminal, wing file, or book-format list located in the periodicals area. Records should clearly indicate whether a given title is held in paper copy or microform. If the microforms are at a distance from the regular periodicals area and the main public catalog, a separate catalog or other periodicals listing should be available in the microforms area. Ideally, a complete holdings record for microform periodicals is readily available at least to the staff. Records for the indexes, reel guides, and other aids that work with the microforms should also be available in or near the microforms area.

A library-prepared guide to the microform periodicals should be developed and made available throughout the library. It should describe what is available, where it is located, and how it is used. Helpful data to include are title, summary of holdings, location, contents, and any missing or illegible sections. This is a good opportunity to publicize the value and purpose of microforms and explain the library's reason for acquiring them.

SERVICES

Services offered will differ from library to library, and depend greatly upon the available resources of each. Basic services in even the smallest library should consist of an easily accessible and correctly filed collection, proper reading and printing machines in good order, and competent staff assistance. The level of service in libraries with only part-time microforms staff can, however, be quite high if everyone in the library is trained to provide basic equipment assistance and answer questions about the microform collections. The importance of posted instructions and diagrams and of descriptive flyers becomes evident. Training for all library staff should also include a thorough understanding of the advantages and disadvantages of microforms so that user resistance can be dealt with effectively.

Making paper copies from microforms is usually done by self-service, and it is preferable that the cost be equal to that charged for photocopying paper materials. Coin-boxes can be purchased from and installed by equipment vendors. If coin boxes are not installed, payment can be on an honor system. Copyright warning notices should be posted on each machine. If there is sufficient staff available, copying can be done for users. This is convenient for some users and inconvenient for others, but in any case it results in less wear and tear on the machines because they are used only by experienced people. Duplicating microfiche is usually a staff function.

The policy for loaning microforms should be the same as for papercopy periodicals. Circulation of microforms is generally not permitted. Some libraries, however, lend not only the microforms but also portable readers. Microforms should be loaned with instructions on packing and care (keep away from moisture, light, and heat), while readers are loaned with use instructions and spare bulbs. A free microfiche copy can be provided in lieu of loaning.

Microform services can be enhanced by cooperation with neighboring libraries. Smaller academic libraries cannot be expected to purchase the large microform sets held by large research libraries. They can, however, provide access to those sets needed by their users by purchasing the paper guides compiled by set micropublishers. They can also work together to share their resources by cooperative buying and Union Listing. Interlibrary loan agreements for borrowing microforms or providing paper copies are impressive to library users who had thought they would not be able to acquire the material they needed.

Other services include orientation tours, bibliographic instruction, one-on-one machine demonstrations, and bulletin board and display case promotions of new or little-used materials.

CONCLUSION

With adequate planning and organization, even the smallest library can and should develop a microform periodicals collection. This chapter has discussed some of the elements of a successful microform periodical service. If users are to be satisfied using microforms, then the library must be committed to fully meeting the many challenges microforms present.

REFERENCES

American Library Association, Resources and Technical Services Division, Committees of the Reproduction of Library Materials Section and Resources Section. 1985.

Microforms in Libraries: A Manual for Evaluation and Management. Edited by Francis Spreitzer. Chicago: American Library Association.

Boss, Richard W., with Deborah Raikes. 1981. *Developing Microform Reading Facilities*. Westport, Conn.: Microform Review.

Folcarelli, Ralph J., Arthur C. Tannenbaum, and Ralph C. Ferragano. 1982. *The Microform Connection: A Basic Guide for Libraries*. New York and London: Bowker.

Hall, Hal W., and George H. Michaels. 1985. ''Microform Reader Maintenance.'' *Microform Review* 14: 24–34 (an excellent brief review of maintenance procedures).

Michaels, George H., Mindy S. Kerber, and Hal W. Hall. 1984. *A Microform Reader Maintenance Manual*. Westport, Conn.: Meckler Publishing.

Saffady, William. 1985. *Micrographics*, 2d ed. Littleton, Colo.: Libraries Unlimited.

Teague, S. John. 1985. *Microform, Video and Electronic Media Librarianship*. London and Boston: Butterworths.

25

Academic Media Selection: A Faculty and Librarian Collaboration

Charmaine B. Tomczyk

Faculty participation in the selection of media is paramount for a good collection. Faculty participation and approval of any specific media acquisition will encourage its steady use. Liaison work between faculty and librarians in identifying, previewing, and selecting appropriate media materials can insure a valuable collection of useful materials that meet the needs of faculty and students.

The scope of media materials is defined here to include nonbook audiovisual materials, excluding microfilm, microfiche, software, and CD-ROM. Most microform materials in small college libraries are representative of the journal collection backfiles, just as the CD-ROM is generally reference materials or indexes. The media format in these cases is an alternative to the printed one. The selection of computer software is addressed throughout the literature, and is deserving of that special attention given its unique format requirements and uses. This chapter will not address that lengthy subject.

WHEREFORE MEDIA?

To collect media or not to collect media? If a library has not had a media collection thrust upon it, nor strong demands for media from its patrons or administration, it is unlikely that librarians will begin such a collection. The cost of the equipment and its electrical requirements, the proper space, shelving, and storage, and the price tags of many media items are not encouraging to a library that is starting a media collection from scratch. As Heery concluded in his survey of British academic libraries, smaller colleges tended to collect more media than the larger universities (1984: 50). He suspects this is due to teacher education programs in smaller settings. The media was collected to support the teacher education programs where future teachers could use elementary- or secondary-level media to build their curriculum units or lesson plans. As with most new technologies, the quality of hardware is more advanced than the software. Increasingly, many disciplines can find valuable media at academic levels. Overall, quality-information sources and educational materials should be made available regardless of format. In particular, media in the areas of art, science, and music lends itself well to stimulating teaching and learning. Media's role can span from assisting the faculty in the classroom to individualized, self-paced instruction for the student. Only 6 of the 179 academic libraries responding to Heery's study had no media at all (1984: 7). Ever since the American Library Association included media in its standards to calculate number of equivalent volumes added to collections, libraries have begun to recognize it as an integral part of their collections and one that "counts."

WHERE IS MEDIA?

The decision to collect depends on the college curriculum's use of media and the college's administrative and educational policies regarding media. The administration may decide that a separate facility is needed to store media if no space exists in the library. For example, many academic computer centers have the responsibility of purchasing software. Some campuses may expand on their media production units to include housing the media as well. Often the college and not the library decides who will collect media. USC-Coastal's library, for example, adopted a learning resources center that was transferred from the School of Education. Most colleges fragment collections due to special needs (or lack of planning). The art department may house a slide collection to serve as a main portion of its classroom teaching. The music department may have its own collection of sheet music. Various departments may have purchased their favorite videocassettes for class viewing. In times like these when library budgets are so slim, the chances of a library beginning a new collection of media on its own are also very slim. Even for those libraries that already have a collection, the book and journal collections, in that order, tend to get priority for purchase.

SETTING THE COLLECTION'S BOUNDARIES

For the library that has the responsibility of collecting media, the first approach is a collection-development policy. The ease with which media can departmentalize or decentralize on campus is alarming. Decide what you can collect, store, and utilize well. The design of the facilities may often dictate the limits of the collection. A small college media collection can not expect to collect actively all formats on all topics, any more than the library's book collection can. If the art department can purchase or produce, store, and use slides (mainly for their own use) more easily and efficiently than the library, then let them continue. If the foreign language department or the music department has audio labs for its students, then do not duplicate their mission in the library's media collection. Librarians are very knowledgeable of the futility of duplication, but may not be aware of the various pockets of media throughout campus. Find out who collects what and where it is by talking with faculty, deans, and department heads, and widely advertise what you are offering. You may find that some media is suited to its nonlibrary location, but other media may be better suited to the library. A transfer should be considered if environmental conditions, such as lack of air-conditioning, are endangering the materials, or if better and more access can be achieved. Typically the library is the building on campus that maintains the longest hours of operation. It may be discovered that a departmental video can be used effectively by another department as well, thereby reducing the item's overall per-use cost. The purchase becomes a better one when housed in the library. If the suggestion of a transfer develops into a tug-of-war, weigh its benefits carefully against the possibility of damaged relations between the library and the department. Political climates cannot be ignored.

COLLECTION DEVELOPMENT POLICY

According to the Audiovisual Committee of the Association of College and Research Libraries guidelines for audiovisual materials in academic libraries, the collection-development policy should specify formats relative to the college's goals and resources, the clientele, curriculum support, and design of the facilities (1987: 535). It recommends the following criteria for selection: scope of curriculum, use, faculty and graduate needs, quality of item, and life expectancy. When appropriate, previewing before purchasing is recommended. The committee also included the need for frequent evaluation of materials for possible weeding and monitoring of purchases in light of college objectives.

Evaluating Media

A qualified media librarian should have the final decision on the purchase of media materials based on the library's approved criteria for selection and the librarian's knowledge of the current media holdings. The evaluation process should include a subject specialist, namely a faculty member from the appropriate discipline. Faculty participation not only judges validity of content but also increases the potential use of the item if purchased. With the high cost of many media items, maximum usage should be a primary goal. Items should be previewed. Most companies will send a full copy or sample (portion) copy for viewing free of charge. Some will charge a preview fee, which might be paid by the department making the request.

Unlike books, media presents several factors to evaluate. A chapter by Clara

DiFelice in *Media Librarianship* proposes a media evaluation form to be used after previewing the media (Ellison 1985: 178–84). The fine points of three major areas, content, utilization and educational value, and technical and physical aspects, are rated by the faculty viewers, who are also asked to score how well the material satisfies their objectives. A final section reserved for the media librarian rates technical and maintenance considerations, such as format compatibility with present media equipment, durability of items for prolonged use, and quality of presentation as compared to other media on the same subject. The form is a vehicle for prioritizing recommendations that can assist in making the final purchase decision.

Sources of Evaluative Reviews

Evaluative reviews that critically judge the item against its competitors should be consulted before or after previewing. Nonevaluative reviews are plentiful, but often do not "pack the punch" needed to decide whether a $350 item is even worth previewing. Review sources vary in amount and type of information. Some are limited to the formats of media, number of reviews printed, or type of library audience. A front-runner in comprehensive listing of reviews is the *Media Review Digest: The Only Complete Guide to Reviews of Non-Book Media* (edited by Leslie Orlin and published annually by Pierian Press). The 1986 edition reviews over fourteen formats in 131 periodicals and services, with some 40,000 review citations and cross-references annually. It provides audience-level indications, such as "C" for college level, and ratings from excellent to poor. However, the book gives a disclaimer that its ratings and reviews should not be the sole source for purchase decisions. *Choice* reviews media, videos and filmstrips in particular, for college collections. *Booklist* also reviews media bimonthly, plus it publishes an annual roundup of outstanding film, video, and filmstrip productions that have been most recommended by their editorial staff. Audience levels are provided too. To date there is not a resource tool for buying "an opening-day collection" for media. Such a compilation would probably be as difficult to assemble as drafting core lists of journals.

The following evaluative review sources are available for the special formats generally found in small academic media collections. (See the various chapters of Ellison and Coty's 1987 book for more complete listings.)

Audiotapes

Record Tape Review Index (annual)

Down Beat

Billboard

Instructional Innovator

Notes

Filmstrips

Science Teacher

Media and Methods

Choice

Library Journal

School Library Journal

Booklist

Maps

American Cartographer

Journal of Geography

Geographical Review

Professional Geographer

Music Scores

First to be considered is *A Basic Music Library* (1983) by the Music Library Association's Committee on Basic Music Collection, edited by Robert Michael Fling (Chicago: ALA).

Notes

Music Review

Other publications devoted to particular instruments, for example, *Piano Quarterly* or *Guitar Review*, should also be included.

Phonograph Records (LPs) and Compact Discs (CDs)

Audio

American Record Guide

Music Journal

Young Children

Rolling Stone

Stereo Review

Videotapes

Choice

American Libraries

Instructor

Jump Cut: A Review of Contemporary Media

Video Librarian
AV Video
E and ITV

CRITERIA FOR SELECTION

The media librarian must first establish whether the nonprint material accomplishes its goal better than a comparable print format. If so, then the quality of the production should be closely examined. This process varies with each type of format. Below are some evaluative points to consider on some of the more common formats of college media.

Audiotapes

The length and thickness of tapes can determine their longevity. Cassette tapes should be sixty minutes or shorter, with minimum thickness of 1 mil (.001 inch). The longer the tape the thinner it is, which makes it more susceptible to getting caught in the machine or stretching. This ruins the sound and eventually breaks the tape. Tapes should be evaluated for good sound levels and clarity, with no background noise. Prerecorded tapes should be played on proper equipment for longer life and better sound. Formats to match against your equipment include the number of tracks (one, two, four, or eight), monaural or stereo, and the Dolby sound system for noise reduction. The faster the speed of the tape, the better the fidelity, for example, 71/2 inches per seconds (ips) is excellent. Lastly, the construction of the cartridge should be durable. Cassette shells that are secured with screws rather than glue are better made.

Filmstrips

For this format, only the suggestion of motion should be well portrayed in the subject matter. If motion must be illustrated to explain or discuss the subject, then a filmstrip is the wrong format to choose. A filmstrip on how to make points in basketball, for example, will not make points with its viewers. The visuals should be clear, appropriate, and interesting, using a variety of graphics, colors, and range of views. We are all too familiar with media plagued by the ''talking heads'' syndrome. Accompanying audio parts should comply with criteria noted in the section above. In addition, sound and images should be suitably matched and synchronized. Captions should be easy to read, given background images and the intended audiences. This format, as all others, should have the educational value to arouse critical thinking.

Maps

Accurate representation is a key factor in judging a quality map. Since the mere interpretation of maps requires some skill by the media librarian, the more complex task of accuracy must rest on the reputation of the publisher. A few of the popular map publishers known to most college libraries are Rand McNally, National Geographic Society, Hammond, American Map Company, Hubbard Scientific Company, and, of course, the National Cartographic Information Center of the U.S. Geological Survey. The printing, colors, scales, and legends should be clear and not blurred, with correct spellings, current names, and adequate explanations. The amount of detail should be appropriate to the intent without appearing confusing or overwhelming to the user.

Phonograph Records (LPs) versus Compact Discs (CDs)

LPs have been the popular medium for audio for over one hundred years. Large collections have been developed and heavily used by patrons, most of whom own stereos. However, technology and consumer markets are changing. The high quality of CDs, despite their slightly increased unit cost over LPs, has made sales soar. The decreasing price of CD players is making them more affordable for most households. While records will continue to be valuable for existing sound collections, the CD is a strong competitor to replace many categories of music previously available only on LPs. CDs appear to have a physical advantage over LPs regarding resistance to warping and damage from humidity or temperature change. CDs are easier to handle, load, play, and store. The CD format is standardized internationally, making it compatible with all CD players. Most importantly, their sound quality is better in terms of lower distortions and surface noise, sharper channel separation, better dynamic range, and higher fidelity. Classical and jazz recordings are areas to consider converting to CD. Spoken word or children's recordings may continue to be suitable in record format. CD manufacturers usually guarantee a longevity of five to ten years. Of course, the choice depends largely on the equipment available in the facility and the patrons' households. When audiocassettes came on the scene, LPs continued to hold their status and usage. The results of the CD revolution are not yet final. The decision of how much to buy in CD format will ultimately depend on the budget, the equipment, and patrons' demand.

Videotapes

When purchasing a motion picture that has been dubbed to tape format, be sure it is the correct, unedited version. Many films have been remade by different directors and, therefore, are substantially different. Regarding novelizations, the fidelity of the video movie to the book may be an important factor for the literature professor who intends to use it in the classroom. The tape speed during recording should be fast to insure a less grainy picture during playing. The grade quality of the tape should insure minimal noise or dropout. Poor quality tape will stretch and wear out quickly.

Videotape can substitute for 16mm films for faculty in the classroom. With the popularity of videotape players at home, students and faculty tend to prefer this format over the awkwardness of the projector and screen. Because of the high cost of educational videotapes, such as those from PBS (Public Broadcasting System) or Time-Life Video productions, checking evaluative reviews and previewing are very important. Some educators foresee the video replacing the sound filmstrip. However, not all subjects are appropriate for this conversion. The "pause" feature on videoplayers gives a grainy, sometimes indistinguishable image. For instruction purposes, the filmstrip allows a better still image for close inspection and discussion, especially in the areas of art or science. In general, this medium is too expensive to consider for recreational purposes. Instead, for guaranteed use, it must fulfill an educational objective within the curriculum.

SUMMARY

Media selection requires a knowledge of the media collection policy and its relation to the overall library collection and other departmental collections. Campus policy at best (or campus sentiment at least) toward media will influence its present handling and future prospects. The library's media collection should complement, not conflict or compete with, other campus media projects.

Evaluative review sources and, whenever possible, firsthand examination or preview of the materials should precede purchase. As technology produces advanced media for educational applications, media librarians have a responsibility to explore, test, and consider the value of new items within the academic goals of their collections and institutions.

REFERENCES

Ellison, John W. 1985. *Media Librarianship*. New York: Neal-Schuman Publishers.

Ellison, John W., and Patricia Ann Coty. 1987. *Non-Book Media: Collection Management and User Services*. Chicago: American Library Association.

Heery, M. J. 1984. *Audiovisual Materials in Academic Libraries*. Leicester, England: Library Association, Audiovisual Group.

Association of College and Research Libraries, Audiovisual Committee. 1987. "Guidelines for Audiovisual Services in Academic Libraries." *College and Research Libraries News* 9: 533–36.

PART VII

Facilities

26

Library Interior Design and Furniture Selection

Robert A. Kuhner

The interior designer handed the head librarian the final architectural layout. The head librarian looked at the drawings and took only a few seconds before announcing them unacceptable. The designer was stunned. The drawings were the outcome of many weeks of discussion that included requests by the designer for information from thc library staff. It was a small library and a modest written program had been worked out. The library staff and the designer had gone over material storage and basic data. A series of preliminary layouts had been discussed with the library staff. The final drawings and specifications were due in two days in order to meet the contract deadline and for work to proceed in a timely fashion. How did this happen? The designer had worked on many library projects and was familiar with libraries from an administrative and managerial viewpoint. The head librarian had appeared hostile to change even though mandated by his supervisor, who had called in a series of consultants. The head librarian had remained silent throughout most of the discussions. Communication among all people involved in planning a new facility is essential. A process that allows the giving, taking, and rejection of ideas is crucial.

The planning process that precedes the actual remodeling should not be taken lightly, nor should the importance of discussion and finalizing of space, furniture, and equipment requirements be underestimated. Remodeling a library or even a section of a library is usually expensive. Besides the cost of remodeling, which includes construction and new furniture and equipment, the planning process will involve staff time and possibly the hiring of a consultant and an interior designer or architect. However, when the facility changes have been completed with careful and thoughtful planning, the remodeling should begin to pay dividends. As Keyes Metcalf stated, "A poorly planned and constructed building may force a institution year after year to spend much more on operation and maintenance than would be required by a better one" (Metcalf 1986: ix).

Planning a remodeled facility differs little from planning a new building. Extensive remodeling can and frequently does involve all the planning and design elements that must be considered in planning a new building. There are certain elements of interior design that must be dealt with no matter what size the project, whether an entire library or a small unit housed in the existing structure.

Planning may be undertaken for a variety of reasons. The impetus may be a determining factor in how the initial phases of planning proceed. Most commonly, space utilization is not examined until space begins to run out. Poor traffic patterns and work flow are not perceived until the books pile up, and then it is attributed to a lack of space. Other reasons for change include new services, shifts in library use, college curricula changes, a need to reorganize the collections, severe cuts in library personnel, and, of course, automation. Whatever the reasons for considering remodeling, the problems in an existing situation should be analyzed clearly and presented to the library staff involved, the college administration, and, depending on the scope of the situation, the students and faculty. Winning support, financial and otherwise, for change from both library staff and college administration is extremely important.

PLANNING PERSONNEL

Once it is decided to embark on a remodeling project, the next step is to decide who will be involved. Who will make which decisions? A formal library planning committee may be established, especially for larger projects. If such a committee is appointed, it must have a clear charge. The key members should involve knowledgeable library staff whose areas of responsibility include the library units affected. Those library staff personnel selected for direct involvement should have experience and expertise that will contribute to discussions and the decision-making process. They must realize that their role will be labor-intensive and that their time away from regular duties may be disruptive to serving library users, but that long-term benefits must take precedence over present staff and user needs. Library staff time should be allocated to planning, and not just taken from normal daily responsibilities. In addition to library staff, it may be appropriate to include college administrators, facility and space planners, building and grounds personnel, teaching faculty, students, and outside community users. The parent institution or funding agency (such as a government or private corporation) may provide some key personnel assistance. When possible, hiring a consultant or interior designer may be necessary for some preliminary planning as well as the design stage.

THE CONSULTANT

The reasons for hiring a consultant are basically twofold: to receive an objective point of view and to obtain experience not available from within the organization. The library staff may not have experience in planning or designing a new facility or in a particular critical area, such as lighting, building structure, or computer facilities. A library consultant will be versed in both library and design matters and can interpret or act as translator between librarian and designer.

Frequently, consultants are hired without an understanding of the role they are to play. When selecting a consultant, make sure that both you and the consultant know specifically what is involved in the consulting work. The library cannot expect a building consultant to recommend and specify a library security system or to submit a detailed interior design solution unless this has been indicated in a contract. If the consultant is hired to assist in writing a library facility program or to review the plans submitted by an interior designer (or both), this must be stated clearly. A worthwhile step in obtaining the services of a consultant is to follow the routine bidding process of the college, sending out invitations for bids to several consultants; a written contract with specific deadlines, based on the bid proposal submitted by the consultant awarded the job, then follows.

At some point, a feasibility study may be advisable to determine the cost of the project. This may involve a campus space planner, structural engineer, or outside contractor.

PLANNING SCHEDULE AND WORK PLAN

Make sure that the library staff and others involved in planning know their respective responsibilities and deadlines. Schedule regular meetings. Set up a timetable. Using the basic techniques of Critical Path Method (CPM) may prove useful in putting the planning process on more than one track where and when possible, and indicates to all involved what deadlines must be met before work can proceed to the next step (see figure 1). All major steps and milestones must be clearly indicated to reach the objectives and goals established for the planning process.

Events (indicated by a number in a circle) are milestones that start or complete an activity; they do not consume time or resources. Numbers do not refer to chronology.

0. Project begins;
1. Building committee's first meeting scheduled;
2. Preliminary goals and objectives completed;
3. List of prospective facility consultants completed;

Figure 1
Work Plan Diagram

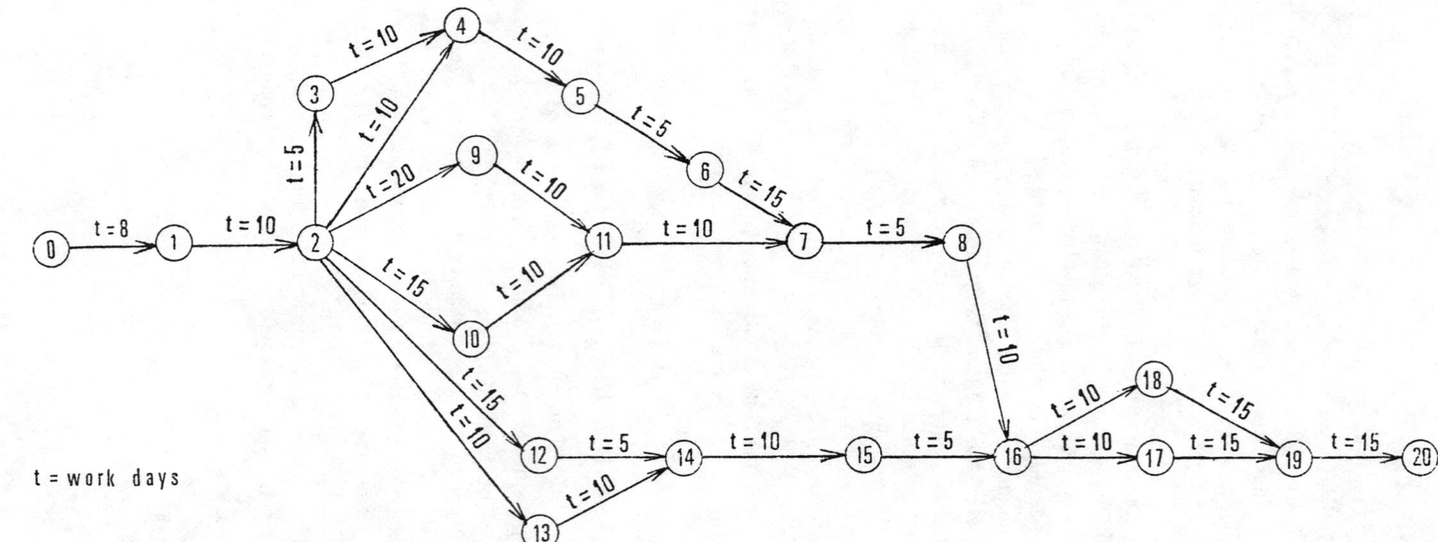

4. Invitation for bids for facility consultants completed;
5. Building consultant contract awarded;
6. First meeting of facility consultant and building committee scheduled;
7. Preliminary report from facility consultant due;
8. Final report and facility program from facility consultant due;
9. Preliminary furniture and equipment list completed;
10. Library units-space worksheets submitted;
11. Worksheets completed;
12. Reports of library visits due;
13. List of prospective interior designers completed;
14. Invitation for bids for interior designer completed;
15. Interior designer contract awarded;
16. First meeting of interior designer and building committee scheduled;
17. Schematic drawings submitted;
18. Final furniture and equipment selection completed;
19. Preliminary architectural drawing submitted;
20. Design phase completed.

Activities require time and preparation between events.

0–1. Write building committee charge; appoint members with areas of responsibilities.

1–2. Formulate objective and goals; discuss facility problems and possible scope of changes with library personnel, college administrators, campus space planner, and appropriate others.

2–3. Identify at least five possible facility consultants.

3–4. Interview prospective facility consultants.

2–4. Prepare invitation for bids for facility consultant.

4–5. Review and evaluate bid responses; select consultant; write contract.

5–6. Set agenda for first meeting with facility consultant; collect and review documentation for facility consultant.

6–7. Schedule facility consultant meetings with appropriate library and college personnel; provide additional documentation as needed, review general findings.

2–9. Arrange for library staff and building committee members to meet with furniture and equipment vendors; visit showrooms and other libraries; send for manufacturer catalogs, price lists; review library literature.

9–11. Discuss furniture and equipment; contact possible vendors for additional information.

2–10. Solicit space and furniture and equipment needs from library units.

10–11. Review preliminary space and furniture and equipment requirements; discuss with library units and on administrative levels.

11–7. Review worksheets and other documentation for facility program.

7–8. Discuss preliminary reports on all levels; make recommendations to facility consultant.

8–16. Review facility final report and facility program for scope of remodeling; solicit comments.

2–12. Schedule building committee members to visit other libraries; discuss and write reports indicating findings.

12–14. Prepare invitation for bids for interior designer.

2–13. Identify possible interior designers and visit some of their completed projects.

13–14. Interview prospective interior designers.

14–15. Review and evaluate bid responses; select interior designer and write contract.

15–16. Set agenda for first meeting with interior designer.

16–17. Review facilities program with interior designer; tour present facility; schedule time for discussion with staff.

17–19. Review schematic drawings; make recommendations.

16–18. Discuss furniture and equipment requirements with designer; visit showrooms; ask for samples for on-site testings (for example, reading chairs); discuss recommendations with appropriate library and college personnel.

18–19. Final review of furniture and equipment selections including colors, fabrics, and so forth.

19–20. Review preliminary drawings and all final furniture and equipment selections; make recommendations.

The above planning strategy is useful from the first stages of planning a remodeling through the shakedown period.

STAFF PREPARATION

Those directly involved should visit other libraries, be familiar with current literature in both library and building- and furniture-design publications, and attend workshops and seminars. Knowledge and advice can also be gained through discussions with furniture and equipment vendors. Talk to as many vendors as possible; ask questions, reflect, and then ask more questions. Visit furniture and equipment manufacturers' showrooms, if accessible, and attend trade shows. Do not rely solely on library conference exhibits or library vendors for information and expertise; these are useful but have limitations.

A FACILITY PROGRAM

The burden for realizing a facility program will fall on library personnel even when a consultant is hired to assist in this responsibility. Nonlibrary personnel hired to design a new facility cannot be expected to assume total responsibility for planning. Outside professionals, whether library consultants, interior designers, or campus planners, need specific information, requirements, and suggestions from library staff.

To assist in writing a program, librarians must first understand their daily work routines and the work plant options available to them before making final recommendations to an interior designer for an improved library facility. Recommendations for any size remodeling should be made in the form of a written program. The program should then be agreed on by all parties involved. In a small project, such as remodeling a single library unit, these may be the head librarian, a small segment of the library staff, and a space planner. In large, costly projects, approval of the facility program must be made by the library administration, the parent institution, and the funding body. The process of writing the facility program, as outlined below, will help the library staff evaluate their needs and carry the planning process beyond redecorating into the realm of designing a practical and esthetically pleasing library work space.

It cannot be overemphasized that preparing a program is perhaps the most important element in the planning process. Certainly in large and costly projects this step must not be treated lightly or left solely to others to execute, whether they are from inside or outside the library and college. Neither the interior designer nor consultants hired by the library should have the final word on the program. The person in charge of the library or library unit should be the primary individual responsible for the contents of the program. This will prevent misunderstandings about the need and scope of the project after the remodeling begins.

The program or guide to the interior designer should be detailed, concise, and very clear. Professional space planners neither need nor want a wordy document. Telegraph style, when possible, is preferable to lengthy prose.

In a large remodeling endeavor, a small pilot project is advisable to avoid subsequent pitfalls in preparing the documentation needed for the program. This can be done by taking a selected library unit through the steps for developing a program and then discussing the difficulties encountered. A general staff meeting can be held to explain amendments in the process.

PARTS OF THE PROGRAM

The Introduction

A clear statement of the goals and objectives should be included, along with a mission statement when it might prove useful. A brief statement is sufficient when a small unit such as an acquisitions unit is the scope of the project. Include information that describes the type of users served (undergraduate or graduate), type of material, formats, variety of media, and the relationship of the library or library unit to other components of the college and outside community. Its function as a support service for the instructional program of the college should be discussed. Include general needs for volume size for each type of collection, number and variety of student stations required, and the number of staff workstations needed.

General Specifications

An overview might include discussion of a centralized library versus a decentralized or subject-division library scheme; service priorities to college community and outside community; access to materials through the catalog; bibliographies including on-line database service; the locations of material storage; desired configurations of reader areas (reading areas scattered throughout library or interspersed among book stack areas); types of reading room furniture (size and number of seats, study carrels, individual research rooms, and lounges); conference and discussion areas; and classrooms needed for library instruction or teaching use. There are standards and methods for determining the number of library seats, but they frequently do not apply to individual circumstances. Using judgment based on local statistics and present and expected patterns of library use may serve better.

The architectural design solution, even in a remodeling, should allow for a high degree of flexibility to meet future needs, and should not preclude rearrangement of space to accommodate new service functions or automation enhancements. Interior partitions should be kept at a minimum and constructed for easy removal. Floor loads should be determined (construction drawings will indicate these). All library live floor loads (that is, weight of furniture and equipment) should be a minimum of 150 pounds per square foot for book stacks and storage files; compact shelving requires 275 to 300 pounds per square foot; music recordings are substantially heavier than books and require shelves that can hold 145 pounds per shelf for LPs and 200 pounds per shelf for 78 records); they may therefore require higher floor loads than shelving for books unless lower shelving heights or wider spaces between shelving units are used in the area housing the record collection. If nonstack areas have live floor loads of only 50 pounds per square foot, this may seriously limit extensive remodeling unless floors are strengthened to hold book shelving, microform cabinets, and so on. A structural engineer should be consulted if there is doubt about the future placement of material storage. Modification of ceiling height including lighting should allow for standard seven-shelf sections of 78 inches high minimum; lighting layout should permit a variety of configurations for library user and staff workstations.

Safety and Security

A central entrance and exit is most desirable; other exits should be kept to a minimum to meet code requirements, and should be alarmed. This is important when using an electronic book-theft detection system.

A statement should be made about the use of sprinkler, heat detection, and alarm systems, and fire extinguishers and fire exits. Local building codes play an important part in the design of a library, and cannot be circumvented. The design must protect against troublesome water damage due to floods, rains, and broken pipes, as well as mold and humidity. It is worthwhile for one library person to have ongoing responsibility for this area.

Individual library staff lockers should be provided in the immediate area in which the personnel are assigned. Give consideration to making lockers available for library users in or directly outside the library.

Stacks

Indicate open and closed book stacks requirements for each part of the collections (see figure 2). The program must spell out the size of collections rather than giving a total library capacity. When the preliminary drawings include stacks layouts, it is important that the interior designer review them with the library staff to ensure that each block of book stacks has the correct capacities corresponding to the individual size of the collection to be housed there. (For example, if the reference collection needs a 5,000-volume shelving capacity and a bound periodical collection needs a 20,000-volume shelving capacity, a layout indicating a reference shelving capacity of 3,000 volumes and a periodical collection of 22,000 volumes shelving capacity may not be acceptable.

Sequence of material by call number should not be impeded by the layout of stacks or architectural barriers (see figure 3). An example is running shelving sections perpendicular to and directly against walls that may restrict direction of the call number sequence. Be aware of special needs for each type of material; for example, because of their size, art and architecture books are generally larger, and when arranging books you must plan on one less shelf per unit of shelving. Atlases, musical scores, and similar references present other shelving problems.

Future Growth

A statement about the future expansion of library facilities should be incorporated to indicate that the library will need to expand and that areas contiguous to the planned facility should not be developed or designed in a manner that will hinder the library from expanding into them in the future.

Movement

Accessing to and shelving of the collection throughout library stacks, reader areas, work and office areas, and so forth should not be impeded by steps or

Figure 2
Stack Capacity

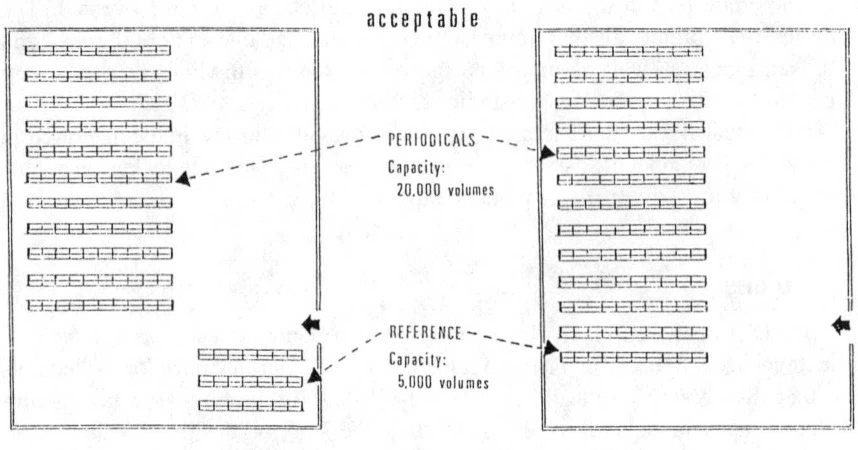

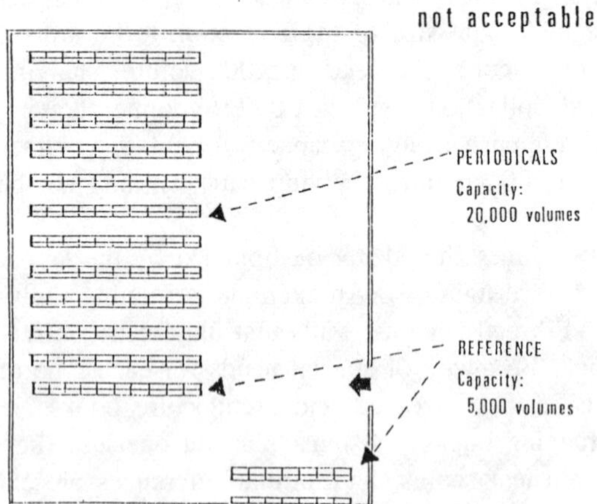

ramps. Movement between levels should be by means of an elevator rather than book or book-truck lifts. Consideration for the handicapped is essential, especially when certain types of governmental funding are requested.

Walls

Generally walls should be kept to a minimum, and where used they should be constructed so that they can be easily and inexpensively removed. Walls are used primarily for security and soundproofing requirements. The computer room requires maximum protection from theft and a controlled environment to ensure properly functioning equipment. A unit head needs an enclosed office for confidential discussions.

Figure 3
Book Sequence

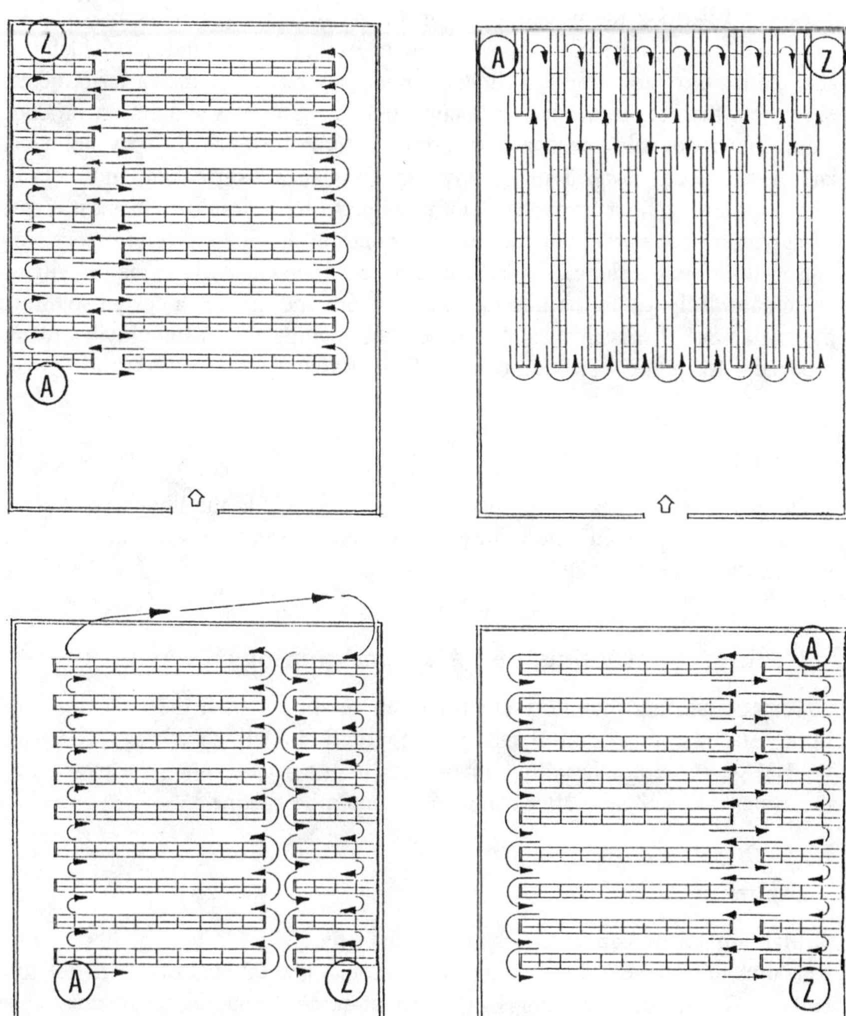

Floors

Carpeting is advisable throughout the library, except when noted for specific areas, both for proper acoustical control and for enhancing the esthetics of the environment. Color coordinate floor covering with furniture and equipment. An overall harmonious effect should be achieved.

Windows

Do not overlook the possibility of installing or removing windows, as well as replacing existing windows. With new energy-efficient windows, which can also reduce ultraviolet light, a capital budget may be one of the easier projects, or aspects thereof, for which to obtain funding. Windows should not produce glare in reader or work areas, nor be harmful to the collections. The psychological and even practical aspects of windows are frequently overlooked. In an era of large, expansive floor areas, it is not possible to have windows in most areas. With windows at a premium, careful consideration should be given to specifying those public and technical areas that require windows. Atriums and skylights bring natural light into the interior of a structure and may be a design solution, but they have disadvantages that should be studied before employing them, especially for purely esthetic or psychological values.

Rest Rooms

Do you want or need public rest rooms located within the library or at some location directly outside the library? How many staff rest rooms and wash-up facilities will there be, and where?

Heating, Ventilating, and Air Conditioning (HVAC)

Temperature and humidity control is important for both the collection and library staff and user comfort and productivity. Remodeling may require altering the HVAC system or installing a new one. In either case, plans for monitoring the system immediately after completion should be routine.

Lighting

Lighting levels can be much higher than required for normal library use. Recommended levels for reading areas should not fall below 50 to 60 foot candles. The level of lighting is a matter of some debate. A satisfactory level should take into consideration the colors and materials selected for the remodeled space. A dark color scheme will take a higher lighting level than a lighter scheme that reflects more light. Higher levels of lighting should be used for certain work or task areas in both public and technical service areas. Indicate any needs under special consideration for the specific area (this will be discussed later). Task lighting is usually needed in carrels, particularly when there is a book shelf. Fluorescent lighting is the norm, and areas where its use is not advisable (for example, because it distorts color) should be indicated. It is very common for designers to use spotlights as general or task lighting, more out of esthetic considerations than any other. Library staff and users find it to be less than satisfactory lighting. Spotlights are also more expensive to maintain and should be kept at a minimum. Lighting may be incorporated into shelving; some fixtures even permit signage to be illuminated through a translucent front panel.

The Library Organization

Organizational structure and functions of the library or library unit should be outlined (an organizational chart is useful), and the functions of each unit described. Show graphically how units should be related to one other spatially. Old patterns and traditions live on beyond their usefulness; automation has introduced such significant changes that spatial relationships among library units and services must be reassessed so that former traffic patterns and work flow do not influence new policies, procedures, and services. Technical services no longer needs to occupy prime space in close proximity to the card catalog, but can be assigned space away from the public areas that is more conducive to technical service activities.

Work Sheets

An important element in determining the type of facility for the library or library unit is the preparation of work sheets for each separate area. The main objective in preparing this documentation is to complete a needs assessment to determine the type of spaces that would work best rather than permitting current space utilization and furniture to dictate the future policies and procedures, including work flow and traffic patterns. Library personnel should objectively present their own and library users' needs. The work sheets clarify the type of space required by the library personnel and users, and indicate those areas that should have direct access or be adjacent to each other for best traffic and work flow. A work sheet for a specific area identifies the purpose and functions, activities, furniture and equipment needs, and any special considerations. Remember that these are the detailed specifications and spatial relationships for your new facility.

Sample Work Sheet

Name of area

Circulation desk

Purpose

Control point for library materials and people entering and leaving library;

Activities

Library materials charged and discharged;

Books placed on hold;

Library user records checked; and

Fines paid and collected.

Special considerations

Area must allow for easy installation for present (see below) and future computer equipment;

Signage; should clearly indicate "Circulation Desk: book charge out and return"; must be seen from library entrance/exit

Spatial relationships

Adjacent to circulation work area (sorting) and circulation office;

Direct access to library lobby;

Direct access to an elevator to upper and lower stack areas;

Direct access to information desk; and

Direct access to elevator.

Furniture and equipment

Charge desk; to include: six linear feet of file drawers, two pencil drawers, one small supply cabinet, six linear feet for books on hold, and lockable cash drawer;

two high stools;

two automated circulation charge-discharge units (dedicated line);

one on-line catalog terminal (dedicated line);

two book detection desensitizing units (dedicated line);

two telephones; and

four book trucks.

Any special structural requirements

Acoustical activities produce high noise level;

Automated circulation and catalog units hardwired to computer room;

Floor should be carpeted; the design solution should consider that this area needs more frequent carpet replacement than other library areas. One possible solution would be to use a different color or shade of carpeting in this area, which can be replaced without concern for an exact carpet match;

Wall between Circulation Desk and work area is not desirable, but work area activities and clutter should not be visible from charge desk;

Note: special structural requirements include considerations about: walls, windows, doors, floors, ceilings, utilities (electrical, plumbing, and HVAC), acoustical, visual, esthetics, audiovisual, and computer. Be sure to indicate computer and special equipment requirements (for example, electrical, cable, and telephone lines, which should be concealed).

ESTHETICS

Do not underestimate the role of esthetics. While function may be an important element to a design solution and the top criterium for the planning librarians, esthetics is also a strong consideration. Esthetics may rightfully, in some cases, upstage the pragmatic point of view. Library users and staff will appreciate and be more considerate of an attractive and well-maintained library.

COLLECTION STATISTICS FOR SPACE PLANNING

Make sure that the collection figures will be useful in estimating future storage needs in a new layout with different furniture and material storage. Also make sure that the figures collected are compatible. Everyone should report storage requirements in the same way. Collecting material storage figures in linear feet is always a good general rule. Your present shelving may include shelving sections that are 2½ feet, 3 feet, and 3½ feet long, with sections containing five, six, or seven shelves per section. Under these circumstances, giving figures in terms of number of shelves or sections is useless. The same is true of other types of storage for other formats. Giving figures in terms of number of pamphlet drawers will be meaningless when moving material from vertical files to lateral files, which have a greater capacity per drawer. Pamphlet files and microforms should be expressed in running feet and inches.

Various methods may be used to determine average number of volumes per shelf or linear foot in order to determine future shelving needs. A simple method is to take random samplings of particular parts of the collection.

ADDITIONAL PLANNING CONSIDERATIONS

Think of future needs. Physical planning, even on a modest scale, always takes a long time from the initial steps until it is realized in bricks and mortar. Planners must think of future storage (that is, projected rate of growth) and needs for growth of material in present formats as well as future formats (for example, CDs, computer tapes, videodiscs, and so on), and consider future changes in the curriculum and student and faculty population.

The planning process must involve more than translating an old work situation into an improved physical plant. An improved work situation is not a matter of getting more space, as some non–space planners are naive enough to think. With tremendous increases in square foot building or rental and maintenance costs, the solution of generous space allowances is not an easy one for which to win support from a college administration or other funding source. Proper space utilization is just as important as obtaining enough net square feet in the designing process.

Attention to the existing mechanicals is crucial. The fewer structural changes, the less costly the project. Moving of plumbing, heating, and air conditioning systems should be kept to a minimum. Do, however, recommend structural changes when after careful evaluation it is clear that they will provide an efficient and effective physical plant.

PROJECT JUSTIFICATION

When justifying the facility program use appropriate standards from professional and educational organizations and, where available and applicable, city, state, or federal government standards. Does the funding agency for the facilities project have standards for office workers? Demonstrate how a standard applies in some work situations and not in others. For example, a cataloger cannot be treated as a typist; specifying special furniture and equipment needs should help justify a proper work space. Use cost figure for every element of the proposal. Call in a contractor to get cost estimates or require that the consultant give the estimates. Do not forget to demonstrate how the plan will save in staffing or make the staff more productive.

WORKING WITH THE DESIGNER

At various points in the designing process, it is necessary for all involved to reach compromises, whether due to net square feet or because possible configurations may not allow every request in the program to be realized. Frequently, a variety of solutions to a library's objectives exist; positive and negative aspects must then be weighed to determine whether a plan is viable—this may be reduced to a question of whether the library staff and users can accept the negative aspects.

Besides the layout of spaces and furniture and equipment, a designer's most valuable contribution is in the area of making selections concerning furniture styles and fabrics, floor, wall, and ceiling treatments, and so forth, which should not be decided by library personnel. Coordinating color selections is important to the success of the total design solution and for the comfort of both the library staff and user in the new facility. Color preferences are too personal and should not be left to the untrained though well-meaning, especially in a public building that is used by many people from diverse backgrounds. There are technical and psychological aspects of color selection that a trained professional designer is qualified to handle. Color selection by the untrained can be a costly disaster. It was not too many years ago that the train stations of a major American city were to get a major and much needed painting. The person in charge enlisted the services of celebrities, untrained in interior design, who were each given a station for which to select a color scheme. The result was an immediate disaster and the project was stopped early on. Millions of riders had to endure the bizarre results. One celebrity's explanation for the failure of her station was that she did not realize that fluorescent lighting changes the quality of colors.

DESIGN STAGE

Remember that a designer will move from the general to the specific. Before a designer provides detailed floor plans, a set of schematic drawings that show general locations and relationships will be submitted (see figure 4). This is the time to mention that the office should be adjacent to the service desk but not the time to worry, if you have written a detailed program that has been approved, that the designer has forgotten a coat closet or locker in your office. General

Figure 4
From Schematic to Final Plan

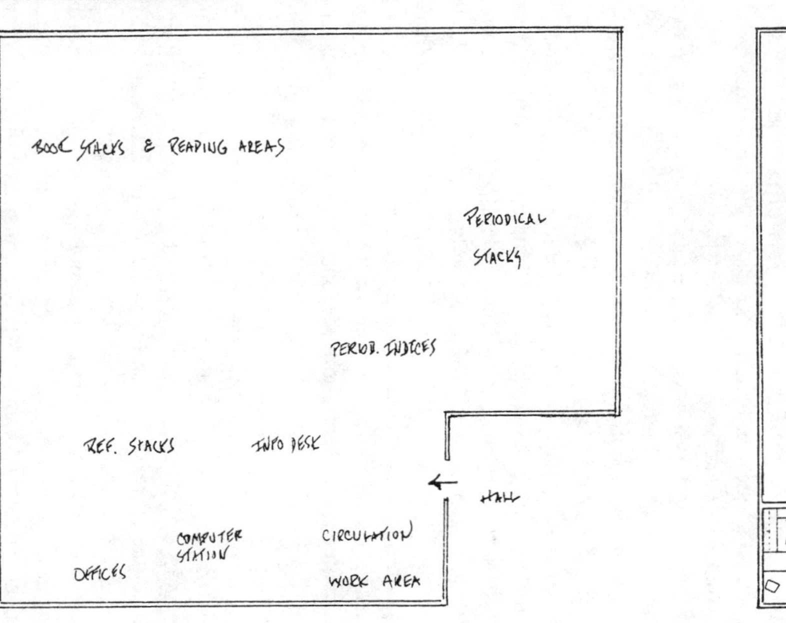

PERIODICAL COLL.
BOOK CIRC. COLL
32 CHAIRS
PERIOD. INDICES
REFERENCE COLL.
INFO/REF DESK
HALL
CLOS
CIRCULATION
SEC. DESK
COMP. WK STATION
OFFICES
OFFICE FILES
WORK AREA
SINK
BUSINESS LIBRARY

spatial questions should always be taken care of first before moving to more specific details. Make sure you know the basics of blueprint reading. Know the difference between a window and a door, the symbol for an outlet, and so on; furthermore, you must read in the scale presented by the architect. The most common scales used are ⅛ inch equals one foot and/or ¼ inch equals one foot; and for detailing, ½ inch equals one foot. If presenting drawings or revisions, work in scale. A designer can not comply with a request for four desks and eight chairs in an office measuring 8 feet by 10 feet.

FURNITURE AND EQUIPMENT (F&E)

Early in the planning process, take an inventory and decide what furniture and equipment can continue to be used before selecting new items. Old furniture, which may also have sentimental value at the library or college, may be serviceable or even enhance a particular setting in the remodeled facility. By salvaging old but valuable reading chairs and tables from the dumpster, refinishing and reupholstering them, a conference or study room may attain a handsome look not achieved with the purchase of new furniture. In the era of postmodernism, designers are only too eager to utilize old furniture. New shelving will cut severely into an F&E budget and may offer little in return. If the designer is concerned about coordinating the shelving with the design scheme, new end panels may serve just as well.

A desk is a desk is a desk, but there are many different styles, as well as a great variety of desk components. A desk should not dictate the worker's routines. The functions of a staff worker should dictate the type of desk. It should not reflect the personal taste of either the individual staff member or the person in charge of purchasing. These principles apply also to other public and staff furniture. Rethink types of furniture and equipment in use. Is the all-too-prevalent twenty-foot long (or longer) circulation desk still functional with an automated circulation system, or has it become merely a place to display handouts and to store supplies? As previously mentioned, do not limit investigations to only just library furniture and equipment vendors. These vendors have improved both the styling and task functions of their product lines, but office furniture and equipment manufacturers have been more responsive to current needs and offer a larger selection. This has been especially true in meeting the requirements of new technologies.

The use of office landscape systems, through which components may be combined, is suitable for both public and staff workstations (see figure 5). The components can be more expensive than traditional furniture lines but they offer a high degree of flexibility for the future. As needs change, existing components can be reconfigured, and if necessary new components can be purchased to alter existing configurations. This furniture and panel system offers a degree of privacy and noise reduction, but, unlike structural walls, it will not require expensive HVAC and lighting fixture alterations when reconfigured. Consider the use of

Figure 5
Office Landscape Workstation

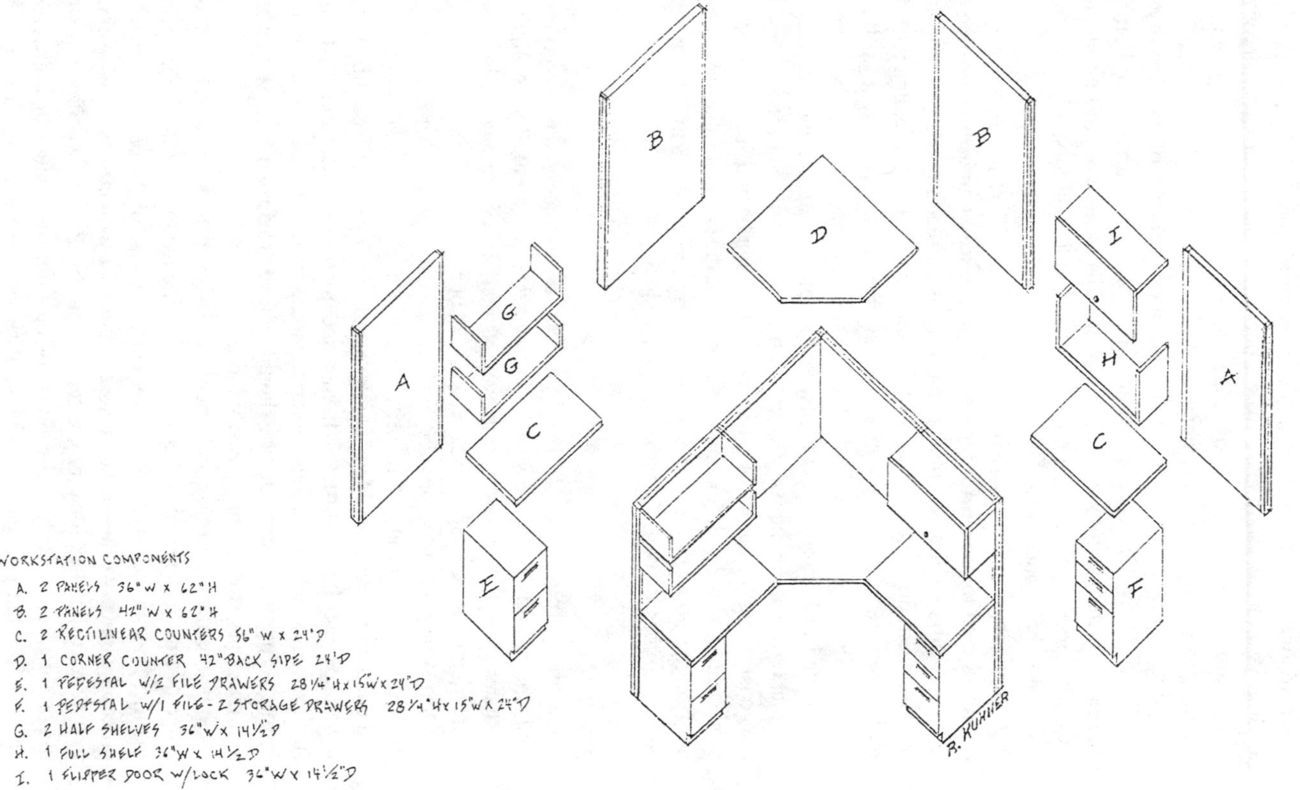

WORKSTATION COMPONENTS

A. 2 PANELS 36" W x 62" H
B. 2 PANELS 42" W x 62" H
C. 2 RECTILINEAR COUNTERS 36" W x 24" D
D. 1 CORNER COUNTER 42" BACK SIDE 24" D
E. 1 PEDESTAL W/2 FILE DRAWERS 28 1/4" H x 15" W x 24" D
F. 1 PEDESTAL W/1 FILE - 2 STORAGE DRAWERS 28 1/4" H x 15" W x 24" D
G. 2 HALF SHELVES 36" W x 14 1/2" D
H. 1 FULL SHELF 36" W x 14 1/2 D
I. 1 FLIPPER DOOR W/LOCK 36" W x 14 1/2" D

custom-made furniture, which sometimes can be made for less than the cost of standard furniture lines. It may also provide a more efficient workstation that will prove more cost-effective over a period of years. The ordering of custom-made furniture requires a knowledgeable person capable of supplying specifications, including scale drawings.

The most important items for consideration, because of the quantity ordered and the use they will receive, are the chairs and work surfaces for library users. In selecting chairs, think again of function. The basic types of seating employed in most libraries are a reading chair, a low stool, a high stool, a lounge chair, a posture chair, and a side chair.

A stool, high or low, may be used at stations where the user is not expected or encouraged to remain for long periods, such as the indices or on-line catalog. Lounge chairs should be comfortable for casual reading and relaxing. It is best to make them difficult to move. Sofas should not be used. Reading chairs should glide easily, and a sled type base is best in order to avoid wear on the carpet. Are chair arms needed? It is always best to use a chair that has been thoroughly field-tested in libraries, restaurants, and similar locations; and that has been on the market for a number of years. Ask the sales representative for the chair you are considering for names of purchasers who have been using the chair for some time. Manufacturers do extensive testing, but design and material problems do not become apparent until items are used by the public. An infinite variety of designs, types of construction, and materials exists. All these factors must be weighed in purchasing a chair so that it is functional, durable, and esthetically pleasing.

General-purpose tables (4 feet by 6 feet) should accommodate no more than four chairs and should have a bull nose edge for durability. A light surface produces glare and is hard on the eyes, as well as being more difficult on which to maintain a clean appearance. It also encourages graffiti artists.

Carrels provide more privacy, and library users prefer them. Carrels are also used to house a variety of items: microform equipment, audiovisual hardware, and computer terminals. Many configurations are available from library vendors; they may also be constructed from standard office landscaping panels, work surfaces, and shelves. College libraries should try to offer individual study carrels or rooms for some users but care should be taken to design them so that activities and materials stored can be easily monitored.

Someone on the library staff must be assigned to become familiar with the range of furniture styles and costs. Purchasing agents and designers may prefer to order one standard type of desk or chair because of the ease in specifying and processing paperwork—one item specification for a quantity of twenty as opposed to five item specifications for the same quantity. Precise specification writing is important to prevent the substitution of an inferior product or a different style or color for the desired item. Make sure you are ordering furniture that will require little maintenance and will stand up well. This means that the furniture should be made from good materials, constructed well, and not require undue work for staff cleaners to maintain a clean appearance. Order contract furniture selected from manufacturers' catalogs that meets your specifications.

The final step for complete control of the project is proper receipt of all merchandise, which includes uncrating, placement, inspection for correctness, breakage, and full delivery of items on orders and packing slips.

REFERENCES

Cohen, Aaron, and Elaine Cohen. 1979. *Designing and Space Planning for Libraries: A Behavioral Guide*. New York: R. Bowker Co. Planning emphasis is on interior design using do-it-yourself techniques with specific sections on furniture and equipment, lighting, color and signage, and acoustics.

Ellsworth, Ralph E. 1973. *Academic Library Buildings: A Guide to Architectural Issues and Solutions*. Boulder, Colo.: The Colorado Associated University Press. This volume presents successful solutions to facility planning through 1,500 annotated photographs from 130 academic libraries. Each chapter discusses the planning problems for a particular design area.

Metcalf, Keyes D. 1986. *Planning Academic and Research Library Buildings*, 2d ed. Edited by Philip C. Leighton and David C. Weber. Chicago: American Library Association. A comprehensive manual that deals with all aspects of library building. It has detailed information including program examples, formulas and tables, and environmental conditions for book preservation. It has been the standard reference work for library facility planning for over twenty years.

Schell, Hal B., ed. 1975. *Reader on the Library Building*. Englewood, Colo.: Microcard Editions Books. Articles on most aspects of library planning from early planning stages through the purchase of furnishing and equipment, written by known authorities.

Snowball, George, and Rosemary Thomson, comps. 1984. *Planning Library Buildings: A Selected Bibliography*, 2d ed. Chicago: Library Administration and Management Association of the American Library Association. A listing of books and articles published from 1948 to 1984 with an emphasis on North America but with some European items as well. ''Besides authoritativeness and quality, accessibility of source, scope, language, date of publication, length of work, and practical application are criteria for inclusion'' (p. i).

27

Effective and Efficient Library Space Planning and Design

Elizabeth C. Habich

EFFECTIVE AND EFFICIENT LIBRARY BUILDINGS

For a library building to succeed, it must work well from both user and staff perspectives: it must both facilitate users' access to information through the library's services and collections, and allow efficient use of staff resources. Although providing effective and efficient access to information involves organizational and service-program design, the library building shapes in lasting, physical ways the interdependent functional relationships comprising the library's organization, and determines the ease with which the organization can respond to changes in service and use patterns.

Function and Form

In the most basic sense, libraries are collections of information and people who know how to provide access to information. Focused around the mission of assessing and meeting users' information needs is a network of both user and staff behaviors, needs, and expectations. This network of behaviors and resources is both influenced by and influences its setting.

The library building encloses the network with form, fixing traffic patterns, defining points of staff and user contact, suggesting future changes that may be made, and shaping both user and staff perceptions of and interactions with the organization. Effective and efficient library buildings result from the synergistic meshing of function and form. Effective use of space enhances the ability of the organization to meet its goals. Efficient use of space means that the building facilitates achieving those goals with the least waste of resources. Since the physical building may place limits on the ease with which the organization can respond to change, planning a new physical environment should begin with an examination of current organizational goals and operations to avoid simply transferring current patterns of interaction to a new setting (Beckman 1982: 203–5). The bubble diagram method described below is a readily understood tool that is useful for reviewing patterns of interaction as the basis for developing physical design.

The purpose of this chapter is twofold: first, to review some issues to consider in configuring library functional areas and major building elements for effectiveness and efficiency, and second, to describe a method for identifying alternative configurations of a particular library's functional areas that will facilitate effectiveness and efficiency. The resulting adjacency (bubble) diagrams will form part of the building program for major projects, providing a visual summary of text that describes both the contents and the relationships between each functional area. Although this chapter focuses on the design of a new library building, the process and many of the concepts may be useful in designing or renovating libraries housed in another building, as well as areas within a library.

The Effective Library

The effective library building supports users' access to information by recognizing patterns and modes of library use, and structuring the physical manifestation of the library organization in a way that anticipates users' needs and expectations. By configuring service and user areas in logical patterns that take into account users' needs and expectations, the effective library building is self-explanatory and allows users to focus more on finding information than on finding their way through the building. The effective building anticipates use patterns through careful planning, and is designed to make library use successful and rewarding for the user through facilities that relate physically to resources, which in turn are related by use or potential use.

Toward these ends, the effective library building:

—Provides nonverbal cues to its use:

—Entrance is accessible from major campus traffic paths;

—High use areas are readily accessible;

—Service points and staff are visible; and

—Collection ribbon can be easily followed.

—Facilitates serendipitous and synergistic use of library resources:

—Service points that are used together are placed together;

—Seats are near stack areas; and

—Related materials are near each other.

—Positions fixed building elements to support rather than dictate intended use and design:

- —Building can respond to anticipated changes in the library's service or use patterns (for example, to new information technology).

The difference between library space that is effective and ineffective library space may be measured in extra staff hours spent giving directions to obscure stack locations and searches filed for material later found on the shelf, and in underutilization of services, as users referred from service point A to B never reach it because the distance and difficulty of getting there are more frustrating than not having the information.

The Efficient Library

The efficient library is efficient both architecturally and operationally. In an architecturally efficient library building, there is a high ratio of net to gross square footage, and the maximum amount of space is available for seating, collections, service, and staff. The operationally efficient building is structured to keep required operating costs low, and can be lightly staffed during off-peak hours without loss of service effectiveness.

Elements of efficient library design include:

- —Building elements
  - —Modular design; and
  - —Fixed building elements that do not intrude, leaving lots of flexible space.
- —Functional areas
  - —Functional area location that minimize steps for users, staff:
    - —High use areas near entrance;
    - —Related service points that are physically proximate; and
    - —Entrance/exit located on main campus pedestrian paths, promoting easy access to the building for the campus community.
- —Service points
  - —Service point locations that permit flexible levels of staffing during peak and off-peak periods.

The difference between efficient and inefficient use of library space may be measure in extra staff required to operate additional entrances or service points at times when use alone would not justify staffing them, or by service points left unstaffed during off-peak hours (Beckman 1982: 204). Inefficient use results in a building that paradoxically appears empty yet has run out of growth space, or that has limited options for reconfiguring service, stack, study, or staff areas in response to changing technology or changing patterns of use.

ADJACENCY (BUBBLE) DIAGRAMS

Since form encloses and defines the perception of function, it is critical to start planning the use of space by reviewing function—the goals of the organization and the best possible way to achieve them. Without a review of current operations, changing the physical environment may replicate existing problems in a new setting. A widely acknowledged need to change the physical environment can open the door to discussing organizational or operational change in a constructive, goal-oriented context of finite time frame.

Adjacency (or bubble) diagrams are a tool for considering relationships between functional areas, and can facilitate discussion of organizational and operational change in the context of space planning. The process of developing bubble diagrams provides the opportunity to review advantages and disadvantages of both existing and possible patterns of interactions between functional areas of the organization (Holt 1986: 84).

The bubble diagrams discussed below comprise circles representing various functional areas, and lines connecting them representing various types and intensities of interrelationships among the functional areas. Some bubble diagrams use mainly circles (or bubbles) to represent the relative size and relationship between functional areas; however, by introducing lines and arrows representing the flow of people or materials between areas, more information may be visually presented, and more factors bearing on the relationships between functional areas may be readily considered.

The distance between bubbles represents the degree of relatedness between the functional areas. Bubble size can be varied to give a general sense of the relative size of functional areas. The type of line connecting the bubbles can be varied to represent different types and intensities of interaction between areas. For instance, a constant stream of referrals from one area to another might be represented as a triple line or a thick line pointing from the referring area to the referred-to area, while less frequent interactions between two areas might be represented as a single line or a thin line. The absence of any line between two areas indicates no interaction. Different types of lines may be used to indicate different types of relationships between areas. A solid line might be used to represent user traffic or referrals between areas, while dotted lines might indicate staff interaction or materials flow. Raymond Holt, Aaron and Elaine Cohen, and Godfrey Thompson discuss adjacency diagrams in more detail (Holt 1986: 83–105; Cohen and Cohen 1979: 73–78; and Thompson 1977: 31–35). Holt offers an extensively illustrated explanation of bubble diagrams that use few lines. Cohen and Cohen and Thompson describe bubble diagrams as part of the process of relating spaces within the library.

Figure 1 illustrates the use of these elements to represent interactions between a hypothetical library's public service functional areas. The double-pointed, solid, triple lines between the entrance and circulation represent a constant stream of library users entering the building and going both directly to the circulation

Figure 1
Sample Adjacency (Bubble) Diagram

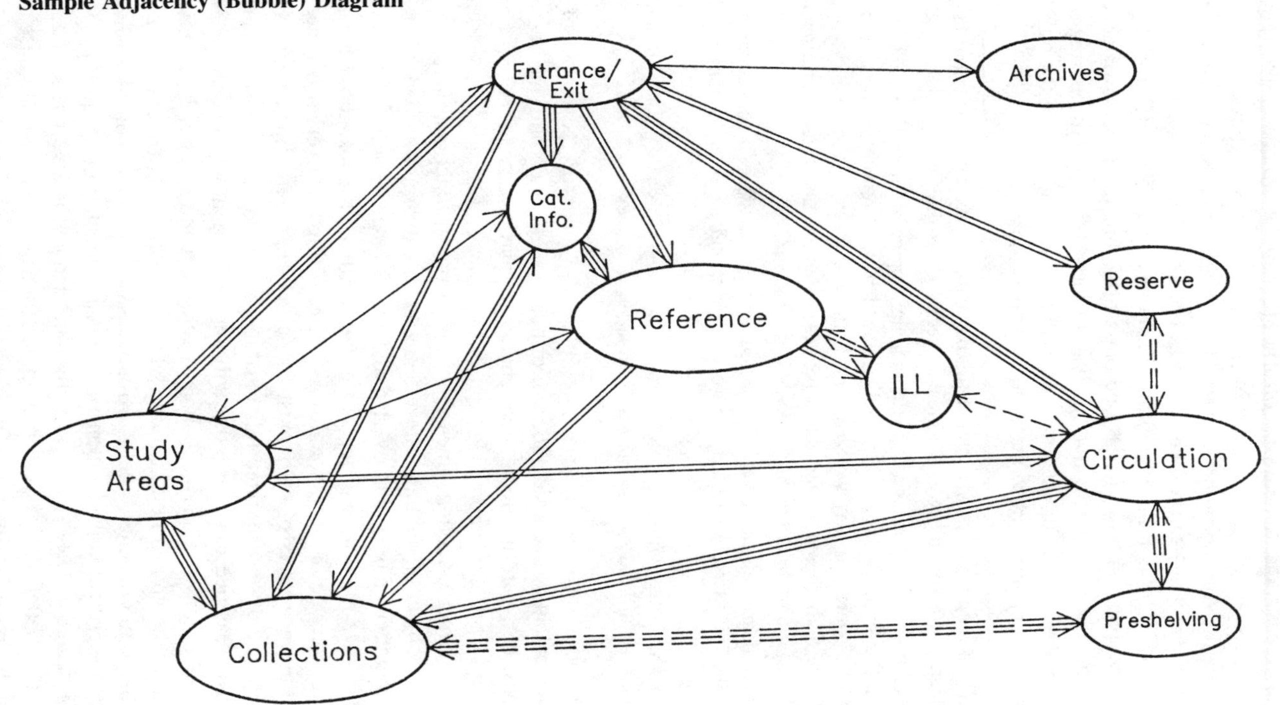

desk to return material and from circulation to the exit after checking material out. Likewise, the double-pointed, triple, solid lines between the entrance and study areas indicate heavy user traffic, perhaps by users coming solely to study. The double-pointed, dotted double line between circulation and preshelving represents the transportation of materials by staff from the circulation area (via the service elevator) to preshelving areas on other floors.

Although the finished bubble diagrams themselves are useful in planning library space and as part of a building program, the process of developing the diagrams is also an effective catalyst for identifying and discussing organization and unit goals and operations. For example, development of the bubble diagram for a library might raise the following questions:

- Which services are most central to this particular library's mission, requiring the greatest degree of accessibility or the greatest degree of visibility?
- Are there staff operations that require a high degree of interaction and that are currently administered and located separately, but which might serve users better or require fewer staff resources if they were combined (Beckman 1982: 205)? For example, in figure 1, the high degree of interaction between reference and catalog information suggests that merging these functions should be considered.
- What degree of interaction is expected between the general collections and reference collection users, particularly between abstract and index collections and bound periodicals?
- To what extent will new technology be integrated with or separated from intellectually related but differently formatted information resources?

In addition to these long-range planning concerns, development of bubble diagrams and the consideration of critical issues concerning the degree of relatedness between functional areas challenges participants to rethink why and how current operations are carried out in the course of deciding where, how thick, and in which directions lines should be between functional areas.

The object of refining a developing bubble diagram on paper is to minimize the number of lines that overlap and the distance between bubbles. In organizational terms, this will tend to bring together on paper those areas that have strong service or operational links. Minimizing the overlap of lines decreases the distance users or staff must travel between areas (increasing efficiency of access), clarifies interarea relationships, and tends to identify clusters of functional areas tied together by heavily interdependent users or staff.

Evaluation of evolving bubble diagrams requires care, both in interpreting what is shown and in identifying what is not shown but should be. If placement of diagram elements "feels" wrong, it is necessary to consider whether this is because critical considerations have been neglected or because the relationship represented between areas is unfamiliar and innovative but sound, and might result in better service to users or more efficient use of staff. Because this process and the resulting diagrams may suggest organizational change, and will form the basis for creating the organization's physical manifestation, the library building, it is important to recognize that the quality of the diagrams is directly proportional to the quality of information they synthesize.

Bubble diagrams can also be used for larger and finer scale planning. On a larger scale, the bubble diagram process might be used during site selection and to determine the location of the building's main and service entrances with respect to other elements of the campus. On a more detailed level, bubble diagrams can be used to aid the development of layout within individual functional areas of the library.

In each case, bubble diagrams should first be completed for major functional areas (for example, reference, circulation, microforms, technical services, collections, and seating), and then translated into physical form or matched against existing or proposed building plans.

From the completed bubble diagram, certain functional areas will readily fall into clusters, others will be relatively free of interdependent relationships, and still others will require further clarification. In figure 1, for example, there are strong interrelations between the Entrance/Exit, Collection, and Study areas; the Reference, Catalog Information, and Interlibrary Loan areas; and the Entrance/Exit, Circulation, and Reserve areas.

Translating bubble diagrams into concrete plans requires collaboration between librarian and architect. The librarian is the expert on why and how functional areas relate to each other. The architect is the expert on building design. As part of the collaborative process of translating bubble diagrams into building plans, the librarian can facilitate the architect's work by developing block layouts for floors of a building. A block layout suggests which functional areas the librarian would prefer to have placed on each floor, and the preferred location of each functional area within each floor.

The first step in translating the bubble diagram into block layouts should be to identify those functional areas that are most strongly related to the entrance/exit, and must be easily or quickly accessible or visible from it. Next, consider other elements related to these key elements, and evaluate the fit between these areas' space requirements and available space. Cohen and Cohen use the concept of placing key services and related elements in a library building's "central square" to illuminate the process of locating these areas (1979: 68–69). In a large and complex building, the process might be conceptualized as fitting together cubes of space in a three-dimensional block so that the highest use areas surround the entrance horizontally and vertically. The goal is to locate high-use and high-profile areas where they increase the efficiency of users' access by minimizing the effort required to reach them.

For example, figure 1 suggests that the elevator and stairs be placed near the entrance/exit to facilitate users' access to study and collection areas, and that the reference desk and catalog information desk be located near each other (or merged) and also close to interlibrary loan. Figure 2 shows one possible trans-

Figure 2
Sample Block Layout for Main Floor Based on Adjacency Diagram

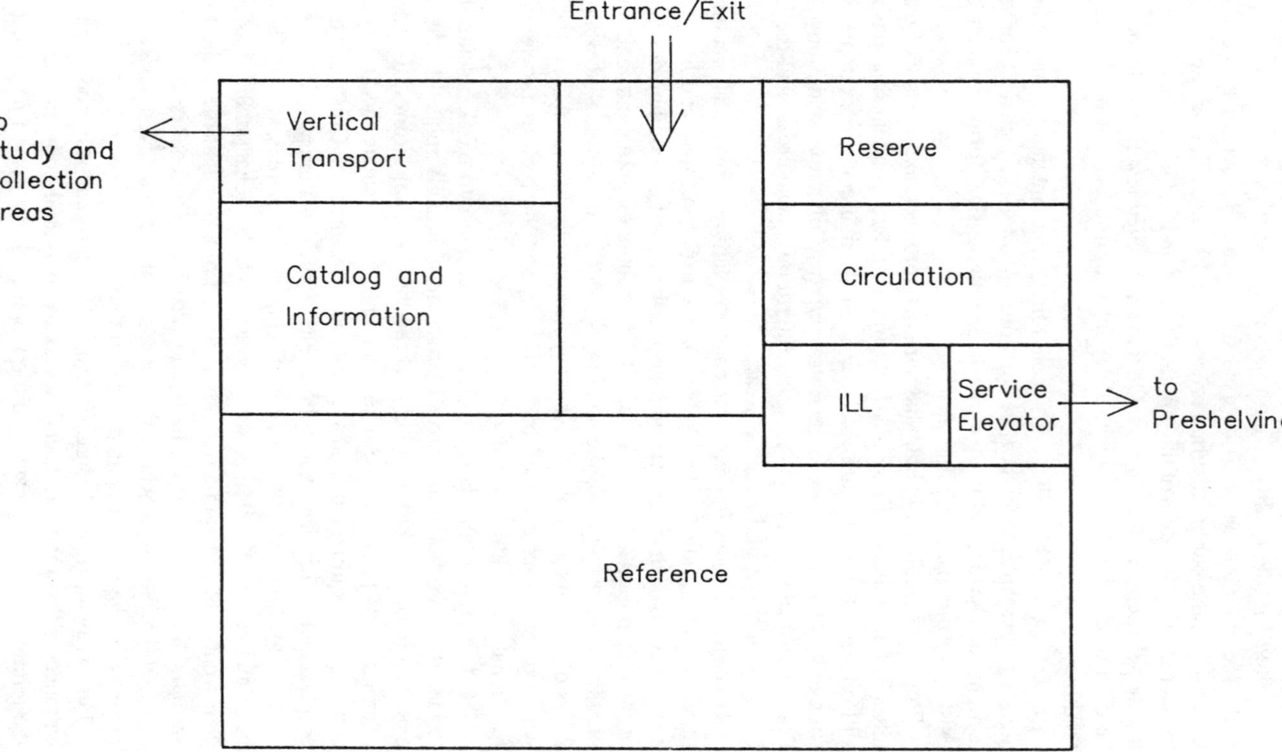

lation of elements of figure 1 into a block layout for the main floor of a hypothetical square building.

Once the functional areas strongly related to the entrance/exit are in place, consider the general characteristics of the remaining available space and the remaining areas to be located. Are there areas (for example, general or special-focus study areas) for which distance from the entrance and high-use service areas might be desirable? Would any areas (for example, an archives or audiovisual area) benefit from the possible absence of natural light in a below-grade location? Consider also service, organizational, and technological changes that may occur over the life of the building.

Building flexibility into library space through clustering staff areas together not only facilitates efficient staff operations and enhanced communication among staff, but also leaves open and uninterrupted by walls the bulk of the library's space devoted to collections and user seating, placing fewer restrictions on later stack and seating rearrangements. Similarly, clustering staff spaces together facilitates the use of open plan layouts within staff areas, easing later changes in workstation layout required to effectively support changes in organization structure, work flow, or technology. (The subject of designing buildings to be adaptive to changes in technology has been addressed extensively in recent publications, for instance in the consultants' symposium edited by Gloria Novak, "The Forgiving Building" [Novak 1987].) Modular building design, with building bays and floor loads designed to accommodate book stacks throughout the library, is recognized as a vital element in assuring building adaptability over the life of a library's occupancy. The reduced efficiency caused by major departures from modular design should be carefully considered (Kaser 1984).

Planning flexibility into the library building assures that the effective and efficient organization reflected in the opening-day building can continue to serve users effectively and efficiently as users' needs, collection size, and technology change the ways in which the organization meets its service goals. The checklist in the appendix summarizes some of these and other issues to consider in arranging functional areas and major building elements.

APPENDIX: MAJOR BUILDING ELEMENTS AND FUNCTIONAL AREAS

Major Building Elements

—Entrance/exit:

—Location should take advantage of existing campus traffic paths to faculty offices, classrooms, and dormitories;

—Location with respect to the building interior should complement location of service, study, collection, and staff areas;

—Number: a single entrance minimizes security and staffing problems, and simplifies user understanding of internal layout.

—Building shape:

—Modular;

—No interior load-bearing walls;

—Minimize intrusiveness of fixed masses (for example, atria, service cores, and vertical transport cores); and

—Consider carefully monumental features and their potential impact on the building's functionality.

—Vertical transport (elevators and stairs):

—Public elevators and stairs:

—Locate close to the entrance to minimize the impact of pedestrian traffic, noise; and activity on the main floor, and permit users to reach other floors with a minimum of effort;

—Consider in conjunction with planning each floor's functions, since elevator and stair locations will anchor the traffic patterns on each floor.

—Locate the service or freight elevator to tie together loading dock, technical services, preshelving, and discharge areas in a configuration that minimizes the length of these frequently travelled routes.

—Areas of technological enhancement (for instance wiring for system expansion, empty ducts, and specially constructed floors or floor systems that accommodate wiring);

—Consider the trade-offs between added initial cost and long-term flexibility;

—Consider where library systems, CD-ROM, end-user searching stations, linkages to local area networks (LAN's), and AV distribution networks are most likely to be located in both user and staff areas; and

—Consider which areas are most likely to benefit from enhanced flexibility in access to wiring because of frequent changes in the type or amount of wiring serving new technologies.

Functional Areas

—Identify among the organization's functional areas:

—High-use areas;

—Areas that require or would benefit from high visibility; and

—Areas that would benefit from relative quiet.

—Explore proposed building plans to identify areas that because of building shape and layout are likely to be:

—Immediately accessible;

—Highly visible; or

—Less heavily travelled.

—Consider how well the proposed building shape and layout can support the organization's requirements and the extent and effect of any required accommodations.

—Reserve immediately accessible and highly visible areas for high-use, high-profile services to:

—Minimize the physical and psychological distance the user must travel to reach these areas; and

—Minimize the impact of pedestrian traffic on others engaged in quiet work or study.

—Consider vertical proximity to the entrance in identifying readily accessible and high-visibility areas; save space adjacent to the stairs and elevators one floor up and down from the entrance for high-use areas that may not fit into the main floor's layout.

Service Points

—Position service points so they make sense to the user and are efficient for staff;

—Consider proximity to the entrance for circulation, reserve, and reference, whose users come to the building specifically to use this service;

—Consider proximity to related support functions; reducing repetitive movement of materials and people allows energy and attention to be focused on more productive work;

—Consider proximity to related service points: what other service points are used in conjunction with this one (for example, reference, catalog information, and interlibrary loan)?

—Considering the level and type of staffing, will service effectiveness or efficiency be enhanced if these service points are combined? By focusing service in a few locations, near the entrance and vertical transport:

—Users are more aware of where to go for help;

—Service points can be more readily staffed (during off-peak hours); and

—The activity associated with service points is concentrated in areas near the entrance and vertical transport, which inevitably have some degree of noise and activity; other areas, away from the entrance and vertical transport can be reserved for quieter seating and stack areas.

REFERENCES

Beckman, Margaret. 1982. "Interaction of Building, Functions and Management." *Canadian Library Journal* 39 (August): 203–5.

Cohen, Aaron, and Elaine Cohen. 1979. *Designing and Space Planning for Libraries*. New York: Bowker.

Holt, Raymond M. 1986. "Using Functional Relationships (Bubble Diagrams) in Your Building Program." In *Planning Library Buildings, From Decision to Design*. Edited by Lester K. Smith, pp. 83–105. Chicago: American Library Association.

Kaser, David. 1984. "Twenty-Five Years of Academic Library Building Planning." *College and Research Libraries* 45 (July): 268–81.

Novak, Gloria, ed. 1987. "The Forgiving Building: A Library Building Consultants' Symposium on the Design, Construction and Remodeling of Libraries to Support a High-Tech Future." *Library Hi Tech* 5 (Winter): 77–99.

Thompson, Godfrey. 1977. *Planning and Design of Library Buildings*. London: The Architectural Press.

Issues in Academic Librarianship: A Bibliographic Essay

Rashelle S. Karp

Change and choice are probably the best words to describe the circumstances over the past five years in smaller academic libraries. This essay summarizes the major changes and choices that are the reality of academic librarianship today, and that have been detailed in the preceding chapters of this book.

PRESERVATION

Academic librarians have the awesome responsibility of deciding which resources in their libraries will be preserved and which will be allowed to deteriorate into oblivion. These decisions are not merely preservation decisions, they are literally decisions that determine which works will survive for the future and which will not.

The usual constants of temperature and humidity controls (Teo 1985) are now coupled with difficult choices regarding differing methods of preservation, which are linked to the age of the resources and to philosophical issues regarding the relative importance of various types of knowledge and format (Thompson 1986). Academic librarians must also decide between developing in-house repair programs for damaged materials (Baker 1986; Dean 1987), or using commercial services (Nainis and Milevski 1987). If they choose to preserve materials in-house, planning involves choices regarding space, equipment, supplies, personnel (Nainis and Milevski 1987), and cost (McClung 1986). Regardless of the location of preservation activities, a policy must be written that includes a disaster plan and guidelines for selection of materials (DeCandido and DeCandido 1985).

Current models for preservation selection range from the very specific, such as "condition-driven" plans (as they fall apart, fix them) and "collection-oriented" programs (title-by-title decisions are made by subject experts on the library's staff); to more generalized models such as "vacuum cleaner" approaches (preserve everything from a particular range of dates, within a particular subject, or from a particular collection), and "bibliographic" models (preserve those items listed in noteworthy bibliographies) (Bagnall and Harris 1987).

Librarians must also pay careful attention to the preservation of newer formats such as in-house databases and computer software, which must be secured with nonprint and print backups (Eddison 1987). For materials in which information is more important than format, choices for preservation revolve around the relative merits of microform, whose evaluation, management, and use is difficult (Saffady 1985; Spreitzer 1985); or optical disc storage, with its advantages of random access, special display features, and durability (Crowley 1988). For materials whose format must be preserved (in addition to the information contained within them), new methods of deacidification include the controversial Library of Congress diethyl zinc process and other processes that use zinc compounds (Nyren 1986), as well as the use of chemical compounds such as morpholine (which has an odor problem), magnesium alkoxides (which are expensive and sometimes dissolve the book's print), cyclophexylamine carbonate (which can cause discoloration), submicron particles of magnesium and calcium oxides (which are effective but not particularly cost-efficient), and nonaqueous book deacidification processes (developed by Wei T'o and promising to be quite efficient) (Cunha 1987). Much of the literature also debates the relative merits of involving faculty, and especially "scholars," in the process of selecting candidates for preservation (Bagnall 1987).

Finally, prevention is the best method of preservation, and much recent literature describes lobbying efforts of librarians to ensure that the original published products (print and nonprint) meet materials standards that will make preservation programs in libraries less costly and less necessary (Welsh 1986).

The responsibilities of preservation choices can become so onerous that sometimes humor is the best defense, as evidenced by one tongue-in-cheek statement regarding the perfect preservation program, where the author claims that librarians' preservation efforts are misdirected and that "instead of expensive deacidification, microphotography, electronic or optical conversion, we should be transcribing our hallowed texts onto clay tablets" (Young 1988: 147).

FACILITIES

The physical plant is, of course, an important element of all library services. Standards of environmental control for preservation purposes have been in the minds of librarians for some time now, but several additional issues have surfaced over the past few years. They include:

1. *Air quality*. Many of the daily routines in libraries cause the quality of the air inside to become dangerously poor. For example, energy conservation through reduced ventilation increases the level of indoor air pollutants, as do smoking, use of cleaning solutions and pesticides, dust on shelves, fungi growing in the books, increased ozone concentrations from photocopy machines (Clark 1985), and asbestos (Stoffel and Koslowski 1985). These irritants have been shown to cause decreased productivity and job dissatisfaction among workers, as well as illness. It is suggested that automated building control systems that regulate energy use and environmental situations might help to alleviate some of these problems (Koelker and Downing 1987).

2. *Work spaces*. It has been demonstrated that worker satisfaction increases with the amount of privacy afforded by an individual's office. The "bullpen" approach, which affords no private office space, is the least desired floor plan. More effective are the "open" floor plan (which allows some privacy via partial partitions), and a floor plan that allows for private offices (Isacco 1985).

3. *Noise*. Noise from students and librarians can be a great irritant, but some patrons must use the library for research and assignments that require verbal communication with others. In an effort to allow both extremes, some librarians have designated areas of the library for noise and others for absolute quiet (Small and Strazdon 1986).

4. *Library furniture*. A great deal of the recent library literature focuses on guidelines for seating in the library and specifications for chairs and tables, particularly as they relate to comfort and good posture (Michaels 1987a, b, c, 1988).

5. *Building flexibility*. Because of new technologies and the concomitant uncertainties of new hardware and space requirements, flexible buildings that can be modified easily and inexpensively (Novak 1987); having a minimum of fixed walls, rooms, and barriers (Lucker 1987); have non–load-bearing interior walls; use raised floors to allow for easy rewiring; provide enough power and communication outlets; and control the amount of natural light that enters the building (Kapp 1987) are essential. Additionally, extensive renovations of older buildings to accommodate modern technology has become a specialization within library architecture (Hudson 1987).

6. *Storage*. Many librarians are making heavy use of the automated warehouse storage of books (Kountz 1987); movable compact shelving (Gorman 1987); and nontraditional shelving methods such as shelving by size, double-shelving, shelving books on the edges of covers with spines parallel to the shelf, decreasing aisle widths, and closing the stacks to public access (Fraley and Anderson 1985). All these storage alternatives have obvious access and preservation problems, but they do allow the librarian to continue to enlarge collections within existing space.

7. *Standards*. The advent of computers and word processing have allowed architectural firms to more easily develop a single library building plan that may be applied to any library. This puts an extra burden on the librarians to carefully examine the qualifications of competing building programs (Manley 1987), and to insist on a partnership between the librarians and the architect that is based on mutual respect and a clear understanding of mutual roles (Carroll 1987). Also of great importance is the development of a detailed "program statement" for the library building project (Metcalf 1986) which incorporates building standards tailored to the specific library (Dahlgren 1985; Palmour, Bellassai, and DeWath 1980).

8. *Other details*. Finally, attention to details such as appropriate landscaping and maximum advantage of views from windows (Michaels 1987a, 1987b) has also been documented as important.

CATALOGING

In the area of automation, catalogers are eagerly looking to automated systems as a way to incorporate data about library resources that is qualitative (Wilson 1983), more thoroughly analytic (Hoffman and Magner 1985; Jones 1987), and that allows for much more sophisticated subject searching (Lewis 1987; Salton and McGill 1983). This is in stark contrast to statistics that demonstrate that cataloging networks ''deprofessionalize'' much of technical services (Hafter 1986; Harrington 1986); that they are too literal (Burke 1987); and that conversion of manual records, although efficient, is very costly (Valentine and McDonald 1986).

One way of decreasing cataloging costs is through a practice referred to as minimal level cataloging (MLC). Proponents cite advantages such as (1) it gets rid of backlogs, (2) some access is better than none, and (3) some materials do not require anything more than minimal level cataloging (Horny 1986). ''Middle of the roaders'' feel that MLC has a place, but only if it is considered minimal level processing, not cataloging (Crowe 1986), and opponents feel that the benefits of MLC are outweighed by the ''increased costs [human and monetary] of providing local reference service to collections with inadequate bibliographic control'' (Rhee 1986: 336). They also point out that many of the materials selected for minimal level cataloging are those that are not cataloged in the OCLC database, for example, materials that are written in lesser-known languages, or that are from third world countries. It is felt that the nature of these unique items actually demands total cataloging in order to provide any access to them (Rhee 1986). Other cited disadvantages of minimal level cataloging include poor authority control, ''loss of access and browsability, lack of concern for national interest, and loss of management information'' (Ross and West 1986: 334).

Fiction is another area that academic librarians have reexamined recently, especially in terms of whether to classify it. It is felt that classification schemes for fiction may increase use (Baker 1988), and that supplemental lists of fiction by category will increase the browsability of these classified collections (Wood 1985).

CIRCULATION

Circulation librarians are concerned with errors in processing returned materials that result in patrons' being charged for books that they have already returned (Weaver-Meyers and Pearson 1986). They are also performing a great deal of operations research to develop more discriminating loan periods to optimize the use of individual titles (Gelman and Sichel 1987). Microcomputers are being integrated into circulation procedures to help determine future stack-space needs (Moreland 1987), as well as to generate sophisticated reports that are extremely useful for collection development, building renovation, and work flow adjustments. The computer seems to be reprofessionalizing the role of the circulation librarian, a position whose professionalism has been questioned in the past (Isom 1986). Finally, circulation policies are being reexamined, especially in terms of who is eligible to borrow materials; how to give extra borrowing privileges and to whom; and how to better handle overdues, billing, and "lockouts" (Dubois 1986).

BUDGETING

Academic library administrators are expanding their sources of funding for operating budgets to include user fees, gifts, bequests, endowments, fines, grants (Shirk 1984), and fund-raising based on donations for creative awards such as library stock certificates, the patron's name on a plaque, and so forth (Clark 1986). These external sources of funding are especially being used to expand special collections (Martin 1987) and to finance on-line searching for which there are multiple users (Dowd, Whaley, and Pankake 1986), although some feel that traditional funding should be used for computer-assisted reference in academic libraries (Beltran 1987). Finally, application of a planning process to budgeting (Ramsey and Ramsey 1986), the use of cost accounting in addition to the more traditional financial accounting (Hyatt 1983), and strict adherence to the 6 percent proportional-funding standard (Madaus 1987) from the Association of College and Research Libraries (1986) have also been issues of importance in recent years.

REFERENCE

The literature still debates the relative merits of using paraprofessionals and/or student assistants at the reference desk. Recent research data indicates conflicting results ranging from the negative to positive. Some data have indicated that allowing paraprofessionals to perform initial screening of requests at the reference desk has resulted in lowered patron satisfaction, lowered patron success rates in finding needed materials, and perceived communication problems (Murfin and Bunge 1988). Other data have indicated that the use of student assistants at the reference desk tends to establish better initial rapport between the patron and the library professional, and that it encourages students to use the library more often (Dawkins and Jackson 1986).

STUDENT ASSISTANTS

Student assistants are a critical part of the library work force because of the financial advantages to the library (that is, they are usually paid minimum wage, they do not get fringe benefits, and so on) (Sichel 1982). Students tend to gravitate toward library jobs because there is less tension, they can "learn and earn," and the library has relatively good working conditions (Rao 1984). Jobs that are typically performed by student assistants include circulation, discharge, shelving, light bibliographical work, and interlibrary loan (Frank 1984). Because of the routine nature of most of the student assistant's duties, librarians have noted that there is an unfortunate tendency to hire students who are "best-suited" for the particular work they will be doing in the library, rather than the most "academically talented individuals" (White 1985). It is often felt that those who are most academically talented will be difficult to manage and will not be motivated, while the less academically talented workers will be more tractable and more easily motivated. Much of the recent literature decries these assumptions, and suggests that formal selection processes, variance in the student assistant's routine (Kathman and Kathman 1985), centralized hiring and training, standardized evaluation (Fuller 1987), and the use of modern teaching aids (Crawford 1988) will counteract the negative effects of routine work.

OFF-CAMPUS PROGRAMS

In terms of extension work, much of the recent literature examines the problems inherent in trying to establish a permanent off-campus resource center. Many suggest that cooperative agreements with already established resource centers in extension locations are a good alternative to permanent centers (J. S. Johnson 1984, 1987) because the resource center then serves not only the students but also the local community (Lessin 1987). Additionally, extension services are making heavy use of the computer to provide dial-up access to main library holdings from off-campus sites (Drake 1987), and for telefacsimilie document delivery (Brown 1985; Gordon 1988).

PERSONNEL

In terms of personnel, major interest areas include a continued interest in the advantages and disadvantages of faculty status for academic librarians (Werrel and Sullivan 1987); problems with motivation of professionals (Shapero 1985); the need for administrators to encourage professionals' active involvement in professional organizations and publication (Stussy 1987); the critical nature of regular performance evaluation (Jones and Jordan 1982); the use of a committee structure for decision making (Association of College and Research Libraries 1986); and the need to promote more women into upper levels of management (Moran 1985). Other concerns have been noted in the areas of proper and legal hiring and recruitment procedures (Dewey 1987; Fielden and Dulek 1982; Isacco 1985); the importance of lifelong learning through formal educational programs at accredited library school programs (Gardner 1987; Weingand 1986); and informal on-the-job training that focuses on "specific information, procedures, or equipment required in the performance of a job'' (Creth 1986: 3). Finally, great concern has been noted regarding the cost of hiring new employees. Research indicates that recruitment costs over one year for one new employee often exceed $64,000 (Roos 1987). In light of this, librarians are urged to recruit well-qualified people who have enough library experience to know that this is what they want to do (Lauer 1984), and to lower staff turnover rates in libraries by hiring people who can cooperate with others and who can ''spread goodwill'' (Leonard 1987).

INTERLIBRARY LOAN

Current issues in interlibrary loan include the need to speed up the OCLC interlibrary loan turnaround time (Budd 1986); the need for better systems of international interlibrary loans (Henshaw 1986); a concern for better interlibrary loan statistical record keeping that can be used for collection development (Beaton and Kirk 1988); simpler reimbursement systems for interlibrary loan which involve less accounting work for the librarians (Wilt 1986); new ways of maintaining control of interlibrary-loaned materials (Ridenour 1987); the effects of fees on interlibrary loan (Everett 1986); expansion of the reference interview to include pertinent questions and answers about interlibrary loan (Boucher 1986); and standards such as those being developed through the linked systems project (Avram 1986) and the linked systems protocol (Buckland and Lynch 1987).

AUDIOVISUAL MATERIALS

Audiovisual (AV) librarians must deal with a host of problems, not the least of which is a negative attitude toward media by faculty who feel that it is unscholarly and only for entertainment purposes (Whichard 1985), and by librarians who do not want AV collections because they do not want to ''encroach upon or duplicate collections or services already established'' within other departments on campus (Dubois 1987: 531). Even if librarians and faculty are committed to AV as an ''established and expected means of transmitting, receiving, and using information'' (Johnson M.A. 1987: 534) for scholarly research (Griffin 1985), they still must navigate a path through other difficulties, including: (1) cataloging of AV materials within current AACR2 guidelines (Graham 1985); (2) circulation, conservation, and maintenance of nonprint media collections (Wall 1985); (3) a lack of frequently updated standards (''AV Standards'' 1986); (4) copyright restrictions and confusions, especially in the areas of duplication, transmission and distribution rights, performances and public domain, fair use, and instructional copying (Bender 1985; Miller 1985); (5) color film fading, incompatible recording, ineffective retrieval systems, and the business failures of many small film distributors (Wiener 1985); (6) storage and display issues such as the merits of intershelving media with print and how to accomplish this (Weihs 1984); (7) administrative issues such as whether to integrate AV into the overall library operations or maintain it as a separate department (Hardy and Sessions 1985); (8) how to involve the entire staff regardless of administrative policies (Association of College and Research Libraries 1982); and (9) how to keep up with the new technologies (Ahlsted 1985).

SERIALS

The escalating cost of serials and serials subscriptions is the number one concern among academic serials librarians. Data indicates that in 1987 serials prices have increased more than five times the U.S. rate of inflation, with the highest categories of increase in science and technology, the social sciences, and the humanities (Knapp and Lenzini 1988). These increases translate into a tripling of prices for serials since 1977 (Clack 1988), which many librarians blame on unethical publishers who charge "what the market will bear" rather than what constitutes an honest profit (Houbeck 1987a). To combat these price increases, academic librarians have suggested that (1) librarians should more heavily engage in cooperative acquisitions and cancellation of serials, especially scientific serials (Roberts 1987); (2) authors should limit the number of articles they write, which would in turn decrease the number of serials being published (Lubans 1987); (3) consumers should increase lobbying efforts against serials publishers for lower prices (Dougherty and Barr 1988); and (4) authors should publish without publishers and make more use of conferences, meetings, electronic mail, computer conferencing, letters and conversations. This would, of course, mean that tenure and promotion considerations for faculty would have to change to look at quality of publishing rather than quantity (Dougherty and Johnson 1988).

Other current issues in serials librarianship include problems cataloging serials within AACR2 guidelines (Williams 1987) and whether to analytically catalog serials (Ferrall and Pinkard 1986); the continuing need to apply research on journal obsolescence for weeding and selection purposes (Wallace 1986); how to deal with sample and unsolicited serials sent by publishers (Randall 1987); whether to buy serials directly from the publishers or through a subscription agent (Stagg 1985); how and where to shelve periodicals and serials (Houbeck 1987b); whether to administer serials by form (with one separate serials department) or function (with discipline-oriented, decentralized serials control) (Harrington 1985/1986); and the use of nontraditional but faster methods of obtaining material from little used periodicals (Ardis 1987) including electronic document delivery (Bosswood 1987). Additionally, serials librarians are using the computer to help select and deselect periodicals by generating statistical reports and other management information which heretofore involved too many variables to analyze manually (Miller and Guilfoyle 1986; Stephenson 1987), and subscription agents are beginning to give librarians less restricted access to their on-line databases, as these become "electronic gateways" between libraries and publishers (Lupone 1987).

COLLECTION DEVELOPMENT

Resource sharing has been and still is a foremost concern of academic collection-development librarians, especially the need to share resources based on careful perusal of collection-use data (Holicky 1984). Other current issues include (1) the need to continue to develop selection criteria for microcomputer software and hardware (Hess 1988); (2) the continued use of scientific formulas to predict budget increases for collection development (Welsh 1988); (3) further development of work originally done by Trueswell (1969), Fussler and Simon (1969), and Buckland (1975) on determining duplication policies for recommended titles (Warwick 1987); (4) the incorporation of reviews of materials into budget allocation formulas (Scudder 1987); (5) determining the most effective mix of librarians and faculty as book selectors (Millson-Martula 1985; Vidor and Futas 1988); (6) continuation of McGrath's (1968) and McGrath and Durand's (1969) work on curricula classification as a scientific basis for allocation of funds to various disciplines (Palais 1987); (7) the use of bibliometric research to determine which 20% of the total universe of resources will best satisfy 80% of user demand (Egghe 1987; Morse 1977; Nicholls 1987); (8) the need to more fully integrate collection analysis, materials selection, collection maintenance, fiscal management, user liaison, resource sharing, program evaluation, planning, and policymaking into collection development (Cogswell 1987); (9) how to "allocate subjects among human resources reasonably, equitably, and advantageously, both for the library and the individual collection developer" (Bryant 1986: 156); (10) how to most effectively use or improve upon guidelines for collection development from the North American Collections Inventory Project (Association of Research Libraries 1987; Henige 1987); and (11) how to use microcomputers in the process of collection development (Emilio 1988).

TECHNOLOGY

Technology has had a considerable impact on all aspects of the academic library. Some factors in this impact have already been discussed; others are difficult to categorize within one department or function.

General issues associated with technology that have yet to be resolved include:

1. How to integrate microcomputers into the library. The advent of public-access microcomputers in the academic library has brought with it a host of issues, including security of hardware (Kelley 1988), software (Costa and Costa 1986), and internal databases that have restricted access (Kelly 1988); how to buy useful software and hardware maintenance contracts (Duke and Hirshon 1986; Hoffman 1987): how to apply vague copyright restrictions for software (Hoffman 1988) and for databases (Drew 1988); and how best to provide public access to microcomputers and to whom (Alberico 1988).
2. How to budget for on-line searching. Currently, on-line searches are billed on the basis of connect hour; the kind of databases being used; when the searching is done;

whether the record is read or merely scanned; how many searches are performed; how much royalty is due to the database supplier; whether the search is on an instructional, personal, academic, or other account (Garman 1988); the number of search terms used; and the number of "hits" (O'Leary 1988). These prices are constantly in flux, as are the number of variables included in their computation. This makes budgeting for on-line searching at the beginning of a fiscal year impossible, and is a great concern to academic library administrators.

3. Whether to charge for on-line searching, and how the charges affect the librarians and users. Librarians are still debating whether to charge individual users for on-line searching; most have devised a combination approach whereby some of the charges are absorbed by the library and others are paid directly by the end user. In some libraries, all charges are absorbed into the library's materials budget (Poole and St. Clair 1986), but severe restrictions are placed on who may use the service and how it may be used (Britten 1987). Some of the effects of direct fees for a library service can be seen in the increase of end-user searching (Ojala 1986), more careful reference interviewing by librarians (Kibirige 1988), and the use of expert systems and artificial intelligence to improve search strategies (Hawkins 1988).
4. How and whether to use CD-ROM. "CD-ROM permits the lowest cost for information provision that has ever occurred" (Lunin and Schipma 1988: 31). It also has the advantages of low replication costs, durability (Co 1987); the ability to be interactive (McQueen and Boss 1986); the ability to integrate text, graphics, and audio (Gale 1987); and the ability to offer local access to highly specialized data never before available (Melin 1986). However, many librarians are questioning its usefulness (Reese 1988), since a disk can only be used by one person at a time (Meyer 1987), CD-ROM has limited ability to write, change, or erase data (Danziger 1987), it is still in its infancy (Quint 1987), and it is still too limited in storage capacity to compete with large on-line databases (Jack 1987). Additionally, there is no industry standard, nor are there standards for access, searching (Hilditch and Schroeder 1987), or evaluation of CD-ROM (Crain 1987; Wall 1986). The issue for academic librarians is not really choosing between CD-ROM or on-line searching, but rather how to use the best of CD-ROM and on-line searching in order to maximize user services (Reinke 1987).
5. How to integrate new technologies within the library. Technology has become the "primary access requirement of the academic library," and it must be understood in this sense (Crowe and Anthes 1988: 124). It has changed the concept of the library from that of a storehouse or location, to a service that is always at hand (Sack 1986), and that integrates all kinds of information systems into one accessible package (Penrod and Witte 1988). It has uncontrollably increased the rate at which changes in procedures occur (Dowlin 1984), while at the same time removing the formulation of new procedures from the individual library's locus of control (Weaver-Meyers and Santizo 1986). It necessitates, more than ever, a participative form of management where failure is considered a positive learning experience (Shaw 1982), and where each member of the staff is constructively and personally involved (Cline and Sinnott 1983; Presley and Robison 1986).

CONCLUSION

"It's easy to make good decisions when there are no bad options" (Half 1985: 1). Only the experiences of another five years will afford us the insight to judge.

REFERENCES

Ahlsted, P. G. 1985. "A Survey of Media Facilities in Academic Libraries." *Library Trends* 34 (Summer): 9–26.

Alberico, R. 1988. "Workstations for Reference and Retrieval. Part One: The Scholar's Workstation." *Small Computers for Libraries* 8 (March): 4–10.

Ardis, S. 1987. "Document Delivery, Cost Containment and Serial Ownership." *College and Research Libraries News* 48 (November): 624–67.

Association of College and Research Libraries, Association for Educational Communications and Technology. 1982. "Guidelines for Two-Year College Learning Resources Programs (Revised)." *College and Research Libraries News* 43 (January): 5–10.

Association of College and Research Libraries, College Library Standards Committee. 1986. "Standards for College Libraries." *College and Research Libraries News* 47 (March): 189–200.

Association of Research Libraries. 1987. *NCIP [North American Collections Inventory Project]: Means to an End: Minutes of the 109th Meeting, Oct. 22–23, 1986.* Washington, D.C.: Association of Research Libraries.

Avram, H. D. 1986. "The Linked Systems Project: Its Implications for Resource Sharing." *Library Resources and Technical Services* 30 (January): 36–46.

"AV Standards: Some Light at the End of a Very Long Tunnel." 1986. *Technicalities* 6: 6–7.

Bagnall, R. S. 1987. "Who Will Save the Books? The Case of the Classicists." *New Library Scene* 6 (April): 16–18.

Bagnall, R. S., and C. L. Harris. 1987. "Involving Scholars in Preservation Decisions: The Case of the Classicists." *The Journal of Academic Librarianship* 13 (July): 140–46.

Baker, B. B. 1986. "Technical Services Report." *Technical Services Quarterly* 4 (Winter): 69–71.

Baker, S. L. 1988. "Will Fiction Classification Schemes Increase Use?" *RQ* 27, no. 3 (Spring): 366–76.

Beaton, B., and J. H. Kirk. 1988. "Applications of an Automated Interlibrary Loan." *The Journal of Academic Librarianship* 14 (March): 24–27.

Beltran, A. B. 1987. "Funding Computer-Assisted Reference in Academic Research Libraries." *The Journal of Academic Librarianship* 13 (March): 4–7.

Bender, I. R. 1985. "Copyright Law and Educational Media." *Library Trends* 34 (Summer): 95–110.

Bosswood, M. 1987. "The Future of Serials, 1976–2000: A Publisher's Perspective." *Serials Librarian* 11 (January): 9–17.

Boucher, V. 1986. "The Interlibrary Loan Interview." *The Reference Librarian* 16 (Winter): 89–95.

Britten, W. A. 1987. "Supply-Side Searching: An Alternative to Fee-Based Online Services." *The Journal of Academic Librarianship* 13 (July): 147–50.

Brown, D. R. 1985. "Three Terminals, a Telefax, and One Dictionary." *College and Research Libraries News* 46 (November): 536–38.

Bryant, B. 1986. "Allocation of Human Resources for Collection Development." *Library Resources and Technical Services* 30 (April/June): 149–62.

Buckland, M. K. 1975. *Book Availability and the Library User*. New York: Pergamon Press.

Buckland, M. K., and C. A. Lynch. 1987. "The Linked Systems Protocol and the Future of Bibliographic Networks and Systems." *Information Technology and Libraries* 6 (June): 83–88.

Budd, John. 1986. "Interlibrary Loan Service: A Study of Turnaround Time." *RQ* 26 (Fall): 75–80.

Burke, M. 1987. "Catalog Tectonics: Reflections on New Technology and Cataloging." *Technicalities* 7 (January): 3–4.

Carroll, R. E. 1987. "Building a Library: The Librarian/Architect Relationship." *New Zealand Libraries* 45 (March): 85–89.

Clack, M. E. 1988. "Price Index for 1988: U.S. Serial Services." *Library Journal* 113 (April 15): 41–42.

Clark, C. 1986. "Private Support for Public Purposes: Library Fundraising." *Wilson Library Bulletin* 60 (February): 18–21.

Clark, S. M. 1985. "Every Breath You Take." *Canadian Library Journal* 42 (December): 327–34.

Cline, H. F., and L. T. Sinnott. 1983. *The Electronic Library*. Lexington, Mass.: Lexington Books.

Co, F. 1987. "CD-ROM and the Library: Problems and Prospects." *Small Computers in Libraries* 7 (November): 42–49.

Cogswell, J. A. 1987. "The Organization of Collection Management Functions in Academic Research Libraries." *The Journal of Academic Librarianship* 13 (November): 268–76.

Costa, B., and M. Costa. 1986. *A Microcomputer Handbook for Small Libraries and Media Centers*, 2d ed. Littleton, Colo.: Libraries Unlimited.

Crain, N. 1987. "Entering Uncharted Territory: Putting CD-ROM in Place." *Wilson Library Bulletin* 62 (December): 28–31.

Crawford, G. A. 1988. "Training Student Employees by Videotape." *College and Research Libraries News* 49 (March): 149–52.

Creth, S. D. 1986. *Effective On-the-Job Training*. Chicago: ALA.

Crowe, L., and S. H. Anthes. 1988. "The Academic Librarian and Information Technology: Ethical Issues." *College and Research Libraries News* 49 (March): 123–30.

Crowe, W. J. 1986. "Local Needs, Shared Responsibilities." *The Journal of Academic Librarianship* 11, no. 6 (January): 337–38.

Crowley, M. J. 1988. "Optical Digital Disk Storage: An Application for News Libraries." *Special Libraries* 79 (Winter): 34–42.

Cunha, G. 1987. "Mass Deacidification for Libraries." *Library Technology Reports* 23, no. 3 (May–June): 361–472.

Dahlgren, A. C. 1985. "An Alternative to Library Building Standards." *Illinois Libraries* 67 (November): 772–76.

Danziger, P. N. 1987. "CD-ROM is the Future Now?" *BASIS* 14 (October/November): 19–20.

Dawkins, W. M., and J. Jackson. 1986. "Financing Reference Services: Students as Assistants." *Technicalities* 6 (August): 4–7.

Dean, J. F. 1987. "The Complete Repair of Bound Volumes." *Serials Review* 13 (Fall): 61–68.

DeCandido, R., and G. A. DeCandido. 1985. "Micro-Preservation: Conserving the Small Library." *Library Resources and Technical Services* 29: 151–60.

Dewey, B. I. 1987. *Library Jobs: How to Fill Them, How to Find Them*. Phoenix, Ariz.: Oryx Press.

Dougherty, Richard M., and B. L. Johnson. 1988. "Periodical Price Escalation: A Library Response." *Library Journal* 113 (May 15): 27–29.

Dougherty, Richard M., and Nancy E. Barr. 1988. "Paying the Piper: ARL Libraries Respond to Skyrocketing Journal Subscription Prices." *The Journal of Academic Librarianship* 14, no. 1 (March): 4–9.

Dowd, S., J. H. Whaley, and M. Pankake. 1986. "Reactions to *Funding Online Services from the Materials Budget*." *College and Research Libraries News* 47 (May): 230–37.

Dowlin, K. E. 1984. *The Electronic Library*. New York: Neal-Schuman Publishers.

Drake, M. 1987. "Library 2000-Georgia Tech: A Glimpse of Information Delivery Now and in the Year 2000." *Online* 11: 45–48.

Drew, S. 1988. "Online Databases: Some Questions of Ownership." *Wilson Library Bulletin* 59 (June): 661–63.

DuBois, H. 1986. "From Leniency to Lockout: Circulation Policies at 43 Academic Libraries." *College and Research Libraries News* 4 (December): 698–702.

———. 1987. "No Room at the Inn: Media Collections and University Libraries." *College and Research Libraries News* 48 (October): 530–32.

Duke, J. K., and A. Hirshon. 1986. "Policies for Microcomputers in Libraries: An Administrative Model." *Information Technology and Libraries* 5: 193–203.

Eddison, B. 1987. "Database Design: Protecting Valuables—Databases and Software." *Database* 10 (December): 88–90.

Egghe, L. 1987. "Pratt's Measure for Some Bibliometric Distributions and Its Relation with the 80/20 Rule." *Journal of the American Society for Information Science* 38: 288–97.

Emilio, B. 1988. "Development of a Computerized Faculty/Staff Interests File." *Small Computers in Libraries* 8 (April): 24–26.

Everett, D. 1986. "On My Mind: Interlibrary Loan Fees: A Different Perspective." *The Journal of Academic Librarianship* 12: 232–233.

Ferrall, E., and M. Pinckard. 1986. "To Analyze or Not to Analyze: Who Makes the Decision?" *Serials Librarian* 10 (Summer): 45–57.

Fielden, J. S., and R. Dulek. 1982. "What Rejection Letters Say about Your Company." *Business Horizons* 25 (September/October): 40–45.

Fraley, R. A., and L. L. Anderson. 1985. *Library Space Planning*. New York: Neal-Schuman Publishers, Inc.

Frank, D. G. 1984. "Management of Student Assistants in a Public Services Setting of an Academic Library." *RQ 24*: 51–57.

Fuller, F. J. 1987. "A Student Assistant Program for the Nineties." *College and Research Libraries News* 48 (December): 688–910.

Fussler, H. H., and J. L. Simon. 1969. *Patterns in the Use of Books in Large Research Libraries*. Chicago: University of Chicago Press.

Gale, J. C. 1987. "Current Trends in the Optical Storage Industry." *Bulletin of the American Society for Information Science* 13 (August/September): 12–14.

Gardner, R. K. 1987. *Education of Library and Information Professionals*. Littleton, Colo.: Libraries Unlimited.

Garman, N. 1988. "The Linear File." *Database* 11 (April): 6–7.

Gelman, E., and H. S. Sichel. 1987. "Library Book Circulation and Beta-Binomial

Distribution.'' *Journal of the American Society for Information Science* 38 (January): 4–12.

Gordon, H. A. 1988. ''Is There a Fax in Your Future?'' *Online* 12 (May): 20–26.

Gorman, M. 1987. ''Movable Compact Shelving: The Current Answer.'' *Library Hi Tech* 20 (Winter): 23–26.

Graham, P. 1985. ''Current Developments in Audiovisual Cataloging.'' *Library Trends* 34 (Summer): 55–66.

Griffin, M. P. 1985. ''Use of Audiovisual Resources for Scholarly Research: A Jazz Archive as a Multidiscipline Resource.'' *Library Trends* 34 (Summer): 111–27.

Hafter, R. 1986. *Academic Libraries and Cataloging Networks*. New York: Greenwood Press.

Half, R. 1985. *Robert Half on Hiring*. New York: Crown Publishers.

Hardy, C. L., and J. A. Sessions. 1985. ''Integrated Media Operations in an Academic Library: A Profile.'' *Library Trends* 34 (Summer): 79–94.

Harrington, S. A. 1985/1986. ''Serials Organization: A Time for Reappraisal.'' *Serials Librarian* 10 (Winter): 19–27.

———. 1986. ''The Changing Environment in Technical Services.'' *Technical Services Quarterly* 4 (Winter): 7–20.

Hawkins, D. T. 1988. ''Applications of Artificial Intelligence (AI) and Expert Systems for Online Searching.'' *Online* 12 (January): 31–43.

Henige, D. P. 1987. ''Epistemological Dead End and Ergonomic Disaster?'' *The Journal of Academic Librarianship* 13 (September): 209–13.

Henshaw, R. 1986. ''Library to Library.'' *Wilson Library Bulletin* 61 (October): 38–39.

Hess, A. 1988. ''Notable Collection of Microcomputer Software and Hardware in Academia.'' *Library Software Review* 7 (March-April): 74–107.

Hilditch, B. M., and E. E. Schroeder. 1987. ''Pertinent Comparisons between CD-ROM and Online.'' *Bulletin of the American Society for Information Science* 14 (October/November): 15–16.

Hoffman, H. H., and J. L. Magner. 1985. ''Future Outlook: Better Retrieval through Analytic Catalogs.'' *The Journal of Academic Librarianship* 11 (July): 151–53.

Hoffman, J. 1987. ''Maintenance Contracts: Should You or Shouldn't You?'' *Small Computers for Libraries* 7 (September): 15–18.

———. 1988. ''The Copyright Issue.'' *Small Computers for Libraries* 8 (January): 20–22.

Holicky, B. H. 1984. ''Collection Development vs. Resource Sharing: The View from the Small Academic Library.'' *The Journal of Academic Librarianship* 10 (July): 146–47.

Horny, Karen L. 1986. ''Minimal Level Cataloging: A Look at the Issues—A Symposium.'' *The Journal of Academic Librarianship* 11, no. 6 (January): 332–34.

Houbeck, R. L., Jr. 1987a. ''If Present Trends Continue: Responding to Journal Price Increases.'' *The Journal of Academic Librarianship* 13 (September): 214–20.

———. 1987b. ''Designing a Periodical Collection with the Patron in Mind: Serials and Users at the University of Michigan's Hatcher Library.'' *Serials Review* 13 (Fall): 57–59.

Hudson, K. 1987. ''Historic Buildings and Modern Technology: The California State Library Remodels for Automation—A Case Study.'' *Library Hi Tech* 20 (Winter): 49–59.

Hyatt, J. A. 1983. *A Cost Accounting Handbook for Colleges and Universities.* Washington, D.C.: National Association of College and Business Officers.

Isacco, J. M. 1985. "Work Spaces, Satisfaction, and Productivity in Libraries." *Library Journal* 110 (May 1): 27–30.

Isacco, J. M., and C. Smith. 1985. "Hiring: A Commonsense Approach." *Journal of Library Administration* 6: 67–82.

Isom, B. V. 1986. "The Circulation Librarian in the University Library." *Illinois Libraries* 68: 440–41.

Jack, R. F. 1987. "Oh, Say Can You CD-ROM?" *Bulletin of the American Society for Information Science* 14 (October/November): 17–18.

Johnson, J. S. 1984. "The Wyoming Experience with the ACRL Guidelines for Extended Campus Library Services." *College and Research Libraries News* 45 (February): 76–82.

———. 1987. "Collection Management for Off-Campus Library Services." *Library Acquisitions* 11: 75–83.

Johnson, M. A. 1987. "Guidelines for Audiovisual Services in Academic Libraries." *College and Research Libraries News* 48 (October): 533–36.

Jones, A. 1987. "Cataloging in Focus." *Special Libraries* 78 (Summer): 177–83.

Jones, N., and P. Jordan. 1982. *Staff Management in Library and Information Work.* Lexington, Mass.: Lexington Books.

Kapp, D. 1987. "Designing Academic Libraries: Balancing Constancy and Change." *Library Hi Tech* 20 (Winter): 82–85.

Kathman, M. D., and J. M. Kathman. 1985. "Integrating Student Employees into the Management Structure of Academic Libraries." *Catholic Library World* 56: 328–30.

Kelley, C. 1988. "Computer Policy and the Law." *Small Computers and Libraries* 8 (March): 30–33.

Kibirige, H. M. 1988. "Computer-Assisted Reference Services: What Computers Will Not Do." *RQ* 27, no. 3, (Spring): 377–83.

Knapp, L. C., and R. T. Lenzini. 1988. "Price Index for 1988: U.S. Periodicals." *Library Journal* 113 (April 15): 35–40.

Koelker, J., and J. Downing. 1987. "Informart: Intelligent Design, Intelligent Use." *Library Hi Tech* 20 (Winter): 29–40.

Kountz, J. 1987. "Industrial Storage Technology Applied to Library Requirements." *Library Hi Tech* 20 (Winter): 13–22.

LaRue, J. 1988. "The Electronic Hermit: Trends in Library Automation." *Wilson Library Bulletin* 62 (February): 24–37.

Lauer, J. D. 1984. "Recruiting for the Profession." *College and Research Libraries News* 45 (September): 388–90.

Leonard, W. F. 1987. "On My Mind: An Alternative Career Path to Academic Administration." *The Journal of Academic Librarianship* 13: 102–3.

Lessin, B. M. 1987. "The Off-Campus Library Services Conference." *College and Research Libraries News* 48 (January): 26–28.

Lewis, D. W. 1987. "Research on the Use of Online Catalogs and its Implications for Library Practice." *The Journal of Academic Librarianship* 13: 152–57.

Lubans, J. 1987. "Scholars and Serials." *American Libraries* 18: 180–82.

Lucker, J. K. 1987. "Adapting Libraries to Current and Future Needs." *Library Hi Tech* 20 (Winter): 85–87.

Lunin, L. F., and P. B. Schipma. 1988. "CD-ROM for Information Storage and Retrieval." *Journal of the American Society for Information Science* 39: 31–33.

Lupone, B. 1987. "The Effect of Local Serials Systems on Subscription Agents: Back to the Basics." *Serials Review* 13 (Fall): 69–71.

McClung, P. A. 1986. "Costs Associated with Preservation Microfilming: Results of the Research Libraries Group Study." *Library Resources and Technical Services* 30 (October/December): 363–74.

McGrath, W. E. 1968. "Measuring Classified Circulation According to Curriculum." *College and Research Libraries News* 24 (September): 347–50.

McGrath, W. E., and N. Durand. 1969. "Classifying Courses in the University Catalog." *College and Research Libraries News* 30 (November): 533–39.

McQueen, J., and R. W. Boss. 1986. *Video Disc and Optical Digital Disk Technologies and Their Applications in Libraries: 1986 Update*. Chicago: ALA.

Madaus, J. R. 1987. "Academic Library Funding and Professional Ethics." *College and Research Libraries News* 48 (November): 606–9.

Manley, W. 1987. "Facing the Public." *Wilson Library Bulletin* 62 (November): 50–51.

Martin, Rebecca R. 1987. "Special Collections: Strategies for Support in an Era of Limited Resources." *College and Research Libraries News* 48 (May): 241–46.

Melin, N. 1986. "The New Alexandria: CD-ROM in the Library." In *CD-ROM: The New Papyrus*. Edited by S. Lambert and S. Ropiequet, pp. 509–16. Ridmond, Wash.: Microsoft.

Metcalf, Keyes D. 1986. *Planning Academic and Research Library Buildings*, 2d ed. Edited by P. C. Leighton and D. C. Weber. Chicago: ALA.

Meyer, R. 1987. "Strategies for Libraries." *Bulletin of the American Society for Information Science* 14 (October/November): 22–23.

Michaels, A. A. 1987a. "Design Today." *Wilson Library Bulletin* 62 (January): 50–51.

———. 1987b. "Design Today." *Wilson Library Bulletin* 62 (February): 31–35.

———. 1987c. "Design Today." *Wilson Library Bulletin* 62 (September): 56–60.

———. 1988. "Standard Lines on Custom-Designed." *American Libraries* 19 (April): 267–69.

Milevski, R. J., and L. Nainis. 1987. "Implementing a Book Repair and Treatment Program." *Library Resources and Technical Services* 31 (April): 159–76.

Miller, J. 1985. "Copyright Consideration in the Duplication, Performance, and Transmission of Television Programs in Educational Institutions." In *Media Librarianship*. Edited by John W. Ellison, pp. 353–74. New York: Neal-Schuman.

Miller, R. H., and M. C. Guilfoyle. 1986. "Computer Assisted Periodicals Selection: Structuring the Subjective." *Serials Librarian* 10 (Spring): 9–22.

Millson-Martula, C. 1985. "The Effectiveness of Book Selection Agents in a Small Academic Library." *College and Research Library News* 46 (November): 504–10.

Moran, B. B. 1985. "The Impact of Affirmative Action on Academic Libraries." *Library Trends* 34: 199–217.

Moreland, R. S. 1987. "Managing Library Stacks Space with a Microcomputer." *Small Computers for Libraries* 7 (June): 38–41.

Morse, P. M. 1977. "Demand for Library Materials: An Exercise in Probability Analysis." *Collection Management* 1: 47–78.

Murfin, M. E., and C. A. Bunge. 1988. "Paraprofessionals at the Reference Desk."

The Journal of Academic Librarianship 14, no. 1 (March): 10–14.

Nainis, L., and R. Milevski. 1987. ''Book Repair: One Component of an Overall Preservation Program.'' *New Library Scene* 6 (April): 1–12.

Nicholls, P. T. 1987. ''Estimation of Zipf Parameters.'' *Journal of the American Society of Information Science* 38 (November): 443–45.

Novak, G. 1987. ''The Forgiving Building.'' *Library Hi Tech* 20 (Winter): 77–82.

Nyren, K. 1986. ''The DEZ Process and the Library of Congress.'' *Library Journal* 111 (September 15): 35–37.

Ojala, M. 1986. ''Views on End-User Searching.'' *Journal of the American Society for Information Science* 37: 197–203.

O'Leary, M. 1988. ''Price versus Value for Online Data.'' *Online* 12 (March): 26–30.

Palais, E. 1987. ''Use of Course Analysis in Compiling a Collection Development Policy Statement for a University Library.'' *The Journal of Academic Librarianship* 13 (March): 8–13.

Palmour, V. E., M. C. Bellassai, and N. V. DeWath. 1980. *A Planning Process for Public Libraries*. Chicago: ALA.

Penrod, J. I., and R. Witte. 1988. ''IAIMS Infrastructure: Technological Base.'' *Journal of the American Society for Information Science* 39: 118–25.

Poole, J. M., and G. St. Clair. 1986. ''Funding Online Services from the Materials Budget.'' *College and Research Libraries News* 47: 225–229.

Presley, R. L., and C. L. Robison. 1986. ''Changing Roles of Support Staff in an Online Environment.'' *Technical Service Quarterly* 4 (Fall): 25–39.

Quint, B. 1987. ''How Is CD-ROM Disappointing? Let Me Count the Ways.'' *Wilson Library Bulletin* 62 (December): 32–34.

Ramsey, I. L., and J. E. Ramsey. 1986. *Library Planning and Budgeting*. New York: Franklin Watts.

Randall, M. H. 1987. ''Controlling Unsolicited Serial Publications in an Automated Environment.'' *Serials Review* 13 (Winter): 63–66.

Rao, D. N. 1984. ''Student Assistants in Libraries.'' *Herald of Library Science* 23, no. 1–2: 3–6.

Reese, C. 1988. ''Manual Indexes versus Computer-Aided Indexes.'' *RQ* 27, no. 3 (Spring): 384–89.

Reinke, S. P. 1987. ''An Online Searching Perspective.'' *Bulletin of the American Society for Information Science* 14 (October/November): 21.

Rhee, S. 1986. ''Minimal-Level Cataloging: Is It the Best Local Solution to a National Problem?'' *The Journal of Academic Librarianship* 11, no. 6 (January): 336–37.

Ridenour, L. 1987. ''Handcarry Interlibrary Loan.'' *Tennessee Librarian* 39 (Fall): 15–18.

Roberts, E. P. 1987. ''Cooperation, Collection Management, and Scientific Journals.'' *College and Research Libraries News* 48 (May): 247–51.

Roos, T. J., and D. W. Shelton. 1987. ''The Cost of Hiring an Academic Librarian.'' *Journal of Library Administration* 8: 81–91.

Ross, R. M., and L. West. 1986. ''MLC: A Contrary View Point.'' *The Journal of Academic Librarianship* 11, no. 6 (January): 334–36.

Rutledge, J., and L. Swindler. 1987. ''The Selection Decision: Defining Criteria and Establishing Priorities.'' *College and Research Libraries News* 48 (March): 123–31.

Sack, J. R. 1986. "Open Systems for Open Minds: Building the Library Without Walls." *College and Research Libraries News* 47 (November): 535–44.

Saffady, W. 1985. *Micrographics*, 2d ed. Littleton, Colo.: Libraries Unlimited.

Salton, G., and M. J. McGill. 1983. *Introduction to Modern Information Retrieval*. New York: McGraw Hill.

Scudder, M. C. 1987. "Using *Choice* in an Allocation Formula in a Small Academic Library." *Choice* 24 (June): 1506–11.

Shapero, A. 1985. *Managing Professional People*. New York: The Free Press.

Shaw, E. E. 1982. "The Courage to Fail." In *Library Leadership: Visualizing the Future*. Edited by D. E. Riggs, pp. 53–65. Phoenix, Ariz.: Oryx Press.

Shirk, G. M. 1984. "Financing New Technologies, Equipment/Furniture Replacement, and Building Renovation: A Survey Report." *College and Research Libraries News* 45: (November): 462–70.

Sichel, B. 1982. "Utilizing Student Assistants in Small Libraries." *Journal of Library Administration* 3: 35–45.

Small, S. S., and M. E. Strazdon. 1986. "Reduction of Noise in Two Campus Libraries of a Major University." In *Energies for Transition*. Edited by D. Nitecki, pp. 194–97. Chicago: ALA.

Spreitzer, F., ed. 1985. *Microforms in Libraries: A Manual for Evaluation and Management*. Chicago: ALA.

Stagg, D. B. 1985. "Serials in a Small College Library." *Library Resources and Technical Services* 29 (April/June): 139–44.

Stephenson, L. E. 1987. "Use of an Automated Serials Central System in a Small Special Library." *Serials Review* 13 (Winter): 21–35.

Stoffel, L., and R. S. Koslowski. 1985. "Asbestos Is Bad News." *Illinois Libraries* 67 (November): 816–17.

Stussy, S. A. 1987. "A Need for the Professional Development of Academic Librarians." *Catholic Library World* 59 (September/October): 82–83.

Teo, E. 1985. "Conservation of Library Materials and the Environment: A Study with Recommendations." *Illinois Libraries* 67 (October): 711–16.

Thompson, H. A. 1986. "Knowledge or Format—Which Comes First?" *Audiovisual Librarian* 12 (November): 184–88.

Trueswell, R. W. 1969. "User Circulation Satisfaction vs. Size of Holdings at Three Academic Libraries." *College and Research Libraries News* 30 (May): 204–13.

Valentine, P. A., and D. R. McDonald. 1986. "Retrospective Conversion: A Question of Time, Standards, and Purpose." *Information Technology and Libraries* 5 (June): 112–20.

Vidor, D. L., and E. Futas. 1988. "Effective Collection Developers: Librarians or Faculty?" *Library Resources and Technical Services* 32 (April): 127–36.

Wall, E. 1986. "An Objective Method of "Weeding" Bibliographic Databases." *Journal of the American Society for Information Science* 37: 256–60.

Wall, T. B. 1985. "Nonprint Materials: A Definition and Some Practical Considerations on Their Maintenance." *Library Trends* 34 (Summer): 129–40.

Wallace, D. P. 1986. "The Relationship between Journal Productivity and Obsolescence." *Journal of the American Society of Information Science* 37: 136–45.

Warwick, J. P. 1987. "Duplication of Texts in Academic Libraries: A Behavioral Model for Library Management." *Journal of Librarianship* 19: 41–52.

Weaver-Meyers, P., and K. W. Pearson. 1986. "Workflow Arrangements and Their

Effect on Discharge Accuracy.'' *College and Research Libraries News* 4 (April): 274–77.

Weaver-Meyers, P., and N. Santizo. 1986. ''The Effect of Automation on the Rate of Changes in Procedures.'' In *Energies for Transition*. Edited by Danuta Nitecki, pp. 240–42. Chicago: ALA.

Weihs, J. 1984. *Accessible Storage of Nonbook Materials*. Phoenix, Ariz.: Oryx Press.

Weingand, D. E. 1986. ''Continuing Education Programs and Activities.'' In *Education for Professional Librarians*. Edited by Herbert S. White, pp. 223–36. White Plains, N.Y.: Industry Publications.

Welsh, E. K. 1988. ''Price versus Coverage: Calculating the Impact on Collection Development.'' *Library Resources and Technical Services* 32 (April): 159–63.

Welsh, W. J. 1986. ''Preserving the Book and Other Library Resources: A Worldwide Plan.'' *Herald of Library Science* 25 (July-October): 171–76.

Werrel, E., and L. Sullivan. 1987. ''Faculty Status for Academic Librarians: A Review of the Literature.'' *College and Research Libraries News* 48: 95–102.

Whichard, M. 1985. ''Collection Development and Nonprint Materials in Academic Libraries.'' *Library Trends* 34 (Summer) 37–54.

White, E. C. 1985. ''Student Assistants in Academic Libraries: From Reluctance to Reliance.'' *The Journal of Academic Librarianship* 11: 93–97.

Wiener, P. 1985. ''Media Librarianship: The State of the Art.'' In *Media Librarianship*. Edited by John W. Ellison, pp. 3–15. New York: Neal-Schuman.

Williams, J. W. 1987. ''Serials Cataloging with AACR2: The Primary Problems and Concerns.'' *Serials Librarian* 12: 27–42.

Wilson, Patrick. 1983. ''The Catalog as Access Mechanism: Background and Concepts.'' *Library Resources and Technical Services* 27 (January/March): 4–17.

Wilt, L. 1986. ''Needed: A National Interlibrary Loan Coupon System.'' *Technicalities* 8 (August): 8.

Wood, R. J. 1985. ''The Experimental Effects of Fiction Book Lists on Circulation in an Academic Library.'' *RQ* 24 (Summer): 427–32.

Young, P. H. 1988. ''Perfect Preservation: A Lesson from the Past?'' *College and Research Libraries News* 49: 147.

Index

About the Editor and Contributors

GERARD B. McCABE is director of libraries at Clarion University of Pennsylvania. He is coeditor of *Advances in Library Administration and Organization: A Research Annual*, and editor of *The Smaller Academic Library* (Greenwood Press, 1988). Mr. McCabe has contributed many articles to professional library publications.

DEBORAH BARREAU is a programmer/analyst with Aspen Systems Corporation in Rockville, Maryland. Prior to this she was systems librarian at Manderino Library, California University of Pennsylvania. She has a master's degree from the School of Information and Library Science, University of North Carolina at Chapel Hill.

JEANNE E. BOYLE is associate director for Public Services for the Library of Science and Medicine and the science branch libraries of Rutgers University, Piscataway. She came to Rutgers as a government documents librarian and has carried out special assignments in acquisitions, cataloging, and automation.

NANCY COURTNEY is a reference librarian at the University of Dayton in Dayton, Ohio.

DAVID R. DOWELL, director of libraries at Illinois Institute of Technology, previously served as assistant university librarian at Duke University and as head of Library Administrative Services at Iowa State University. He holds an M.L.S. from the University of Illinois and a Ph.D. from the University of North Carolina.

EDWARD D. GARTEN is director of university libraries and professor at the University of Dayton. He holds a Ph.D. in higher education administration. He has served as visiting professor with the Kent State University School of Library Science since 1987, is active with numerous ALA and LAMA committees, and has served as consultant to over forty colleges and universities since 1977.

GARY A. GOLDEN is director of the Camden Library at Rutgers–The State University of New Jersey. He has worked in various administrative and public services positions at both the University of Illinois at Urbana-Champaign and Southern Illinois University at Carbondale.

PATRICIA R. GUYETTE is head of Interlibrary Loan and Special Services at East Carolina University. She has been in charge of Interlibrary Loan for eleven years and has implemented the changes necessary for dealing with the extraordinary growth that has occurred in this particular operation.

ELIZABETH C. HABICH is building projects officer for the Northeastern University Libraries.

RONALD P. HASELHUHN is a faculty member of the School of Library and Information Management, Emporia State University, Emporia, Kansas. His areas of teaching include administration, information transfer and government publications, and collection management. Since 1985, Mr. Haselhuhn and Henry R. Stewart have been conducting joint research in the areas of administration and collection management in academic libraries.

JAMIE WEBSTER HASTREITER is currently the coordinator of serials and technical services at Eckerd College. Formerly she was a branch manager of a busy public library in the Buffalo and Erie County Public Library System.

J. J. HAYDEN III has a bachelor's degree in computer science and statistics from the University of Southern Mississippi. He has worked for many years in the information systems development and support and user training. For the past several years he has been assisting libraries and information centers to automate. He has worked at INCOLSA (Indiana Cooperative Library Services Authority) and is currently employed by SOLINET (Southeastern Library Network).

FRED HEATH is director of the Texas Christian University Libraries in Fort Worth, Texas. He served previously as an academic library administrator in Alabama and Virginia.

BARBARA B. HUNSBERGER has been acquisitions librarian at Millersville University of Pennsylvania since 1976. She has graduate degrees from Villanova University and Pennsylvania State University.

BARBARA JONES has been a library director in two small academic libraries: library director at the Fashion Institute of Technology in New York City; and director of library services at the University of Northern Iowa in Cedar Falls when this chapter was written. Currently she serves as head of reference at the Minnesota Historical Society while pursuing graduate study. Her interest in collection management comes from her academic background in history and her professional interest in preserving the physical book and unrestricted access to its contents.

RASHELLE S. KARP is an assistant professor at the Clarion University College of Library Science. She has worked as a children's librarian, a special librarian, a cataloger, and the state librarian for the blind in Rhode Island. Her special interests include collections development, library services to special groups, special libraries, and library automation.

DEON KNICKERBOCKER is a graduate of Washington State University and holds a master's degree in library science from Clarion University. She is currently a reference librarian at Carlson Library, Clarion University.

ROBERT A. KUHNER is a library building consultant with training in interior design. He is presently library planning officer at the City College of the City University of New York and has work experience in all facets of librarianship. He is an active member of the American Library Association, serving on the Library Administration and Management Association and Library Instruction Round Table committees.

EVELYN LYONS is a reference librarian at Millersville University of Pennsylvania, where for eight years she served as supervisor of student assistants. Lyons hold a B.A. degree from Smith College and an M.L.S. from Columbia University; she has done additional graduate work at Drexel University.

TERRENCE MECH, director of the library at King's College, Wilkes-Barre, Pennsylvania, was formerly director of library services at the College of the Ozarks.

MARILYN E. MILLER is assistant director of academic library services at East Carolina University in Greenville, North Carolina, having held previous library positions in Connecticut, Massachusetts, and Virginia. She is the author of a recently published interlibrary loan article, "Interlibrary Loan in the North Carolina Information Network: the Impact of Selective Users on a Net-Lender University Library."

CHERYL TERRASS NASLUND has been committed to preservation planning and education since experiencing several major library disasters. In addition to writing and speaking about disaster planning and the administration of preservation programs in libraries, she serves on a committee in the American Library Association Preservation of Library Materials section.

DAVID G. SCHAPPERT is the director of the Keystone Junior College Library in La Plume, Pennsylvania. In addition to library research, he is currently working on projects in eighteenth-century literature.

MARY SELLEN has been a director of small libraries in Pennsylvania, Alabama, and California. She developed a small computerized circulation system and has worked extensively with microcomputers in the small academic library. She has also published articles about the various aspects of administering academic libraries of this size.

SHEILA A. SMYTH is associate director and technical services director of the Lorette Wilmot Library, Nazareth College of Rochester, Rochester, New York. She earned her M.S.L.S. from Catholic University of America and her M.A. in English from State College of New York at Geneseo. Ms. Smyth is the liaison representative between the American Library Association's Resources and Technical Services Division/AudioVisual Section and On-Line Audiovisual Cataloguers, Inc. She has made presentations to local and national library groups.

HENRY R. STEWART is director of library services, Emporia State University, Emporia, Kansas. He earned his Ph.D. at the Indiana University graduate library school, served as associate dean for management and public services, Old Dominion University Library, Norfolk, Virginia, and taught in the library school of the University of Alabama. He and Ron Haselhuhn have conducted research together since 1985.

RONNIE C. SWANNER is the assistant library director for instructional media services at Trinity University. He has been a consultant to the U.S. Army and Air Force and several other business and educational institutions. He is the current president of the Division of Interactive Systems and Computers of the Association for Educational Communications and Technology.

SALLIEANN C. SWANNER has worked for over fifteen years in the field of library automation. She is the assistant director for systems and technical services at the University of Texas Health Science Center, San Antonio. She has both technical and public service experience from a public library, an academic library and currently a large medical library.

KATHLEEN TILLER is a reference librarian at the University of Dayton in Dayton, Ohio, and also coordinates off-campus library services.

CHARMAINE B. TOMCZYK earned her B.A. from the University of Connecticut and her M.L.S. from Southern Connecticut State University. She is currently associate librarian for technical services at the University of South Carolina–Coastal Campus. She is a former chairperson of the South Carolina Library Association's Technical Services Section.

LOIS N. UPHAM holds the bachelor's degree from the University of Maryland; the M.S. in L.S. from the University of North Carolina, Chapel Hill; and the Ph.D. degree from North Texas State University. Before beginning her teaching career, she worked for many years in technical services positions in libraries and networks. She has taught at the University of Southern Mississippi, Emory University, and currently at the University of South Carolina College of Library and Information Science.

DELMUS E. WILLIAMS is the director of the library at the University of Alabama in Huntsville. He holds an M.S.L.S. from the University of Kentucky and a Ph.D. in library science from the University of North Carolina.